Jewish Identity on the Suburban Frontier

A Study of
Group Survival in
the Open Society

JEWISH IDENTITY ON THE SUBURBAN FRONTIER

Second Edition

MARSHALL SKLARE
and JOSEPH GREENBLUM

THE UNIVERSITY OF CHICAGO PRESS
Chicago and London

The University of Chicago Press, Chicago 60637
The University of Chicago Press, Ltd., London
© 1967, 1979 by The American Jewish Committee
All rights reserved. Published 1967
Second Edition 1979
Printed in the United States of America
86 85 84 83 82 81 80 79   5 4 3 2 1
ISBN: 0-226-76175-4 (cloth); 0-226-76176-2 (paper)
LCN: 78-74165

CONTENTS

FOREWORD

This book and its companion volume, *The Edge of Friendliness: A Study of Jewish-Gentile Relations,* continue a long-standing pursuit of the American Jewish Committee: the support of social-science research and its use in the practice of intergroup relations.

The origins of this pursuit go back to the 1930's. During that decade, in an unprecedented step, the Committee began to take periodic polls of public opinion concerning Jews—initially for the purpose of obtaining guidance in combating Nazi influence, which was then a serious problem in the United States. Opinion polling quickly proved useful in planning program activity of this and other kinds and has been continued since that time.

The accumulated findings were eventually compiled and reanalyzed in book form for whatever broad insights they might reveal when considered together. The first such reanalysis, *Education and Attitude Change* (1961), by Charles Herbert Stember, explored the relationship between formal education and prejudice. It was followed by a more comprehensive work, *Jews in the Mind of America* (1966). In this volume Mr. Stember reviewed virtually all public opinion data concerning Jews from 1937 to 1962, demonstrating the over-all trends of public attitudes during that quarter century; a symposium of distinguished sociologists, social psychologists, demographers, and historians interpreted the trends he found in the light of their respective disciplines.

A major scientific endeavor of another kind was launched by the American Jewish Committee in 1944. That year, a Scientific Research Department began to operate, under the direction of Max Horkheimer, who had previously organized and headed the Institute for Social Research at Frankfurt, Germany. The new department, established in the wake of a conference of leading social scientists, embarked on a group of research projects eventually published as *Studies in Prejudice* (1949–1950). The basic volume in this series, *The Authoritarian Personality*, by T. W. Adorno and others, proved a milestone in social science and exerted an enormous influence on the entire field of the psychology of prejudice.

For more than twenty-five years, the American Jewish Committee has involved itself with questions of Jewish identity and continuity in the United States. As overt hostility against Jews declined and the society became more and more open, these issues came to loom increasingly large. Eventually, they were to stimulate important research in new directions.

When the Committee began to work on questions of Jewish identity, the chief impetus came from the agency's activities in intergroup relations. It was felt that the relations of Jews to other groups, though primarily determined by outside forces (such as the nature of the society, or the intensity of anti-Jewish feeling), depended also on the Jew's attitude toward himself. To be treated as an equal, it was reasoned, a man had to consider himself an equal, and he probably could do so more effectively if he knew his traditions and the meaning of his group identity.

As time went on, the Committee shifted to what might be termed a "personality health" viewpoint. It was now stressed that a Jew needed to be surefooted in his identity and to accept himself for what he was, not only for the sake of his relations with non-Jews, but also in order to preserve or attain an integrated personality. Knowledge and understanding of the group heritage appeared essential to achieve this goal.

During the past decade, the American Jewish Committee's work on Jewish identity has been chiefly inspired by still another line of thought: the conviction that Judaism as a way of life can be an invaluable guide to modern living and human progress. Making Jewish tradition relevant to the ethical and moral issues of the day became the paramount task.

For planning program activity along this line, information was needed on such matters as the social characteristics of Jews, their adherence to religious practices, Jewish education of the young, the Jewish home, Jewish institutions, and Jewish-Gentile intermarriage. The Committee's Scientific Research Department accordingly expanded its program to include studies of the internal life of American Jewry. The first such inquiry focused on an East Coast City ("Riverton"); it was conducted by Marc Vosk and Marshall Sklare, who were then, respectively, Director and Associate Director of Research. The *Riverton Study* has been published in summary form (1957). It deals with a community consisting mostly of second-generation Jews, exploring their own and their children's feelings about their Jewish heritage, as well as their attitudes toward Gentiles, toward Israel, and toward various other matters of significance to American Jewry.

But, in addition, an even broader undertaking was needed: a large-scale community study that would embrace Jews of the third and fourth generations, as well as the second, thereby giving us further insights into the future and direction of Jewish life in the increasingly open society of the United States. That study, conducted in a midwestern suburb known in these pages as "Lakeville," now appears in this volume, the first of a series of two. It is the work of Marshall Sklare, until recently Director of the American Jewish Committee's Division of Scientific Research, and Joseph Greenblum, Study Director in the Division.

Volume II of *The Lakeville Studies* deals with a different but closely related set of factors in the life of the same Jewish community. It examines relations between Jews and Gentiles, portrays their attitudes toward each other, and scrutinizes the behavior patterns and value systems that enter into the experience of living together in the community. The author, Benjamin B. Ringer, was associated with the Committee's Scientific Research Division for many years.

These two volumes, based on field data painstakingly acquired and carefully analyzed, represent the labor of nearly a decade. We believe they will stand as a significant contribution to social science. Even more important, we hope that they will shed new light on the entire problem of Jewish integration—the question of how American Jewry can achieve full participation in all areas of this nation's life while retaining its religio-cultural identity. In this sense, the studies should prove of service to Jewish educators, synagogue groups, Jewish community center workers, and communal planners. But they should also be of interest to intergroup relations practitioners, social scientists, and all who are concerned with the status of minority groups in America. It is with these hopes that the American Jewish Committee presents *The Lakeville Studies* to the Jewish and the larger American community.

New York
January 1967

JOHN SLAWSON
Executive Vice President
The American Jewish Committee

PREFACE TO THE SECOND EDITION

Data for the Lakeville Studies were gathered in 1957–58, and two volumes on the studies were published in 1967. The first, entitled *Jewish Identity on the Suburban Frontier,* was primarily devoted to behavior and attitudes in respect to the Jewishness of Jewish residents of this prestigious suburb of a midwestern metropolis. The second volume, entitled *The Edge of Friendliness,* was primarily devoted to the interaction of Jews and Gentiles in Lakeville and to their attitudes toward one another.

There are two possible reactions when one completes the field work for a project of the magnitude of the Lakeville Studies. The first is joy that one is free to return to home base and need never spend another moment at the scene of the studies. The other is regret that one cannot stay longer and reap the benefits of the investment which one has made in the community. Since my feelings about Lakeville fell into the second category, I cherished information about Lakeville which came my way in subsequent years.

Lakeville was on my mind and I welcomed any opportunity to return there. In 1968 I was asked by the American Jewish Committee, which had sponsored the original research, to spend a short period in Lakeville and assess reactions to the Six-Day War as well as to other, less dramatic developments, which had taken place in the community. In the mid-1970's I took the initiative and collected a substantial amount of data on the evolution of Lakeville as a suburban Jewish community. Most recently, I sought to assess the latest changes in Lakeville's Jewish community. An extensive amount of material was collected and is summarized in Chapter 11. The emphasis is on the evolution of community institutions rather than on changes in individual attitudes and behavior.

x

In the effort to preserve anonymity, certain details have been altered or deleted.

I have had to rely upon personal resources to gather this new material. As a consequence, it is based upon observations made during brief trips to Lakeville and a series of loosely-structured interviews with Lakeville politicians, real estate agents, educators, rabbis, officials of Jewish organizations, and strategically-situated residents. Perhaps at some future time the resources will be available to interview as many of the 432 Jewish members of the original sample as are still alive and well in Lakeville or residing in other communities, the surviving members of the original Gentile sample, and a sample of the Jewish and Gentile families who have become residents of the community since the time that the original studies were done.

This new edition would not have been possible without the help of Arden Geldman, who served as my research assistant when he was a graduate student at Brandeis University. Not only did he do considerable interviewing for me, but he was generous enough to aid me in obtaining the answers to questions which arose in the course of writing. His skill as an interviewer will be evident in the pages which follow. But equally impressive was the enthusiasm with which he joined me in seeking to comprehend the changes which had taken place in Lakeville in recent years.

I am also grateful to David Bamberger, who as a Brandeis undergraduate took an independent study course with me in which he reviewed the changing character of Lakeville and the relationships between Jews and Gentiles. I also appreciate the secretarial assistance rendered by Doris Lelchook, Jane Tillis, and most recently by Elaine Cohen. As noted in the first edition of *Jewish Identity on the Suburban Frontier*, the frustrating aspect of writing these acknowledgments is that the obligation to preserve anonymity precludes naming individuals who were good enough to consent to be interviewed or who offered to help in other ways.

As before, the last are frequently the most dear. The present edition would not have been completed without the help and presence of my wife, Rose.

Brandeis University   MARSHALL SKLARE
Waltham, Massachusetts
August 30, 1978
27th of Av, 5738

PREFACE TO THE FIRST EDITION

The spectacular development of archeology in Israel during recent decades, highlighted this year by the opening of Masada, demonstrates the disparity between the amount of scholarship on the Jewish past and on the Jewish present. The disparity is partly a function of the thrust of Jewish scholarship itself, with its strong classical emphasis. But a portion of the difference—particularly as it applies to the study of the Jews of the United States—is a tribute of sorts to the position of American Jewry. There being no Jewish problem in the conventional sense, the study of Jewish life is not a preoccupation of contemporary social science as much as it is an enterprise of specialists. Would that some other groups in American society occupied the same enviable position!

But if there is no conventional Jewish problem in America—American Jews not constituting a social problem for the society as a whole—Jews do have their own Jewish problem: the problem of Jewish identity. They are confronted with the question of how to guarantee their survival in a society which is on the one hand pluralistic but on the other hand is so hospitable as to make group survival difficult. This being the case, the need of the hour is to provide members of the Jewish group with a clear assessment of their situation.

While many have recognized the need, fewer have been in a position to offer sound and detailed analysis. In undertaking the task of clarifying the present problem of Jewish identity, we have been guided by the perspectives and methods of the social sciences in the belief that these are essential keys for obtaining the knowledge of contemporary Jewish life required for self-understanding. We hope that we have fulfilled this promise as well as two other—more usual—objectives: to contribute a significant study for those interested in intergroup relations and in the sociology of religious and ethnic groups, and to produce a useful document for the agency which sponsored the project.

The provision of self-understanding involves as weighty a responsibility as the more conventional ambition of making a contribution to the social sciences. In seeking to supply self-understanding the analyst confronts a host of problems, including the fact that almost inevitably he tends to study his subjects from the single perspective of their Jewish identity. But since Jewish scholars conduct the great bulk of investigations in this particular area of scholarship there is an even more disturbing problem which is endemic to the study of contemporary Jewry. It concerns the fact that while such scholars may easily develop empathy with immigrant Jews residing in the area of first settlement and struggling to gain a foothold in a world they never made, similar empathy is more difficult to come by when Jews of the type who form the bulk of the subjects in the present research are under scrutiny. Success interferes with empathy: it is easier to treat the Jews of the "ghetto" sympathetically than it is to do the same for those of the "gilded ghetto." And this in spite of the fact that an objective assessment might suggest that it is the inhabitants of the "gilded ghetto" who are in more difficult straits. Since psychological pressure can be more fearsome and enduring than physical deprivation, it is the situation of the privileged Jew, the successful Jew, the college-educated Jew which should evoke the most sympathetic response.

Frequently the Jewish social scientist is in conflict: he prides himself on accepting his group identity but he wishes to separate himself from a community which does not seem to honor his values. He upholds universalism, but at the same time he may be unconsciously ethnocentric, expecting Jews to uphold standards which he does not seriously expect Gentiles to embody. The end of the matter is that his research may constitute an obstacle as well as an avenue toward self-understanding.

The present enterprise, we trust, was conceived more in empathy than in hostility. We have consciously sought to avoid the temptation of adopting a stance of superiority toward a community where so many successful people reside. Hopefully the knowledge that all modern Jews, ourselves included, face much the same problem which the Jews of Lakeville confront has been sufficiently humbling so as to prevent any distaste with certain outward manifestations of Jewish life—manifestations which might detract from empathy toward Lakeville and its residents, and from an understanding of the type of life which they have created. Analyst or subject, expert or layman, outsider or resident, all of us are—as the traditional phrase has it—"flesh and blood."

A negative bias is dangerous but a positive bias can be just as deadly. What is the source of positive bias in the study of contemporary Jewry? Rather than unalloyed ethnocentrism it has generally been the desire to defend Jews and Judaism against detractors, whether scholarly or popular. In fact so pervasive has been the motivation of defense that it played a significant role during the birth of modern Jewish scholarship, whose goal was to accurately reconstruct the Jewish past. If the study of the past has been affected how much more vulnerable is research on the Jewish present.

Given the improved climate of intergroup relations there may be less of a temptation to commit the unwitting error of manifesting positive bias. Nevertheless, barriers to objectivity may be strong even if subtle. Thus in an age of mounting anti-Semitism the responsible social scientist will hesitate to publish anything which might be seized upon as an excuse for agitation or be used in the validation of prejudicial claims. But in an age of declining anti-Semitism there is also a temptation to censor material which might be misinterpreted by those who would retard or halt the trend toward the achievement of equal status. Self-censorship is both the enemy of objectivity and of Jewish self-understanding. Aware that the telling of half of the truth can be a greater sin than telling nothing, we have sought to reveal the full story of Jewish life in Lakeville.

If both a positive and negative bias are successfully avoided the Jewish scholar who feels a strong commitment to Jewish life must wrestle with a special problem endemic to his particular stance: the temptation toward unbridled optimism. Wanting the group to survive, he may look for signs of health when he should focus on pathology. He may hesitate to analyze a decline of Jewish life out of a fear of discovering the truth, or he may hesitate to publish his material out of concern that it will weaken Jewish morale and may itself contrbute in some subtle way to increased alienation and paralysis of group will. When he comes to feel that his efforts must make an immediate and direct impact on the Jewish will to survive, this attitude immensely complicates his scholarly responsibilities. If there has been a lachrymose conception of Jewish history, as Salo W. Baron has maintained, we can also find its opposite: expressions of unbridled optimism about the future of Jewish life in the United States. Mindful of this problem we have sought to resist the temptation to think positively and thereby to write an inspirational tract.

The cynic claims that gratitude is the anticipation of future favors. We have no more favors to ask of our respondents, only a feeling of profound gratitude to them. Our Jewish respondents in particular subjected themselves to extraordinarily long interviews. Why did they do so? Merely because we structured the situation so that it was easier for them to respond to our importunings than to turn us away? Did they continue to answer question after question because it was highly satisfying to be the object of attention by a skilled and attractive interviewer? Such motives undoubtedly came into play, but the interest of Lakeville Jews in talking about themselves for a period of between three and four hours—in many cases at one sitting—can also be interpreted as indicating a concern with Jewish identity. The discussion of Jewish identity may, in fact, constitute for the modern Jew a kind of pious act of the type which he is not capable of performing in respect to certain more traditional manifestations of his identity. From this perspective talking about Jewish identity is an act of affirmation, and Jewishness remains alive as long as the individual is troubled by the problem of identity.

We have tried to acknowledge our debt to our respondents in two ways. The first has been to treat their answers with the utmost seriousness. The second has been to treat them confidentially. Regrettably, both researchers and respondents are sometimes guilty of a breach of confidence. For our part we have gone to considerable lengths to preserve the anonymity of the community and of the identity of respondents and informants. Efforts to preserve such anonymity necessarily constitute a compromise: alterations in the description of individual persons, of community facilities and institutions, and of historical events must be kept within certain boundaries if their character is to be preserved.

It is our hope that our efforts in behalf of anonymity will be complemented by the community itself. We trust that all who are quoted or portrayed on these pages, or who play a prominent role in the community, will recognize the wisdom of preserving anonymity and will resist the temptation to identify the site of this particular research project.

If research requires cooperative respondents it also requires faithful supporters. Since the problem of Jewish identity is ever-increasingly a problem for the Jew more than it is a problem for American society, support for research on contemporary Jewish problems must come largely from Jewish organizations rather than from government instrumentalities or large public-service-type foundations. Admittedly, organizations are not ideal sponsors—by their nature they are interested rather than disinterested, political rather than scholarly. Furthermore, any organization committed to advancing the interests of a minority group magnifies such tendencies. Given these dangers and frailties a particular debt of gratitude is owed to the American Jewish Committee, which is one of the few agencies where a study of this type could have been initiated and executed. The faith and forbearance of its executive vice president, Dr. John Slawson, has played a major role in bringing the study to fruition. It was his conception that the AJC could not rest on its contributions to the field of "prejudice research" alone, but rather should go forward into the study of Jewish identity and thus complement the traditional emphasis of AJC's program. AJC's sponsorship has been exemplary, for the agency gave its staff freedom to design the investigation as well as to draw their own conclusions from the data they collected. Accordingly, AJC bears no responsibility for either factual or interpretative statements made in these volumes.

A debt is owed to one other institution: the American Foundation in Israel, for granting a Fulbright lectureship which enabled me to spend the academic year 1965–1966 at the Hebrew University. Jewish tradition has it that a stay in the Holy Land makes one wiser. It is not for me to say whether there is warrant for this view in the present instance. But I can attest to the fact that my stay served the purpose of providing a retreat from the pressures of New York City and thus enabling me to bring this volume to conclusion. Admittedly, writing about Lakeville in the city of Jerusalem constitutes something of a reversal of Yehuda Halevi's well-known phrase: "My heart is in the East and I am in the uttermost West." But there is excuse enough for doing so by virtue of the fact that Jews exist in Lakeville today because of events which occurred in these very hills millennia ago. It may be appropriate, then, that this volume—which concerns a community so removed from this city in so many ways—be brought to completion in the Holy City.

If my institutional debts are considerable my personal debts are also numerous. From the very beginning Benjamin B. Ringer, now of Hunter College, was involved in this project. I am grateful for all of his efforts; he played a major role in the development of the questionnaires, in the field work, and in the preparation of data for analysis. Specializing in the material bearing on intergroup relations, he is the author of Volume II of this series, entitled *The Edge of Friendliness: A Study of Jewish-Gentile Relations.* Joseph Greenblum joined the staff of the American Jewish Committee after the study was initiated, but he too has been involved with this effort through many phases. He made a significant contribution to the analysis of the data on Jewish identity and to the writing of this volume. Because of his intelligence and devotion it is a pleasure to acknowledge his contribution on the title page as well as in this preface. I should also like to thank two former colleagues who were involved in the study, Alfred E. Levin and David Ryan. The efforts of these professionals would have been in vain if not for the devoted efforts of those who served at one time or another on the secretarial staff of AJC's Division of Scientific Research: Ruth Ballan, Judith Gimple, Sally Hoffman, Elizabeth Keller, Alice Saitzeff and Nancy Schmiderer. They did much of the work of preparation of tabular materials and the typing of manuscript. Anne Biderman and Malka Kroll rendered similar assistance in Israel.

While AJC staff directed the field work for the Jewish sample the interviewing of Gentile respondents was conducted by the National Opinion Research Center of the University of Chicago. AJC has utilized the services of this organization on many occasions and it is a pleasure once again to thank them for their able assistance. The other agency which assisted us was SRDS Data, Inc. We are grateful to this firm for their tabulating services and particularly to Hugh Rogers, who was on the SRDS staff at the time.

Two colleagues in a related division of AJC, Milton Himmelfarb and Lucy Dawidowicz, have assisted me in more ways than they know. The staff of AJC's Blaustein Library has helped on this occasion as on so many others and it is a pleasure to acknowledge the assistance of Harry Alderman and Iva Cohen. I should also like to thank another member of the AJC staff, Morris Fine, for facilitating the appearance of these volumes. Moshe Davis and Simon Herman of the Institute of Contemporary Jewry of the Hebrew University have been of help to me during my stay at the Hebrew University. And I am especially grateful for the hospitality extended by another institution in Jerusalem: the Student Center of the Jewish Theological Seminary of America. Raphael Posner and Yaakov and Galilit Penini of the Center were helpful to me in diverse ways.

The frustrating aspect of these acknowledgments is that the obligation to preserve anonymity precludes naming individuals in Lakeville and in Lake City who were of assistance. These include staff members and lay leaders of AJC, several donors who supported an extension of the study, individuals who served as key informants and as members of our sponsoring committee, and our interviewers, many of whom reside in communities adjacent to Lakeville. Most of all it precludes acknowledging by name a local resident whose help was invaluable. Not only did he find the solution to many problems which we as outsiders could not solve for ourselves, but his cheerfulness and interest acted as a spur to all of us. I hope that these volumes will serve as some recompense for the efforts he made in our behalf.

The last are frequently the first. My wife, Rose, has borne part of the burden of this project in Lakeville itself, in New York City, and in Jerusalem. Without her help and presence this publication would not have been completed.

Neve Shaanan   MARSHALL SKLARE
Jerusalem
July 12, 1966
24th of Tammuz, 5726

Jewish Identity on the Suburban Frontier

1

INTRODUCTION

In 1900, Jacob David Wilowsky, the famous rabbi of Slutsk, Russia, told an audience in New York City that any Jew who came to the United States was a sinner. In his view, Judaism had no chance of survival on American soil. "It was not only home that the Jews left behind in Europe," he said, "it was their Torah, their Talmud, their *yeshivot*—in a word, their *Yiddishkeit,* their entire Jewish way of life." [1] The Slutsker Rav implied not only that observant Jews placed themselves and their children in peril by coming to the United States but that their presence in the country condoned the heresy of America.

In view of the rise of Nazism some three decades later, it was providential that few acted upon his inference that American Jews should return whence they had come; emigration was so exceptional that the Jewish group became noteworthy for its extraordinarily low percentage of returnees. Furthermore, the overwhelming majority of immigrants did not feel that they were committing an act of rebelliousness against *Yiddishkeit* when they made the decision to come to America and remain here. In fact, rather than viewing America as the future graveyard of Judaism, some saw it as the place where a Jewish renaissance would occur. In particular, those who were not strictly Orthodox felt that in the "first new nation" Judaism would be able to flourish in a way that was impossible in the traditionalistic societies of Europe. Others were more guarded: they saw the future of American Judaism as highly promising, yet fraught with difficulties.

Many religious leaders felt the call to America. Isaac Mayer Wise, who was to become the leading American Reform rabbi of his time, emigrated from Bohemia on the assumption that the future of the Jewish religion in general, and of liberal Judaism in particular, was in the New World. Solomon Schechter, the leader of Conservative Judaism, came to the United States both because he desired a more Jewish environment for himself and his children than was available in the English university town where he resided and because he felt that America represented the wave of the Jewish future. He was convinced that his particular approach to Jewish tradition could flourish in the New World.

However, committed Jews soon discovered that while there was liberty and equality for Jews in America, the state of Judaism was perilous. Even as great a believer in the future of American Judaism as Isaac Mayer Wise was appalled when he arrived in 1846. He found that among the Jews of New York City:

> . . . there was not one leader who could read unpunctuated Hebrew or . . . had the least knowledge of Judaism, its history and literature. [There were] but three men in private life who possessed any Jewish or any Talmudic learning. . . . Otherwise ignorance swayed the scepter, and darkness ruled.[2]

Laymen experienced the challenge of the new environment even while they were still in Europe. A good example is Abraham Kohn. Leaving his village of Mönchsroth in 1842, when he was twenty-three years of age, Kohn broke with his accustomed mode of life before he passed through the last town of his native Bavaria:

> Friday night we were in Volkach, and on Saturday morning at 3 o'clock set out for Schweinfurt, where we arrived to refresh ourselves with some remarkable wine. At noon we stopped at Poppenhausen and arrived, in the evening, at Münnerstadt. For the first time in my life I desecrated the Sabbath in such a manner, but circumstances left me no choice. May God forgive me![3]

Kohn's American loyalties and his ability to adjust to a new way of life were exemplary: he was later to become a strong supporter of Lincoln, to achieve prominence in the political life of his community, and to assume the presidency of the first synagogue established in the Middle West. But like thousands of other Jewish immigrants, he started his business career as a peddler, and in doing so he departed even further from the ways of his fathers:

> . . . leading such a life, none of us is able to observe the smallest commandment. Thousands of peddlers wander about America; young, strong men, they waste their strength by carrying heavy loads in the summer's heat; they lose their health in the icy cold of winter. And they forget completely their Creator. They no longer put on the phylacteries; they pray neither on working day nor on the Sabbath. In truth, they have given up their religion for the pack which is on their backs. Is such a life not slavery rather than liberty? [4]

Kohn begged forgiveness for his libertarian behavior:

> God in Heaven, Father of our ancestors, Thou who hast protected the little band of Jews unto this day, Thou knowest my thoughts. Thou alone knowest of my grief when, on the Sabbath's eve, I must retire to my lodging and on Saturday morning carry my pack on my back, profaning the holy day, God's gift to His people, Israel. I can't live as a Jew. [5]

While the leaders of Judaism did not suffer the same kind of agonies that men like Abraham Kohn felt, they were sensitive to the struggle that he and so many others experienced as they sought to maintain personal and group identity in a new culture. Solomon Schechter, for example—a patriot long before he arrived on American shores in 1902 and, like Kohn, a great admirer of Lincoln—came to fear for the survival of *Yiddishkeit* as soon as he became acquainted with local conditions. He noticed even more sophisticated challenges to the retention of identity than did his predecessors. So concerned did he become that in 1912 he resigned from the board of directors of the Educational Alliance—the great settlement house in New York City established by "uptown" Jews to help "downtown" Jews—because he felt that while the institution was stressing Americanization, the immigrant Jew became acculturated so quickly that the real need was for what he termed "Judaisation." Failing to convince his colleagues on the Alliance board, he wrote in his letter of resignation:

> The great question before the Jewish community at present is not so much the Americanising of the Russian Jew as his Judaising. We have now quite sufficient agencies for his Americanisation. But the problem is whether we are able to keep the immigrant within Judaism after he has

become Americanised. Nor is there any need on our part of civilising him, as the general phrase is. Our public schools are overcrowded with Russian young men and women, and so are our Colleges. . . . Most of them join Ethical Culture or other sociological societies, whilst a minority entertain even anarchistic views . . .

Time and economic conditions compel the immigrant to grow constantly in his Americanism and to develop it, unfortunately not always for his good. Any close observer of the conditions downtown will find that one of the most pernicious influences on the immigrant, as soon as he is able to read American papers, is the sensational press, developing a tendency in him towards objectionable individualism and realism as well as towards a certain license in action and thought, which he never knew before. . . . There cannot be the least doubt that what the immigrant loses quickest in this country is his Judaism. . . .

However, my views on this and cognate matters are not shared by the Board. Heaven knows, we never had too much Hebrew [taught at the Alliance] but even this little is to be reduced in favour of something which is called Ethics and Religion. . . . I have sufficient experience to know that it will terminate in representing the religion of the Settlement kind, made up of obsolete philosophies, intermixed with sociology and political economy, interspersed with epigrams from Emerson, obscure lines from Browning, and exclamations about evolution and progress, proving that we, the heroes of modernity, are the promise and fulfillment of civilisation. I have heard and read enough of this sort of lecture to know that, in the best case, it is an "unsectarian religion," bringing us nearer with every day to the abyss; or the great "melting pot," which will devour Judaism ruthlessly as soon as the social prejudice on the part of our neighbours will sufficiently relax.[6]

If Schechter was correct in 1912 in feeling that Jewish identity could not be taken for granted even among immigrant Jews whose class position was very close to the bottom of the social hierarchy and who resided in a thickly settled Jewish area located in the most Jewishly populated city in America, the question of today is: What are the nature and the level of the Jewish identity of the American Jew? The question is doubly pressing in light of the fact that the "social prejudice" to which Schechter alluded has noticeably relaxed in the intervening decades.

This volume, then, is a study in contemporary Jewish identity. Its compass is limited to an analysis of certain aspects of Jewish identity as they occur in a community located in the Middle West, which we call "Lakeville." Our concern with this community is as a case study in problems of Jewishness and Jewish identity, rather than in terms of any special interest in local questions. Our assumption is that what is experienced by Jews in Lakeville is shared, to a greater or lesser extent, by most American Jews, and in fact by modern Jews wherever they reside. And we feel that certain aspects of the problem of identity among the Jews of Lakeville are experienced by members of other minority groups, while others are shared by all modern men who are in search of cultural continuity and community.

The Choice of a Community

It is possible to study the state of the Jewishness of the American Jew in a number of settings. Thus we could seek to locate a community or neighborhood which would be the present-day equivalent of the Lower East Side of a half-century ago. But such a choice would result in minimizing certain important demographic and sociological trends in American Jewish life. Our preference was to proceed in the opposite direction, seeking a community where such trends would be magnified. Our objective in doing so was to locate a place where the Jew who would be increasingly encountered in tomorrow's Jewish community was presently widely represented.

Social mobility was one very important trend that concerned us: it is well known that American Jews have moved upward faster and further than any comparable group. Thus, while we sought a community which had a variety of economic groups, we preferred one with a good proportion of vocationally successful individuals. Another distinguishing tendency among American Jews is their high level of secular education. Therefore, although we wished to avoid a university town where individuals professionally involved in higher education made their residence, we sought a community which had a particularly strong representation of citizens who had been exposed to higher learning. Another distinguishing characteristic of the American Jew is his consumption of "culture": his role as a theatergoer, a music lover, a patron of the arts. Thus we sought a community where such endeavors were widespread and where Jews were accepted as participants and supporters of cultural enterprises.

We also sought a community where different strands of the American-Jewish population were represented. What we particularly had in mind was locating a community where the descendants of both "uptown" Jews and "downtown" Jews were to be found. Although most of American Jewry are "downtown" descendants, our assumption was that the sociological significance of "uptown" descendants is larger than their numerical significance would indicate. As a consequence, we required that our community have a fair representation of families of German descent. Another qualification was that the community contain the grandchildren and great-grandchildren of immigrants, thus allowing us to study the impact of the process of acculturation over a longer time span than is customary. Finally, we sought a community populated by youthful families; we wished to avoid one where there would be a concentration of newly married couples in favor of a community with a high representation of families with children of grammar-school and high-school age.

The presence of children in this age group would mean that parents would necessarily be involved in making choices regarding the transmission of group identity. By overrepresenting individuals who were confronted with such decisions, we hoped to be in a strategic position to gain understanding of the way in which the problem of Jewishness is handled in contemporary life.

It became apparent to us that, while individuals possessing the characteristics in which we were interested are spread too thinly throughout any given metropolitan area to make the study of an entire city economically feasible, such individuals are concentrated in suburban areas. As a consequence, our project became a study of Jews who resided in suburbia. Suburbanization has been a major trend among American Jews since the mid-forties. But our interest was not in suburbia as such. Rather, we chose a suburb because the individuals whom we were interested in studying were concentrated there. Nevertheless, our study throws considerable light on the attitudes and patterns of life of suburban Jews.

In making the choice of a particular suburb, we looked for an older community—one which was an established area before it received a major influx of Jewish population. We wished to avoid a suburb settled after World War II; in such suburbs, Jews are frequently numbered among the earlier residents. Inasmuch as the bulk of the American-Jewish population arrived in the United States after the basic institutions of the society were formed, we thought that an older suburb would more closely approximate the situation of the American Jew.

We also desired a suburb where the size of the Jewish community was large enough so that it would have to be reckoned with, but small enough so that it did not constitute a majority. While the more typical situation of the suburban Jew is that he constitutes the majority in his particular community, we felt that a suburb in which Jews were in a minority would reflect more faithfully the Jew's overall situation in American society. Minority status was not only advisable in respect to the in-group aspect of the project but especially important for that part of our study dealing with intergroup problems and attitudes. In this connection, we required a community characterized by what local residents thought were good intergroup relationships. This would allow us to study Jewish-Gentile interaction under favorable conditions as well as to analyze the nature of in-group attitudes in a benign intergroup climate.

Desiring to locate strongly acculturated respondents who were nevertheless within the mainstream of American Jewish life, we decided on a location in the Middle West.* We required a medium-sized suburb small enough to be investigated with the means available to us, but large enough to offer challenging variety. And we required that our suburb have an institutional structure autonomous enough to allow it to be treated as a distinctive community.

Our choice was Lakeville, a community with a population of approximately 25,000, in which the Jewish population numbers about 8,000. Lakeville is a suburb of "Lake City," one of the leading industrial and commercial centers of the nation.

Suburbanization in Lake City

Suburbanization is an old story in Lake City. Members of the middle and upper classes, many of whom in past decades had a rural or village upbringing, have long sought to escape the metropolis. And spurred by the growth of industry in the outlying areas of Lake City, working-class and lower-middle-class suburbs have come into being in recent years.

Of all the suburban locations which surround the city, the one having top status is the "Heights"—the section in which Lakeville is situated. A number of social classes established residence on the Heights; certain sections were pre-empted by the upper class, by the solid middle class, by the lower middle class, or by servants and others who worked for the upper class. In any case, the Heights suburbs developed a reputation as the place of residence of Lake City's upper class; for whoever else might live on the Heights, it became the favored place of residence of Lake City society. Thus an issue of the Social Register during the 1920's indicates that over 80 per cent of those listed as living in the suburbs of Lake City

---

* Another consideration in this connection was that the Riverton Study, also sponsored by the American Jewish Committee, was conducted in an eastern seaboard community. Consequently, we preferred to study a community located in a different area of the country.

resided in one or another of the Heights communities. There have been changes in the intervening decades, however. Some of the descendants of the old elite have moved to new locations, particularly to exurbia. Among other motivations, such families prefer larger plots of land than can easily be purchased in the Heights. Also they prefer to reside in less elaborate establishments than their parents occupied. But in spite of such changes, the elite reputation of the Heights has been retained.

At the beginning of the century, relatively few Jews lived on the Heights. Those who did were as likely to be local merchants as they were to be wealthy estate owners. During this period and for years afterward, the preference of the Lake City Jew was for an apartment in the city. His aspiration to better himself did not involve a move to the suburbs, but rather a shift to a better neighborhood within the city: he changed his residence from a smaller and older flat to a newer and more commodious apartment. Although the Jewish upper class frequently owned their own homes, they preferred residences situated along tree-lined boulevards located within easy reach of the hub of Lake City. But Lake City, like so many other communities, became afflicted with urban blight. And the neighborhoods in which the Jewish upper class had established themselves deteriorated even more rapidly than did many others; they were located especially close to the sections into which Negro newcomers from the South moved.

The upper-class Jews who decided to leave the city followed the example of the Gentile elite; they too favored the Heights. Shortly before World War I, the industrialist who was the richest, most public-spirited, and most widely respected member of the Jewish community of Lake City, both by his fellow Jews and by Gentiles, bought an estate on the Heights. It was located in one of the most picturesque areas of Lakeville. His choice signified both to upper-class Jews and to other Jews that for their group the Heights was the most preferable of all the suburban areas surrounding Lake City.

The purchase of property on the Heights was not a simple matter, however. Restrictions existed. To this day, Jews are the victims of discrimination. Thus one of the smaller Heights communities—essentially an upper-middle-class area with very few residents who are members of the Social Register—has been able to maintain its *judenrein* status. Another Heights suburb—a larger town where many socialites make their home—has a long history of restriction and even today has relatively few residents who are Jewish. Nevertheless, because of the diversity of communities on the

Heights, property has always been available for purchase. And of all the Heights communities, it is Lakeville that has been the most free of anti-Jewish discrimination.

Lakeville's History

The first phase of Lakeville's development began in the 1850's, a decade or so after the area was opened for settlement. Initially, efforts were made to develop the community as a port for transporting cargo to inland markets. Although the scheme collapsed after the advent of the railroad and in the face of the increasing predominance of Lake City, it gave impetus to the development of Lakeville as a commercial center for the immediate hinterland as well as a site for some light industry.

During the 1870's, certain local business and real estate interests, aware of the uncertain future of their small community as either an industrial or commercial center, decided to make the most of its secluded atmosphere, rolling hills, pleasant vistas, and lake front by promoting the town as a recreational and residential community for wealthy families from Lake City. The town was plotted on a park system to help preserve its natural beauty. New plank sidewalks were built for the business district, transportation facilities were improved, and various public buildings were constructed. Within a relatively short span of years, the plan began to succeed, and Lakeville became a fashionable summer resort.

As Lakeville's appeal grew, desirable land sold for as much as $10,000 an acre. Mansion after mansion arose along the lake front. Country clubs were organized, establishing Lakeville's reputation as a golfing community. A luxury hotel was built and a harbor created for pleasure craft. A tract of land was rescued from becoming a beer garden and was turned into a center for the performing arts. The center attracted major musical and theatrical artists and fashionable audiences.

The summer elite had no concern with the commercial life of the community. Their business interests, frequently of a large-scale character, were centered in Lake City. Many of Lakeville's local businessmen viewed the summer elite with mixed feelings: they were happy with the progress of the community, but unhappy with the fact that they could not compete socially with the summer people. In any case, they felt only a commercial stake in Lakeville property; they had no interest in introducing a restrictive policy concerning its sale. By way of contrast, many of the other fashionable communities on the Heights which had no prior history as commercial towns were quick to adopt discriminatory practices. Thus, despite its growth during an era when the exclusion of Jews was commonplace in communities where upper-class Protestants resided, Lakeville continued to rely on the impersonal workings of the marketplace. A real estate circular of the time characterized Lakeville as a "democratic place, considerably more so than some of her sister towns . . . which have much the air of exclusiveness about them. Nevertheless, Lakeville numbers among its residents many of the wealthy business and professional men of [Lake City] and people who stand high on the social scale." A columnist in the local newspaper came more directly to the point of the prevailing attitude: "We hear some very fine people are a bit disturbed over the settlement among us of some excellent families of the Hebrew faith. Tastes do differ, but why object? . . . rather we commend them for they pay their bills 100 per cent on the dollar every time and that kind of thing goes a long way with us. We welcome them."

During the 1910's, more and more families began to make the community their year-round place of residence, although some of the wealthiest of these families maintained an apartment in Lake City as well. In the 1920's, suburbanization took an even stronger hold, and the population grew from 6,000 to 12,000. Some of Lakeville's new permanent residents came from the old summer elite, but the majority were middle-class "White Anglo-Saxon Protestants" who preferred a house and a garden among congenial neighbors in the suburbs to an apartment in the city. They brought with them the values of strong family life and responsible citizenship. Under their influence, Lakeville underwent a major expansion and improvement of its educational, religious, philanthropic, and community institutions, becoming one of the more attractive and progressive communities on the Heights.

Although population growth lagged during the depression and the war years, it took on a powerful impetus in the late 1940's. Because of its excellent facilities, especially in education, as well as its traditions of leisure and culture, Lakeville was particularly attractive to the younger generation of middle-class residents of Lake City. These individuals had grown up in the metropolis, but like their counterparts throughout the country they were intent upon leaving their urban neighborhoods and making a different life for themselves in the suburbs. Lakeville also received some new, if impermanent, residents from the ranks of middle-level executives employed by large corporations and transferred to offices or factories located in the Lake City area.

Jews in Lakeville

With the exception of corporation employees, one of the salient characteristics of this influx was that many of the newcomers were Jewish. This was due, in good part, to the "democratic" tradition that we have already noted. There had always been Jews living in Lakeville, and though their number was never very large, they had been part of each phase of its development. Thus among the early businessmen there were a Jewish jeweler and clothier. Lakeville's first theater had been built by a Jew, who became relatively prominent in the community.

When Lakeville became a summer resort, it attracted a small number of Jewish millionaires who bought or built mansions along the lake front or small estates in the wooded areas of the community. These members of the German-Jewish elite were joined by other prosperous Jewish families. Finding that they were excluded from elite Gentile clubs and facilities, they tended to form a summer colony of their own. These families were responsible for the first Jewish communal institution in Lakeville: having adopted many aspects of the style of life of their peers, and in response to the discrimination against them, they established a golf club—the Wildacres Country Club. Consequently, the initial evidence of organized Jewish group life in Lakeville differs from most other places, as, for example, in the nineteenth-century city where the first evidence of such organized life is generally the purchase of land for a cemetery, or in the twentieth-century suburb where it is usually a piece of property on which to build a synagogue.

In time, many of the members of the Wildacres Country Club became year-round residents of Lakeville. However, in the 1920's population growth was predominantly Gentile. Moreover, during this period the elite class of Gentiles who took up permanent residence in the community became increasingly influential in the political and social life of the town. Since the main thrust of discrimination came from the Gentile elite, the effect of this development was to make the Jewish group even more isolated. Accepting their marginal position in Lakeville, Jews discreetly kept their distance while making substantial contributions to the cultural, educational, and philanthropic institutions of the community. The 1920's also saw a number of Lakeville residents joining with other Jews on the Heights to organize the first Jewish religious institution in the area: the Isaac Mayer Wise Temple. But aside from their activities in the temple and the country club, Jews did not develop a strong Jewish community; they feared to increase their conspicuousness as an out-group. Rather, they preferred to remain a small body of wealthy and accommodating citizens who had adapted to the norms of Lakeville, one of which was that Jews led a separate social life and did not disturb the prevailing Gentile tone of the community.

These grounds of mutual adjustment were dramatically altered after World War II with the heavy migration of Lake City Jews to the community. Within a decade, the Jewish population grew from an insignificant minority to the point where close to one out of every three households in Lakeville was Jewish. But while some of the oldtime Gentile residents felt that their town was about to be inundated by Jews from Lake City, in actuality the major line of Jewish suburban movement was not in the direction of the Heights. Lakeville's drawing power was limited to special groups. Thus it attracted only the more prosperous and the most highly educated of the new Jewish suburbanites. It was also of special interest to those who had a particular style of leisure-time activities. And the reputation of its school system served as a magnet for some families who were especially concerned about the deterioration of city schools and particularly desirous of a school system known for its quality education. Most Lake City Jews who adhered to a relatively traditional Jewish way of life avoided the community, choosing instead a suburban location at some remove from the Heights—generally one of the newer suburbs where there was no strong existing community pattern to which they would be under pressure to conform.

Although on the whole wealthier, better educated, more urbane, less traditionally Jewish, and less ethnocentric than the average new Jewish suburbanite, the majority of Jewish newcomers to Lakeville were different from the Jewish oldtimers of the town. For one thing, they were from East European stock, rather than from the more acculturated German-Jewish one. And on the whole they were much less inclined to take an inconspicuous place in the community. They were more willing to play an active role in community affairs, to maintain the manners and mores they had acquired in the urban Jewish neighborhoods, and to organize purely sectarian associations and institutions. Thus they established new temples or reinvigorated old ones, and they founded chapters of several national Jewish organizations. Within a short time, a quite visible and variegated structure of Jewish communal life developed in the town. Many of the older residents remained in Lakeville, rather than move back to the city after their children were grown. Strong differences arose between Jewish newcomers and Jewish oldtimers.

During this same period, a significant number of the elite Gentile residents left Lakeville. It is difficult to determine to what extent their departure was provoked by the influx of Jews, by the growth and alteration of the community in general, or by the attraction of an exurban rather than a suburban location. There is no question, however, that many of the Gentiles who remained in the community believed that this exodus was in response to the Jewish migration, and there seems little reason to believe that many of the elite families who left would have been more willing to share Lakeville with the Jewish newcomers than they had been to share their clubs with the older Jewish residents. Be that as it may, their emigration, combined with the influx of Jews, inevitably altered the social character of the town. While wealthy and influential Jews continued to move into Lakeville, Gentile newcomers tended to be young, middle-class families, and as a consequence the ranks of the elite Gentile group were not replenished. In sum, the Jewish influx meant that Lakeville had lost its social *éclat* for the Gentile.

Contemporary Lakeville

Almost all Lakeville Jews are solidly middle-class or upper-class in occupation or income. And surprisingly enough, Lakeville Jews tend to conform to the image held of the suburbanite in American culture to a greater extent than do Lakeville Gentiles. Although the latter include a substantial number of middle-class business and professional men who commute to Lake City, there is also a significant proportion of working-class families who are employed in the community. Some of these working-class families have their roots in Lakeville's history as a town rather than a suburb, and in its functions as a service center for the surrounding communities. The breadwinner of such a family may be employed, for example, by the local electric or telephone company or by the railroad which serves Lakeville's commuters. Other working-class families have their roots in Lakeville as an elite area of summer homes and year-round residences. This group continues to work at a variety of crafts and occupations needed for the maintenance of the community's homes and gardens.

The residences of Lakeville reflect some of these differences. Recent Jewish families are likely to live in newly constructed houses of modern ranch design. Gentiles occupy a range of dwellings, ranging from inexpensive frame houses in the center of town to early American or early modern houses in the more affluent neighborhoods. The wealthy group of longtime Jewish residents occupy older, elaborate homes or radically modern dwellings that rest on stilts in the hilly areas of the town. Most of the neighborhoods, however, have developed a variety of housing designs which bespeak the heterogeneous mixture of Jews and Gentiles, longtime residents and newcomers, who now make up Lakeville.

There is no heavy industry and relatively little light industry in the community. But what Lakeville does possess in abundance is retail establishments. They number over two hundred and cater to the full range of consumer needs. The business district reflects both the old and the new Lakeville. Although the main street has modern fluorescent lighting, the side streets still use old-fashioned lamps. Venerable stores that evoke an atmosphere of the nineteenth century are interspersed with sleek, contemporary shops that bespeak the sophistication of the modern suburb. Even though business flourishes, local merchants fear that the growth and prosperity of the town may result in the establishment of shopping centers in outlying districts.

The Jewish influx has had some impact on shopping facilities. A kosher butcher shop has opened on a side street and a Jewish delicatessen on the main street. The appearance of Chinese restaurants is also probably due to the Jewish influx—a pattern carried to Lakeville from the Jewish neighborhoods of Lake City. But an even more apparent aspect of Jewish influence is the fact that long-established merchants of conservative inclinations have found themselves forced to adapt to the tastes of their young, style-conscious, and affluent Jewish customers.

In respect to local government, the political structure of Lakeville was overhauled in the 1950's. Under the new plan, policies are set by an elected mayor and a City Council of six members and are executed by a professionally trained city manager who assumes responsibility for the day-to-day operation of the city. This change has been successful, and today Lakeville is governed more efficiently than in the past. With its revamped structure and competent manager, the community has been able to cope with the municipal problems created by its growth and to contain the stresses bred by rapid social change. Lakeville residents attempt to steer clear of larger political loyalties in the running of their community, and in theory fidelity to national political parties does not enter into non-partisan local elections.

Adoption of the council-manager form of government was primarily due to the spirited action of a variety of civic groups, including the Lakeville Voters' Association, the Lakeville Civic Association, and the Lakeville League of Women Voters. These groups operate a continuous program aimed at arousing public interest and action in community affairs. Perhaps the most effective of these organizations and the one which especially attempts to foster a non-partisan approach to local issues is the Lakeville League of Women Voters, considered one of the most enlightened and active chapters in the state. The League's activities include a variety of civic projects, ranging from school and health surveys to public meetings about political affairs. The efforts of the League to register voters have enabled the town to maintain one of the highest percentages of registered voters in the nation.

In addition to the League and to other typical community-wide civic groups such as the Lions and Kiwanis, during the past two decades Lakeville has developed a number of neighborhood improvement associations. Although they focus on the particular interests of their members, these associations inevitably become involved in general community affairs. The associations typify the wide desire in the community to protect it from creeping commercialism and suburban blight; they exemplify Lakeville's will to maintain itself as a desirable residential area populated by public-spirited citizens.

Lakeville's school system is reputed to be among its most desirable features, constituting an inducement for Jewish families, traditionally oriented toward education, to move into the community. The school system has long been a source of pride to the residents of Lakeville. Its high rating was achieved by years of painstaking effort and liberal expenditures of public funds. During the postwar boom, when other community services deteriorated, the schools were able not only to maintain their standards but even to improve them, a fact that testifies to the public investment in education.

The system is divided into districts. Each is governed by an independent board of education consisting of five elected members who serve without compensation. Candidates for the board are nominated in an open caucus formed by representatives of the PTA's (Parent-Teacher Associations) within the school district. School board elections and education appropriations are of considerable interest to Lakeville residents. The elementary-school districts, only one of which lies completely within the boundaries of Lakeville, include over a dozen schools. The schools reflect the ethnic, religious, and class composition of their neighborhood. Since there are virtually no Negroes in Lakeville and few in immediately adjacent areas, the districts have not had to face the problem of racial integration.

The Lakeville High School serves the local community and some neigh-boring areas, and it draws its students from the graduates of Catholic parochial schools as well as from the public schools. The high school brings together diverse economic, religious, and ethnic groups: children of low-income Italian Catholic families from the small community to the southeast of Lakeville, native American Protestants in modest circum-stances from central Lakeville, and the children of affluent Jews and Gentiles from the preferred residential areas. Despite this heterogeneity, the major emphasis of the curriculum and teaching is preparation for college, and four out of five of its graduates go on to an institution of higher learning.

From its earliest beginnings, religious life was firmly established in Lakeville. Sometime after the Civil War there was an attempt to make Lakeville a Baptist community, but Presbyterian, Episcopalian, Metho-dist, and Lutheran congregations came to be established in rapid suc-cession. Although Protestants have constituted the preponderant majority in the past, they make up somewhat less than one-half of the present population. Today there are seven Protestant churches in the community, the largest and most prestigious being Presbyterian and Episcopalian. Lakeville Protestants are chiefly of English, German, and Scandinavian descent.

Despite the early dominance of the Protestant faith, Catholics have resided in Lakeville for many years. The first Catholic parish was organ-ized in the 1870's. At one time, the local church supported a parochial high school, but financial difficulties caused it to close. The parish con-tinues to operate an elementary school. Catholics comprise about one-fifth of the Lakeville population and are chiefly of Italian and Irish descent. The Jews were the last of the three major faiths to organize a congregation. At present, one Conservative and four Reform congrega-tions are located either in Lakeville proper or in immediately adjacent areas.

Relations between the various religious groups are considered to be cordial. In recent years, the Lakeville Ministerial Fellowship has spon-sored an interdenominational Thanksgiving Eve service in which a num-ber of Jewish and Protestant congregations have participated. Ministers and rabbis have also tried to work out a compromise on the perennial question of how Christmas is to be celebrated in the public schools.

Most Lakeville residents are typically devoted to a variety of humani-tarian and philanthropic causes and institutions. The most important local philanthropy is the Lakeville Community Hospital, which now has over 150 beds and a million-dollar budget. A Women's Auxiliary of the hospital was organized in the 1920's and has since become one of the most important health and welfare associations in the community. It provides the hospital with many thousands of hours of volunteer service, runs a profitable gift shop and snack bar in the building, and contributes significant sums of money to the institution. Membership in the Auxiliary is open to all women in the area, but its officers and board members tend to be drawn from the affluent class of the community.

An array of other organizations are active in meeting health and welfare needs. Chief among these are the Family Service (which was organized in the depression years as the Social Service Committee), a Mental Health Association, a Golden Circle for Senior Citizens, a Visiting Nurse Association, local chapters of the Red Cross, and a wide spectrum of organizations which raise funds for the treatment and research of "dread diseases." A particularly illustrious association in Lakeville is the Infant Welfare League, which raises funds for baby clinics and settlement work in Lake City. Along with such non-sectarian health and welfare activities, Lakeville citizens are also involved in a range of sectarian philanthropies.

In spite of the many changes that have taken place in the community during recent decades, Lakeville's past as a summer resort is still very evident. The community boasts five private golf clubs as well as a yacht club. Its public facilities include bathing beaches, boating facilities, tennis courts, golf courses, and playgrounds. In addition to the park district which manages these facilities, Lakeville also has a playground and recreation board. The site of many of the indoor activities sponsored by the board is a community recreation building which features a large gymnasium, a commodious auditorium complete with stage facilities, a game room with a soda bar, various club and conference rooms, a workshop with power and hand tools, and a well-outfitted kitchen. During the fall, winter, and spring, the facilities of the recreation building are in intensive use, and during the warm weather the board conducts a variety of recreational programs for several different age levels at its playgrounds, parks, and swimming pools.

Just as Lakeville's unusual recreational facilities can be traced to its history as a summer resort, the extent and quality of its present-day cultural activities also have their roots in its elite past. The outstanding facility in the community is its center for the performing arts, which continues to provide first-rate musical and theatrical programs during the summer season. Lakeville also boasts a community concert series, held in the high school during the winter, a music club that provides entertainment at community gatherings, and even a barbershop quartet. Through the support of the Library Board and of the Friends of the Library, the public library has become a vital force in the cultural life of the community. It has good facilities for young people, and borrowers have a choice of over 140,000 volumes. The library also boasts an active music department. Great Books discussion groups as well as other community enterprises of an intellectual nature are held in the library's comfortable building, well situated near the center of Lakeville.

Every year, an adult education program is presented at the Lakeville High School. Courses range from sewing to municipal government and from woodworking to foreign languages. There are also formally organized associations such as an art league and film society, and informal ones such as literary clubs and play-reading groups. The community's present role as a place of residence of the educated and affluent thus complements its past as an elite summer resort, with the result that diversified cultural and intellectual activities are available to its residents.

In short, Lakeville's pleasing physical characteristics, its public spirit and clean government, its balanced population, its good intergroup relations, its active community organizations, its excellent schools, its variegated and harmonious religious life, its philanthropic orientation, its emphasis on fine recreational facilities and cultural activities, all bespeak a model community. How, we wonder, does Jewishness fare in a community that typifies so much of American aspiration?

Before we turn to this problem, we must analyze the social characteristics of the 208 men and 224 women of Lakeville whom we interviewed. Knowledge of their demographic profile will provide us with a basis for evaluating their behavior in respect to a variety of aspects of Jewishness as well as for understanding their responses to the questions we put to them about their attitudes toward Jewish identity.

2

THE JEWS OF LAKEVILLE:
THEIR SOCIAL
CHARACTERISTICS

In this chapter, the 432 respondents who compose our representative sample of Lakeville's Jews, and who thereby reflect the demographic profile of Lakeville Jewry, are described in respect to such commonly analyzed characteristics as age, family composition, occupation, education, income, and length of residence in the community.*

Since our study is concerned with the question of acculturation and its relationship to group identity, we are also obliged to give careful attention to the generational status of our respondents. Furthermore, it is necessary that we focus on an issue that is special to the Jewish situation. While members of other ethnic groups may have come from different sections of the same country, Jews came to America from diverse areas of the European continent. Because of the acculturation of the first generation, as well as the emergence of the second and succeeding generations, the old regional differences have eroded away. Nevertheless, we must seek to ascertain whether any distinctions remain between those

* See the Appendix for a description of the method by which the sample of Lakeville Jews (as well as of Gentiles) was selected.

whose families originated in Germany and the countries dominated by German culture (whom we shall designate as "Germans") and those who originated in Eastern Europe (whom we shall designate as "East Europeans"). Finally, we must review the whole question of how our respondents compare with other Jews in the Lake City metropolitan area and, more importantly, in the nation at large.

Age and Family Composition

When we consider the factor of age, we find that the great majority of our respondents, men as well as women, are located in the 30 to 49 age group. The median age of the men is 43.1 years; for women, it is 37.6 years (see Table 2–1).[1]

TABLE 2–1. AGE OF RESPONDENTS BY SEX

Age		Men	Women
20–29		3%	15%
30–39		36	46
40–49		36	29
50–59		22	9
60 and over		3	1
	N	(208)	(224)
MEDIAN AGE		43.1	37.6

That only about a tenth of our respondents are below 30 years of age underscores the character of the community, particularly the fact that Lakeville existed as a suburb long before those of the mass-produced, post–World War II variety were established. It has not, therefore, attracted large numbers of very young families which typically require housing modest in size and inexpensive in price. The settlement of families at the opposite end of the spectrum has also been limited: Lakeville is not a place to which people move at an advanced stage in the life cycle.

Lakeville holds no attraction for single persons: some 96 per cent of our respondents are married, and the balance are either widowed or divorced. As we would expect in a suburban area, relatively few childless couples are encountered. But less typical for suburbia is the fact that there are no really large families. Only 6 per cent of our respondents have as many as four children, less than 1 per cent have five children; there are no couples with six or more children.[2] As indicated in Table 2–2, the mean number of children per family is 2.2. Given the age distribution of our respondents and what we know about the proclivities of younger Jewish couples in the suburbs, this figure may be expected to climb somewhat.[3]

TABLE 2–2. NUMBER OF CHILDREN PER RESPONDENT

Number of Children	
0	2%
1	13
2	56
3	23
4	6
5	*
MEAN NUMBER OF CHILDREN	2.2

* Less than 0.5 per cent.

Eventual family size in Lakeville and in hundreds of other communities in the country will be one of the decisive factors in the question of whether Jews survive as a group in American society. Yet from the perspective of our present inquiry, it is the youthfulness of the children that interests us most. This is because when children are young parents are forced to play an active role in the socialization process. And while other socialization agents are extremely powerful, the influence of parents extends even beyond the home, for their decisions structure the world in which the youngster moves.

It is apparent that Lakeville Jews are very much involved in the socialization process: in half of our families the mean age of the children is 10 years or less. In nearly three-quarters of our families the mean age of the children is less than 15 years (see Table 2–3). Thus Lakeville presents us with an excellent situation for the study of Jewish identity: the fact that most families have young children means that the problem is on the doorstep, rather than at a remote distance. The question of the identity of the younger generation will be analyzed at various points in the following chapters, and Chapter 9 is devoted entirely to a discussion of this issue.

TABLE 2-3. MEAN AGE OF CHILDREN OF RESPONDENTS

Mean Age of Children	
0–2	6%
3–5	22
6–8	17
9–11	15
12–14	13
15–17	8
18–23	9
24–29	6
30 and over	4
TOTAL RESPONDENTS WITH CHILDREN	(424)

Occupation

Turning to the area of socio-economic status, we shall examine first the occupations of our respondents, then their level of education, and finally their income.

While to the Jew in Lakeville it seems that a wide variety of occupations is represented among his peers, to the student of social stratification, who tends to think in terms of occupational classifications, the range is not very considerable. Almost all our respondents work as (*a*) professionals or technicians, (*b*) managers, officials, or proprietors, or (*c*) sales workers (see Table 2–4). None of them work as clerks, operatives, service workers, or laborers. A mere 1 per cent were classified as craftsmen or foremen.[4] If not by their own conceptions, then by any general standard our respondents may be said to constitute an occupational elite.

The leading occupational classification—"managers, officials, and proprietors"—includes 52 per cent of those who are the main earners of their households. The predominant group falling under this rubric (those categorized as "other managers, officials, and proprietors") exhibits considerable heterogeneity. Included are senior officials of large enterprises as well as junior members of small firms, owners of important retail chains, and proprietors of prosperous retail shops which draw their labor force mainly from members of the owners' own family. The professional and technical group, which includes 34 per cent of the main earners,

TABLE 2–4. OCCUPATIONAL CLASSIFICATION OF
MAIN EARNER *

Occupation		
Professional and technical workers	34%	
Lawyers, judges		11
Physicians, surgeons, dentists		8
Engineers		4
Accountants		3
Other		8
Managers, officials, and proprietors	52	
Sales managers, buyers		6
Bankers, stockbrokers		3
Other		43
Sales workers	13	
Insurance agents and brokers;		
real estate agents and brokers		3
Salesmen; sales representatives		10
Craftsmen and foremen	1	
Retired, no answer	†	

* Based on occupational classification of the U.S. Census Bureau.
† Less than 0.5 per cent.

covers a somewhat narrower spectrum, although it too has variety: some
are professionals known throughout the metropolitan area and even
beyond, while others are professionals who practice in relative obscurity.
Two areas are pre-eminent—law and medicine—and thus our professional and technical workers are concentrated in some of the most statusful fields of specialization.

While few Jews in Lakeville work at "blue-collar" jobs or in lower-
status "white-collar" occupations, we find that they have another very
distinctive characteristic: 61 per cent are either self-employed or the
owner or part-owner of a business. The figure seems anomalous. In a
mature capitalistic age in which ever-increasing numbers of individuals
—be they professional or technical workers, managers, or officials—work
for enterprises which they do not themselves own, Lakeville Jews follow
quite a different pattern. Viewed in historical perspective, their proclivities seem characteristic of an earlier capitalistic era—an era when enterprises were small or at least family-owned, when professionals were
"free" rather than salaried, when each man was the captain of his own
economic ship, and when—if he served as someone's first or second mate

—he was doing so only against the day when he would strike out on his own.

Poverty is frequently the price paid for economic backwardness. And even if it is not exacted, the individual may suffer from psychological ills: he may feel alienated from an economic order which has fossilized him. Our respondents, however, do not seem to display either tendency; they are both prosperous and satisfied with the economic order and the place they occupy in it. Perhaps many are the last of their breed; it is problematic whether their children will be capable, or even desirous, of achieving the same level of self-employment. In any case, their employment pattern surely involves a wide range of correlates and effects, many of which are of a subtle kind and await research.

TABLE 2–5. INDUSTRY IN WHICH MAIN EARNER IS EMPLOYED *

Kind of Business or Industry	
Professional and related services	22%
Manufacturing, non-durable goods	16
Manufacturing, durable goods	11
Wholesale trade	14
Retail trade	11
Finance, insurance, and real estate	11
Advertising, publicity, public relations	4
Publishing	3
Construction	3
Personal services	2
Other fields	3
No answer	†

* Based on industry classification of the U.S. Census Bureau.
† Less than 0.5 per cent.

To complete our analysis of occupational characteristics, we turn to the industrial composition of our sample. We find that almost three-quarters of our respondents can be classified under the following rubrics: (*a*) manufacturing, (*b*) trade, or (*c*) professional and related services (see Table 2–5). Most are thus concentrated in a handful of industrial classifications, and, accordingly, few are employed in certain fields which engage significant segments of the general population, such as public utilities (including transportation and communication) and public administration.

In spite of the fact that the Lake City metropolitan area serves as a major center of heavy industry, the majority of our respondents engaged in manufacturing make their living from the production of non-durable goods. On the other hand, the image of the American Jew as connected exclusively with the production of "soft" goods is not sustained in our sample; a substantial minority is engaged in the production of durable goods. Another important facet of the occupational picture is that more of our respondents are engaged in wholesale as distinct from retail trade. While the metropolitan area is an important wholesale center, such a concentration is notable, inasmuch as retailing customarily employs far more people than wholesaling.

Education

By any yardstick, the educational level of our respondents must be judged as high.[5] All the men have finished grammar school; only 4 per cent lack a high-school diploma (see Table 2–6). Even more extraordinary is the fact that a full 89 per cent have had a year or more of higher education. Finally, some 34 per cent have been enrolled in a graduate or professional school.[6]

The educational attainment of the women generally parallels that of the men. As we should expect, there is some measure of discrepancy: only 82 per cent of the women have been enrolled in college, as compared with 89 per cent of the men. Also, a larger proportion of the women

TABLE 2–6. EDUCATIONAL ATTAINMENT OF MEN AND WOMEN RESPONDENTS AND OF THEIR FATHERS

Level of Education	Men	Women	All Respondents	Respondents' Fathers
No formal education	—%	—%	—%	16%
Some grammar school	—	—	—	16
Completed grammar school	—	—	—	11
Some high school	4	2	3	11
Completed high school	7	16	11	18
Some college	24	40	33	8
Completed college	31	28	29	10
Beyond college	34	14	24	7
No answer	—	—	—	3
N	(208)	(224)	(432)	(432)

have failed to complete the requirements for an undergraduate degree. But it is at the graduate level that the gap is most noticeable: less than half as many women as men have taken such training.

Whatever the extent of these disparities, they are minor in comparison with the differences between the respondents and their parents. Even if parent–child differences are minimized by confining the comparison to the fathers, the gulf between the generations is still very wide. For example, while all our respondents have completed grammar school, some 32 per cent of their fathers lack a grammar-school diploma.[7] And at the other end of the educational spectrum, we note that only 25 per cent of the parents were enrolled in a college or university, in contrast to 86 per cent of their children.

Differences between the generations, then, are vast. However, the significance of the college-educated parental group should not be overlooked, for it means that there is one segment of our sample where the educational gulf between the generations may not be overly wide. Although a son in such a family may have gone on to graduate school, whereas the father halted at the undergraduate level, both parent and child may share the same universe of educational discourse.

We have no way of knowing the significance of educational discrepancies between parent and child. From the size of such discrepancies, and from what we know about Jewish attitudes toward education, it is apparent that they are more frequently the result of parental encouragement than the product of rifts between juvenile aspirations and parental proclivities. Of course, while our inference that parental encouragement was present may be entirely correct, it may nevertheless be true that the educational gap between the generations may be productive of unanticipated consequences in parent–child relationships.

Income

It may be appropriate at this point to analyze the income of our respondents, for the linkage between education and income is commonly made by students of social stratification as well as by those with less disinterested motives. For example, the insurance companies, eager to sell college-endowment policies, have given extensive publicity to the income differentials that exist between the college-educated and those with a lower level of schooling.

The median total family income reported by our respondents is sizable:

$18,112 (see Table 2–7). Some 40 per cent report that they have incomes of $20,000 or more, while 9 per cent report an income of $50,000 and over. Only 12 per cent report an income of less than $10,000 per year.[8]

TABLE 2–7. TOTAL FAMILY INCOME

Income	
Less than $5,000	1%
$5,000–$7,499	3
$7,500–$9,999	8
$10,000–$14,999	24
$15,000–$19,999	23
$20,000–$29,999	17
$30,000–$49,999	14
$50,000 and over	9
No answer	1
MEDIAN TOTAL FAMILY INCOME	$18,112

As we should expect in a group that includes many young and well-educated persons, the tendency is for income to be on the rise. Thus we find that the family income of our respondents has been increasing at about $1,000 per year: five years ago the median figure was approximately $13,000. In contrast to the 12 per cent who now have incomes of less than $10,000, five years ago some 34 per cent were in this category.

Given favorable economic conditions, most of our respondents should continue to increase their income during the next few years. We find, for example, that respondents of ages 40 to 49 have a considerably higher income than those under 40. Thus, while 33 per cent of the 40–49 group attain an income of $30,000 and over, only 8 per cent of the under–40 group are in the same category (see Table 2–8). Even more significantly, the group aged 50 years and over is more prosperous than the 40–49 group. However, the margin between them and the 40–49 group is not nearly so marked as is the contrast between the under–40 group and those in the 40–49 category.

In addition to the age factor, occupation is an important influence on income. While it is true that the greatest range tends to be within occupational groupings rather than between them, and that some occupations are notably better rewarded than others, we find that there are sizable income differences between occupational categories. Thus the median total family income of managers, officials, and proprietors is about $24,000, while for sales workers it is only $16,000. The professionals are located between these two extremes. Here the income range within the occupational category is considerable. Thus the approximate median for physicians—$23,000—is almost as high as for managers, officials, and proprietors. Lawyers follow at some distance ($20,000), while engineers are not especially prosperous ($18,000).

TABLE 2–8. TOTAL FAMILY INCOME BY AGE *

Income	Age		
	Under 40	40–49	50 and over
Under $10,000	16%	3%	6%
$10,000–$14,999	32	19	17
$15,000–$19,999	21	24	13
$20,000–$29,999	22	20	21
$30,000 and over	8	33	39
No answer	1	1	4
N	(81)	(74)	(53)

* Based on men respondents.

There is one very special aspect to income differentials in Lakeville, namely, that no correlation exists between level of education and income. Thus the relationship that analysts have documented time after time in studies of the population at large is not present in this instance. Specifically, 42 per cent of the men over 50 who did not enter college have an income of $30,000 or more. Approximately the same proportion, or 41 per cent, of the men of the same age who completed college have attained the same level of income. The same lack of correlation between education and income is found among younger age groups as well.

Does Lakeville Jewry negate the argument of those who preach that the road to prosperity is paved with education? Not really. We may think in terms of two escalators which help individuals attain high levels of income. One is the escalator of education, so common at present in the larger society. The other is business enterprise—the kind utilized by the self-made man whose main assets are aggressiveness, imagination, and optimism. While this escalator has slowed perceptibly in the general community, our data suggest that it still operates at comparatively high speed in this particular segment of the Jewish community.[9]

It should be pointed out that not all our respondents who lack a college education are truly self-made men. A small proportion come from well-established families—families so prosperous that, in a sense, they could afford *not* to send their sons to college, or if they did enroll their offspring, there was no economic incentive to complete the requirements for a degree. These families aside, the significant fact is that self-made men—individuals who have created a modest business empire without benefit of sheepskin or inherited wealth—are encountered in Lakeville. They are, of course, exceptional people. Many of their Jewish peers attempted the same risky journey without a similar measure of success; the less successful have remained in Lake City or have located in suburbs of lesser reputation.

If our self-made respondents are exceptional people, they are in all probability part of a dying breed. Thus the younger age groups in our sample have substantially fewer individuals who are only elementary or high-school graduates than the oldest age group. The trend is clear enough: as time goes on, men who succeed in the business world and who have only a high-school diploma will be highly exceptional. The man who lacks capital will at least have the asset of a college education.

If we look at our data on education and income in perspective, the type of selection process operating in Lakeville becomes clear. The community attracts those who have (*a*) considerable education and high income, (*b*) high income and middling or poor education, or (*c*) considerable education and a middling income. Thus it seems necessary to be richly endowed with either education or income if one is to make his home in the community; few come who are middling or low in both education and income. Furthermore, we may assume that those who manage to settle in Lakeville and who suffer from a deficiency in both characteristics find it difficult to adjust. We did not study the problem of what kinds of Jewish families leave Lakeville, but we infer that the departure rate among those who are middling or low in both income and education must be high.

Generation and Descent

The largest group of our respondents (39 per cent) are second-generation Americans (see Table 2–9).[10] Next in order of magnitude is the third generation, constituting 31 per cent of our respondents. The fourth generation totals 19 per cent. It is followed by the immigrant generation, which contributes a mere 8 per cent to the total. Not only is this first-generation group a small one but it does not perfectly conform to the image of an immigrant generation, for most of the respondents in this group came to this country as children—before or during their early adolescent years—and were therefore educated and acculturated here during their formative period; also included in the first-generation group are well-educated and sophisticated persons who came here as refugees in the 1930's.

In summary, our sample is dominated by the second and third generation. It also includes a sufficiently sizable fourth-generation group to enable us to study, if only in a preliminary way, a generational group which has rarely been represented in other studies of Jewish populations.

TABLE 2–9. GENERATION IN THE UNITED STATES

Generation		
First	8%	
Second	39	
Third	31	
Partly Third		17
Fully Third		14
Fourth Plus	19	
Partly Fourth		16
Fully Fourth		3
No answer, indeterminate	3	

For Jews, the problem of generational differences is complicated by distinctions arising from place of origin: what we term "descent." Some feel that there is little justification for devoting special attention to this factor; they believe that while differences between German Jews and East European Jews were once highly significant, by now they have been reduced to the vanishing point. Others, while conceding that differences remain, contend that they are a function of generational level rather than descent, for they believe that Germans and East Europeans who are of the same generation display identical attitudes and behavior patterns. Inasmuch as three-fifths of our respondents are East European, one-fifth are German, and most of those remaining can be classified as "mixed" (their ancestors came from both groups), we have an opportunity to study the question of the influence of descent on attitudes and behavior patterns (see Table 2–10).[12]

TABLE 2-10. DESCENT BY SEX OF RESPONDENT

Descent	Men	Women	Total
German	16%	23%	20%
Mixed	15	14	14
East European	67	57	62
No answer, indeterminate	2	6	4
N	(208)	(224)	(432)

Interestingly enough, we find that a somewhat greater proportion of the women than of the men in our sample are of German descent. Since more women than men belong to the third and fourth generation, the cross-descent marriage pattern which suggests itself is that of a German girl who is younger and more advanced in generational status marrying an older (and presumably occupationally successful) man of East European descent who is less advanced in generational status.

Although the subject of who marries whom is a fascinating one, for us the more crucial question is the generational status of each descent group. We find that while a majority of the Germans (as well as those who are mixed) are third-generation or higher, a majority of the East Europeans are second-generation (see Table 2–11). A large minority of the East Europeans are of the more advanced generations, primarily the third generation. Both groups have an equal proportion of immigrants (9 per cent), the Germans constituting the more recent arrivals.

TABLE 2-11. GENERATION BY DESCENT

	Descent		
Generation	German	Mixed	East European
First	9%	2%	9%
Second	15	26	53
Third	30	37	32
Fourth plus	46	32	4
No answer, indeterminate	—	3	2
N	(86)	(62)	(266)

Turning to a specification of relationships in the area of descent—as, for example, the correlation between educational attainment and descent —it soon becomes apparent that descent is a factor of some significance.

It is not superseded by generational status. The expectation that Germans, with their preponderance of third- and fourth-generation individuals, would have a level of educational attainment distinctly superior to that of the East Europeans turns out to be false. In actuality, not only do the Germans lack such superiority but they are inferior to East Europeans in educational attainment (see Table 2–12).* For example, about four times as many East Europeans as Germans have taken graduate training. In contrast to East Europeans, many of the Germans who enrolled in college did not complete their education, and this in spite of the fact that, as we shall see, their parents were generally much better off than were the parents of East Europeans.[12] It is also worth noting that in spite of a fiscal advantage, a higher proportion of Germans stayed away from college. It is true that the German group is slightly older than the East European and therefore might be expected to lag somewhat in education; the median age of Germans is 45.1 years, compared to 41.8 for East Europeans. However, the age differential is not very large and must be balanced against the more advanced generational status and the superior financial position of the parents of our German respondents.[13]

TABLE 2–12.   EDUCATIONAL ATTAINMENT BY DESCENT *

	Descent		
	German	Mixed	East European
Level of Education			
Completed high school or less	15%	3%	11%
Some college	40	23	22
Completed college	36	26	30
Beyond college	9	48	37
N	(33)	(31)	(139)

* Based on men respondents.

As we should expect on the basis of these contrasting levels of educational attainment, East Europeans surpass Germans in the proportion of professional and technical workers (see Table 2–13). Furthermore, occupational choice in the two groups is different; the proportion of East Europeans practicing medicine and law—professions very popular and

* In order to simplify our presentation in this section, analysis is limited to men respondents.

esteemed among Jews—is almost twice that of the Germans. The Germans, in turn, outnumber the East Europeans in engineering, a profession which has traditionally attracted relatively few Jews.[14]

The East Europeans are exceeded by the Germans in the "managers, officials, and proprietors" category and particularly in respect to the proportion of "sales workers." The occupational distribution of the mixed-descent group is closer to the Germans than to the East Europeans.

TABLE 2–13. OCCUPATION BY DESCENT *

				Descent		
Occupation	German		Mixed		East European	
Professional and technical workers	27%		26%		42%	
Lawyers, judges		6		13		12
Physicians, surgeons, dentists		6		—		11
Engineers		9		—		5
Accountants and others		6		13		14
Managers, officials, proprietors	52		55		45	
Sales workers	21		19		11	
Craftsmen and foremen	—		—		2	
N	(33)		(31)		(139)	

* Based on men respondents.

How do the descent groups compare in respect to income? Inasmuch as we have noticed that our older respondents have somewhat larger incomes than our younger respondents and that our businessmen do better than our professionals, we should expect the Germans to be more prosperous than East Europeans. But even if these and other relevant differentials are taken into consideration, the contrasts are very sharp. Germans have a median family income of almost $29,000, compared to less than $18,000 for East Europeans. (The mixed group is located between, having a median income of $20,000.) Furthermore, only 9 per cent of the Germans, in contrast to 36 per cent of the East Europeans, have incomes of under $15,000; some 46 per cent of the German group have incomes of $30,000 or more, whereas only 20 per cent of the East Europeans are in the same category.

In considering the impact of these differences, it is well to bear in mind that because of their greater numbers East Europeans who possess sizable incomes constitute a larger group than similarly situated Germans. Thus, while the relative class position of the Germans is much higher than that of the East Europeans, the latter need not always be dominated by the former.[15] For example, there may be a sufficiently large number of prosperous East Europeans to enable the group to establish a distinctive set of Jewish institutions and to maintain them without the help of Germans.

Impact aside, how may we explain the fiscal superiority of the Germans? The answer is not immediately apparent, for some of the factors that influence income do not explain the variance. Thus, even when we control for age, the East Europeans lag behind: 64 per cent of the Germans age 50 and over have an income of $30,000 or more, but only 28 per cent of the East Europeans in the same age bracket are that prosperous. Among the younger age groups, a similar income lag is found. The greater affluence of the Germans cannot be explained by their inferior educational achievement: while 50 per cent of the Germans who have some college or less possess an income of $30,000 or over, only 20 per cent of the East Europeans in the same educational bracket are that affluent. The financial gap is just as significant among those who have completed college. Furthermore, the factor of occupation does not account for the variance: within every occupational category, the income level of the Germans exceeds that of East Europeans.

If age, occupation, and education are not helpful, generation may provide a better starting point for analysis. We may select the third generation for special attention, for both descent groups have a significant proportion of their members in this category. We find that income differences are magnified in this crucial generation: Germans have a median income of more than $50,000, in contrast to about $17,000 for East Europeans. (The income of the mixed-descent group is $23,000.) It is true that age differences contribute to the disparity: the mean age of third-generation Germans is about fourteen years higher than for East Europeans, and thus the latter (with a median age of 37.8) have yet to reach the peak of their earning power. Nevertheless, it is exceedingly dubious whether they will attain the present level of the Germans fourteen years hence.

Is the financial eminence of the Germans of the third generation a new or an old superiority? And if old, is German eminence a result of the fact that the value system of their immigrant grandparents was more conducive to mobility than the value system of the grandparents of East Europeans? [16]

In lieu of hard data on value differences between German and East European immigrants, we are better advised to think in terms of other factors. For example, from what we know of the tempo and character of nineteenth-century Jewish immigration to the United States, it is probable that the grandfathers of our German respondents were preceded by friends, relatives, and other individuals coming from their village or province. These earlier immigrants had already progressed economically by the time the grandparents of our third-generation respondents arrived in the United States. The significance of this development is the possibility that such grandparents were assisted by these earlier immigrants and their rate of mobility consequently speeded. It is doubtful whether the grandparents of third-generation East Europeans had available to them a similar network of already-established countrymen.

Another, and even more significant, possibility is that the particular occupations to which Germans were attracted expanded very rapidly during the crucial years of their early settlement and that the rate of expansion for analogous East European occupations was more gradual.* It may be that the East European grandparents encountered a slightly more mature economy—one which was more difficult to penetrate.

Finally, we know that the East Europeans came in comparatively large numbers and settled in compact areas; it may be that they began to compete with one another, rather than operate as a small middle class serving a larger Gentile public, as the Germans seem to have done. We know that not only was the immigration of Germans much smaller but their spread throughout the country was more even. They hardly went through a prolonged proletarian phase, for they entered the middle class speedily and in a body. [17]

Whether it was the size and concentration of the immigrant group, the tempo of economic development, or the type of assistance rendered by relatives and friends, our data suggest that present-day discrepancies between Germans and East Europeans have existed for at least a single generation and presumably for more. Thus, when our respondents were asked to compare their present economic standing with that of their parents, [18] it was found that 56 per cent of the Germans (a group having a median family income of almost $29,000) said that their economic

---

* This seems like a better possibility than the obvious point that, since the German Jews came from a more Westernized area than East Europeans, they were able to make a speedier adjustment to American conditions.

standing, compared with that of their parents, was either lower or the same (see Table 2–14). But 62 per cent of the East Europeans said they occupied a higher rank than their parents.[19] It will be recalled that East European median income is less than $18,000.

It is thus apparent that the bulk of second-, third-, and fourth-generation Germans were launched into the economic world from a much higher platform than were the East Europeans and that the latter, although highly mobile, have not been able to overtake them. It is difficult to say whether the East Europeans will be able to leave substantial capital to their children or whether the education they are providing their offspring can substitute for such capital. In any case, whether the disparities between the two groups will be reduced in future generations depends as much on the ability of the Germans to maintain their favorable position as it does on further advances on the part of the East Europeans.

TABLE 2–14. Economic Mobility by Descent *

Present Economic Standing of Respondent Relative to Parents	German	Mixed	East European
Higher	44%	61%	62%
Same	20	11	20
Lower	36	28	18
N	(25)	(28)	(124)

* Based on men respondents.

It would be surprising if the contrasting economic and social histories of our two descent groups did not create a certain amount of tension between them. Part of such tension might result from the fact that in spite of their highly favorable economic position, Germans could feel dissatisfied or insecure about their class or status position. Certainly they have the classic problem of those who possess "old money" and who must indicate a willingness to share status with the owners of "new money"— in this case the East European group. Their situation is complicated by the fact that some of the East Europeans who are their financial inferiors equal or surpass them in the realm of formal education. In any case, it is possible that because of the class and status mobility of the East Europeans some Germans have become highly anxious about their own position. As a consequence they manifest hostile attitudes to fellow Jews in Lakeville.[20]

Length of Residence

The matter of length of residence is an important social characteristic in and of itself as well as a significant aspect of the descent problem. We find that although Lakeville is an old suburb, most of our respondents are relative newcomers: their median length of residence is only 4.5 years [21] (see Table 2–15). Given this recency of arrival, the 11 per cent who have resided in the community for seventeen years or more—long before the heavy postwar migration of Jews to Lakeville—may be considered longtime residents.

TABLE 2–15. LENGTH OF RESIDENCE IN LAKEVILLE

Years of Residence	
1–2	26%
3–4	24
5–8	24
9–16	15
17–24	6
25 or more	5
MEDIAN YEARS OF RESIDENCE	4.5

What are the differences between German Jews and East European Jews in respect to length of residence? We find that in contrast to 4.2 years for East Europeans, the median length of residence of German Jewish men is 7.8 years; the mixed-descent group is intermediate at 6.1 years (see Table 2–16). Some 34 per cent of the East European Jews, in contrast to 12 per cent of the German Jews, have been in the community for less than 3 years. The difference between the two groups is thus marked; nevertheless, Lakeville is not a clear-cut case of a confrontation between East European newcomers and German oldtimers. German Jews have continued to move into the community at a steady pace, and thus the German group consists of both newcomers and longtime residents. And while East Europeans have a low percentage of longtime residents, in terms of absolute numbers there are as many East Europeans as Germans who can claim to be longtime residents.

The relationship between length of residence and descent is a subtle one. Thus the figures in Table 2–16 underplay the historic role of Germans in the community. Some of the German Jews who resided in Lake-

TABLE 2-16. LENGTH OF RESIDENCE IN LAKEVILLE
BY DESCENT *

	Descent		
Years of Residence	German	Mixed	East European
1–2	12%	19%	34%
3–4	12	26	27
5–8	37	19	17
9–16	12	16	15
17–24	12	10	3
25 or more	15	10	4
N	(33)	(31)	(139)
MEDIAN YEARS OF RESIDENCE	7.8	6.1	4.2

* Based on men respondents.

ville prior to World War II have died, while others moved back to Lake City when their children married and established independent households. Upon retirement, others moved to cities in the South or West which are favored with a salubrious climate. The point is that, whether living or dead, these families may have left an imprint on the Gentiles of the community, on the present German residents, and on the East European longtime residents. A possible avenue of influence is through the institutions which this group established. While others may now control these institutions, they do so within the framework constructed by German pioneers. Finally, the imprint of this older group may live on in a negative way: in terms of the institutions which they did *not* initiate.

In viewing the present German group as a mixture of newcomers and longtime residents, it is well to consider the possibility that German newcomers may become more speedily integrated into established circles and thus begin to feel like oldtimers much more rapidly than East Europeans. Since the East European newcomer group is so large, few would have any acquaintance with East European longtime residents. German newcomers, on the other hand, hold a better chance of having relatives or friends among longtime residents. Furthermore, German newcomers might have the advantage of being "wanted." That is, if German longtime residents had a feeling of being threatened by East European newcomers, it is conceivable that in their desire to reinforce their position in the community they would overlook the newness of the German newcomer and invite his collaboration. Thus invited, the German newcomer could conceivably overcome his newness much more rapidly than the East European.

In subsequent chapters, we shall comment on various aspects of the cleavage between Germans and East Europeans, especially in respect to religious attitudes and institutions. Certain aspects of the problem of intragroup tensions—particularly feelings between Jewish oldtimers and Jewish newcomers as they relate to intergroup relationships—are discussed in Volume II.

Lakeville and the Nation at Large

As is apparent from the discussion in Chapter 1 concerning the choice of community, Lakeville Jewry is not representative of either the Jewish or the general population of the nation at large.

In what does the specialness of Lakeville Jewry reside? Partly in their Jewishness. That is, Jews deviate sharply from the population at large in such social characteristics as birth rate, occupation, income, and urbanization. (Many such differences between Jews and Gentiles are in the process of being reduced, rather than magnified.) But there is a second aspect to the specialness of our study population: the fact that they differ sharply even from their fellow Jews. Part of the disparity is accounted for by geography; the Jews of the Midwest do not have exactly the same social characteristics as the Jews of the Middle Atlantic and New England states, the sections of the country where the bulk of the Jewish population is located. But the largest part of the discrepancy is accounted for by the fact that Lakeville does not attract a cross section of the Jews who live in the Midwest generally or in Lake City in particular.

Since there is no demographic study of the Jews of Lake City, the exact degree of deviation between those who reside in Lakeville and in the metropolitan area cannot be specified. But it is obvious that Lakeville's elite reputation has discouraged the settlement of whole segments of the Jewish population of Lake City. Furthermore, the cost of homes in Lakeville places the community beyond the reach of many. And some of those who *can* afford to live there prefer to remain in the city; others prefer suburbs that are located nearer to the center of the city.

The fact that Lakeville—at least for its Jewish residents—is a "bedroom suburb" results in maximizing the selective recruitment process. Very few earn their livelihood in Lakeville or in the immediate area, and thus practically nobody has settled in Lakeville because of employment opportunities. Furthermore, the majority of our respondents were reared outside of Lakeville, and thus they chose to settle there as an act of conscious will. Since they could have settled in a variety of other suburbs, we may conclude that they purchased a home in Lakeville because the community possessed a certain combination of characteristics that they found appealing.

Others would not find Lakeville equally attractive. Leaving aside the financial costs involved, we should expect that Jews who are Yiddish-speaking, or are religiously Orthodox, or wish to follow traditional Jewish culture patterns would be wary of Lakeville. Or to shift to another cause of selectivity, the limited choice of housing in the community means that those who prefer apartment living must go elsewhere. And then there is the hard fact that the high cost of housing in Lakeville is out of reach for all Jews of the lower class and for most of the lower middle class. Lakeville thus attracts selectively on the basis of style of life, religious orientation, and economic standing.

If selectivity operates so strongly, how, then, do the Jews of Lakeville compare to the Jews of the country at large on some selected social characteristics? Because of the paucity of Jewish demographic information, there is no easy answer. Furthermore, what knowledge we do have is derived, not from sample studies of the Jewish group, but from studies of a cross section of the total American population. Since Jews constitute less than 4 per cent of the population, the number of Jewish interviews in such studies tends to be small, thus increasing the possibility of sampling error. Nevertheless, comparisons with our data are worthwhile in order to provide some notion of the magnitude of the difference between our respondents and the Jews of the nation at large.

We shall utilize two sources for our comparisons, both based on surveys which took place at about the same time as our own. They were conducted by the Survey Research Center of the University of Michigan (SRC) and the National Opinion Research Center of the University of Chicago (NORC).[22]

In respect to nativity, the SRC data indicate that 31 per cent of the Jews of the nation are foreign-born; in our sample, only 8 per cent are in the same category. In respect to education, SRC and NORC indicate that 33 per cent of the Jews of the nation have had at least some college education; in our sample, the comparable figure is 86 per cent. While our respondents have all had at least some high school, 26 per cent of the NORC respondents and 21 per cent of the SRC respondents received only eight years of schooling or less.

In respect to occupation, our sample contains about twice as many professional and technical workers as in the nation at large; 18 per cent of the Jews of the country, according to NORC, and 19 per cent, according to SRC, are professional and technical workers, while in our sample the figure is 34 per cent. Although 52 per cent of household heads in Lakeville are managers, officials, and proprietors, only 36 per cent (NORC) and 32 per cent (SRC) of the Jews of the nation are in the same category. Finally, NORC found that 21 per cent of the Jews of the nation are craftsmen, operatives, or non-farm laborers, while SRC found that 19 per cent are in this category. This is in marked contrast to the 1 per cent in our sample.

The wide differences in income between the Jews of Lakeville and those in the country at large are summarized in Table 2–17.

TABLE 2–17. TOTAL FAMILY INCOME OF JEWS IN THE U.S. AND IN LAKEVILLE

Income	United States (NORC)	(SRC)	Lakeville
Less than $5,000	38%	27%	1%
$5,000–$7,499	32	31	3
$7,500–$9,999	11 }	42 {	8
$10,000 and over	19		88

In respect to age distribution, the contrasts between our respondents and the Jews of the nation are somewhat reduced. Nevertheless, in our group there is a large concentration between ages 30 and 49, whereas in the nation as a whole only slightly more individuals are in this age group than in the other adult age categories combined (see Table 2–18).

The wide gap between Lakeville Jews and those in the nation at large

TABLE 2–18. AGE OF ADULT JEWS IN THE U. S. AND IN LAKEVILLE

Age	United States (SRC)	Lakeville
20–29 *	14%	9%
30–39	29	42
40–49	24	32
50–59	19	15
60 and over	14	2

* The SRC tabulation starts with age 21.

suggests that whatever internal differences are found among our respondents—as, for example, the contrast in educational levels of German and East European Jews or in income levels of salesmen and of managers, officials, and proprietors—must be understood within the context of the particular character of our sample. That character is easily delineated: sociologically considered, our Lakeville respondents are an elite group of American Jews. They must be so conceived since they exceed, by such a wide margin, the national average in respect to generational position, level of education, occupational status, and income. The data on age grading which we have cited reinforce the notion of their elite position, underlining the idea that contrasts between them and other Jews are not simply a matter of life-cycle differences. Finally, the favored position of Lakeville Jewry would be especially apparent were a measure of socioeconomic status constructed and the Jews of the nation distributed in equal quarters. In that event, the great majority of our respondents would be located in the highest quarter of the distribution.

If the Jews of Lakeville are so clearly an elite group, will they more closely resemble a cross section of tomorrow's American Jewry? Or, to state the question differently, in time to come will the Jews of the nation at large more closely resemble today's Lakeville Jews?

Of course, certain characteristics, such as region of origin in Europe and generation, are "frozen." Nevertheless, our expectation is that while the gap in respect to certain important social characteristics will not be closed, it will be narrowed; just as differences in social characteristics between Jews and Gentiles are in the process of diminishing, so do we expect that in the decades ahead the Jews of the nation at large will increasingly come to resemble today's Lakeville Jews. True, the lack of certain segments of the Jewish population, such as Orthodox Jews, means that such resemblance will at best be approximate. But the following projections are persuasive: while the present level of education in Lakeville is considerably in advance of the Jews of the nation, it will be less so in the future; while the proportion of foreign-born is much smaller, it will be less so in the future; while the income level is much higher, it will be less so in the future. Thus we may say that if present trends continue, the social characteristics presently encountered in Lakeville will typify ever wider segments of American Jewry. And since important attitudinal and behavioral differences sometimes correlate with these characteristics, our study has a double interest: as research into a present elite group and also as affording us a glimpse, albeit an imperfect one, into the possible shape of the future.

3

THE LAKEVILLE JEW
AND RELIGION

Religion is the logical starting point for an analysis of Jewish identity in Lakeville. Jewish tradition teaches that Jews are a group only by virtue of their having embraced the Torah, and thus religion is conceived of as the keystone of group identity. But there is contemporary warrant, in addition to historical justification, for taking religion as our starting point. Because of the special character of American pluralism, Jews increasingly conceive of themselves in terms of constituting a religious group. Thus contemporary life as well as hoary tradition magnifies the religious component in the Jew's Jewishness.

The Sacramental Tradition of Judaism

To be a member of a group with a long tradition means that the individual must define his stance in respect to that tradition. For the Jew, this means confronting a religion which is strongly sacramental in orientation.* Since the sacraments—what the Jew calls *mitzvot*—are divinely ordained, their performance has sacred significance.† Observance of the *mitzvot* is pleasing to God. Such observance demonstrates obedience to His will. By pleasing Him, the world is preserved from destruction.

The thrust of Jewish sacramentalism is to diminish the sacred-secular dichotomy by investing all routines of life with sacred significance. To insure ritualistic correctness, a "fence" of supplementary observances and prohibitions is elaborated. Whether by virtue of the original revelation or of later elaborations, Jewish sacramentalism makes radical demands on the individual: it requires that he follow an all-encompassing way of life. The way of life is incumbent on every member of the group; lacking different standards for cleric and layman, Jewish sacramentalism is equally obligatory for all.

The dietary laws are a striking illustration of Judaism's sacramental tradition. They invest the act of eating with sacred significance, and they provide every believer with recurring opportunities to show his obedience to God's will. Having no hygienic or other instrumental purpose, their justification is that they are pleasing in God's sight. Their observance affects the individual in the most profound ways; *kashrut* may influence his choice of neighborhood, friends, and occupation. In sum, adherence to sacramentalism controls the very rhythm of the individual's life.

A religion characterized by high sacramentalism creates problems for

---

* In this and the following chapters, "sacramental" is used in the sense of ceremonial, legalistic, or ritualistic, rather than in the sense in which the term is used in Christianity or even in reference to pre-Talmudic Judaism. It should be kept in mind that all religions have a sacramental tradition. By designating the Jewish religion as "strongly sacramental," we mean to highlight the contrast between traditional Judaism and the orientation of American Protestantism—the normative religious approach in Lakeville and in the country at large.

† Of the two categories of *mitzvot*—those between man and God and those between man and man—it is the man–God *mitzvot* with which we shall be concerned in the following pages. Among the factors leading to this emphasis is that the thrust of Judaism's system of man–man *mitzvot* approaches certain significant aspects of American culture. Thus the motivation of the Lakeville Jew to make a philanthropic contribution may not only be the desire to conform with the Jewish sacred system; it may also be strongly influenced by the normative pattern of American philanthropy, which derives in large part from the Protestant tradition of "good works." But in his observance of *kashrut* there is considerably less ambiguity about the intention of his act.

The term *mitzvah*, the singular of *mitzvot*, is also frequently employed in the following pages.

its followers who live under conditions different from those under which the religion was originally elaborated. As the historian Jacob Katz has emphasized, even the most pious Jew of medieval times found it difficult to observe halachic * precepts relating to economic life and occupational activities. Such precepts presupposed "the existence of a large Jewish population . . . able to dispense with contact with [Gentiles] or at least able to tolerate restrictions on free intercourse with them." [1] In contrast to conditions which obtained when the laws were formulated,

> The Jewish settlers in France, Germany, and, for that matter, in almost every other country of Europe were tiny groups who succeeded in acquiring some position in society at large through discharging specialized functions—chiefly as merchants, moneylenders, and the like. In exchange for fulfilling these functions they were dependent on the other sections of society to provide their most basic needs. The Jew bought his food as well as his clothing from non-Jews and had to rely upon them for various kinds of services. Under such circumstances voluntary abstinence from business dealings with Gentiles for certain periods, or restrictions involving certain types of merchandise, would have had disastrous consequences for his economic existence.[2]

With the coming of Emancipation, the Jewish sacred system was shaken to its foundations. So great was the tension between the old sacramentalism and the new modernism that no mere reinterpretation or amendment of halachah, such as was done during medieval times, could suffice to legitimate the way of life which the new Jew wished to follow. Unlike the medieval Jew, who was obedient to the past but confronted by unforeseen difficulties in respect to his observance of halachah, in the modern era men came to feel that the sacramental system under which their ancestors had lived was inappropriate for their own times—that it had no claim on them. Even if they affirmed the existence of God, they did not feel that He must be served by following the old observances. In terms of our earlier example of *kashrut,* they began to wonder whether God was interested in what they ate or whether His hegemony needed to be acknowledged by their dietary choices.[3]

Nevertheless, sacramentalism is not easily discarded; to some degree, at least, it is necessarily involved in the practice of any religion. And when the religion that one inherits is characterized by high sacramentalism, any reformation necessarily starts out from the sacramental frame-

* Relating to halachah: the Jewish legal tradition, based on talmudic law, which has been developed through the decisions of rabbinic sages.

work and is inevitably influenced by it. Furthermore, not all Jews experience the pull of modernism in quite the same way or to the same degree. The presence of the more traditionally oriented inevitably creates pressure on the less traditionally oriented. Not only must innovators justify their conduct before traditionalists but they must seek to keep the gap between themselves and their conservative brethren from widening, lest they become sectarians who have no alternative but to establish a new religious movement.

In sum, the post-Emancipation Jew may be a modern man, but he is not a new man. He must wrestle with Judaism's sacramental emphasis. He must seek to discover what *mitzvot* he can still embrace out of the vast storehouse of his sacramental heritage. Whatever the results of his striving, the *mitzvot* he settles on may not conform to the inner dynamics of the sacred system, for what was hallowed in traditional life may conflict sharply with the secularistic mode of his daily life. In fact, his very secularism and his adherence to the norms of the general community may motivate him to emphasize *mitzvot* which an earlier generation performed as a matter of course, even while he neglects *mitzvot* which were previously considered essential and were invested with considerable affect.

The medieval Jew was guided by prescription: by the attitude that he must embrace all that had been handed down to him. His deviations or shifts in emphasis—be they motivated by changed circumstances of life, by new religious conceptions such as Hasidism, by contact with the surrounding culture—did not affect the basic integrity of the system. All is different with the modern Jew, who exercises a kind of personalism in contrast to the prescriptionism of earlier generations. That is, the modern Jew selects from the vast storehouse of the past what is not only objectively possible for him to practice but subjectively possible for him to "identify" with. Of course, his personalism is not really individualistic: it is influenced by his spouse, his children, his parents, his friends, his neighbors, his community, his class position, his times. These forces help assure that the selection from the sacramental heritage will not be a random one, but that a limited number of patterns of observance will emerge which will characterize entire segments of the population.

It is thus apparent that because of Judaism's high sacramentalism we must turn first to the study of religiosity in terms of religious practice. If our respondents' heritage were different, we might give priority to the study of religious beliefs (the "ideological" dimension of religion) or to religious experiences (the "experiential" dimension of religion).[4]

Mitzvot in the Lakeville Home

Given our objective of analyzing religious practice, we could study observance of the *mitzvot* by our respondents in a variety of settings: their synagogues, their places of business, the meetings of their Jewish organizations, or their homes. The home is by far the best starting point. Unlike the Jewish organization, where directives from the national office may influence local practice, what the family does is formulated and instituted by a group of intimates. Unlike a synagogue, where procedures are necessarily a compromise between contending conceptions (or where someone may attend a religious service to be "seen" or because one has been invited by a relative or friend), religious practice in the home is a more nearly perfect reflection of individual conviction and desire. And unlike the house of worship, where practice may be influenced by a religious specialist, the home has no professionals.

The unique importance of the home for our analysis is also connected with the secularism that characterizes the general society. Observance of Jewish sacramentalism is rendered difficult by such secularism, especially for those who desire to participate in the general society. But even if there is no such impetus, a prescriptive approach to observance is rendered difficult. As we have seen, in medieval days economic relationships between Jew and Gentile made it difficult to observe the old norms. In our day, the problem is compounded: the very practice of business has become strongly secularized. One aspect of this change is commented on in the other volume: that business is routinely conducted in social settings, or that there is at least the attempt to diminish social distance in the pursuit of occupational objectives.

The aspect of this sociability which is of particular interest to us is the serving of food. The business lunch, the dinner at the club, the banquet of the trade or professional association, all mean that, unless the individual has a very firm commitment to the practice of *kashrut* and is willing to be excluded from the prevailing sociability pattern, he will violate the dietary laws in the course of his occupational activities. But the individual who has some commitment to the dietary laws may continue to observe them in his home, for there sacred values can be implemented without modifying expected occupational routines. Because it is by definition the most personal of all institutional settings, at least theoretically the home can remain a fortress of sacramentalism, even if surrounded by a highly secularized society.

The further fact is that if any one institutional setting is the focus of Jewish sacramentalism, it is the home. Since Judaism constitutes a way of life, it must by definition center in the home. There the individual's earliest Jewish experiences take place; there he spends much of his time, in spite of the fact that under modern conditions occupational duties are performed almost entirely outside his domicile. For the traditional Jew the synagogue is, in a sense, merely the lengthened shadow of his home, rather than the central institution of cultic worship.

Because of these reasons for concentrating on religious practice in the Lakeville home, we presented our respondents with a list of eleven observances and asked, "Which of the following observances are practiced more or less regularly in your home?" To establish changing levels and patterns, we also inquired into which of the rituals were practiced in their parental home when the parents "were about your present age." The list is as follows:

> Bacon or ham never served.
> Kosher meat bought regularly.
> Kasher the meat.
> Special dinner on Friday night.
> Lighting of candles on Friday night.
> *Kiddush* on Friday night.*
> No smoking allowed in house on Sabbath.
> Seder on Passover.
> Bread not eaten in home on Passover.
> Either or both parents fast on Yom Kippur.
> Candles lit on Hanukkah.

This list is, of course, merely a selection from a vast number of regulations constituting the "prepared table" of Jewish sacramentalism. It emphasizes the observance of holidays and festivals, particularly (1) the Sabbath, (2) the High Holidays, (3) Passover, and (4) Hanukkah.† In addition to whatever dietary regulations are observed in connection with these occasions, it includes some items on the general observance of *kashrut*. Furthermore, all the items represent only primary aspects of religious practice rather than finer points of observance.[5] For example, the one on Passover dietary observance concerns whether or not bread

---

* *Kiddush:* sanctification, i.e., the prayer recited over wine before the Sabbath meal and on other special occasions.

† The Sabbath, being a weekly holiday in Jewish tradition, is however often treated separately from the annual Jewish holidays in the discussion which follows.

is eaten in the home; it does not inquire into the extent to which the home is freed of *chametz.**

We find that of the eleven practices, the mean number observed are 2.8 (see Table 3–1). Some 19 per cent of the respondents observe none of the rituals, while only 10 per cent observe seven or more. The largest group of respondents observe only one or two rituals. The conclusion to be drawn from Table 3–1 is that religious practice in most of the homes is at a very low level and that observance of the traditional sacramental pattern by the Lakeville Jew is minimal.

TABLE 3–1. LEVEL OF HOME OBSERVANCE AMONG RESPONDENTS AND THEIR PARENTS

Per cent practice following number of observances	Parents	Respondents
11	14	1
9–10	18	2
7–8	9	7
5–6	10	14
3–4	12	20
1–2	16	37
0	21	19
MEAN OBSERVANCE	5.2	2.8

In their deviation from tradition, our respondents are not merely following the pattern of observance which they knew as children, for they were reared in homes where a considerably higher level of observance was practiced. In contrast to their 2.8 observances, the mean number of rituals followed in their parental homes is 5.2. Inasmuch as a total of 41 per cent of the older generation practiced seven or more rituals, many of our respondents were raised in homes which by present Lakeville standards are quite observant. On the other hand, in only a relatively small group of homes was there really a prescriptive orientation, for only 14 per cent of the parents observed all eleven rituals.

Since we do not have information about the ritualistic orientation of grandparents and great-grandparents, we cannot say exactly at what point modernism made its initial inroads. Thus we do not know when observance became more personalistic than prescriptive, but it is appar-

---

* *Chametz:* leavened food (and utensils used with them) proscribed during Passover and which must be ritualistically removed from the home.

ent that our respondents have merely continued a process initiated by prior generations. They may be said to exemplify an intensified personalism, rather than a break from prescriptivism to personalism.

Given the contrast between the 2.8 mean of Lakeville and the 5.2 mean of the older generation, the question arises as to whether our respondents constitute the last generation in which the Jewish home has any recognizable religious character. Based on the fact that nonobservance has not grown (whereas 21 per cent of the older generation abstained from any ritualistic observance, only 19 per cent of the present generation does so), we have no grounds for projecting such a trend. Rather, our data suggest the possibility of the stabilization of religious practice, of course at very minimal levels. We shall have more to say about this at a later point, where we consider the influence of generational status on religious observance.

Since parents and children differ, we must ask which rituals have survived and which have withered away. In Table 3–2, we see that the ritual most frequently observed by our respondents is the lighting of the candles on Hanukkah, a *mitzvah* observed in 68 per cent of the homes.

TABLE 3–2. SPECIFIC HOME OBSERVANCES AMONG RESPONDENTS AND THEIR PARENTS

Per cent practice specified observance	Parents	Respondents	Per Cent Difference
Hanukkah			
Light candles	60	68	+8
Passover			
Seder	67	60	−7
No bread eaten	54	22	−32
Yom Kippur			
Parents fast	60	34	−26
Sabbath			
Special dinner Friday night	52	30	−22
Light candles Friday night	47	32	−15
Kiddush	29	16	−13
No smoking	19	1	−18
Dietary Laws			
No bacon or ham	45	9	−36
Kosher meat bought	46	5	−41
Kasher the meat	39	4	−35

One other ritual is practiced by a majority: the holding of a Seder on Passover in 60 per cent of the homes.

In contrast to Hanukkah and Passover, the Sabbath is marked by only a minority. While according to Jewish tradition observance of the Sabbath is of cardinal importance, in only 32 per cent of the homes are the Sabbath candles lit. Other Sabbath rituals are observed by a smaller group.

Dietary observance is maintained in but a few Lakeville homes. The most minimal observance—that of abstaining from serving pork products—is practiced by 9 per cent. While dietary observance per se is highly exceptional, when a dietary observance is connected with a holiday or festival—as, for example, refraining from eating bread in the home on Passover or fasting on Yom Kippur—it is observed more widely than the daily dietary laws. The lack of appeal of the dietary laws can be understood by contrasting the 32 per cent in whose home the candles are lit on Friday nights, the 30 per cent who have a special meal, and the 16 per cent who make the benediction over the wine (*Kiddush*) with the 5 per cent who purchase and serve kosher meat at the Sabbath meal.

Turning to parents, we find that not only were Hanukkah and Passover celebrated in a majority of their homes but the Sabbath was observed in some form in one-half of their homes, and some of the daily dietary laws were followed in almost half of their homes. In contrast to the present generation, where a special dinner on Friday is observed much more frequently than is the serving of kosher meat, almost as many parents observed the latter as the former. In any case, the greatest differences between the generations are in daily dietary observances such as the purchase of kosher meat: 46 per cent of the older generation did this, in contrast to 5 per cent of the younger generation. But even dietary observances connected with holidays or festivals were observed more frequently by the older generation: considerably more parents than children fasted on Yom Kippur or refrained from eating bread on Passover.

Our respondents in Lakeville thus demonstrate a declining sacramentalism when their religious observance is contrasted with that of their parents. It is notable that, in spite of this shift, observance of the Seder and of the lighting of the Hanukkah candles remains relatively stable. In fact, the lighting of candles on Hanukkah has increased somewhat in the present generation; it is the single religious practice that registers any gain. Paradoxically, this ceremony does not bulk large according to traditional norms. The prominence of Hanukkah, however, is not entirely the work of our respondents, for the trend is evident even among the parents, where observance of Hanukkah is exceeded only by that of Passover. And in the parental generation, fasting on such a pre-eminent occasion as Yom Kippur is no more frequent than lighting the candles on Hanukkah.

TABLE 3–3. SPECIFIC HOME OBSERVANCES AMONG RESPONDENTS AND PARENTS WITH SIMILAR LEVEL OF OBSERVANCE

Per cent practice specified observance	8–10 Observances		5–7 Observances	
	Parents	Respond-ents	Parents	Respond-ents
Light Hanukkah candles	93	95	75	96
Passover Seder	95	100	89	97
No bread on Passover	98	95	84	55
Yom Kippur fast	97	95	90	80
Special dinner Friday night	98	95	71	86
Light candles Friday night	94	91	59	92
Kiddush	54	82	14	50
No smoking on Sabbath	17	14	6	—
No bacon or ham	98	82	41	9
Kosher meat bought	100	68	44	5
Kasher the meat	91	50	27	5
N	(98)	(22)	(63)	(80)

	2–4 Observances		1 Observance	
	Parents	Respond-ents	Parents	Respond-ents
Light Hanukkah candles	50	89	22	58
Passover Seder	79	85	41	18
No bread on Passover	26	13	6	4
Yom Kippur fast	50	30	12	12
Special dinner Friday night	24	20	6	4
Light candles Friday night	15	23	3	3
Kiddush	—	5	—	—
No smoking on Sabbath	1	—	—	—
No bacon or ham	12	5	3	1
Kosher meat bought	11	1	6	—
Kasher the meat	2	—	—	—
N	(84)	(168)	(32)	(77)

The trend that we have noticed toward declining sacramentalism needs to be supplemented by a comparison of the two generations at similar levels of observance. We have selected four such levels: 1, 2–4, 5–7, and 8–10 observances.[6] Bearing in mind that parents average 5.2 rituals and our respondents 2.8, the present analysis will enable us to determine whether there has occurred any change in the pattern of observance of specific rituals between the two generations with the same level of observance.

The results of Table 3–3 indicate that the younger generation exhibits greater consensus in terms of the rituals they observe. Thus, whatever customs each of the two generations emphasizes, except at the 8–10 level more of the younger generation practice their high-priority customs than did the older generation. In essence, the parents observed a diversified ritual pattern, while the younger generation observes a specialized pattern.

Turning to specifics, we find that the younger generation tends toward (1) increased emphasis on Hanukkah, (2) increased emphasis on the Passover Seder, (3) maintenance or even increased observance of some Sabbath ritual, and (4) sharply decreased observance of the dietary laws. Reviewing these trends in greater detail, we find that there is:

1. *Increased emphasis on Hanukkah.* Among the younger generation, the lighting of the *menorah* * ranks either first or second at all levels of observance, but among the older generation other holidays received greater emphasis. The contrast between the generations is sharpest at lower observance levels. Thus, 89 per cent of the younger generation who observe only 2 to 4 rituals celebrate Hanukkah, compared to 50 per cent of the older generation. Furthermore, in marked contrast to the older generation, the majority of our respondents who practice only a single ritual rely on Hanukkah.

2. *Increased emphasis on the Passover Seder.* With the exception of those who observe only one ceremony, the predominance of Hanukkah among our respondents does not mean less emphasis on the holding of a Seder. Even at the 2–4 observances level, 85 per cent of the present generation celebrate Passover by participating in a Seder.

3. *Maintenance or even increased observance of some Sabbath ritual.* With the exception of the single-observance family, at all levels the younger generation observe Sabbath rituals as frequently as did their

---

* *Menorah:* the eight-branched candelabrum lighted on each night of Hanukkah; also generally refers to the seven-branched candelabrum that is frequently used as a symbol of Judaism.

parents. Sometimes they even exceed them. The recitation of the *Kiddush* was not stressed among the older generation; it is recited in 50 to 80 per cent of the more observant younger homes in contrast to only 14 to 54 per cent of parental homes. In more observant younger homes, the lighting of Sabbath candles and a special Friday night dinner are also widely observed. The tendency to Sabbath observance among that minority of the younger generation who are at the higher levels of observance does not extend, however, to the prohibition against the lighting of a fire; only among those at the very highest observance level is a home encountered where smoking is avoided on the Sabbath.

4. *Uniform decline in observance of dietary laws.* Whatever the level of observance, fewer of the younger generation observe the dietary laws. The *kashrut* situation is most apparent at higher observance levels. For example, at the 5–7 observances level, 50 per cent recite the *Kiddush* on Friday evening, but only 5 per cent buy kosher meat. In the parental generation, this relationship is reversed: some 44 per cent bought kosher meat, but only 14 per cent recited the *Kiddush*.

Of these four trends, perhaps the most notable one is Sabbath observance. On an overall basis, fewer of the younger generation observe any Sabbath ritual than did their parents, but those younger people who are at the higher levels of religiosity continue to remember the Sabbath. Their Sabbath observance is, of course, not fully traditional; practically no one refrains from lighting a fire. But on the other hand, the pattern of the older settlers in Lakeville—who neglected such rituals and, as we shall see, were even willing to observe Sunday as their Sabbath—has not prevailed. True, very few of those who perform Sabbath rituals are the offspring of these first families. Nevertheless, it may be considered remarkable that there is a group of residents who continue with these rituals. They persist in their remembrance of the Jewish Sabbath despite the fact that the Sabbath is not part of Lakeville's mode of living. After sunset on Friday, life in the community goes on as usual.

To the traditional Jew, a home where the burning lights of the Sabbath candles are on display while *kashrut* is neglected constitutes an anomaly. But to the Lakeville Jew who remembers the Sabbath, it is the "Kitchen Judaism" of his parents or grandparents which is the anomaly. Whatever the effect of the disintegration of *kashrut* observance on the ultimate destiny of the Judaism practiced by our respondents and their descendants, the proclivity of the more observant to mark the arrival of Queen Sabbath is notable.

Criteria for Ritual Retention

Why are some home observances retained more frequently than others? It would be unproductive to seek an answer to this question by employing criteria internal to the Jewish religion or even by having recourse to established perspectives in the sociology and psychology of religion. While such approaches might help us learn why the Lakeville Jew has retained some small measure of ritualism in his home, we should not be able to explain the particularity of his ritual pattern.

A more rewarding approach is to think of our respondents' ritual pattern as emerging from the pull of two forces: (*a*) the pervasive impact of the modern, Christian, secularist environment and (*b*) their desire to express Jewish identity and continuity in familiar forms. But which familiar forms? Five criteria emerge as important in explaining retention of specific home rituals. Thus the highest degree of retention will occur when a ritual: (1) is capable of effective redefinition in modern terms, (2) does not demand social isolation or the adoption of a unique life style, (3) accords with the religious culture of the larger community and provides a "Jewish" alternative when such is felt to be needed, (4) is centered on the child, and (5) is performed annually or infrequently.

To review these criteria in detail:

1. *Capable of effective redefinition in modern terms.* We might expect that neither Hanukkah nor Passover would be attractive to the Lakeville Jew. These holidays have at their center the celebration of a miracle: in the case of Hanukkah, the cruse of oil normally sufficient for one day which lasted for eight days; in the case of Passover, the exodus from Egypt accomplished by divine intervention. However, now the miraculous elements inherent in both holidays are muted in favor of a theme that appeals to the modern Jew of Lakeville: both holidays are said to symbolize man's unquenchable desire for freedom. The focus is no longer on God's benevolence, but on the struggle of the ancient Jewish people and their heroic leaders to overcome slavery in the case of Passover and religious intolerance in the case of Hanukkah.

As the dietary laws attest, not all reinterpretations are equally successful. One familiar approach is that they have hygienic significance. But the idea has had little appeal for individuals who live in a publicly enforced sanitary environment and who, furthermore, conceive of food prohibitions as primitive taboos. Indeed, the success of this particular reinterpretation has been so limited that the hygienic value of *kashrut* is rarely voiced in Lakeville.

2. *Does not demand social isolation and the following of a unique life style.*   Were the Lakeville Jew to observe all eleven rituals on our list, he would find that he had separated himself to some extent from the general community; were he to observe the full round of traditional rituals, he would find himself following a separate and highly distinctive life style. Valuing his acculturation and disinclined to lead a distinctive way of life, the Lakeville Jew is interested only in those rituals which demand minimal separation and deviation from the general community. Thus we find that the traditional observance of the Sabbath, as indexed by the item on the prohibition against lighting a fire, withers away. It is replaced by the observance, on the part of the more devout in Lakeville, of a highly specific set of rituals centering on Friday evening. These rituals neither demand social isolation nor constitute a distinctive life style.

3. *Accords with the religious culture of the larger community and provides a "Jewish" alternative when such is felt to be needed.*   This criterion refers to convergent characteristics in each of the major American religions that form the basis of the "tri-faith" culture which has been noted by many commentators. The aspects of Hanukkah observance currently emphasized—the exchange of gifts and the lighting and display of the *menorah* in the windows of homes—offer ready parallels to the general mode of Christmas observance as well as provide a "Jewish" alternative to the holiday. Instead of alienating the Jew from the general culture, Hanukkah helps to situate him as a participant in that culture. Hanukkah, in short, becomes for some the Jewish Christmas.

4. *Centered on the child.*   Both the Passover Seder and the lighting of Hanukkah candles have traditionally been among the most child-centered observances in the Jewish calendar. Not only is the Passover Seder a personal religious experience for adults but it also has the purpose of conveying to the next generation the experience of the Exodus. While the ritual of Hanukkah is not explicitly child-centered, its mode of celebration inclined in this direction even before the encounter with America; witness *dreydl* games * and the giving of Hanukkah *gelt* in Europe. In essence, then, the recitation of the Haggadah and the lighting of the *menorah* constitute religious acts performed by the adults to satisfy

* *Dreydl:* a spinning top on the four sides of which are engraved the Hebrew initials of the phrase "a great miracle happened there."

personal religious requirements as well as ritual occasions which are made doubly meaningful by the participation of the younger generation.

While the retention of these rituals may be stimulated by the child's eagerness, the motivation of the parent does not rest on their child-centeredness alone. These occasions appeal to the parent because they accord with his desire to transmit Jewish identity to his offspring. Hanukkah and Passover, which provide ready-made forms and techniques for involving the child at major points in their celebration, carry the imputation and the hope that when the child becomes a parent he will be performing these rituals for himself and for *his* children.

The mood of a child-centered holiday must be appropriate. Passover and Hanukkah have special appeal in this connection, for both commemorate joyous occasions. Their tenor is in keeping with the norms of optimism and fun which the general culture holds in respect to the atmosphere in which children should be reared. And the parent feels that having provided his child with "positive" associations with Jewishness, the child will have no cause to reject his heritage.

5. *Performed annually or infrequently.* The fact that both Passover and Hanukkah are annual rather than weekly or daily occasions undoubtedly serves to maintain observance. The Sabbath activities—including the lighting of candles, the preparation of a special meal, the attendance at the meal by all members of the family, the recitation of *Kiddush* —involve something of a religious regimen. They make regular demands on each member of the family; they appeal only to the more pious. But the lighting of the *menorah* (even if done faithfully on eight successive evenings) and the holding of a Seder (even if it includes the reading of all of the Haggadah) are unusual occasions. As holidays, they are a relief from the routine.

Infrequently performed rituals harmonize more with the secular component in modern American life than daily or weekly rituals. Secularization affects the scope of religion. It restricts the application of religion to fewer and fewer areas of the individual's life. It results in limitations on regular, routine, daily performance of religious sacraments. Given the pervasiveness of secularization, the yearly ritual will persist more than the seasonal, the seasonal more than the monthly, the monthly more than the weekly, the weekly more than the daily. In essence, secularization undercuts the emphasis of Jewish sacramentalism on the sanctification of the routine and imperils the continuation of those rituals which do not celebrate an extraordinary occasion.

Synagogue Attendance

Since some 19 per cent of our respondents observe no rituals in their home and another 37 per cent observe only one or two practices, we must conclude that the majority of Jewish homes in Lakeville lack a distinctive religious character. If the Jewish home is not a fortress of sacredness in a secular society, the possibility exists that the focus of sacramentalism has shifted to the synagogue and that this is now the prime sanctuary of Jewish faith and future. If this is, indeed, the case, it indicates the high acculturation of our respondents and their adherence to the prevailing pattern of American religiosity—a pattern in which religious activities are centered in an institution specifically dedicated to religious ends, which in turn is surrounded by other institutions dedicated to secular ends. If this shift has, in fact, taken place, it should be evidenced by a high degree of membership in congregations and by a higher level of attendance at synagogue services than of home observance. As we shall see in Chapter 5, the first qualification is fulfilled, for the majority of the Jews of Lakeville belong to a synagogue. Our present interest is the extent of attendance at religious services.

In inquiring about attendance, we did not ask about daily services; we were aware that such services are held in only one of the synagogues in the community and that this synagogue finds difficulty in gathering the quorum necessary for public worship. Thus the most frequently conducted service about which we asked was that held on the Sabbath. Additionally we asked about the Festivals—specifically about attendance at the services held during Sukkot—and also about attendance at the High Holiday services of Rosh Hashanah and Yom Kippur. An index of synagogue attendance was constructed, with zero representing those who never attend and 9 representing those who have attended High Holiday and Sukkot services for each of the past three years and a Sabbath service every week, or almost every week, during the past year.[7]

Only 3 per cent of our respondents, we find, are in the highest category, and only an additional 10 per cent are in the next-highest category (see Table 3–4). Thus a total of 13 per cent may be considered as regular worshipers by Lakeville standards: generally they attend High Holiday services each year, they come to Festival services occasionally or regularly, and they attend Sabbath services at least twice a month. The majority of our respondents—74 per cent—are irregular worshipers: they are located in the 1–2 group (generally those who attend High

TABLE 3–4. LEVEL OF SYNAGOGUE ATTENDANCE AMONG RESPONDENTS AND THEIR PARENTS

Per cent at following attendance level	Parents	Respondents
9	24	3
7–8	13	10
5–6	21	20
3–4	22	35
1–2	4	19
0	16	13
MEAN ATTENDANCE	5.0	3.7

Holiday services in some years but not others, or who attend regularly on Yom Kippur), the 3–4 group (generally those who attend High Holiday services regularly and Sabbath services a few times each year), and the 5–6 group (generally those who attend High Holiday services regularly, Festival services occasionally, and Sabbath services either monthly or a few times each year). Almost half of the 74 per cent group are located in the 3–4 category. Finally, there are the nonattenders: the 13 per cent who never come to any service.[8]

How does this picture of synagogue attendance compare with what we already know about home observance? Any such comparison has an element of arbitrariness, but when we contrast Table 3–4 with Table 3–1 it is evident that a greater number of respondents abstain from home observance than absent themselves from synagogue attendance. The relationship between home and synagogue is detailed in Table 3–5, where we find that more than half (59 per cent) of those who do not perform

TABLE 3–5. LEVEL OF SYNAGOGUE ATTENDANCE BY LEVEL OF HOME OBSERVANCE

Per cent at following attendance level	Number of Home Observances			
	5+	3–4	1–2	0
7–9	33	13	7	1
5–6	38	21	14	5
3–4	23	48	44	20
1–2	6	13	24	33
0	—	5	11	41
N	(105)	(86)	(159)	(82)

any rituals in their home *do* attend religious services on occasion. In the majority of cases, such attendance is confined to the High Holidays. Further, many of those whose home observance is minimal attain more than a minimal level of synagogue attendance.

To be sure, there are also cases where home observance exceeds synagogue attendance. But those whose synagogue attendance exceeds their home observance are more numerous. It is this group which engages our attention, since their pattern indicates the impact of a pervasive acculturation and represents a decisive break with the Jewish sacramentalism of old. The most striking example of such a break is the type of Lakeville woman who joins the congregation for Sabbath worship but does not perform the mandatory ritual of lighting the Sabbath candles in her home. According to Jewish tradition, such behavior is anomalous. It would seem that her sacramental pattern has been influenced by the environment, with its stress on public worship, for instead of observing one of the three mandatory "womanly" *mitzvot,* this woman performs an act which is optional for her sex: that of attending a religious service.

In regard to generational differences, we see in Table 3–4 that our respondents participate in public worship considerably less frequently than did their parents. This decline does not result from a growth in nonattendance but rather is a consequence of the diminishing number of regular worshipers: while 37 per cent of the parents attended services regularly (scoring 7–8 and 9), only 13 per cent of our respondents do so. The contrast between the generations is not so sharp as we noticed in respect to home observance, but it still constitutes a decline of sizable magnitude.

When we analyze the particular religious services that appeal to Lakeville Jews, we see nothing like the emergence in the synagogue of anything which resembles Hanukkah in the home, that is, an occasion of minor significance which has been escalated into major significance. While the older generation exceeds the younger in High Holiday attendance, these services still outrank all others by a wide margin. Thus more than seven out of ten of our respondents attend services on both Rosh Hashanah and Yom Kippur every year or almost every year (see Table 3–6).

The relatively high level of attendance at High Holiday services suggests the unique character and appeal of Rosh Hashanah and Yom Kippur as well as the operation of one of our criteria for ritual retention: the annual and the infrequently performed ritual. It appears that the criteria

TABLE 3-6. ATTENDANCE AT SPECIFIC SYNAGOGUE SERVICES
AMONG RESPONDENTS AND THEIR PARENTS

Per cent attend on	Parents	Respondents	Per Cent Difference
Yom Kippur			
Every year	79	59	−20
Twice in 3 years *	2	12	+10
Once in 3 years	1	11	+10
Less often or never	18	18	0
Rosh Hashanah			
Every year	78	57	−21
Twice in 3 years *	2	14	+12
Once in 3 years	2	11	+9
Less often or never	18	18	0
Festivals †			
Every year	44	10	−34
Twice in 3 years *	2	8	+6
Once in 3 years	2	10	+8
Less often or never	52	72	+20
Sabbath ‡			
Every week	29	5	−24
2–3 times a month	11	11	0
Once a month	8	13	+5
Less often	13	36	+23
Never	39	35	−4

* The question regarding the parents' attendance referred to "once every two years."
† Questions were asked about Sukkot and included a specific reference to Simchat Torah.
‡ Among men and their fathers only.

are operative both in synagogue attendance and in home observance, for despite the fact that according to traditional norms attendance at weekly Sabbath services is of crucial significance (observance of the Sabbath is no less important than observance of the High Holidays), only 5 per cent of our male respondents attend services each week. Of course, just as with home observances, the break with prescriptive Judaism occurred two or more generations ago: only 29 per cent of the fathers of our men respondents attended Sabbath services each week.* In the parental generation, 39 per cent abstained from all Sabbath worship. Thus the pattern

* Sabbath attendance figures are for men only since in the traditional pattern the attendance of women at these services was not stressed.

was either regular attendance or nonattendance. Among the Lakeville generation, however, sporadic attendance, as distinct from regular attendance, is encountered more frequently.[9]

If the pre-eminence of the Sabbath as an occasion for synagogue attendance has declined, it is the Festival services which have suffered the greatest attrition; since 72 per cent of the Jews of Lakeville never come to these services, nonattendance is the dominant pattern. The contrast between the generations is strong: while 46 per cent of the parents attended these services at least fairly regularly, only 18 per cent of our respondents do so. In sum, the Jews of Lakeville retain the High Holidays as a major event in the Jewish calendar, they attend Sabbath services very irregularly, and they ignore the Festivals as occasions for public worship.[10]

Can we say, then, that Lakeville Judaism is a synagogue Judaism rather than a home Judaism? Not entirely; but the trend in this direction is unmistakable. There is the fact that some of those who observe little or no ritual in their homes attend religious services. There is the additional fact that while the Jewish home in Lakeville is ritualistically very weak, the synagogue is strong and growing stronger. True, it must struggle to attract worshipers; its religious services do not draw the majority of the Jews of Lakeville on a daily, weekly, or even monthly basis. Nevertheless, the synagogue as an institution prospers. We are certainly justified in saying that the growing strength of the Lakeville synagogue does not derive from the Jewishness of the Lakeville home; if it were dependent on that home, synagogue attendance would be at a considerably lower level than it is at present.

The changing relationship between home and synagogue sets the stage for the development of a new pattern: home observance as derivative from synagogue involvement. Rather than conceiving of the synagogue as an extension of the home, those in Lakeville who seek to arrest the decline in observance think in terms of remaking the home through the influence of the synagogue. They feel that the synagogue is the only place where the new Jew will learn how to be a Jew—the only place where he can be impressed with the importance of conducting a Jewish home, inspired to observe rituals which he presently neglects, and instructed in their performance. However, even the rabbis and the synagogue leaders of Lakeville do not seek to return to the old ritualism, with its tendency to encompass all of life within the realm of the sacred. Rather they seek to narrow the wide chasm between the synagogue and the Jewishly denuded home of Lakeville.

Influences on Religious Observance

Whatever the changing role of the synagogue as an institution, we are still confronted with the question of why the level of synagogue attendance and home observance in Lakeville, albeit low, is lower for some respondents than others. What is the explanation for different levels of observance of the *mitzvot*?

PARENTAL HOME

One of the key factors—perhaps the largest single one—which influences religious practice, we find, is the Jewishness of the parental home. While our respondents live in independent households (generally having left their parental homes either at the time of marriage or before), the home environment in which they were reared constitutes an important influence in their adult religious life. As we see in Figure 3–1, the mean number of observances followed by the Lakeville generation is related to the rituals observed in the parental home: the more observant the parent, the more observant the child. To be sure, the great majority of children are considerably less observant than their parents. Thus the parental pattern does not serve as a model which the child duplicates, but rather as a base line from which he initiates changes.[11]

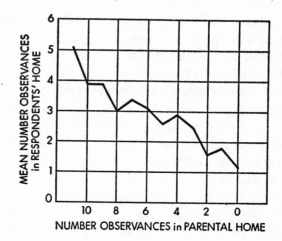

FIGURE 3–1. LEVEL OF OBSERVANCE IN RE-
SPONDENT'S HOME BY LEVEL OF
OBSERVANCE IN PARENTAL HOME

The influence of the parental home can be discerned even in those deviant cases where the offspring is more traditional in ritualistic behavior than his parents. Such cases occur most frequently among those raised in homes where the level of observance is below the Lakeville norm. However, the influence of the parental home is present even in such instances, for these respondents rarely attain as high a level of ritual observance as those reared in more traditional homes.

The influence of the parental home is independent of generation and descent. For example, those reared in a less observant East European immigrant home are less observant than those reared in a more traditional East European immigrant home; those reared in a more observant second- or third-generation home and who are of German or mixed descent are more observant than those reared in a less observant home of similar generation and descent.

Furthermore, the importance of the parental pattern of observance is independent of other Jewish influences to which our respondents were exposed in childhood: the type and amount of Jewish education, the percentage of Jews in their neighborhood, the character of their parents' friendship ties, and the extent to which their parents socialized with relatives. For example, given a similar type of schooling (whether Hebrew school, or Sunday school, or no Jewish education) and controlling for amount of exposure, we find that respondents whose parents maintained a more traditional home are more observant than those whose parents were less traditional.

The influence of the parental home is also strikingly apparent when observance of specific rituals is considered. With the possible exception of the dietary laws, the probability of a given individual's observing any particular *mitzvah* is greatly increased if it was practiced by his parents (see Table 3–7). For example, the influence of parental practice is visibly evident in the case of the Passover Seder: although this ritual is practiced by 26 per cent of those who did not inherit it, it is observed by 77 per cent of those who were exposed to it as children. The impact of the parental example on observance of the Sabbath eve rituals and of the dietary laws relating to Passover and Yom Kippur is also considerable: while they are practiced by 5 to 18 per cent of those who did not inherit them, they are performed by 35 to 50 per cent of those who witnessed them in their childhood. Similarly, while 15 to 31 per cent acquire the pattern of regular synagogue attendance on the Sabbath (once a month or more) and on the High Holidays, 43 to 67 per cent of those who inherit these patterns follow them. Even the lighting of the Hanukkah candles—the ritual most widely observed by those who did not witness it in their parental home—is inherited more frequently than it is acquired.

TABLE 3–7. SPECIFIC RELIGIOUS OBSERVANCES AMONG RESPONDENTS BY SPECIFIC OBSERVANCES AMONG PARENTS

	Specified Observance	
	Practiced by Parents	Not Practiced by Parents
Per cent practice specified observance	N	N
Light Hanukkah candles	80 (259)	51 (173)
Passover Seder	77 (290)	26 (142)
No bread on Passover	36 (235)	5 (197)
Yom Kippur fast	50 (260)	9 (172)
Special dinner Friday night	47 (225)	12 (207)
Light candles Friday night	47 (205)	18 (227)
Kiddush	35 (124)	9 (308)
No smoking on Sabbath	7 (84)	— (348)
No bacon or ham	15 (195)	3 (237)
Kosher meat bought	11 (199)	— (233)
Kasher the meat	9 (170)	1 (262)
Per cent attend synagogue services on		
Yom Kippur (every year)	67 (337)	31 (88)
Rosh Hashanah (every year)	66 (334)	28 (92)
Festivals (every year)	20 (184)	2 (237)
Sabbath (once a month or more) *	43 (101)	15 (107)

* Men and their fathers only.

It is, of course, quite remarkable that in a period of declining sacramentalism we encounter instances of children performing rituals that were neglected by their parents. For the most part, however, present ritual wealth depends on the size of one's ritual inheritance; while the Lakeville Jew dissipates some of the religious capital received from the parents, he also conserves a portion of his patrimony. Although we encounter instances where those who were born into ritually indigent families have managed to acquire a modest ritual competence, few such individuals overcome their initial disadvantages. In sum, while Lakeville has an extraordinary number of self-made men in the economic realm as well as a multitude of individuals who are fiscally more potent than their parents, comparable success stories are encountered much less often in the religious arena.

The size of one's ritual patrimony is not the entire picture, however. *Mitzvot* practiced in the parental home are experienced by individuals with varying intensity and feeling, and such experience is remembered in adulthood with different degrees of sentiment.[12] In response to the question "Do you have any memories of things you experienced or ate or did in your home as a child which you associate with a Jewish way of life?", we find that virtually all who were reared in homes with any degree of observance can recall such memories. Furthermore, when probed as to their feelings about these memories, more than nine in ten say that their memories are "mostly pleasant."

While the great majority of our respondents have memories, and pleasant ones at that, the degree of sentiment they attach to these memories is quite distinct at different levels of religious rearing. Asked "How sentimental do you get over these pleasant memories at times?", those of our respondents raised in highly observant homes are by far the most sentimental. Some 78 per cent coming from highly observant homes (9–11 rituals) admit to becoming "very" or "moderately" sentimental, while those from progressively less observant homes show a steady decline in feeling. For example, only 45 per cent of those raised in homes which are low in observance (1–4 rituals) ever feel "very" or "moderately" sentimental.

The relationship between parental pattern, degree of sentiment, and personal observance is specified in Table 3–8. We find that the attachment to childhood memories reinforces the influence of the parental example and in so doing has an effect on present levels of observance. This effect, however, is limited to those reared in highly or moderately observant homes. Strength of attachment to memories of one's Jewish childhood has no consistent effect in raising the level of religious observance among those who come from low or nonobservant homes, for respondents reared in such homes who feel sentimental about memories of their Jewish childhood do not have a higher level of religious observance than those with little or no sentiment. We conclude that only when exposure to a Jewish way of life is above minimum levels is the individual impressed with sufficient depth of feeling to influence his religious behavior as an adult.

These childhood memories are religious in more than a limited sense.

TABLE 3-8. LEVEL OF RELIGIOUS OBSERVANCE BY
ATTACHMENT TO JEWISHNESS OF CHILDHOOD
HOME AND PARENTS' LEVEL OF
HOME OBSERVANCE

	Degree of Sentimentality about Childhood Jewish Memories			
	Very	Moderate	Slight	None
Among those reared by highly observant parents (9–11), per cent with				
5+ home observances	55	40	28	*
5+ synagogue attendance	58	45	28	*
N	(63)	(49)	(21)	(*)
Among those reared by moderately observant parents (5–8), per cent with				
5+ home observances	39	29	27	—
5+ synagogue attendance	39	32	18	20
N	(13)	(31)	(22)	(10)
Among those reared by low observant parents (1–4), per cent with				
3+ home observances	28	30	17	37
3+ synagogue attendance	58	74	55	69
N	(24)	(23)	(23)	(27)
Among those reared by non-observant parents, per cent with				
3+ home observances		6		20
3+ synagogue attendance		31		41
N		(16)		(15)

* Too few cases.

They embrace and fuse a variety of things past, but primarily those connected with the observance of the Sabbath and the Jewish holidays: ceremonial activities; feelings about mother, father, and other relatives; emotions expressed when meals were eaten or new clothes worn. One example is mentioned by a young lawyer whose immigrant father owned a corner grocery and who has discarded certain of the dietary laws, while practicing most other rituals. Reared in an observant household, he feels warmly about the memories of his childhood. He recalls the Sabbath in the following terms:

It was pleasant when we came home from school on Friday and celebrated *Shabbes;* we lit the candles and had real meals. We ate at all hours during the week.

An observant middle-aged owner of a clothing store remembers best the distinctive scent of the traditional foods that were prepared for the Friday evening meal in his highly Orthodox childhood home. Often feeling very sentimental about his memories, he recalls

Friday afternoon and the smell of *Shabbes* in the house—the fresh baked *challah,* the gefilte fish.

Respondents often retain pleasant memories of several Jewish holidays simultaneously. A mother of two preadolescent children, who maintains the average Lakeville pattern of religious practice, is very attached to the memories of her highly traditional childhood. As she puts it,

Oh, the excitement of the holidays! We always had lots of people for the Seder and on Sukkos. I used to enjoy the singing and the gaiety.

A garment manufacturer who is observant by Lakeville standards came to the United States from Eastern Europe when he was a boy. Raised by Orthodox parents, he feels warmly about his childhood. He particularly remembers getting

a new suit for Pesach. And Simchas Torah—what a thrill!

Of all the Jewish holidays recalled in the framework of pleasant memories, Passover is most frequent, and of all the occasions remembered—not only about this festival but also in relation to all other Jewish memories—the Seder is cited the most often. The blending of the ceremonial and familial aspects of this occasion is quite apparent in the childhood impressions of another manufacturer, also highly observant by Lakeville standards. This respondent, who relates that he often becomes quite sentimental about his memories of his parents' home, remembers most of all that

the rituals at Passover were most pleasant. All my relatives would be there, including fourteen children. . . . My oldest uncle would say *Kiddish.*

While we find that it is predominantly the memories of a more traditional childhood which influence present religious observance, we also encounter some fairly observant respondents who retain a warm attachment to a childhood in which only minimum levels of Jewishness were experienced. One such case is a woman of German descent who attends services regularly at one of Lakeville's Reform temples. Born into an aristocratic Southern family, she surpasses the religious observance of her parents. She has very positive memories of the few religious ceremonies practiced in her childhood home and particularly remembers that

> My grandfather said a prayer before dinner Friday night and didn't smoke until after Saturday. Daddy fasted every year [on Yom Kippur] and said it was good for the stomach.

SPOUSE

In a noticeable number of cases, the husband or wife of a respondent was raised in a home with a different religious orientation from that of the respondent's parental home. In such instances, the respondent's religious observance—particularly the level of ritualism in his home—is influenced not only by his parental pattern but by that of his spouse's parents as well, whether these standards were lower or higher than those in which he was reared.

While we did not gather data on the home observance of in-laws, we can approximate the situation by utilizing data on the spouse's generation and descent.[13] We know that the more advanced the generation, the fewer the observances to which individuals were exposed in their home. We know, furthermore, that those whose descent is German or mixed were raised in less observant homes than those of East European descent.

We find in Table 3–9 * that the highest proportion of observant households are those in which an East European respondent, reared by observant parents, takes a first- or second-generation East European as his spouse. Marriage to a spouse of a more advanced generation reduces somewhat the proportion of observant households, while marriage to a spouse of mixed or German descent means a sharp drop in the proportion of observant households.

We obtain an even better understanding of this process when the respondent's home is compared to that of his parents. As we know, the overall trend is toward a decline in religious observance. However, we find that the religious background of the spouse influences the *amount* of decline that occurs. A first- or second-generation East European spouse limits this decline, while a spouse from a less observant back-

* We shall analyze respondents of Eastern European descent only; they, of course, constitute the largest single group.

TABLE 3-9. PRESENT LEVEL AND INTERGENERATIONAL CHANGE OF HOME OBSERVANCE BY PARENTS' LEVEL OF HOME OBSERVANCE AND SPOUSE'S DESCENT AND GENERATION *

	Spouse's Descent and Generation		
	East European of First–Second Generation	Third–Fourth Plus Generation	German or Mixed Descent
Among respondents reared by highly observant parents (9–11), per cent with			
5+ observances	53	45	16
More or same	9	5	—
Somewhat less (1–5)	48	35	8
Much less (6–11) observances than parents	43	60	92
N	(56)	(20)	(13)
Among respondents reared by low or nonobservant parents (0–4), per cent with			
3+ observances	54	27	
More	61	35	
Same	12	26	
Less observances than parents	27	39	
N	(33)	(34)	

* Based on second- and third-generation East European respondents.

ground accelerates it. There is a very steep decline if the spouse is of German or mixed descent.

Whether the East European respondent is of the second or third generation (more frequently he is second-generation) does not alter the influence of his spouse. Thus, second-generation respondents are pulled just as strongly as third toward lower levels of home observance if their spouses are of a more advanced generation or of German or mixed descent. Similarly, third-generation respondents must accommodate to higher levels of observance if their East European spouses are of a less advanced generation.

When a respondent was reared in an observant home and is married to a first- or second-generation spouse, the spouse plays a supportive role vis-à-vis religious observance. On the other hand, in families where the respondent was reared in an unobservant home and is married to the same type of spouse, the spouse may play an innovative role in the family's religious life. As we see in the lower segment of Table 3–9, some spouses do fulfill this role; predominantly they are first- or second-generation individuals of East European descent, and they tend to increase both the absolute and relative levels of home observance. Thus, 54 per cent of the families in which respondents were reared in unobservant or low observant homes and married a first- or second-generation spouse of East European descent practice three or more observances; this compares to only 27 per cent of those families in which the spouse is of a more advanced generation or of German or mixed descent. And in contrast to only 35 per cent of those married to a spouse of more advanced generation or of German or mixed descent, 61 per cent of those married to first- or second-generation East European spouses have a level of home observance which exceeds that of their parents. Finally, the religious influence of the spouse persists, whether the respondent is of the second or third generation.

We do not know how diversity in religious background is handled by our respondents. And we do not know how families in which husband and wife were raised in different kinds of homes resolve their religious differences. But what we do know is that the presence of children in the household is a factor that motivates husband and wife to arrive at a common ritual front as well as an important influence on ritual practice generally. It is to this subject that we now turn.

LIFE CYCLE

In seeking to transmit Jewish identity to their children, parents must face the problem of the observance of the *mitzvot*. Rituals which they had taken for granted in their childhood and may have rejected or set aside as irrelevant to their immediate life commitments in the transitional years of adolescence and early adulthood come up for reconsideration. Parents have no choice but to formulate and then to exemplify a model of religious behavior to which they will expose their offspring.

Some students of the subject who have noticed a rise in observance during these early years of parenthood describe the observance pattern as "child-oriented," in contrast to the "adult-oriented" (or, more properly, the "God-oriented") pattern of Jewish sacramentalism. Thus the traditional Jew performs rituals because they are pleasing in the sight of God, while the new Jew, it is said, performs them as a child-rearing device and as a result of secular rather than sacred drives. His behavior is viewed as deriving not so much from inner conviction as from community pressures. He is subject to the coercion of rabbis, religious-school teachers, and other "professional Jews." [14]

Whatever increase in ritualism occurs in the child-rearing years may be viewed, on the other hand, in somewhat different terms. It may be seen more as a consequence of the assumption of the parental role and thus as a result of inner as much as of outer pressures. It can be viewed in a sacred rather than a secular context, for in impressing on his child the importance of Jewish survival, the parent is involved in making an ultimate commitment. And from the vantage point of Jewish tradition, a ritual which is performed to impress and instruct one's child is not thereby profaned.

The years of late adolescence, college, and the start of a career and household are transitional and relatively unstable: the childhood family bonds supporting religious practice have been loosened, and new bonds have yet to be forged.[15] Resolution of the problem of religious commitment can be postponed only as long as one does not have to be concerned about the transmission of culture. The issue of whether what is dormant in one's background is to be activated comes alive when a new household is established and particularly when, with the arrival of children, the household becomes a family unit in which the function of cultural transmission must be performed.

When the function of transmission is encountered by the parent, it must be confronted in a very concrete and palpable way. The weighty responsibility of rearing the next generation is thrust upon the parent, moving him away from the relatively more abstract religious issues which might have concerned him at an earlier stage in the life cycle into more concrete questions. Among these is the question of ritual, one of the most palpable of all issues in the area of religious loyalty and a question which has special significance for the Jew.

How, then, do our respondents behave ritualistically at different points in the life cycle?[16] We find that home observance and synagogue attendance are at relatively low levels in the earliest phase of parenthood (see Table 3–10). Observance rises as children reach school age, and it attains its peak when children are of Bar Mitzvah or Confirmation age. When children become mature, parental observance declines.[17]

TABLE 3-10. LEVEL OF RELIGIOUS OBSERVANCE BY FAMILY LIFE CYCLE

	Life-Cycle Phase				
Per cent practice following number of home observances	Pre-School	Early-School	Peak-School	Late-School	Post-School
5+	19	23	26	27	25
3–4	14	25	22	18	12
1–2	38	41	40	37	25
0	29	11	12	18	38
MEAN OBSERVANCE	2.4	2.9	3.2	3.1	2.3
Per cent at following synagogue attendance level					
5+	14	31	44	32	31
3–4	35	37	30	60	36
1–2	30	21	17	4	12
0	21	11	9	4	21
MEAN ATTENDANCE	2.5	3.6	4.3	4.3	3.3
N	(68)	(103)	(162)	(22)	(67)

The decline at the end of the child-rearing years does not occur with the consistency or magnitude which attended its rise, however. The level of synagogue attendance among older parents, for example, exceeds that of younger parents: while 14 per cent of those with very young children attend services with some regularity, compared to 44 per cent of those with children aged 10 to 14, fully 31 per cent of those with adult children attend regularly. And the proportion observing five or more home rituals among parents who have adult children exceeds that of parents with very young children.[18]

Furthermore, a significant portion of the decline in religious observance among parents of grown children is accounted for by the influence of advanced-generation respondents of German descent. There appears to be no decrease at the end of the child-rearing years among those of East European descent: there is even a slight increase in observance among the second-generation parents, while among the handful of third-generation parents who have reached this phase of the life cycle a similar trend appears to be developing.

Further light on the influence of the life cycle is found in the responses to the item: "Are there any questions of a religious nature that you have thought about or discussed during the past year?" We find that while a minority of our respondents say that they have confronted questions of religious observance in particular, the parents who have done the most thinking and discussing are those whose oldest child is below the age of 6 (see Table 3–11). This is the group, it will be recalled, that has a very modest level of home observance and synagogue attendance. Thus the high point in wrestling with the problem of ritualism occurs before children are ready for formal Jewish education and thus before parents are subject to the prodding of rabbis, religious-school teachers, or for that matter the children themselves who, having learned about Jewish ritual at religious school, can, if they so wish, use their special powers of persuasion to induce their parents to be more observant. The highest point of concern occurs when the pattern of the family is still half-formed, but must now begin to take on shape so that children may be socialized in a culture which expresses their parents' real commitments. Appropriately, those who have the most firmly established pattern and are least active in the socialization role—the parents of adult children—do very little thinking and discussing in respect to religious observance.

TABLE 3–11. CONCERNS ABOUT RELIGIOUS OBSERVANCE BY FAMILY LIFE CYCLE

	Life-Cycle Phase				
	Pre-School	Early-School	Peak-School	Late-School	Post-School
Per cent thought about or discussed questions of observance in past year	37	26	20	23	12
Per cent mention exposing children to observance out of concern for providing them with background in Jewish life	18	35	28	18	10
N	(68)	(103)	(162)	(22)	(67)

In analyzing the way parents respond who are thinking about questions of religious observance, we find that there is a tentativeness and uncertainty behind their seemingly assertive formulations. They appear to be exploring the precise role of ritual in the family's religious scheme. They are particularly concerned with locating the limits of observance. Aware of Judaism's ritualistic emphasis and its orientation to the sacred-secular dichotomy, they wonder to what extent they can accommodate themselves to these traditions. A good example of this uncertainty is a third-generation businessman, not yet turned 30, whose parents are highly observant. His oldest child is a three-year-old; his level of both home observance and synagogue attendance is minimal. He has been discussing with friends

> Questions about keeping a kosher home and observing holidays. We all perhaps would like to [be more observant], but we have excuses, so we talk about it.

Another member of the third generation is a mother whose oldest child is 5 and whose husband is one of Lakeville's most successful young entrepreneurs. She was reared in a very traditional household and conducts her own home in a more traditional manner than most of her neighbors. But she has not resolved the question of what claim ritualism has upon her. She has been thinking about

> How much observance is necessary to be a good Jew. . . . I feel Judaism is changing. Some people only think of religion in terms of ritual. I don't.

A further example is a young matron whose father was a successful professional man and served as the president of an important Reform temple in Lake City. While she maintains the average Lakeville pattern of observance, she admits to going "through a cycle of doubting" from which she has yet to emerge. She has been concerned with

> The importance of making tradition more meaningful—re-evaluating the importance of tradition in religious services.

A third-generation woman in her early twenties whose only child is still a toddler has a minimal pattern of religious observance. But she has been discussing with her friends

> whether to celebrate various observances or not, and why.

In a very small number of cases, we encounter concern with religious questions which stems from the desire to repel Christian influence. A mother of two pre-schoolers is one such case. Although raised in an unobservant home, she has introduced the celebration of Hanukkah in her household—her only manifestation of religious observance. The husband has acquiesced, but has made known his desire to have a Christmas tree as well, on the basis that otherwise the children might experience a feeling of deprivation. While thus far she has successfully opposed him, she is uncertain whether she can continue to do so in the future. This particular woman is seeking some way to make the observance of Hanukkah so meaningful and significant that the importance of Christmas will recede. Thus her thinking and discussion have focused on "whether we should celebrate Christmas and *how* to celebrate Hanukkah."

The seeking after an adequate ritual model by parents of pre-school-age children is followed by the resolution of the issue as the family matures and hardens its religious pattern. It is the parents of grammar-school-age children who, when they are asked how they manifest their concern to provide their children with a background in Jewish life, most frequently mention that they observe the *mitzvot* (see Table 3–11).

But whatever the motivation for observance, it is the parent who leads; only occasionally do we find cases where a parent feels coerced by his offspring. A third-generation mother of two young daughters who are attending Sunday School is one such case. The mother retains the same home observances followed in her parental home. However, her regular attendance at Sabbath and Festival services far exceeds the pattern set by her parents. Her attendance is due to her children's prodding:

> The children wanted to see us going to synagogue so we went.

Another mother of two girls, whose own father was Gentile and whose Jewish mother rejected all religious observance except attendance at High Holiday services, finds herself observing the Seder ritual, lighting the Hanukkah *menorah,* and attending services occasionally. She complains,

> We sent our daughters to Sunday school, but often they take the words of religious education too seriously and demand too much.

GENERATION

Much recent writing in the field of the sociology of religion proceeds on the assumption that the main determinant of religiosity is generational status, rather than parental patterns or the influence of the life cycle. As exemplified by Will Herberg, this approach stresses that the second generation deviates maximally from the religious pattern of the first generation, while the third generation experiences a "return." The second generation attempts to evade the traditions of its immigrant parents, but the third is attracted to that which the second attempted to reject. The second generation, dissociating itself from the heritage of its immigrant past, concentrates on seeking acceptance and status in the larger society and in doing so refuses to embrace traditions dear to the parents. The third generation, however, feeling greater security because of its acculturation, seeks a more particularistic group identity and social location within the structure of American religious pluralism. It is attracted to the religious—if not the ethnic—heritage of its grandparents.[19]

Since our respondents are not representative of Jews in the nation at large, we are not in a position to settle definitely the dispute about the effect of generational status. Our effort will rather be to discover whether, within the context and the limits of the religious pattern of our respondents, each generation in Lakeville evidences a distinctive response. The case for the existence of such a response seems plausible, for each generation has a particular status in American society and a different level of acculturation. Furthermore, since social change has been so rapid, each generation is distinctive in that the religious legacy it inherits differs both in size and kind from that received by prior generations.

Our procedure for studying generational differences is to analyze the religious observance of our respondents against the background of what prevailed in the parental home.[20] As a consequence, we are able to compare the religious observances not only of respondents who happen to belong to different generations but also of each such generation and its parents.[21] Most sociologists who have studied the religious influence of generational position have not presented family-linked statistics.[22] Because we gathered data on the religious observance of the parents as well as of our respondents themselves, we do not have to treat our first-generation interviewees as if they were the parents of our second-generation respondents, or the latter as if they were the parents of the third-generation respondents.

In order to eliminate any religious influences which derive from differing social and cultural heritages rather than from generational status, we shall follow the procedure of controlling for descent. This control is based on the assumption that the generational concept is meaningful only if it involves a comparison between groups who are fairly homogeneous. The contrasts which we have noted in Chapter 2 in the social characteristics of our descent groups, even in the third generation, suggest that those descended from German and East European Jews have different personal histories and inherit different social and religious legacies. Furthermore, German-origin Jews are overrepresented in the more advanced generations and underrepresented in the less advanced generations. As a consequence, were all our respondents of the same generation considered as a single unit, rather than divided into three descent groups, some important differences may be obscured.

It will be recalled that our respondents are at a level of religious observance much inferior to the one occupied by their parents: their mean of home observance is 2.8, compared to 5.2 for their parents; their mean score on synagogue attendance is 3.7, compared to 5.0 for their parents. In Table 3–12 and in Figure 3–2, the level of religious observance achieved by each Lakeville generation is presented against the base line of the observance level of their parents. We find, of course, that first-generation Lakeville respondents of East European descent were exposed to by far the most traditional pattern of observance: their parents practiced an average of 9.2 out of a possible 11 home rituals and

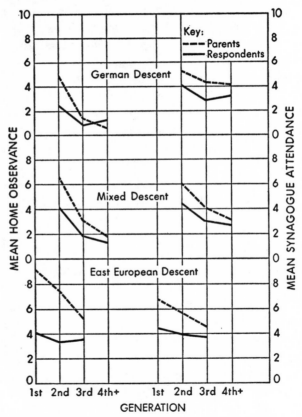

FIGURE 3–2.   MEAN LEVEL OF RELIGIOUS OBSERVANCE
OF RESPONDENTS AND THEIR PARENTS BY
RESPONDENT'S GENERATION AND DESCENT

TABLE 3–12. MEAN LEVEL OF RELIGIOUS OBSERVANCE OF RESPONDENTS AND THEIR PARENTS BY RESPONDENTS' GENERATION AND DESCENT

		Generation		
Among those of German descent	First	Second	Third	Fourth Plus
Mean home observance				
Parents	*	4.9	1.4	0.6
Respondents	*	2.5	0.9	1.3
Difference		−2.4	−0.5	+0.7
Mean synagogue attendance				
Parents	*	5.3	4.3	4.1
Respondents	*	4.1	2.9	3.2
Difference		−1.2	−1.4	−0.9
N	(*)	(13)	(26)	(39)
Among those of mixed descent				
Mean home observance				
Parents	*	6.6	3.1	1.8
Respondents	*	4.2	1.8	1.3
Difference		−2.4	−1.3	−0.5
Mean synagogue attendance				
Parents	*	6.2	4.1	3.2
Respondents	*	4.6	3.0	2.7
Difference		−1.6	−1.1	−0.5
N	(*)	(16)	(23)	(20)
Among those of East European descent				
Mean home observance				
Parents	9.2	7.5	5.2	*
Respondents	4.1	3.3	3.5	*
Difference	−5.1	−4.2	−1.7	
Mean synagogue attendance				
Parents	6.8	5.6	4.5	*
Respondents	4.4	3.9	3.7	*
Difference	−2.4	−1.7	−0.8	
N	(25)	(140)	(85)	(*)

* Too few cases.

had an average score for synagogue attendance of 6.8 out of a possible 9.[23] The respondents, however, observe only 4.1 home rituals and score only 4.4 on synagogue attendance. Thus, instead of the observant new-comer pictured by the generational school of thought, the Lakeville immigrant is a highly acculturated individual.

While the differences between first-generation East Europeans and their parents are the largest of all, the gap between second-generation East Europeans and their parents is also considerable. Since the second-generation East Europeans are numerically the most prominent, their response is of special significance. Among those of German and mixed descent, the gap between the least advanced generation (the second generation) and their parents is also sizable. Furthermore, each succes-sive generation in each descent group is reared in an increasingly more restricted pattern of home observance and synagogue attendance. Never-theless, we find that while each generation in Lakeville almost always fol-lows an observance pattern more limited than the one in which it was reared,[24] the deviations from the parental pattern among the more advanced generations are generally not as sizable as among the less advanced generations.[25] For example, while differences between second-generation respondents of East European descent and their parents are wide, the gap is much reduced in the case of the third generation of the same descent group and their parents.

The smaller deviations from the parental pattern by the more advanced generations in Lakeville suggest, then, that generational status *does* have an influence on religious performance. Indeed, if the performance of each generation were solely responsive to the base line established by the parents, second-generation respondents of East European descent should exhibit a much higher level of religious observance than they actually do. Instead of occupying substantially the same level of home observance and synagogue attendance as their third-generation contem-poraries, they should exceed them. Or looked at from a different perspec-tive, the third generation should occupy a much lower level of religious observance than they actually do. A similar logic would apply to the third generation of German descent, compared to their fourth-generation contemporaries, and to similar generations among those of mixed descent. However, with the possible exception of the latter, the religious observance of the most advanced generations is no less than that of their contemporaries in the preceding generation. Whether expressed in mean figures (Table 3–12) or in proportions at given observance levels (Table 3–13), both home rituals and synagogue attendance are found to be either at about the same level or at a higher level. *In the more advanced generations, then, the trend toward declining religious observance is halted. Within each descent group the overall trend is for stabilization to set in.*

TABLE 3–13. LEVEL OF RELIGIOUS OBSERVANCE BY GENERATION AND DESCENT

	Generation			
Among those of German descent, per cent with	First	Second	Third	Fourth Plus
3+ home observance	*	39	8	11
1+ home observance	*	85	38	63
5+ synagogue attendance	*	39	30	25
3+ synagogue attendance	*	85	45	58
N	(*)	(13)	(26)	(39)
Among those of mixed descent, per cent with				
3+ home observance	*	62	18	.10
1+ home observance	*	93	70	65
5+ synagogue attendance	*	56	31	15
3+ synagogue attendance	*	75	57	.45
N	(*)	(16)	(23)	(20)
Among those of East European descent, per cent with				
5+ home observance	44	30	30	*
3+ home observance	68	53	60	*
5+ synagogue attendance	44	35	32	*
3+ synagogue attendance	84	76	72	*
N	(25)	(140)	(85)	(*)

* Too few cases.

We reason that among second-generation East Europeans the orientation to the parents' religious way of life is more ambivalent than that of their third-generation contemporaries and that this greater ambivalence holds true for third-generation Germans, as compared with their fourth-generation contemporaries. We see that while the less advanced generation is subject to stronger childhood religious influences than the more advanced generation, it pulls away from them more sharply. This greater deviation seems to be due to the influence of generational position. Such a negative pull appears to reflect the cleavage that occurs when parents, particularly of an early generation, follow a traditional pattern of religious observance. The more advanced generation, exposed to a less demanding religious regimen, narrows the gap between itself and its parents. In extreme instances of religious neglect, it may even exceed its parents.

While family-linked generational comparisons tell us part of the story, the effect of generational status becomes even clearer when the influence of disparate patterns of religious rearing is controlled. For example, third-generation East Europeans were reared in less observant homes than second-generation East Europeans, but there is considerable overlap of the childhood observance patterns of the two generations. If our data are so arranged that each generation is given an equal religious start, we shall be in a better position to gauge the effect of generational

TABLE 3-14. LEVEL OF RELIGIOUS OBSERVANCE BY GENERATION, DESCENT, AND PARENTS' LEVEL OF HOME OBSERVANCE

	German Descent		Generation of East European Descent	
	Third	Fourth Plus	Second	Third
Among those reared by highly observant parents (9–11), per cent with				
3+ home observance	*	*	67	85
5+ synagogue attendance	*	*	45	50
N	(*)	(*)	(76)	(20)
Among those reared by moderately observant parents (5–8), per cent with				
3+ home observance	*	*	42	60
5+ synagogue attendance	*	*	23	28
N	(*)	(*)	(34)	(25)
Among those reared by low or nonobservant parents (0–4), per cent with				
3+ home observance	4	10	30	47
1+ home observance	33	61	73	90
3+ synagogue attendance	46	59	46	63
1+ synagogue attendance	63	85	83	93
N	(24)	(39)	(30)	(40)

* Too few cases.

status on religious performance independent of the influence of the parental pattern.

We note in Table 3–14 that third-generation East Europeans exceed their second-generation contemporaries who had a similar childhood exposure to religious observances. This superiority is consistent, whatever the level of observance which prevailed in the home of the respondents' parents. For example, among those reared in highly observant homes, over eight out of ten of the third generation preserve three or more home observances; only two-thirds of their second-generation contemporaries do so. Among those reared in minimally or unobservant homes, only three in ten of the second generation observe a similar number of rituals, compared to almost half of the third generation. Furthermore, fourth-generation respondents of German descent are more observant even when they share with the prior generation the same low level of religious exposure.

Among those with minimal religious rearing, the higher level of observance achieved by more advanced generations applies both to home practices and synagogue attendance. But those from more traditional parental homes do not achieve a substantially higher level of synagogue attendance. This suggests that when the East European immigrant parents are observant, the changes initiated by the second generation result in a less radical reduction in synagogue attendance than in home observance. This reflects the trend to a synagogue-centered Judaism, with which we are already familiar.

The strains experienced by second-generation respondents of East European descent are highlighted in Table 3–15, which compares the home observance and synagogue attendance of each respondent with that of his own parents (rather than between all respondents of a particular generation and all their parents). We find that among those whose East European parents were moderately or highly observant, the decrease in home observance—but not synagogue attendance—of the second generation is more extreme than that of the third generation.* It is also significant that among those with little or no religious rearing, both Germans and East Europeans of more advanced generations have a consistently greater increase over their parents' level of both home and synagogue observance than is true for less advanced generations.

This effect persists despite the fact that the more advanced genera-

---

* The finding holds true for men as well as for women. Because of the lack of emphasis on synagogue attendance among immigrant mothers, one would not expect so steep a decrease in their daughters' attendance.

TABLE 3-15. Intergenerational Change of Religious Observance by Generation, Descent, and Parents' Level of Home Observance

	German Descent		Generation of East European Descent	
	Third	Fourth Plus	Second	Third
Among those reared by highly observant parents (9–11), per cent with				
Same	*	*	4	15
Somewhat less (1–5)	*	*	37	40
Much less (6–11)	*	*	59	45
home observance than parents				
More or same	*	*	23	32
Somewhat less (1–3)	*	*	40	21
Much less (4–9)	*	*	37	47
synagogue attendance than parents				
N	(*)	(*)	(76)	(20)
Among those reared by moderately observant parents (5–8), per cent with				
Same or slightly less (1–3)	*	*	33	64
Somewhat less (4–5)	*	*	34	16
Much less (6–8)	*	*	33	20
home observance than parents				
More or same	*	*	37	35
Somewhat less (1–3)	*	*	44	39
Much less (4–9)	*	*	19	26
synagogue attendance than parents				
N	(*)	(*)	(34)	(25)
Among those reared by low or nonobservant parents (0–4), per cent with				
More	4	44	40	55
Same	79	41	30	13
Less	17	15	30	32
home observance than parents				
More	16	35	38	49
Same	37	11	14	15
Less	47	54	48	36
synagogue attendance than parents				
N	(24)	(39)	(30)	(40)

* Too few cases.

tions are younger and therefore have a higher proportion of families in the earlier, and thus in the least observant, phases of the life cycle. We find, in fact, that in each phase of the life cycle more advanced generations exceed less advanced generations. This difference is maximized when religious rearing is also controlled. Among respondents of East European origin who have had similar levels of childhood religious exposure and are in the early-school or peak-school phases of the life cycle,[26] the third generation shows a consistently higher level of home observance and synagogue attendance than the second generation. Furthermore, the decline of the third generation from high or moderate parental observance levels is not so steep as that of the second, while its increase over minimal or nonobservant parental levels is greater (see Table 3–16).[27]

In sum, generational position has dynamic religious effects. With descent, parents' observance level, and life cycle controlled, a persuasive case can be made for the influence of generational status. Admittedly, the picture is sharper with our respondents than it would be for others. Since Lakeville residents have risen so far, have acculturated so fast, and have done so in an era of particularly rapid social change, we should expect them to maximize any generational effect: the world of most Lakeville sons is quite different from that of their fathers. The picture of stabilization and increased observance that emerges would be described by some—in our opinion, inaccurately—as a "return" to religious observance.

In any case, the picture is quite remarkable in one respect: the more advanced generations maintain a higher observance level, despite the fact that their educational achievement is considerable. If we make the assumption that general education contributed to the ambivalence of the second-generation East Europeans toward their parents' religious heritage, it is apparent that it did not produce a similar result in the religious life of the third generation. The formal education of the second generation may have provided them with ideological support for their rejection or radical modification of the "foreign" elements in the religious system of their immigrant parents. For the third generation, general learning no longer presented such a stark contrast with the more acculturated religious pattern of *their* parents.

Whatever influences we can discern which speed, retard, or stabilize changes in religious behavior, it is apparent that sacramentalism in Lakeville is in crisis. In such a situation, there will be denial of the authority

TABLE 3-16. LEVEL AND INTERGENERATIONAL CHANGE OF RELIGIOUS OBSERVANCE BY GENERATION AND PARENTS' LEVEL OF HOME OBSERVANCE: AMONG EAST EUROPEAN–ORIGIN RESPONDENTS WITH CHILDREN AGES 6 TO 14

	Generation of East European Descent	
	Second	Third
Among those reared by highly observant parents (9–11), per cent with		
3+ home observance	76	86
5+ synagogue attendance	49	65
Much less home observance (6–11) than parents	55	43
Much less synagogue attendance (4–9)	33	29
Less synagogue attendance (1–9) than parents	71	57
N	(49)	(14)
Among those reared by moderately observant parents (5–8), per cent with		
3+ home observance	30	64
5+ synagogue attendance	20	43
Much less home observance (6–8) than parents	30	14
Much less synagogue attendance (4–9)	22	17
Less synagogue attendance (1–9) than parents	61	50
N	(20)	(14)
Among those reared by low or nonobservant parents (0–4), per cent with		
3+ home observance	30	61
5+ synagogue attendance	20	35
More home observance than parents	45	65
More synagogue attendance than parents	37	57
N	(20)	(23)

of the past and the call for a new measuring rod of religiosity. It will be remembered that one of the interviewees has been quoted as saying (page 77 above): "I feel Judaism is changing. Some people only think of religion in terms of ritual. I don't." It is to this reconceptualization of the Jewish religion that we now turn.

The Shift from Sacramentalism

Like all religions, Judaism contains many elements in addition to sacramentalism. If Jews in other centuries were not always satisfied with the centrality of sacramentalism, we can expect that those of Lakeville are certainly motivated to emphasize a variety of other aspects. Of course, in his impatience with the performance of the man–God *mitzvot,* we should not expect the Lakeville Jew to bring into being a fervent religious movement such as Hasidism. Rather we should expect his response to be more appropriate to his particular religious temperature. And because of his acculturation, we should also expect the response to be strongly influenced by the religious culture of the general community.

In our society, the main alternative to sacramentalism is moralism. By the standards of moralism, the religious man is distinguished not by his observance of rituals but rather by the scrupulousness of his ethical behavior. While the follower of sacramentalism sees ethical conduct as an integral part of observance, the follower of moralism feels that such conduct may be impeded rather than stimulated by the stress on sacramentalism. At the very least, sacramentalism is seen as irrelevant to motivating ethical conduct. Furthermore, some moralists view sacramentalism as a screen used by the unethical to mask their hypocritical conduct. In sum, in the eyes of those who hold to the position of moralism, sacramentalism does not advance the realization of what they conceive to be the true purpose of religion: that of teaching man how to deal justly with his fellow man.

All religions are both moralistic and sacramental, but they vary in the balance between the two. However the scale is weighted, there is tension. If the balance is in the sacramental direction, there remains doubt as to the degree of ethical perfection of those whose normative observance is high. And if the scale is balanced toward moralism, questions occur such as (a) the viability of a religious system that has little ceremonial framework and (b) to what extent ethical conduct can be realized if it is not elaborated in a code of religious law. Since a mere 1 per cent of our respondents observe the eleven rituals about which we inquired, we can assume that there will be a tendency on their part to square theory with practice: to redefine the criteria of religiosity and to do so in the direction of moralism. At the same time, we should expect that some of those who are not very observant are still traditional enough in their thinking, if not their practice, to maintain sacramentalism as the crucial dimension of religiosity.

In addition to the new emphasis on moralism, two other approaches to religiosity should emerge. One is the dimension of religious feeling—of subjective experience as the measuring rod of religiosity, in contrast to the performance of rituals. The other is the dimension of religious belief: the affirmation of the existence of God and of the power of inscrutable supernatural forces in human life.[28] According to this view, the religious man is not so much the observant as the believing man—he who keeps faith in God's plan for his children in the face of human and personal tragedy. In this view, it is faith alone which gives meaning to the performance of rituals and good deeds. Faith, in fact, transcends rituals and good deeds. While the sacramentalist holds that more is required of a religious man than belief in the power of a Divine Being and the experiencing of His nearness, to nonsacramentalists belief in God and the experiencing of His presence are all that is needed. In their view, ritualism is optional; it is only for those who feel the need for it.

In order to ascertain changing criteria of religiosity, we asked our respondents to answer a question which encouraged them to think in dimensions other than the sacramental: "Irrespective of whether you follow religious practices or attend synagogue, do you consider yourself to be a religious person? Would you say that you are very religious, moderately religious, somewhat religious, or not religious at all? Why do you feel this way?" Some 15 per cent consider themselves "very religious," and another 15 per cent feel that they are "not at all religious," while 46 per cent consider themselves to be "moderately religious" and 24 per cent consider themselves to be "somewhat religious." [29]

We find that respondents who consider themselves "very religious" most frequently conceive of religion in terms of moralism (see Table 3–17). Moreover, the "very religious" are generally satisfied with their level of moralistic behavior. Also, they rarely feel themselves wanting in other dimensions of religiosity. Those who consider themselves "moderately religious" most frequently conceive of religion in terms of sacramentalism; about one-fourth consider their performance to be inadequate, but twice as many feel that it is adequate. The "moderately religious" also mention the criteria of moralism, religious feeling, and belief in God. The "somewhat religious" mention these dimensions as well, but they focus particularly on their sacramental deficiencies. Those who consider themselves "not at all religious" hold this image primarily because they judge themselves deficient in religious feeling and belief. To

TABLE 3-17. CRITERIA USED IN EVALUATION
OF OWN RELIGIOSITY

	Consider Themselves			
Per cent * who feel	Very Religious	Moderately Religious	Somewhat Religious	Not at all Religious
Adequate in				
Sacramentalism	29	46	23	3
Moralism	62	35	19	14
Religious feeling	23	24	17	6
Belief in God	23	22	16	3
Deficient in				
Sacramentalism	6	25	39	19
Moralism	—	—	1	—
Religious feeling	—	2	10	33
Belief in God	3	2	4	25
N	(64)	(198)	(106)	(63)

* Since more than one criterion is possible, percentages add to more than 100.

a much lesser extent, they rate themselves as weak in sacramentalism.

The drift away from sacramentalism as the pre-eminent criterion of religiosity can be seen in Table 3–18. Some 16 per cent of the non-observant consider themselves to be "very religious," and another 27 per cent believe they are "moderately religious." Only 27 per cent of the nonobservant feel that they are "not at all religious." Less observant persons tend to claim a somewhat lower level of religiosity than do more observant individuals. However, only up to a point do those who practice more observances consider themselves to be more religious than the

TABLE 3-18. EVALUATION OF OWN RELIGIOSITY
BY LEVEL OF HOME OBSERVANCE

	Number of Observances		
Per cent consider themselves	5+	1–4	None
Very religious	16	14	16
Moderately religious	68	43	27
Somewhat religious	13	28	30
Not at all religious	3	15	27
N	(105)	(245)	(81)

less observant; nonobservant and less observant respondents see themselves as "very religious" just as often as do the more observant.[30] The majority of those at the higher observance level see themselves as "moderately religious."

The drift from sacramentalism is further demonstrated by the more observant respondents who consider themselves "very religious." While 47 per cent of them mention sacramentalism as important in the formation of the image of their religiosity, 53 per cent mention moralism (see Table 3–19). For the less observant and the nonobservant who rank themselves as "very religious," the trend to moralism is even stronger; in the case of such respondents, moralism far outranks other criteria of religiosity.

TABLE 3–19. CRITERIA OF HIGH RELIGIOSITY
BY LEVEL OF HOME OBSERVANCE

Of those who say they are "very religious," per cent who feel adequate in	Number of Observances		
	5+	1–4	None
Sacramentalism	47	21	23
Moralism	53	65	69
Religious feeling	35	21	15
Belief in God	23	18	38
N	(17)	(34)	(13)

The drift from sacramentalism is found even among the large "moderately religious" group. As we noted, this group is the one which most frequently conceives of religiosity in terms of going to worship and performing rituals. However, this trend is striking only among the more observant of the "moderately religious" (see Table 3–20). While 63 per cent of the more observant stress sacramentalism, only 39 per cent of the more numerous less observant and 32 per cent of the nonobservant feel the same way. Nor do these latter groups, despite their lower observance levels, feel any more deficient in sacramentalism. Instead, they stress adequacy in the other criteria about as often as, or more often than, do the more observant. Among the less observant group, moralism receives as much emphasis as does sacramentalism.

Furthermore, even the most observant of our respondents are conscious of the strain on Judaism's age-old sacramental tradition. A young architect, newly settled in Lakeville, who is part of the minuscule group

TABLE 3–20. CRITERIA OF MODERATE RELIGIOSITY
BY LEVEL OF HOME OBSERVANCE

Of those who say they are "moderately religious," per cent who feel	Number of Observances		
	5+	1–4	None
Adequate in			
Sacramentalism	63	39	32
Moralism	31	39	27
Religious feeling	22	23	32
Belief in God	13	26	32
Deficient in sacramentalism	28	25	23
N	(71)	(105)	(22)

observing all the *mitzvot,* says, "I'm an observant Jew, and that's the only way I know how to be a religious Jew." He states without prompting, however, that "a person can be moral without being observant." But he also adds, "He cannot be religious without being observant."

While traditionalists defend sacramentalism as the true measuring rod of religiosity, others attack it with impunity, including those who consider themselves "very religious." A respondent who places himself in this category, although he attends services only occasionally and neglects some of the rituals to which he was exposed in his parents' traditional home, is convinced that sacramentalism has been superseded by moralism, by religious feeling, and by the importance of belief in God:

> My mother had a *fleyshedik* stove and *milchedik* stove. Working on Sabbath was the mortal sin, and we ate breakfast only after morning prayers, wearing *tallis* and *t'fillin*. But it's just not rituals [that are important]. They disappear, but not the innate very personal belief in God. There's a very close and personal and direct relationship between me and God. I wouldn't hurt anyone, can't turn anyone down, and no one will walk out of my house hungry. . . . My belief in religion is not in the hereafter, but rather in the hell and heaven here on earth and now. I don't believe in putting money into a church or *shul* as a premium on an insurance policy for the hereafter. I don't even have to go to *shul.*

A physician raised in an Orthodox home, who attends services more frequently than the previous respondent, but is less observant in his home, considers himself "very religious." He believes that the essence of Judaism is moralism, and he implies that Judaism is superior in this respect to Christianity:

> I try to live by the morals set down by the Jewish religion: Do unto others as you would like others to do unto you. I believe in live and let live. The Jewish religion is wonderful because we don't emphasize life after death but we live morally now. It teaches us how to live and not how to die.

Another respondent who considers herself "very religious" was also reared by Orthodox parents. She has departed even more sharply from the religious orientation of her childhood. She attends services only on the High Holidays and observes but one out of the eleven home rituals. Not only is she convinced of the superiority of moralism, but in addition she feels that it can make an important contribution to interfaith relations:

> My concept of being a good Jew is being a good person. I wouldn't do anything to hurt anyone. Just being religious [i.e., observant] doesn't make one a good person. Showing a non-Jew what a good person a Jew can be without ceremonials is what I believe. I have a belief in the Ten Commandments part of religion and live it without joining the functional part. I also have a deep feeling, even if it's based on supernatural fear. But there is a God.

There are, of course, nonobservant respondents who rate themselves as "very religious," but who were not exposed to Orthodoxy in childhood. A longtime Lakeville resident, now retired from the presidency of a manufacturing company, is one of these. He was raised by Reform parents who neither attended services nor observed any rituals at home. He belongs to a Reform temple and follows the same pattern as his parents. He considers himself "very religious"

> Because of the manner in which I conduct myself—all my life I've been careful to lead my life in such a way that I don't have to be ashamed of myself. I deal honestly and perform charity—that is my entire religion.

Belief in God is irrelevant for this respondent, as it is for some others who are nonobservant but consider themselves "very religious." In their view, God has been supplemented by ethics, and ethical performance is the real measure of religiosity.

Some who situate themselves in the "very religious" category stress religious belief, rather than moralism. This approach is typified by a woman who has resided in Lakeville for quite a few years, is married to a prosperous businessman, and is highly concerned about the type of Jew currently settling in the community. Like the previous respondent, she observes no rituals in her home. Nor were any performed by her Reform parents. She does, however, attend services on the High Holidays. She considers herself "very religious" because

I have complete faith in God, and this is all you need.

In the "moderately religious" group, not only do we find many more observant individuals than among the "very religious," but among such observant respondents we find a group who betray little need to support and sanction sacramentalism with moralistic or other criteria. In fact, they value sacramentalism as a criterion of religiosity, regardless of the reason for observance. There is the example of the young mother whose husband's income is modest by Lakeville standards. The family belongs to the Conservative synagogue in the community. The woman, who was reared in an Orthodox home, feels very much at ease in the synagogue religiously, but regards herself as an outsider socially, apparently because of her financial condition. Considering herself "moderately religious," her frame of reference reflects the sacramental emphasis:

> There are certain traditions that I like to follow, such as lighting the Friday night candles and the Hanukkah candles and observing the holidays and having the Seders. My children attend Sunday school, but I am not an avid *shul*-goer myself.

Not all "moderately religious" respondents who are more observant were raised in Orthodox homes, however. A third-generation respondent who is the wife of a public-relations man feels that her father could best be described as a Reform Jew and her mother as Conservative. Nevertheless, she thinks much in sacramental terms:

> I wouldn't say I'm very religious because I'm not very observant and I don't attend temple with great frequency, but neither am I only somewhat religious, because I'm glad I'm a Jew. I'm always trying to find out about Judaism, and I follow certain observances.

The effect of evaluating oneself according to the traditional model of Jewish piety is apparent in the response of some of our "moderately religious" respondents. A chemist who is more observant than his parents and much more traditional than the great majority of Jews in the community nevertheless considers himself only "moderately religious" because of his neglect of several observances:

> I don't attend synagogue every Saturday. I ride on Saturday and carry money on Saturday.

His model of religiosity is a highly observant grandmother of whom he was very fond.

The group considering itself "not at all religious" is a conglomeration of several types. Some have been exposed to a religious education, but without profit. A case in point is the wife of a prosperous businessman of Reform lineage. While religious observance in her parental home was minimal, she was enrolled in Sunday School at an early age and was confirmed. She feels "not at all religious" because

> It's just never meant anything to me and I've had the training.

The same reaction is apparent in the response of another woman raised in a similar environment, who received very much the same kind of Jewish education:

> I never attend temple. I'm just not religious. Both my parents were very Reformed Jews, and I've never felt the need of it.

Some respondents whose parents provided them with little in the way of a Jewish home environment have turned to religion at moments of crisis, but generally with unsatisfactory results. A prominent clubwoman, who is a longtime resident and the wife of a prosperous business executive, rarely goes to services. When she does,

> I am bored to death. I look at prayers objectively. I can only think of what I thought when my wedding was performed. Words. Words. Words. I tried to do something after the death of my five-year-old nephew. I read prayer books for solace, but I couldn't get any.

The "not at all religious" group also includes individuals who do not have a Reform background. One such case is the son of Russian-born parents, who grew up in a Yiddish-speaking, nonreligious home. His acculturation is extensive: his home is English-speaking, and he displayed a Christmas tree in the living room when his children were younger. In other respects, he is different from his Gentile neighbors: he votes the Democratic ticket, and he would give aid and comfort to the Socialist Party if he felt it could be a more significant political force. While his self-righteous tone makes him sound more like a conservative than a liberal, he typifies the Jew detached from Judaism's sacramental tradition:

> My religion? It's a love of nature. I mind my own business. I'm a damn good citizen.

4

THE SYNAGOGUES
OF LAKEVILLE:
INSTITUTIONAL ANALYSIS

We have seen that the typical Jewish resident of Lakeville neither attends services with any regularity nor observes basic Jewish rituals in his home. Nevertheless, he is affiliated with a religious institution: some 66 per cent of our respondents are members of a synagogue. In fact, the synagogue's reach into the Jewish community is far more extensive than is indicated by the two-thirds who are currently affiliated. More than four in five Lakeville families, or 83 per cent, are past or present members. And even more striking is the fact that almost everyone will be a member at some time in his life. Thus, more than nine in ten, or 93 per cent, of the families whose children are all age 18 or over are past or present members. This high level of present or past affiliation is as true of third- and fourth-generation Jews of German descent as it is of second-generation Jews of East European descent.

The five synagogues in the community and the percentage of our affiliated respondents who belong to each are as follows:

Isaac Mayer Wise Temple	38%
Solomon Schechter Synagogue	27

97

David Einhorn Temple	14
Samuel Hirsch Temple	8
Max Lilienthal Temple	8

Four of these institutions are Reform, while one—the Solomon Schechter Synagogue—is Conservative. Although an attempt was made to form an Orthodox synagogue, the community was unreceptive. Since institutionalized Jewish life in the community is centered in these congregations, an understanding of them (and of the abortive attempt to establish an Orthodox congregation as well) will tell us much about the Lakeville Jew. And since the synagogues must be understood in historical as well as contemporary terms, we shall not only analyze the present program of each congregation but also inquire into the circumstances that brought it into being.

The Isaac Mayer Wise Temple

EARLY HISTORY

The Isaac Mayer Wise Temple was the first Jewish congregation to be established in the Lakeville area. It is also the largest and best-known synagogue on the Heights. In contrast to some of the country's pioneer Reform congregations, the early history of the Temple lacks apparent drama, for neither was it established as a result of the gradual transformation of an Orthodox institution nor was it founded as a result of a revolt led by younger people who had sought—fruitlessly—a spiritual home in a religious institution controlled by their elders.

The relative placidity surrounding the establishment of the Isaac Mayer Wise Temple is traceable to the fact that many of its founders were either first-generation Reform Jews who had been affiliated with a Reform congregation before moving to the Heights or the offspring of Reform families. Even those who lacked such rearing or affiliation were no strangers to Reform Judaism; many of their relatives or friends were Reform Jews. Thus the founders of the Wise Temple were not seeking to discover new truths or establish new forms in order to give expression to their spiritual yearnings. They were, in the main, a group of veteran Reform Jews who saw their task as recreating in Lakeville what they had known in Lake City.

Many of the founders had belonged to (and some still retained an affiliation with) a particular Reform congregation of Lake City: the

Samuel Holdheim Temple. A leading Reform institution whose membership was primarily German-Jewish, Holdheim was widely known in Lake City. It attracted attention because of the great wealth and high status of some of its members, the prominence of its rabbis, and its strict adherence to the doctrines and practices of Classical Reform.[1]

While the early days of the Wise Temple are deficient in the kind of high drama that surrounded the establishment of certain pioneer Reform temples, the seemingly unruffled history of its establishment is deceptive. Such placidity masks a strong inner tension—a tension which provides us with significant clues into the world of the Jewish first families of Lakeville.

The question of the establishment of a congregation arose when the Heights began to attract year-round Jewish residents in the early part of the century. According to Jewish tradition, the procedure to be followed was clear: the first ten male householders should form themselves into a *minyan,* thereby providing the nucleus for a formally organized congregation. Nevertheless, in actual fact over a decade passed before a synagogue was in full operation. In the meantime, several hundred Jewish families had become residents of the Heights.

The ostensible reason for the delay was the fact that some of the families residing on the Heights continued their affiliation with congregations in Lake City, especially with the Holdheim Temple. But they could at best attend religious services or participate in congregational life irregularly; the round-trip travel time to Holdheim totaled about four hours. Most of the other German Reform temples in Lake City were similarly inaccessible.

The lack of religiosity of some of those who chose to reside on the Heights was a highly important factor which inhibited the establishment of a congregation. Such individuals had given up regular attendance at services and did not feel uncomfortable about living in a community that lacked a Jewish house of worship. Nevertheless, there were undoubtedly a sufficient number of more traditionally oriented persons to form a congregation, especially if we consider that the wealth of the longtime Jewish residents was such that a congregation could be adequately supported by a mere handful of families. There was really no need to wait until a broad base of support was assured.

The decade of delay becomes understandable when we realize that the establishment of a congregation would be a public declaration that Jews not only were permanent residents of Lakeville but had constituted themselves into a separate segment of the community. True, the country club had already proclaimed Jewish separatism. But this institution was basically a summer facility. Furthermore, its existence could be explained away as a consequence of Gentile exclusion rather than Jewish divisiveness. The first families, we infer, felt compelled to ask the question: Granted that the community accepted individual Jews and a Jewish country club, would it also tolerate the establishment of a Jewish community?

Anxiety about the reaction which the establishment of a synagogue might provoke may constitute only part of the story. An alternative explanation is that—whether nominally committed to the maintenance of Jewish identity or not—unconsciously many of the first families hoped that a new beginning was on the horizon: that Lakeville, unlike Lake City, might come to constitute a community in which traditional religious distinctions would pass into limbo. We wonder whether the Wise Temple was organized only after it became evident that while the traditions of Lakeville were different from those of Lake City, the townspeople were Christian in orientation, and hence the community did not offer the alternative of honorable assimilation.

Lack of evidence does not allow us to resolve the question of whether the Wise Temple was organized as much out of disillusionment with the dream of a new non-sectarianism as out of conviction about the unique value of Judaism. What we do know is that there were always individuals in the community who were at least nominally committed to Jewish survival. This is evidenced by the fact that religious classes for Jewish children were organized on the Heights during the pre–World War I period. The impetus for the classes was the feeling that children should be instructed in their faith. The particular fear was that if the younger generation were allowed to go uninstructed, they would not receive the rite of Confirmation. Adults, if they were so minded, could go occasionally to Lake City for religious services, but commutation for religious instruction in the case of the children was not feasible.

Why was Confirmation viewed so seriously? At the time, many Jews in Lake City considered it an unimportant, even objectionable, ritual. However, to the followers of Classical Reform the ceremony had great significance. It was considered a prime religious rite, for without Confirmation the child was not really a member in good standing of the Jewish faith. Confirmation was thus the admission ticket to an adult Jewish identity. It was felt that to allow one's children to grow up without being confirmed was to engage in active assimilation.

The Isaac Mayer Wise Temple traces back to the privately organized classes designed to prepare children for Confirmation. The Temple, then, emerged from a school, rather than from a quorum of ten males who worshiped together. Its mode of formation indicates the break with sacramentalism which the early families had made. One other aspect also represents a break with Jewish tradition. This is the fact that the classes were established and maintained by women. In Judaism, the spiritual nurture of the child, especially the male child, has traditionally been both the obligation and the prerogative of the father. The shift to the mother represents a radical departure, indicative of the high acculturation of the early families in the area of the sacred. It also suggests a decided modification of the family structure and the sex roles traditional in the Jewish group. Finally, the role of the woman in forming and maintaining these religious-school classes foreshadows certain aspects of contemporary Jewish life in Lakeville.

While the children who completed the course of study could be confirmed in a Lake City temple, the existence of an instructional program in Lakeville served to highlight the absence of a synagogue. Furthermore, the interaction attendant upon the establishment and maintenance of the classes had the effect of strengthening interpersonal relationships between Jewish families residing on the Heights.

In the early 1920's, a series of meetings were held which resulted in the decision to organize a religious institution. However, the majority felt that it was unwise to organize an independent synagogue; it was resolved that a branch of the Holdheim Temple be formed. This unusual arrangement, essentially a compromise between establishing a congregation and delaying such a move, indicates the ambiguities experienced by the early Jewish residents.

While men were elected to the posts of president and vice-president, in contrast to the practice in other Reform temples at the time a full third of the officials of the new institution were women. This unusual amount of representation constituted acknowledgment of the role of the women in sparking the group's formation.

The classes which the women had organized were incorporated into the new congregation. Sessions of the school were held on Sunday morning. The program was not very intensive; classes lasted for only a portion of the morning. Guidance on teaching methods was supplied by a non-Jewish educator on the staff of a Lake City university. No classes for high-school youth or for adults were organized. In addition to the school, the new branch congregation also held religious services. These were conducted by the rabbi of the Holdheim Temple and had to be scheduled for Friday evening, inasmuch as the rabbi was obliged to conduct services at Holdheim on Sunday morning.

While this was a minimal program even for a new congregation, the group did sponsor an additional activity during its first year: a lecture series featuring nationally known speakers who discussed topics of general interest. All the speakers were non-Jews. The activity was not designed primarily as a service to the membership. Neither was its function that of earning money for congregational coffers nor that of bringing the Temple to the attention of the public. Rather, the objective was to offer a service to the general community. The series represented the desire to sponsor an activity which, unlike the religious school or the religious services, was non-sectarian in character. The activity was designed to convey the idea that while Lakeville Jewry had proceeded to organize, it had no desire to be considered an alien element. The activity celebrated the community's toleration of the newly established institution: Lakeville had allowed the Temple the right to organize, and the Temple reciprocated by offering the community a feature which it lacked. Appropriately, only a nominal charge was made for admission: while nationally known speakers were brought from New York and other cities, the admission fee for the entire series was only one dollar. In sum, the group felt compelled to initiate a non-sectarian program, instead of first turning all its energies inward and seeking to establish the new institution on as solid a foundation as possible. As a demonstration of gratitude for Lakeville's tolerance and as a rejection of a strong in-group orientation, the lecture series is another item of evidence which suggests that the decision to organize was not unambiguous and came after some inner turmoil.[2]

THE ESTABLISHMENT OF AN
INDEPENDENT CONGREGATION

Although the Holdheim Temple cooperated with the group on the Heights, the establishment of a branch congregation created many difficulties for the parent institution. The officers found it difficult to meet the needs of the new group. The rabbinical situation was particularly troublesome, since a single rabbi served the Holdheim Temple. He was widely known to residents of the Heights; he had held his post for several decades and had officiated at the Confirmation and nuptials of some of the Heights families. But he was advanced in years and in poor health, and his doctors finally prevailed on him to discontinue his trips. Rabbis who had no connection with the Holdheim Temple had to be enlisted to substitute for him.

There was no precedent in Jewish tradition for the branch-congregation arrangement. In spite of Protestant influences on the worship patterns of Classical Reform Judaism, the leadership of the Holdheim Temple lacked familiarity with such arrangements as chapels or missions functioning as extensions of mother congregations. Despite their acculturation, they began to revert to the traditional Jewish notion of considering each *minyan* both equal and independent. Thus as time passed it became evident even to those who were hesitant about establishing an independent congregation that the arrangement could only be temporary. Nevertheless, the device of a branch congregation had allowed the Jews of Lakeville additional time to adjust to the fact that they constituted a separate part of the community. By blunting reality, the branch congregation had served an important function: it could be claimed that all that had been started in the town was an extension program of an already-existing institution.

Another important factor impelling clarification of the status of the branch congregation was the need for a congregational home. The practice of the group was to rent space in lodge halls, clubrooms, public schools, and churches. This practice could not go on indefinitely. Furthermore, an incongruity existed between such makeshift accommodations, some of them decidedly unluxurious, and the fiscal potency of the group. While the membership was smaller than most of the Reform congregations in the metropolis, it included several of the wealthiest Jews of the metropolitan area. And the median income of the membership was undoubtedly higher than that of any other congregation. Why, then, were proper accommodations lacking for so long?

In our view, the hesitancy to erect a suitable edifice constitutes another example of the difficulty which the congregation experienced in proclaiming to the community at large that the Jews constituted a separate group. As part of this difficulty, there was fear of an adverse reaction on the part of non-Jews to a Jewish house of worship. So unsure of their acceptability were the first families that they wished to test public reaction. The lack of a building served to obviate the unpleasant prospect of retreating under pressure in the event of a hostile reception.

But as the years passed, it became increasingly enervating to shift from one meeting place to another. Furthermore, the procedure came to constitute a grave embarrassment: Jews were the only religious group without permanent headquarters, and thus they had to impose on the good will of the general community, and specifically on some of the Protestant churches. The decision to build was thus inevitable. However, before the funds for an edifice were raised, it was necessary to come to a decision about the future status of the group. After a series of meetings, it was decided to form an independent congregation: the Isaac Mayer Wise Temple. The roster of the newly established institution soon numbered approximately 250 families.

Once the decision to become independent and to build a temple was made, the necessary funds were raised without difficulty: in a relatively short time a structure was erected. Certain aspects of the physical form of the building are of significance. While in doctrine and ritual the Wise Temple modeled itself on the Holdheim Temple, the building erected in Lakeville was quite different from the one in Lake City. The Holdheim building possessed a monumental quality. It drew the eye both because of its bulk and the fact that it stood on a main traffic artery. The structure built in Lakeville, on the other hand, was inconspicuous. It tended toward understatement and was located in a comparatively unobtrusive location. It differed from the style of the residences of many of its leading supporters, whose homes did not tend toward understatement and were generally built on a larger scale than the domiciles in which these families had resided in Lake City. While the residences did not attempt to conserve space (they generally included facilities for entertaining large numbers of guests), the Temple building leaned toward compactness. Furthermore, the modesty of the new building was in contrast to the luxurious synagogue structures created during the 1920's in Lake City and many other metropolitan communities. Conceived at the height of the building boom, the structure built in Lakeville did not express the speculative temper of the period or the tendency of the times toward erecting grandiose structures.

There is one other aspect of the building's size that is significant. Since the founding families did not wish to encourage the establishment of a second synagogue on the Heights, it would have been logical to erect a larger building. The size of the building thus suggests that the founders were not interested in encouraging more Jewish families to move into the vicinity. Rather than feeling the need to strengthen their foothold in a strongly Gentile area, the building seems to suggest that the longtime residents believed that the absorptive capacity of the Heights in respect to Jewish population had already been reached.

By the time the building was erected and dedicated, scores of new families had joined the Temple; the facility seemed to be on the way toward becoming outmoded. The fact that attendance was irregular kept it from being cramped, but the real reason why enlargement was not needed at once was the onset of the depression. Home construction in Lakeville came to a halt, and some families even moved back to Lake City.

Another aspect of the Temple building provides insight into the world of the early families. While the modesty of the original structure has become obscured by later additions, the fact that it was not located on a main traffic artery remains apparent even today. We surmise that its placement was not accidental, but rather served the purpose of de-emphasizing the existence and importance of the Jewish segment in the community at large.[3]

Modesty of physical plant and unobtrusiveness of location aside, a member of the Holdheim Temple would have found the newly established Isaac Mayer Wise Temple highly familiar. At the weekly religious services, the rabbi's sermon, rather than the Torah service or the prayers, was the central feature. The services took place on Sunday morning; the membership strongly approved of Sunday, rather than the traditional Jewish Sabbath. Those with young children were able to emulate the pattern of Protestant churches in the community: both parents and children could arrive and leave together. Since religious-school classes met for about half of the morning and the services were similarly brief, the schedules dovetailed. The curriculum of the school continued to be geared to preparing the child for Confirmation, which generally coincided with graduation from grammar school. The ceremony of Bar Mitzvah was not permitted.

Aside from the flurry of activity on Sunday morning, the building was not very busy. The community-wide lecture series was continued, but it did not constitute an intensive kind of program. The leisure-time activities of the membership were centered in the various Jewish city and country clubs to which they belonged; social affairs were held in these clubs, in the better hotels of the metropolis, or in spacious private homes. But while the Temple was not a very active institution, its stability seemed assured. There were no competing synagogues to dilute support. Even during the depression, the fiscal condition of the institution was not troublesome; the group was able to raise the comparatively modest funds needed for the maintenance of its compact building and for other congregational expenses.

FROM CLASSICAL REFORM TO NEO-REFORM

While the Holdheim Temple in Lake City has continued to espouse the position of Classical Reform, the Wise Temple is now a Neo-Reform institution. The practiced eye may notice a few survivals of Classical Reform at the Wise Temple, but the shift has been complete enough so that only those familiar with the history of the congregation are aware of its original emphasis. How did it happen that stability was retained in the mother congregation, while innovation prevailed at the daughter congregation?

The potentiality for change was created by the fact that the Wise Temple was the only synagogue on the Heights. Although the Jewish population did not increase during the early years of the depression, the lag in population growth was only temporary. A slow but steady stream of Jewish families arrived in Lakeville during the late 1930's and 1940's. Many of these families were neither German Jewish by descent nor Classical Reform by conviction. Those who were interested in a synagogue affiliation had no alternative but that of joining the Wise Temple.

The Temple, on its part, had no device for excluding deviants; unlike some Protestant groups, which require a creedal affirmation as a condition for membership, the institution followed the usual Jewish practice in the United States of enrolling any Jew who was desirous of joining. Whether because they were hesitant about diluting support, or because they feared that the establishment of another congregation would call the attention of the community at large to the growth of the Jewish population, the officials of the Temple did nothing about encouraging the establishment of a separate synagogue for those who were ideologically uncommitted to Classical Reform.

While deviants were admitted to the Temple, no real effort was made to convert them. Nothing in the experience of the leadership had prepared them for handling such a problem. In Lake City, the multiplicity of congregations encouraged self-selection: individuals chose a congregation on the basis of affinity as well as location. Not only did the long-time residents make no real effort to change the ideological predilections of the new group; they did not integrate them into the various Jewish organizations and social clubs which they dominated. Their procedure was to uphold Classical Reform norms and to hope that, through exposure, reconciliation to such norms would occur.

The attitudes of the newcomers—many having an Orthodox, Conservative, Zionist, Yiddishist, or nondescript Jewish background—were undoubtedly affected by the general culture of the Heights, by joining the Wise Temple, and by sending their children to its religious school. On the whole, however, they did not become committed to Classical Reform. Their heterodox tendencies were reinforced by the fact that they interacted among themselves, forming their own social cliques and organizations. The policy adopted by the oldtimers of neither excluding nor integrating deviants might not have posed a problem during the expansionist period of Classical Reform. It was fraught with danger, however, during the 1930's and 1940's.

While it is sometimes necessary to either integrate or exclude deviant groups in order to assure institutional continuity, far more crucial at times is organizational prosperity. That is, when an institution is flourishing, the pressure for change is minimal. Although the Wise Temple was financially solvent, as a religious institution it was subject to evaluation by other than fiscal standards. For example, the services were not very well attended. Institutional morale was not very high: longtime residents seemed to lack the *élan* which characterized the early period of Classical Reform. Missionary zeal was absent: there was no effort to use the building as a base from which to bring the message of Classical Reform to all who might be induced to listen.

Institutional drift at the Wise Temple contrasted with the activism which prevailed at the Holdheim Temple. This congregation, as a historic institution, could call forth familial loyalties; the sons of the founding families could be induced to accept leadership even as they had accepted the privileges of their birth. For them, loyalty to the family dictated that one's obligations to Holdheim be met. Concomitantly, no deviants joined the congregation; other synagogues in the area absorbed those who were unsympathetic with Classical Reform. Furthermore, the number of worshipers at Holdheim was not solely dependent on the religious enthusiasm of the institution's membership. While attendance at the Wise services was confined to affiliated families, the Holdheim services drew upon the interest and curiosity of a city-wide audience, Gentile as well as Jewish.

Holdheim also sponsored a community-center program. Situated adjacent to a heavily populated area which was deficient in recreational facilities, the institution conducted a variety of clubs, forums, and classes. Participation of non-members in such activities was encouraged. The Holdheim Temple also invited community agencies to use its building as a meeting place. It took these steps more out of a sense of *noblesse oblige* than out of a desire to repay the general community for its tolerance.

A community-center approach was unworkable in Lakeville, where there was no similar shortage of recreational facilities. And while the women of the Holdheim Temple participated in various charitable endeavors which were integrated into the congregational program, the Wise Temple, removed as it was from the poverty of Lake City, never developed an appealing program of welfare activities.

The lack of well-attended services and of a lively temple program encouraged those who were uncommitted to Classical Reform to suggest that if certain changes were made, interest in the Temple would grow. The most radical innovation suggested was that of shifting the schedule of weekly services: they proposed these be held Friday evening, instead of Sunday morning. While the plan was advanced as a practical technique for increasing attendance rather than as an ideological break with Classical Reform, both groups were aware of its implications. When longtime residents demurred, the newcomers charged that they were unwilling to experiment in the best interests of the institution. They accused the longtime residents of developing their own form of orthodoxy and thereby of not being authentic Reform Jews.

Neither the partial vacuum created by the wavering enthusiasm of longtime residents nor the thrust coming from the direction of the newcomers would by itself have been powerful enough to bring institutional change. Events taking place on the national and international front were a crucial influence. The rise of Nazism was perhaps even more important than the depression. To those with strong Jewish commitments, the events occurring outside of Lakeville encouraged skepticism about the assumptions of Classical Reform, especially its faith in the irresistible and well-nigh automatic perfectibility of man and the forward march of his social system. Normal social change would have meant the growth of skepticism in respect to Classical Reform, but the traumatic events of the 1930's greatly increased feelings about the lack of relevance of its ideology.

The ferment of the period made a deep impact on Rabbi Benjamin Finkelstein, the spiritual leader who had been engaged as the rabbi of the Wise Temple in the early 1930's after the unexpected death of the Temple's previous rabbi. Rabbi Finkelstein was a comparatively young man. He was conversant both with general affairs and Jewish problems, highly sophisticated in his tastes, very handsome, and a talented writer as well as an engaging speaker. To the chagrin of the longtime families, he developed an abiding interest in Zionism: he came to believe that Palestine should be not only a place of settlement for Jewish refugees but also a Jewish national homeland. Simultaneously, he became convinced that Reform had gone much too far in severing its links with the Jewish past. In short, Rabbi Finkelstein became a proponent of Neo-Reform. While he subsequently claimed that he had always held Neo-Reform convictions, some of the longtime residents were convinced that Rabbi Finkelstein had deliberately misled them. Others, who granted the sincerity of his convictions, felt that he had unwittingly become infected with the virus of Neo-Reformism.

Some of the changes that Rabbi Finkelstein advocated could be initiated without great controversy. The introduction of Hebrew classes for children and the celebration of Bar Mitzvah are relevant examples; both of these changes were finally agreed to. They were, however, made optional "extras" to be utilized only by those who were so inclined. To underline the point, the Hebrew classes were not fully integrated into the religious-school curriculum, and a separate charge was made for them. Tuition was set at a figure large enough to make the classes in theory self-sustaining, thereby precluding the possibility that membership dues would be devoted to spreading knowledge of the Hebrew language. In regard to Bar Mitzvah, it was stipulated that Confirmation remained the norm and that Bar Mitzvah candidates were obliged to undergo Confirmation as well. Thus, from the point of view of the Temple leadership, if not the boy himself, Confirmation was reaffirmed as the prime ceremony of induction into the household of Israel.

The proposal to shift the weekly service to Friday evening could not be settled so agreeably. It became, in fact, the prime issue on which Classical Reformers and Neo-Reformers divided. Neither side believed that all that was at stake was merely settling upon the most convenient and appealing time for worship, for shifting to Friday evening symbolized a return to the traditional Jewish Sabbath and, concomitantly, a rejection of the day of rest observed by the general community. Furthermore, the shift implied that the founding fathers of the Wise Temple were subject to criticism: that in their desire to adapt Judaism to the contemporary scene they had done violence to some of its fundamentals.

The Neo-Reformers won their case. While the details of their strategy are not clear, the effect of their victory is plain: the split in the congregation between Classical Reformers and Neo-Reformers became a matter of public rather than of private discussion. It became impossible to continue the fiction of a united congregation.

Resolution of the conflict was delayed for a time: during World War II the two factions arranged a "cease fire." With the coming of V-J Day, however, the conflict was renewed. As a result, additional efforts were made to arrange a compromise between Classical and Neo-Reformers and thus to retain a measure of institutional cohesion. The device utilized for this purpose was that of engaging two rabbis instead of one. The proposal for hiring an additional rabbi was presented as a natural consequence of the growth of the congregation, but its function was obvious to both sides. Rabbi Finkelstein was to represent Neo-Reform, and his associate was to represent Classical Reform.

The arrangement proved to be unworkable. Instead of bringing harmony, it dramatized the split between the two groups. Disagreement between the rabbis was chronic, and even greater polarization resulted as each group rallied around their man. When an impasse had been reached, both rabbis were asked to resign. The board of directors abolished the office of associate rabbi and proceeded to seek a single spiritual leader who would be acceptable to both factions. The new rabbi would have to espouse a middle-of-the-road approach on religious doctrine and practice and be neutral on the issue of a Jewish homeland, neither favoring the pro-Zionist position of the Neo-Reform element nor the anti-Zionist stand of the Classical Reform group.

THE TRIUMPH OF NEO-REFORM

Although the quest for an acceptable spiritual leader appeared foredoomed, the board succeeded in locating a candidate who received the enthusiastic endorsement of both Classical Reformers and Neo-Reformers. True, Rabbi Herbert Greenberg was not strongly identified with either school of thought, but his unique appeal cannot be explained merely on the basis of his moderation. Rather, it was his personal qualities as much as his ideological stance that made him appealing.

Rabbi Greenberg was an East European Jew. He made no attempt to hide this fact. He did not seek to pass himself off as of German descent; on the contrary, he was proud of his background. To him, differences between Eastern and Western Jews were no longer salient. Actually he represented qualities which both longtime residents and newcomers, Germans and East Europeans, esteemed but lacked—qualities which they could not themselves encompass, but which they could only hope to attain in their children. Rabbi Greenberg was very tall and very lean; most members of the congregation were not so tall or lean. Rabbi

Greenberg's clothes were beautifully casual and very tweedy; the tailoring of the membership was only solid and expensive. Rabbi Greenberg's manner was that of a sophisticated Easterner; they were provincial Midwesterners. Rabbi Greenberg's aloofness fascinated the longtime residents who, although living in a culture dominated by Rotarianism, were vaguely acquainted with the manners of Boston Brahmins and Philadelphia gentlemen. And Rabbi Greenberg's manner was not unattractive to the newcomers. While they knew little about Boston or Philadelphia society, they were eager to discard the emotionality which was part of their background. The newcomers were proud to identify with Rabbi Greenberg, who had come from a background which they thought of as their own.

Finally, neither old nor new families had any reservations about Rabbi Greenberg's acceptability to the Gentile community. In discussing the Wise Temple, a local resident who has served various Jewish agencies in a professional capacity declared, "Rabbi Greenberg is the perfect symbol of the way the congregation would like the Gentile world to see them." What he was expressing was the fact that to the Jews of the Heights the Rabbi's appearance and manner represented the very antithesis of the stereotype which they believed was imputed to them by some of their Gentile neighbors.

Contrary to all expectations, Rabbi Greenberg did not seek to mediate between the two factions. Instead of moving the partisans of Classical Reform and Neo-Reform into a new unity, he precipitated the final split between the two groups. This he did in a much more rapid and final way than his predecessors—rabbis who had much stronger ideological convictions than his own. Under his leadership, the Wise Temple completed its transformation into a Neo-Reform institution.

After surveying the situation, Rabbi Greenberg concluded that the congregation would be able to achieve its potential only if cohesiveness were increased. This conclusion meant that a clear choice between Classical Reform and Neo-Reform was required. Rabbi Greenberg noted that the Heights was enjoying a steady influx of Jewish families, and he estimated that the process would continue; as an outsider, he had no reason to underestimate the potentiality of the area for growth and was able to gauge the situation much more accurately than either the longtime residents or the newcomers. He believed that because of the coming increase of Jewish population in the Heights, the congregation would quickly recover from any temporary loss of membership or support.

Rabbi Greenberg cast his lot with the Neo-Reformers and presented the Classical Reform group with the option of either going along or leaving the congregation. Most left and proceeded to join forces with those who had already resigned because of their objections to Neo-Reform innovations in general and to Rabbi Finkelstein in particular. These families, together with new arrivals who had a background in Classical Reform, established their own institution: the David Einhorn Temple.

In spite of the passage of time, Rabbi Greenberg remains a topic of conversation among former members of the Wise Temple. He is portrayed by them as a man devoid of spiritual depth or ethical principles, a cynic interested only in building a giant institution and prepared to sacrifice his beliefs for the purpose of personal aggrandizement. But to his many supporters at the Wise Temple, Rabbi Greenberg is esteemed as a religious leader whose complete and utter devotion has been responsible for making Isaac Mayer Wise the leading Reform Temple in the metropolitan area. He is thought of as in large measure responsible for the evolution of a congregation whose program, it is claimed, sets a standard not only for the Lake City area but for the nation as well.

A CLASSICAL REFORMER IN A NEO-REFORM INSTITUTION

Not all adherents of Classical Reform have left the Wise Temple. One group that has remained consists of elderly individuals who hesitate to shift to a new institution. Their involvement with the congregation tends to be minimal; they generally confine their participation to attending services on the High Holidays. A second group consists of both younger and older individuals. Some are longtime residents, while others are younger persons whose parents were among the founders of the institution. A number of these members are active in the congregation itself, while others are active in Reform Jewish affairs on a city-wide, regional, or national level. Classical Reformers who are willing to adjust to Neo-Reform and will take part in congregational affairs without attempting to form a Classical Reform faction receive much encouragement from Rabbi Greenberg.

George Bloch, a wealthy manufacturer of German descent, is an example of a man from a Classical Reform background who is active in the congregation. The Bloch family moved to Lakeville from Lake City long before the arrival of the newcomers. In Lake City, they had been affiliated with an important Reform congregation, although not with the Holdheim Temple. Members of various branches of the Bloch family have been identified with the Wise Temple since its founding.

George Bloch is proud of the leadership which his family has supplied to the Wise Temple, to Lakeville, and to Lake City. He has endowed a number of foundations which perpetuate the memory of some of the more outstanding members of his family, and he feels an obligation to further the causes they espoused. He looks askance at his friends and acquaintances who have resigned from the Wise Temple. George Bloch is determined to remain at the Wise Temple, for he feels that loyalties to a religious institution are not easily sundered. Terming himself a member of the "old guard" in spite of being a comparatively young man, he conceives of his role at the Temple in the following terms:

I do my best to uphold the ideals of the original founders of the Temple. People know how I stand on matters. Some of the members of the board have called me a "Tory," but I think they really appreciate what I stand for. A man once came up to me and said that it was good that there is a George Bloch around to remind the congregation of its past history.

In specifying how he seeks to remind the congregation of its history, Bloch cited the following example:

I was out of town several months ago and missed a board meeting. When I got back, I noticed in the minutes that a resolution had passed permitting members to wear hats during services. I reopened the question at the next board meeting. They appointed a subcommittee to look into the matter.

I presented my case before the subcommittee and was able to sway them to the idea that wearing a hat was against our tradition. The board reconsidered the matter and actually rescinded the resolution, although they did make a compromise. The policy now is that members aren't permitted to wear hats, but that if a guest does so he won't be disturbed. This matter of wearing hats shows how far this thing can go and how far it will go someday.

George Bloch's explanation of his attitude toward covering the head during worship conforms to the approach of Classical Reform, namely, that Jewish customs which are out of keeping with Western norms and are not patently spiritual should be discarded:

A hat really has no place in Western civilization. When we want to show respect, we take our hats off, not put them on. In fact, I believe that originally the custom was not a Jewish one and that it has no religious significance. It is simply an Orthodox practice that has no place in Reform Judaism. It is not that the hat worries me so much; it's the idea that it's a leak in the dike. If things are allowed to continue, the dike will weaken and crumble. Kosher meat is another custom which could have the same effect. It has outlived its usefulness. Once it was a health measure, but now you don't get trichinosis from eating pork.

Although trying to hold the line against Neo-Reform, George Bloch has refrained from organizing a general counterattack. Furthermore, as a highly loyal member of the congregation he has manifested his devotion by contributing his time as well as his money to the institution.

While George Bloch's loyalty to the Wise Temple has served to endear him to Rabbi Greenberg as well as to many lay leaders of the congregation, it has also been responsible for considerable strain between him and his friends. His friendship circle, which is strongly Jewish in composition, has its source in the young people with whom he grew up in Lakeville. Although he still receives some invitations from his old friends, they look askance at his tolerance of Neo-Reformism. He has lost the easy camaraderie which he knew as a youngster:

> When I go to a party, people tend to change the topic of conversation when I come into the room. The men will be discussing the Einhorn Temple or how they feel about Rabbi Greenberg. When they see me, they start talking about baseball. Some of my old friends actually feel that I have horns.

CONGREGATIONAL PROGRAM

The Wise Temple has the facilities, the resources, and the desire to sponsor a widely ranging program of activities. As noted previously the leadership feel that their Temple's program is outstanding—that it sets the standard for the nation as a whole. A former member of the Temple's staff characterized the particular form which the pursuit of excellence takes as follows: "Not only must they have the best at Wise but they must know that they have the best." Outside observers in a position to make comparisons with other congregations agree that while the Wise program is broad in scope, it is more or less typical of the large, prosperous, Neo-Reform, suburban congregation. They feel that while the highest standards are observed in respect to office procedures, building maintenance, and matters of form, the content of the program is not extraordinary.

As with other congregations, the schedule of religious services occupies the front page of the Temple's expertly edited and well-printed weekly bulletin. The membership of the Temple is so large that on the High Holidays the main services must be held in the auditorium of the local high school, which has the largest hall on the Heights. But even so, the membership cannot be accommodated at a single sitting; a double service must be held. However, a fair proportion of the worshipers are not interested in attending services on the morning of Rosh Hashanah, and only a single session is held at that time. A number of separate services are conducted for the children of the congregation on the High Holidays. An additional adult service is also held in the Temple building. Many of those who attend are elderly. They find it easier to come to the Temple, for here there is less walking, no steps to climb, and familiar surroundings.

In contrast to the High Holidays, the Festival and Sabbath services pose no problem of fitting too many worshipers into too few pews. Except for the yearly Shavuot service, at which about 150 children are confirmed, seats at the Festival services are readily available. What is especially notable about the Festival services is that they tend to be children's services, rather than adult services. Thus a service on the first day of Passover was described by an observer as follows:

The service was designated in the Temple bulletin as "Passover Family Worship Service." There were few unattached adults present—the vast majority of the congregation was composed of children and their parents, plus a few grandparents. I received the definite impression that without the children and the motivation which they provided for the adults to come, the service would have drawn a very minimal crowd.

Actually, Rabbi Greenberg revolved the whole service around the children. They conducted the Torah service very largely, they read a number of prayers from the pulpit, and his sermon was in the form of a story which was geared to the grammar-school age level. However, while the service was for the children, the children did not really take over. Rabbi Greenberg was still the central figure, and this was in no sense a service conducted by a junior congregation.

One of the most interesting aspects of the service was the April birthday greetings. The rabbi stated that the birthday greetings would now be held, and about forty-five children ascended the pulpit. Presumably, this is a regular monthly feature of the Saturday morning service. Rabbi Greenberg first gave a general benediction for the entire group of forty-five, most of whom seemed to be under the age of twelve. After his general benediction, he spent a moment with each child individually. He seemed to whisper in their ear and kiss them at the side of the head at the same time. He was a most impressive figure as he bent down in his robe and *tallit* to kiss the small children. The children seemed to enjoy this aspect of the service, the parents seemed to enjoy it, and Rabbi Greenberg seemed to enjoy it.

Sabbath services are held on Friday evening and Saturday morning. The same sanctuary in which services were held when the Temple had a membership of only a few hundred families is used for these services and is adequate in size. The more important of the two services is the one on Friday evening. In spite of the fact that the Wise membership numbers well over fifteen hundred families, attendance at Friday night services cannot be taken for granted, and techniques to stimulate interest are continually employed. An important feature of the service is the rabbi's sermon, the subject of which is attractively phrased and is announced in the weekly bulletin.

The Friday evening service involves a corps of lay members of the congregation. Upon entering the Temple, one is greeted by an usher, who is easily distinguishable by his boutonnière. The usher hands each worshiper a prayer book; if the worshiper arrives after the service has started, he must wait until the usher precedes him down the aisle and shows him to a seat. Considerable stress is placed on expert ushering, and a committee exists to supervise the activity.

The additional participants at the Friday evening service, whose names are listed in the bulletin together with the ushers, include the woman who blesses the candles and the men who serve as "pulpit assistants." Also listed are the women who act as hostesses at the social hour following the service. Not all who come to the service stay for this function; its appeal to the peripheral person is limited. But for the individual who knows others in the congregation, the social hour can be an important feature of the evening.

Since the number of people for whom prayer is central—or who attend the service as a matter of duty or habit—is limited, there is need for various features to counteract boredom and attract people with special interests, concerns, and loyalties. One type of special service on Friday evening is that sponsored by a group affiliated with the Temple. At such a service, many more laymen than usual are involved, particularly in reading the service. Another type of special service is family worship night, which begins earlier than usual and lasts less than an hour. An appeal is made to parents to bring their children to these services. Other special services are scheduled to reach those with particular interests, such as music or another one of the fine arts.

Another important aspect of the Friday evening service is the Kaddish prayer. This feature is quite lengthy by traditional standards, since not only is the prayer itself recited but the names of the deceased are read. A reminder to be present is sent to the family. The newly born are also named and blessed by the rabbi at the Friday evening service.

The Saturday morning service is very different in character. There is no advertisement of a sermon topic, no special features, no attempt to involve the membership. The keynote of this service is not prayer, but rather the celebration of a Bar Mitzvah (or occasionally of a Bat Mitzvah). Without the ceremony, it would be difficult to sustain the service. Rabbi Greenberg has elaborated several dramatic features in connection with the ceremony. For example, the Bar Mitzvah walks to the pulpit at an appropriate point in the service, accompanied by his mother. She presents him to the rabbi, symbolically handing over to him the fruit of her womb. Later, the boy's father comes to the pulpit and publicly performs the ceremony of blessing his son. The son is doubly blessed: he also receives a benediction from Rabbi Greenberg. Rather than delivering a sermon, Rabbi Greenberg gives a short address in the form of a charge to the Bar Mitzvah. Since there is no junior congregational service, children may attend the Saturday morning service.

Instead of meeting only on Sunday morning, religious-school classes are held during the week as well. While parents prefer to send their children on Sunday morning, the size of the student body is so large in relationship to the number of rooms that it is impossible to schedule all classes at the same time. The religious school begins with kindergarten and culminates with Confirmation. There are no classes for the post-Confirmation group, but the more interested graduates are utilized as student teachers. Hebrew classes are held in midweek. Although during the earlier period in the congregation's history only a handful of students were enrolled, the classes have grown with the demand for Bar Mitzvah. The newest feature of the educational program is the nursery school, whose registration is growing rapidly.

It is questionable whether the congregation could function at anything like its present level without the religious school. One official of the Temple believes it to be the strongest feature attracting people to the congregation. He has noticed that families wait until their children are of Sunday School age before joining and that there are some resignations after the child is confirmed. He has also noticed that there are instances where parents send their children to the religious school, but do not themselves attend services on the High Holidays.

The Temple sponsors an active youth program led by experienced group workers. There is also an organization for young adults, but much more popular is the Couples Club, composed of the "young marrieds." After this part of the life cycle, the sexes divide: mature men and women have the Men's Club and the Sisterhood, respectively. Both are active organizations running elaborate programs. The Men's Club, for example, is the sponsor of a bowling league, a class for social dancing where the latest steps are taught, and a Sunday morning discussion series devoted to topics of serious interest. Overlapping in age cycle with the Men's Club and the Sisterhood is the Parent–Teacher Association of the religious school. Finally there is the Golden Age Club.

The Temple's facilities are used round the clock: various Jewish organizations occupy meeting rooms in the building, a Red Cross sewing group gathers regularly, temple committees as well as committees of the Men's Club, Sisterhood, and other Temple affiliates hold regular sessions, and various special-interest groups such as a theater workshop are constantly being organized. All of this activity is in sharp contrast to the situation that obtained during the Temple's Classical-Reform period. In one sense, this lively interest resembles what took place at the old Holdheim Temple, except that it is generally members of the Temple rather than residents of the community at large who are involved. Furthermore, even when non-members attend a function in the Temple, they are likely to be on the same class and status level as the membership itself.

While the activities of the Wise Temple involve only Jews, the institution has a more active and imaginative interfaith program than any of the other congregations. Rabbi Greenberg is the focus of this effort. He is recognized by the Gentile community as the leading rabbi on the Heights. The culmination of the interfaith program is the Passover Seder which is sponsored each year for a different Lake City Protestant theological seminary. While other interfaith activities may involve only the rabbi's occupancy of the pulpit of a church in Lakeville or in one of the neighboring suburbs, the interfaith Seder involves large numbers of members of the Temple. Each Christian seminarian is sponsored by a member of Wise; Christian visitor and Jewish host sit side by side throughout the evening. As he leads the Seder, Rabbi Greenberg points out the relationship of the holiday to the Christian tradition and to the life of Jesus.

The assumption is that in addition to Rabbi Greenberg's explanations, the Jewish sponsor will be able to enlighten his Christian guest about particular aspects of the Passover symbolism and the Haggadah. Less elaborate Sedarim are held for the youth groups of churches in the area.

The adult education program which the Temple sponsors is designed to give the member who lacks Jewish knowledge an opportunity to acquaint himself with certain important aspects of the Jewish heritage. Several courses are offered each year in such subjects as the Hebrew language, the Bible, great Jewish books, Jewish customs and ceremonies, current Jewish and general issues, and problems of family living. The classes are concentrated on one evening during the week, and an effort is made to avoid scheduling overlapping activities. While the adult education classes are a staple of the Temple's program, only a limited number attend in comparison with other activities.

Further opportunities for the pursuit of Jewish knowledge are available in the Temple's library, which is separately endowed. The library is housed in a large and handsome room, which doubles as a board room. A collection of Jewish ceremonial art, expertly exhibited, is also located in the Temple. The lecture series initiated by the founders of the Temple is still continued. It consists of five evenings each year and now constitutes a very minor part of the Temple's program.

Most of the leaders feel that the size of the membership and the extent of the Temple's program require that further facilities be constructed. Some would prefer to select a new site where the congregation could begin a multimillion-dollar project and erect a complex of synagogue buildings which would be recognized as the most outstanding Jewish religious structure in the Lake City area, if not in the nation at large. Others, such as George Bloch, would be satisfied to buy property adjacent to the present site and build some additional classrooms, parking facilities, and meeting rooms. Bloch and others are satisfied with the arrangement of utilizing the auditorium of a local school for the High Holidays; they point out that there is really no need for additional seats during services held at other times during the year. They feel that the additions which were made to the original structure after World War II are still serviceable. They would prefer to keep the membership at about its present size. While Rabbi Greenberg has not made his wishes known to the board, he is giving encouragement to those who want to start afresh and build a new and greater Isaac Mayer Wise Temple.

The Solomon Schechter Synagogue

THE FORMATION OF A
CONSERVATIVE SYNAGOGUE

We noticed that prior to World War II, even those residents of Lakeville who were of East European background and retained a measure of traditionalism joined the Wise Temple. Many began to consider themselves Reform Jews and were influential in tipping the scales at Wise in the direction of Neo-Reform. However, some families did not come to consider themselves Reform, but justified their affiliation on the basis that Wise was the only Jewish religious institution in the community. In addition, there were a number of traditionally minded families who stayed away from Wise entirely. They preferred to retain their affiliation with the congregation in Lake City to which they had belonged prior to their move to Lakeville.

The very same issue which had confronted the longtime residents who were religious liberals confronted traditionalists as well: the Jewish education of their children. Instead of relying on the religious school of the Wise Temple, traditionally oriented families utilized a type of instruction which had been popular in the United States during the immigrant era, but had declined as communal and congregational Hebrew schools were organized: they hired a Hebrew teacher to come to their homes to give private lessons to their children. Dut to referrals, most of the families employed the same teacher. He was soon going to Lakeville several times each week to meet his students. His instruction was geared primarily to preparing boys for Bar Mitzvah.

The activity of the Hebrew teacher served to underline the fact that there were Jews in the area who were traditionally minded. A number of new families of this type settled in Lakeville immediately after World War II. Among them were several prosperous businessmen who had been leaders of large and prestigious Conservative congregations in Lake City. They possessed a strong image of themselves as Conservative Jews and were not inclined to shift their religious identity. Accustomed to synagogue life, they soon began to entertain the idea of establishing a congregation. They had none of the conflicts about the wisdom of such a move which the longtime residents had evidenced at an earlier period. They were highly confident of their ability to establish and maintain a synagogue and willing to assume the obligations such a venture would impose on them. Members of Wise who did not consider themselves Reform Jews joined forces with this group of newcomers.

The Conservative nucleus in Lakeville received considerable encouragement from outside the community, especially from several Conservative rabbis in Lake City who were concerned both about Jewish indifferentism in the Heights and about the monopoly enjoyed by Reform Judaism. The rabbis feared that should upwardly mobile Conservative Jews move to the Heights, they would be lost to traditional influence. The encouragement of one particularly well-known Conservative rabbi was especially important. Some of the new residents had been, or were still, affiliated with his congregation. He was held in the same type of esteem by them as had been the rabbi of Holdheim by the founders of the Wise Temple. But in spite of their respect for the rabbi, the new group, being more traditionally minded, entertained only momentarily the notion of becoming a branch of the synagogue which he served. Furthermore, the rabbi's congregation did not look with favor on the idea. In addition to the interest of this rabbi and other Conservative rabbis in Lake City, the new group also received help from the national institutions of the Conservative movement—the Jewish Theological Seminary of America and the United Synagogue of America. Realizing the magnetic pull of Lakeville, they too were eager to establish a traditional synagogue in the community.

A series of parlor meetings held in the early 1950's concluded with the establishment of Lakeville's first Conservative congregation: the Solomon Schechter Synagogue. The meetings went off smoothly. They were devoted almost entirely to organizational questions; no one posed any problems of religious doctrine or practice which required protracted discussion. The tone of the meetings was set by several of the energetic and successful businessmen who had been active in Lake City congregations. While there were some professional men in the group, they were mostly lawyers with very close business connections, and they too concentrated on organizational problems, rather than ideological questions. Fifty families were enrolled as a result of the parlor meetings.

The first regular activity of the congregation was a weekly religious service held on Friday evening. The possibility of conducting services on Sunday morning was never considered. On the other hand, neither did the group follow traditional norms and schedule the service for Saturday morning. The services were first held in the homes of the organizers of the congregation; later a public hall was rented. After a hiatus during the summer, the group organized its first High Holiday services. These were successful; almost a hundred families attended. The leaders of the congregation were encouraged; they felt that their belief that a demand for Conservative Judaism existed in Lakeville had been justified. Classes for children were started during the first year of the congregation's existence; they grew rapidly and provided a strong focus of support. The classes were of two types. One was a Sunday School which enrolled the majority of the students and met at rented quarters. The other was a Hebrew school which was housed at the Wise Temple. The Hebrew classes were taught by the same tutor who had previously given private lessons. One additional activity was initiated: a Sisterhood. Like their husbands, the women who took the leadership were highly experienced in organizational affairs and were prepared to work hard to insure success.

CONFLICT: EXTERNAL AND INTERNAL

The approach of the founders of the Solomon Schechter Synagogue was almost precisely the opposite to that of the Wise Temple. Instead of proceeding cautiously and making modest plans, the group thought in ambitious terms. Rather than content themselves with guest rabbis and a part-time staff, they engaged a full-time rabbi, an educational director, and a cantor during the first year of the congregation's existence. While at the Wise Temple the decision to erect an edifice was delayed for a number of years, they immediately began to look for a permanent home. Viewing makeshift quarters as a highly temporary expedient, the officers soon began to discuss where their building should be located and whether it would be better to erect a new structure or to renovate an old one.

In spite of the energy of the leaders, the problem of a congregational home was not easily solved. The first site in which they were interested suddenly became unavailable; it had been hastily purchased by some of the Gentile property owners in the area. Another site was located, and this time a purchase was consummated. However, the obvious opposition of some Gentiles in the neighborhood motivated the officers to look elsewhere, and the property was disposed of at a loss. The founders of the Wise Temple had feared that the establishment of a congregation would be resented; peculiarly, it came to pass more than two decades later. By then the Jewish population of Lakeville had grown appreciably and the Gentile residents had come to suspect that the Jewish group would not remain a small and inconspicuous segment of the community. The projected establishment of another synagogue was apparently interpreted by some as a sign that Protestant dominance of the community would be lost if events were left to run their course.

The leaders of the Synagogue were not deterred by the hostility they encountered. They decided, however, to shift tactics and thus minimize the risk of failure. They would purchase property not in the name of the institution, but rather in the name of an individual. They discovered that an estate consisting of a mansion, several smaller residences, and a large plot of land by Lakeville standards was about to come on the market. It was located on a street on which some of the finest homes in the community were situated. Rather than being disturbed by the conspicuous location of the property (as would have been the case with the early leaders of the Wise Temple), officers of the Solomon Schechter Synagogue viewed this as an advantage. The estate had the further attraction that instead of having to wait until a building was erected, the congregation could move in and begin activities immediately. The leaders felt confident that this time they would be tolerated, if not welcomed. Gentile residents would adjust to a *fait accompli*.

The negotiations for the estate turned out to be more complicated than originally thought. The property was jointly owned by a family characterized by deep rifts; only one member was willing to sell, and he did so more to spite his relatives than for any other reason. On the assumption that other family members would later capitulate, the congregation decided to buy. The purchase was in the name of one of the members of the Synagogue, ostensibly for the purpose of making the estate his private residence. The purchaser was a highly successful businessman who had lived in the community for some time, and thus the sale did not attract undue attention. He entered into protracted negotiations with other members of the family and was finally successful in attaining full ownership of the property. He then transferred the title to the Solomon Schechter Synagogue.

When the intended purpose of the purchase became clear, Jewish objections turned out to be more vehement than those of Gentiles. Some of the older German Jewish families, hostile to the influx of new Jewish families, seized upon the incident and claimed that a group which would use subterfuge to gain their ends had no place in the community. They believed that by using subterfuge, the Schechter group had committed the blunder of reinforcing hostile stereotypy about Jewish business practices.

The purchase of the estate brought to a head the feeling of some of the longtime Jewish residents about being overwhelmed by Jewish newcomers. As they viewed it, Lakeville would no longer be a quiet community composed of like-minded Jews and Gentiles. Furthermore, the presence of a new synagogue would serve to attract an additional influx of Jewish families, making Jews an ever-larger proportion in the community. And while the earlier East Europeans had at least been satisfied to join the Wise Temple, the newcomers and their allies not only wished to establish another congregation but wanted to flaunt their presence in the general community. Instead of beginning in appropriately modest quarters, they had shown what kind of people they were by seizing one of the show places of the community.[4]

The stratification pattern in the Jewish group and the resulting communications network prevented these reactions from directly reaching the attention of most of the families affiliated with the Solomon Schechter Synagogue. However, some of the longtime residents who were critical of the Synagogue decided to do more than make their feelings known in Lakeville itself. They approached the leading Jewish community-relations agency in Lake City and requested them to intercede. In the interest of preserving the excellent intergroup relations which, they said, had characterized Lakeville throughout its history, the agency was asked to dissuade the Solomon Schechter Synagogue from occupying its new premises.

When asked why they believed conflict would ensue, the objections focused on the location of the property. It was stated that the street on which the property was situated could not accommodate additional automobiles: a traffic bottleneck would result. This would be resented by the Gentiles, and all the Jews in the community would be blamed. Executives of the agency were aware of the hidden purpose of those who objected and viewed their motives unsympathetically. The agency also realized that should it go along with the request, it would contravene its own objective of enlarging opportunities for Jews to settle in all sections of the metropolitan area. The agency refused to intervene.[5]

Since the longtime Jewish residents were stymied and the Gentiles were less overtly hostile than after the previous attempt to purchase a site, the Synagogue was free to occupy the property. Given the value of the land and the buildings, the price of the estate was reasonable; but considering the size and wealth of the membership, the financial commitment was sizable. True, a successful fund-raising campaign was concluded, but most of the proceeds were in the form of pledges. Although a mortgage was arranged for, unless there was a constant flow of cash to meet the payments there was the danger that ownership, which had been acquired through much travail, would revert to the bank.

The leaders of the Schechter Synagogue were optimistic. They had built their own businesses by risk-taking, and they were confident that they could succeed in a religious enterprise as well. And unlike the long-time residents who had no desire to see the Jewish population grow and had set their sights low when they built the Wise Temple, the leaders of the Synagogue both expected and welcomed a population increase. They believed that some of the new families would surely be attracted to their synagogue, and they saw their problem as tiding themselves over until new families arrived. The technique which they settled upon to solve their fiscal problem was that of a coupon book: one much like those utilized for the payment of a mortgage on a home. Each member received his book with his pledge divided into appropriate monthly payments. The officers stressed that remittances had to be made promptly so that the Synagogue's obligations to the bank could be met. The technique was successful. The schedule of payments was maintained, and the possibility of a foreclosure did not arise.

Conflict developed on a different front, however. The man who had been chosen as rabbi had a successful record in another community, but after a few months it became apparent that he was unable to cope with his new congregants. Having been affiliated with leading Conservative congregations in Lake City, officers and board members of the congregation were accustomed to highly talented and very forceful rabbis. While the man they had chosen as spiritual leader was competent, he was not a commanding personality or an esteemed leader. As soon as the congregation was established in its own home and the crisis of institutional birth was past, the leaders began to bicker among themselves. The rabbi was not able to mediate; lacking a forceful personality, he could not impose his will on the emotional, talented, and hard-driving men who constituted the lay leadership of the Solomon Schechter Synagogue.

Conflict among the laity had its counterpart in a difference of opinion that developed between the rabbi and the Hebrew teacher who had taught the offspring of the traditionally minded families in Lakeville prior to the establishment of the Synagogue. The subsequent discharge of the teacher became a cause of dissension in the congregation.

GROWTH AND COHESION

In spite of these and other conflicts, growth continued. The location of the congregation and the fact that it possessed a building of its own constituted an inducement for affiliation. While disputes among the leaders were discouraging, the property which the congregation owned served to give a feeling of stability and the promise of future possibilities. School enrollment climbed steadily and constituted a further stabilizing element.

Factionalism was reduced by the need to initiate a building program. The school grew so rapidly that the bedrooms of the mansion, which had been turned into classrooms, could no longer hold the entire student body. Space had to be rented at a local public school. Furthermore, while the rooms on the first floor of the mansion could take care of meetings of the Sisterhood and other groups as well as the worshipers on the Festivals and on Friday evening and Saturday morning, accommodations were insufficient for the High Holidays. One year, a tent was erected on the Synagogue's grounds. While clear skies prevailed on Rosh Hashanah, a violent rainstorm arose on Yom Kippur, and the drenched worshipers were forced to retreat to the mansion. In other years, public halls were rented for the High Holidays, but leaders of the congregation were unhappy about utilizing such facilities. They felt that at the earliest possible moment all activities should be housed in the congregation's own buildings.

Greater cohesion developed under the leadership of a new rabbi, David Ginzberg. Rabbi Ginzberg approached his job enthusiastically, viewing it as a challenge. Emotionally, he was similar to those who had founded the congregation: he too was an aggressive and self-confident individual who felt capable of coping with any difficulties that might confront him.

Rabbi Ginzberg differs quite markedly from the spiritual leader of the Wise Temple, Rabbi Greenberg. A gregarious person with a ready sense of humor, Rabbi Ginzberg is cast in the mold of the self-made man. Some of those outside of the congregation, or even on its fringes, find him deficient in spirituality. Members of Wise and of other Reform congregations have commented that Rabbi Ginzberg lacks taste and bearing; several have intimated that he is all too typical of the objectionable element which has settled in the community in recent years. On the other hand, many members of the Schechter Synagogue have discovered in Rabbi Ginzberg a sagacious counselor who understands their difficulties, a rabbi who is highly approachable and "human," and a spiritual leader who gives of himself without stint so that the Solomon Schechter Synagogue may become an institution to which they will be proud to belong. At times firm and at other times yielding, Rabbi Ginzberg has been able to steer a successful course between the contentious men who established the congregation. He has also been able to mediate various disputes which have arisen among the aggressive women who have led the Sisterhood.

Rabbi Ginzberg has concentrated his attention on pressing matters of synagogue financing, building, and organization. He has emphasized projects on which consensus could be obtained, rather than on ideological issues that might divide the congregation. In his early years, he was aided in this policy by a president of the Synagogue who had originally been attracted to the congregation because some of his friends were members. This president was not very concerned with Conservative Judaism as a religious system, but he had strong feelings about the need for a well-run and adequately financed synagogue.

In his decision to avoid ideological issues that might cause dissension, Rabbi Ginzberg discovered that by and large the membership was apathetic about reforms which in other congregations could provoke differences of opinion. For example, when he shortened the weekly Torah portion by shifting to the triennial cycle, he discovered that the innovation produced no critical comment.

Rabbi Ginzberg has been aware that other changes might not be so well received. Feeling that conflict is something which the congregation can ill afford, when he has sensed that animosity might be engendered he has compromised. For example, an organ had been installed during the ministry of the previous rabbi. Although disapproving of the performance of instrumental music at religious services, Rabbi Ginzberg has not sought to have it removed. Rather, he has endeavored to limit its use and has won agreement that the organ would be played only at one service each week (Friday evening) and on one Festival (Shavuot). By proceeding as he did, Rabbi Ginzberg forestalled the formation of pro-organ and anti-organ factions in the congregation.

In another instance, Rabbi Ginzberg discovered that there was no room for compromise. It was his conviction that synagogue membership should involve more than a financial commitment. He felt that members should be asked to uphold congregational principles by agreeing to follow certain minimal standards of religious observance. When he sounded out congregational sentiment, he found that there was very little sympathy for his position, undoubtedly because so many had departed so far from the sacramental tradition. Fearful of endangering the harmonious atmosphere which he had sought to create, the rabbi decided not to press the issue. His hope is that at a more propitious time the proposal can be reintroduced without harming congregational unity.

Rabbi Ginzberg's ability to reinforce institutional loyalties is reflected by the success of the building campaigns he has helped to organize. The first structure that was added to the old mansion was a school building.

The increase of the student body, the attraction that such a building would have for new members, and the desire to dispense with use of public facilities all played a part in the decision to give this structure priority. The second addition was a complex consisting of a very spacious auditorium, an activities room, a lounge, and a kitchen.

The congregation still lacks a sanctuary. It utilizes the auditorium for the High Holidays as well as for some of the other services. Plans have been drawn for a sanctuary, and a fund-raising campaign will soon be initiated. The plans call for a structure of rather limited seating capacity, considering the spaciousness of other portions of the building. However, the size of the sanctuary is being scaled to the expected number of Sabbath and Festival worshipers. On the High Holidays and other occasions, capacity will be increased by combining the auditorium and the sanctuary. Since the latter is being built in front of the auditorium, the plan calls for moving the eastern wall of the sanctuary on the High Holidays, as well as on other occasions when maximum capacity is required. In spite of the sanctity with which the eastern wall is invested in Jewish tradition, the architect's plans have been favorably received.

CONGREGATIONAL PROGRAM AND TENSIONS

While the membership of the Schechter Synagogue is considerably smaller than that of the Wise Temple, its present program is already more intensive. One reason for this intensiveness is that there is less concern about self-segregation at Schechter. Another is that the religious and educational program there is closer to traditional norms.

The Schechter Synagogue is the sole congregation in Lakeville that conducts a daily service. This is held only during the morning, however; except on the Sabbath, there is no afternoon or evening service. It is at these daily services, attended by a handful of members, that the culture of traditional Judaism can still be glimpsed in Lakeville. The Sabbath afternoon service was described by an observer as follows:

> The service was held in what was once probably the conservatory of the mansion. The room now functions as a *bet midrash*. The men drifted in slowly, a number of them parking their cars in the lot which adjoins the synagogue. Attendance was very small, and the service had to be delayed until the tenth man appeared. The age of the worshipers ranged from the late 20's to the early 60's. While very heterogeneous in age, the worshipers obviously knew each other well. The men were as different in

appearance as in age: one or two of the older men looked like *shul yidn,* while some of the younger men looked like "go-getters."

The services were conducted very informally and the *davening* was strongly traditional. Rabbi Ginzberg served as *baal k'riyah.* Because of the small attendance, every man had a role in the service.

After *Minchah,* the group adjourned to another room where tables had been prepared. The "Third Meal" was served. There were bottles of soda of various flavors, and plenty of lox, smoked fish, herring, American cheese and other *milchiks,* as well as cake. At the conclusion of the meal, *Chumashim* with *Rashi* were passed out, and under Rabbi Ginzberg's direction the group began to study the portion of the week. About ten to fifteen lines were reviewed. The questions asked of Rabbi Ginzberg hardly taxed his knowledge or ingenuity. The session was on an elementary level, with the discussion carried on in English. Rabbi Ginzberg translated from the Hebrew as he read each line of the portion of the week.

At the conclusion of the study session, the *minyan* adjourned to the *bet midrash,* where *Havdalah* was held and the *Maariv* service conducted.

While it is a struggle to maintain the daily *minyan,* the High Holidays are well attended. Unlike the Wise Temple, the congregation worships together, rather than in shifts. In addition to the service conducted for adults, three additional services are held. One is for children under 8, a second for ages 8 to 12, and a third for those 13 and over. A *Selichot* service is held before Rosh Hashanah, starting with a social at 10:30 P.M.*

The Festival services are poorly attended. But in spite of the comparative paucity of worshipers, the Synagogue does not reinforce attendance by discontinuing the separate services conducted for children. Thus, in contrast to the Wise Temple, the Festival services at Schechter retain their adult character.

Each week, a late Friday evening service as well as a Saturday morning service is held. The former parallels the Wise service in many respects. The Saturday morning service also parallels the Wise service in the emphasis placed on Bar Mitzvah. Nevertheless, the service retains some of its traditional character; since the congregation sponsors a junior congregation on Saturday morning, the service is not as child-oriented.

The educational program for children begins with nursery-school classes, where an attempt is made to conduct a program with Jewish content in addition to the usual nursery-school routine. Sunday School classes are held for children from kindergarten age through second year

* *Selichot:* the penitential prayers recited before the High Holidays, especially on the Saturday midnight preceding Rosh Hashanah.

high school, at which point Confirmation is held. When children reach the age of 7, 8, or 9, the congregation seeks to influence parents to enroll them in the Hebrew school and thereby to discontinue their attendance at Sunday School. In contrast to Wise, where Hebrew classes supplement the Sunday School, at Schechter the leadership look upon the Sunday School as an introduction to Hebrew school. Most of the children who remain in the Sunday School are girls; about 85 per cent of the Confirmation class is female. According to a brochure issued by the Synagogue, the Hebrew school alone can give the child "the happy feeling of being a Jew that comes from the knowledge, understanding and appreciation of his heritage and the problems of his people." The Hebrew school meets three times a week. The school has a small high-school department for those students who continue after Bar or Bat Mitzvah.

As with the other congregations, the educational program for adults is much less elaborate than that for children. The Synagogue sponsors a number of study groups which meet at the homes of members, two courses in the Hebrew language, and a forum series devoted to topics of Jewish interest.

Like those at the Wise Temple, the clubs affiliated with the Schechter Synagogue are an intimate part of the congregational program. The program starts with several "tween clubs" for children of 12 to 13 years of age. There is also a Tephilin Club made up of boys who recently celebrated their Bar Mitzvah. It meets on Sunday morning for services and is followed by breakfast; the club conducts several other activities as well. A Bat Mitzvah club also meets for services on Sunday and follows prayer with lunch. In addition to these religiously oriented clubs, there is an overall teen-age program with a varied set of activities. Among other features projected by the youth director, the program includes a film festival, a photography club, science club, glee club, Israeli dance club, and conversational Hebrew and Yiddish clubs.

For adults there are the Mr. and Mrs. Club (the "young marrieds"), the Sisterhood, and the Men's Club. The first is less active than the second or third, but all have a variety of activities. The program of the Men's Club, for example, rivals that conducted by the same group at the Wise Temple. The club sponsors a bowling league and a golf tournament, holds many social affairs, including a "Matzo Ball," and sponsors a religious retreat led by Rabbi Ginzberg.

The approach of the Synagogue leadership, and particularly of the rabbi, is to continue to expand congregational activities and facilities in order to give the institution a continuing appeal to every member of the family. Thus, in addition to the nursery school, the Synagogue sponsors a day camp during the summer for very young children. On another front, Rabbi Ginzberg is attempting to persuade the membership to use the Synagogue for family celebrations. He was highly gratified when he persuaded a prominent family in the congregation to hold their daughter's wedding in the social hall of the Synagogue, rather than in the ballroom of a hotel. The hall was decorated with special floral displays at a cost of several thousand dollars. Another example of the rabbi's approach is the annual dinner dance of the congregation, which was also held at the Synagogue, rather than at a hotel in Lake City as in previous years. Rabbi Ginzberg, who had strongly advocated the shift, stressed in the congregational bulletin that the membership would be even happier at the Synagogue than they had been at the hotel. Although the occasion was strongly secular in orientation (the featured performer of the evening was George Jessel), the Rabbi gave it a sacred interpretation:

> Time grows near for the biggest social event of the year. It being true that "the increase of multitudes exalteth the king," the King of Kings will be exalted when the largest gathering of the year in the social life of the congregation will take place on Sunday evening.
>
> Why shouldn't it be the biggest? We have the largest membership ever. No longer will people be in a fever of haste to drive into Lake City, to weave through the snarls of traffic, in order to arrive on time. No longer will they have to leave early because of the loss of an hour's time in travel. No longer will they fret about sitting at a "good table" because the openness of our auditorium makes every corner of it desirable, and good friends sitting together make a "good table." No longer will they chafe under the restrictions because of alien auspices. No expense is being spared to make the auditorium decorative, the atmosphere soft and beautiful, the mood festive.

While on the surface the Solomon Schechter Synagogue seems placid enough—the personality conflicts that characterized the institution during an earlier period being now merely an unpleasant memory—in actuality it is an institution with strong and abiding tensions. These tensions inhere in the nature of the position which the institution espouses. Although these tensions may not always be apparent to, or experienced by, the members of the Synagogue, they are inevitably present, since there is at Schechter a very strong desire to be at once traditional and modern and to simultaneously integrate into the overall American culture while preserving something of Jewish culture. Thus the purity of Jewish family life is exalted at religious services and Sisterhood programs, while the entertainer featured at the congregational dinner has led a notorious sex life. The women of the congregation are exhorted to prepare their homes for Passover by removing all *chametz* and by kashering kitchen utensils, while a mother-daughter trip to a modeling and charm school is organized by one of the Synagogue's auxiliaries. The solemnity of the *Neilah* service, which concludes the observance of Yom Kippur, is followed a few scant hours later by a "Yom Kippur Nite Dance" in honor of new members.

The Schechter Synagogue is close enough to Jewish tradition to feel the pressure of sacramentalism. Consequently, if the member of the Synagogue is to conduct himself in accordance with the norms for which the institution stands, he must be more alienated from the general culture than are his peers at the Wise Temple. An example of such alienation is a poignant open letter written by Rabbi Ginzberg to parents of high-school students. The rabbi called upon the parents to keep children in Lakeville rather than to allow them to make a trip that the schools had planned—a trip that coincided with Passover. But simultaneously he suggested to the parents that they plan activities for their children which would be so attractive that their offspring would not experience any feeling of deprivation. If Rabbi Ginzberg's position is shared by the membership, what it suggests is a realization of the inevitability of alienation—given a sacramental stance—and grave conflict over the deprivation which such alienation necessarily involves:

> It has come to our attention that some of the schools in the area have planned a trip to New York and Washington for their students during the spring vacation. In view of the fact that the spring vacation falls during the Passover Season this year it poses a serious problem and a strong temptation to Jewish students.
>
> Apart from the problem of food, which is an almost insuperable obstacle, it would mean that Jewish students would be away from home . . . when they should be with family and loved ones for the observance of the traditional Passover Seder Services. While we cannot tell the schools how and when to arrange their affairs, we do call upon Jewish students to display courage and inner pride by refraining from participation in a program that menaces their Jewish loyalties. Passover rings out a call to freedom. For Jewish students who are affected, it bids them free themselves from bondage to conformity and to firmly say "no" to a program that can only inflict a spiritual hurt upon them and disrupt time-honored home practices.
>
> We call upon Jewish parents to follow an admirable example of one of our families which is helping strengthen their daughter's resistance to

temptation by so planning the week of Passover for her that the joys she would experience by staying at home with them will more than compensate her for the disappointment in not going with her classmates. This is an hour that calls for steadfastness by Jewish students and resourcefulness by their parents. May they both emerge triumphant.

The David Einhorn Temple

THE RE-ESTABLISHMENT OF CLASSICAL REFORM IN LAKEVILLE

The David Einhorn Temple is one of a small number of American synagogues which continue to reflect the traditions of Classical Reform. To its supporters, the Einhorn Temple is the only synagogue in Lakeville which has the right to call itself "Reform." [6] To some of the members of other synagogues in the area, however, the Einhorn Temple conjures up a far different image: it is thought of as an institution which violates Jewish tradition so flagrantly that it cannot be considered a bona fide synagogue. While all the religious institutions in the community have their detractors as well as supporters, none has given rise to such heated controversy as Einhorn.

As with the Wise Temple at a previous period, the beginnings of the Einhorn Temple can be traced to the desire of parents to provide their children with a Jewish education. But unlike the situation three decades earlier, Jewish religious instruction was available in Lakeville. However, some parents in the community felt disinclined to expose their children to the Neo-Reformism of the Wise Temple. Not only did they object to the content of the Wise curriculum and their mode of celebrating Jewish holidays but they were loath to give any sanction to the Temple's departure from Classical Reform norms by sending their children to its religious school. As was the case at an earlier period, such parents were troubled by the fact that their children would attain maturity without being confirmed. While they were much less concerned with establishing a religious institution that would cater to their personal spiritual needs, the religious school they founded, like the one established earlier, ultimately gave rise to a full-fledged congregation.

The religious school established in the post–World War II period differed from the one started several decades earlier in that it was not entirely the result of local initiative. A national Jewish organization, the American Council for Judaism, had come into existence during the

interim, and it supplied considerable assistance to the group in Lakeville. The Council had been founded in 1943 for the purpose of com-
batting Zionism; its broader aim was that of rallying adherents of
Classical Reform in the face of the growing power of Neo-Reformism.[7]
Among other aspects of its program, the Council sought to promote the
establishment of a network of religious schools designed to transmit the
heritage of Classical Reform to the younger generation. Lakeville, where
adherents of Classical Reform lived in significant numbers, was a natural
site for such a school.

The ACJ-assisted school was opened in the early 1950's and quickly
proved to be a success. Registration grew from year to year. Families of
German descent who had been affiliated with the Wise Temple were
attracted to the school, and as a consequence the student body came to
include grandchildren of the early members of the Wise Temple. The
school also attracted newcomers who were interested in a suburban
version of the Classical Reform Judaism available to them in Lake City.

A third group found the school appealing. These were parents who
lacked a commitment to Classical Reform but wished simply to expose
their children to a Jewish educational experience. Some of these parents
were consciously survivalistic. Others spoke in terms of giving their
children the opportunity to become acquainted with the Jewish religion
so that when the child was mature he would have a basis for making an
intelligent decision about his religious identity. Whatever differences
characterized these parents, they were united in their desire for a religious
school that would confine itself to a minimal program of study, would
not embarrass them because of their disregard of Jewish ritual, and would
avoid calling on them to affirm uncongenial theological ideas before their
children. Furthermore, since they were concerned about already-existing
cleavages between Jews and Gentiles, they were attracted to a school
that would avoid inculcating strong in-group sentiments. Finally, they
were interested in an institution that promised to make only very modest
financial demands on them.

The very success of the religious school confronted parents of all
types with the question of whether—inasmuch as they had enrolled their
children in a religious school—they did not have an obligation to join
a synagogue.[8] The answer became evident to them more quickly than it
had to the founders of the Wise Temple, for the role accorded religion
in the post–World War II period placed unsynagogued Jews in an even
more anomalous position than before. Furthermore, those who were
close to the American Council for Judaism—an agency which continu-

ally reiterated that Jews were Jewish solely by virtue of religious identification—were under pressure to form a congregation and thus to square their actions with their affirmations.

In spite of the weight of these factors, reluctance was nevertheless present; it was several years before a congregation was established. We infer that the fear of separatism as well as the old yearning for a non-sectarian community was still operative. Also present was an emotion which the previous generation had not experienced quite so keenly: the resistance to assuming the financial, religious, and psychic obligations entailed by the establishment of a congregation. But in the end, even those who were primarily interested in the religious school came around: they agreed that a school could not stand by itself and that the formation of a congregation was a natural development.

The initial form of organization was the very same one conceived by the founders of the Wise Temple: the group should constitute itself into a branch of the Holdheim Temple. Once again the rabbi of Holdheim was asked to come to Lakeville to preach, to organize, and to guide. But the idea of a branch congregation turned out to be as impractical in the 1950's as it had been in the 1920's, and as a consequence an independent institution was formed. Upon its establishment, the links with Holdheim as well as with the American Council for Judaism were severed. The Council's religious school became the educational arm of the Einhorn Temple.

The leadership of Einhorn has continually stressed that the institution is independent of the Council. Aware of the disesteem in which the Council is held by wide segments of American Jewry, even those congregational officials who are officers or supporters of the Council stress that there is no link between the two institutions. But in spite of their efforts at disassociating the Temple from the Council, many local residents believe that a strong linkage exists. This view has been strengthened by the fact that the Einhorn Temple has refrained from affiliating with the national body of Reform Judaism, the Union of American Hebrew Congregations.*

THE SCHOOL AND THE SERVICE

In contrast to those of the Wise Temple and the Solomon Schechter Synagogue, the program at Einhorn consists almost entirely of two activi-

---

* The dominant point of view at the Union is Neo-Reform.

ties: the religious school and the services. To the casual observer, the school appears unexceptional. However, upon closer examination a number of special features become discernible. Perhaps the chief of these is that the school is highly ideological: of all the institutions in Lakeville, the Einhorn Temple is the only one preoccupied with indoctrinating its students with a given point of view, rather than familiarizing them with a body of knowledge acceptable to wide segments of the Jewish community. Accordingly, the Temple goes to considerable lengths to guard its students from outside influence. It makes a continuous review of the content of its textbooks, supplementary reading materials, and curriculum aids. It leans heavily on the curriculum recommended by the American Council for Judaism, and among the texts it utilizes are those employed in the Unitarian-Universalist Church. But perhaps even more important is the manner in which the teaching staff is selected.

The teaching staffs of the other synagogues tend to come from diverse backgrounds. Some teachers live in Lake City, rather than in Lakeville or in the Heights. Some occupy a different class position from the one held by their students. Some are not affiliated with any congregation, while others have an affinity for a different wing of Judaism than the one represented by the congregation in which they teach. The prime qualifications for service are academic training, both general and Jewish, teaching experience, and pedagogic ability. At the Einhorn Temple, on the other hand, the ideological proclivities of the prospective teacher are a central qualification. Ideological correctness is particularly stressed for the teaching staff of the higher classes. A discussion in the seventh grade is reported by an observer as follows:

> The discussion which completed the class period was touched off by a girl who said that she had had an argument in public school over the following matter. Someone had given a report and had classified the Jews as a nationality. She objected to this and felt that it was "pitiful that people think of a religion as a race." This led to the question of whether Jews were a race, religion, or nationality.
>
> Mr. Kohn [the teacher] stressed time and time again that Judaism is a religion and nothing more. He pointed out that if you practice the Christian religion you are a Christian, and if you practice the Jewish religion you are a Jew. He said that if he wanted to change his religion tomorrow, he would cease being a Jew and would become a Christian. Being Jewish thus meant being a member of a religious group.
>
> He asked the class whether Jews were ever a nation. They seemed unresponsive to this question, and he indicated his surprise at their lack of

a ready answer. He proceeded to point out that Jews were once a nation, but that in the last 2,500 years Jews have been a religion. Religion and nationality have been divorced, he said, for a very long time. He pointed out that some Jews think that being Jewish is being a member of a nationality. He said that these people have a right to their opinion and that they were sincere in this belief, but that he felt otherwise and he was sure that most of the class agreed with him.

The teaching staff is recruited from the membership of the Temple itself and is unsalaried. While the result of this procedure is ideological conformity (as well as social-class homophyly), it also results in the appointment of instructors who lack familiarity with the subject matter they are charged with teaching. For example, while most of the staff have received a higher education in secular subjects, few if any have advanced training in Jewish studies. Critics of the institution insist that there are members of the teaching staff who lack even an elementary Jewish education. George Bloch, admittedly an interested party, commented,

> I don't think much of the Einhorn religious school. I say that because I know some of the people teaching there. They went to Sunday school with me at the Wise Temple. They were such poor students they flunked out.

In order to remedy these defects, attempts have been made at in-service training. Several teachers have been asked to engage in a reading program. Teachers' meetings are utilized for the purpose of enriching the Jewish knowledge of the staff.

Another distinguishing characteristic of the Einhorn Temple religious school is the lack of provision for learning the rudiments of the Hebrew language. The entire curriculum is geared to presenting Jewish knowledge in English; no real effort is made to teach even the most basic prayers in the Hebrew original. There is no motivation to familiarize even a minority of the male students with the Hebrew language, for the ceremony of Bar Mitzvah is not permitted.

Turning to the weekly religious services, perhaps their most striking feature is that they are held on Sunday morning. The Einhorn Temple is different in this respect from all other congregations in Lakeville; it is, in fact, one of the few temples in the nation to preserve this aspect of Classical Reform practice. In keeping with the original procedure which held sway at Wise, the schedule of the children and the adults is coordinated. However, since the religious school now meets for a full morning, the program of the adults has been expanded: the first part of the morning consists of a coffee hour, thus filling the gap between the start of classes and the beginning of services.

The services generally draw a fair-sized crowd of worshipers. One of the factors that sustains attendance is the school itself. Most of the students do not live within walking distance, and no public transportation is available. Since the congregation does not provide private bus service, a considerable number of parents must transport their children to and from the school. The leadership of the Temple is unwilling to admit that the traffic generated by the religious school is an important factor in enlarging attendance at services, although during school holidays the size of the congregation drops off sharply. The success of the weekly service is pointed to by officials of the institution as validating the idea that Sunday morning is both an appropriate and an attractive time for Jewish worship.

One of the most distinctive aspects of the service is the prominent place occupied by the rabbi's sermon. This is partly a result of the proclivities of Rabbi Edward Isaacs, Einhorn's spiritual leader, but it also seems connected with a theological issue: the explicit rejection of the idea of a personal God.* When coupled with alienation from the Hebrew language and from the traditional prayer book, this theological stance results in a de-emphasis on prayer. The resulting void is compensated for by the sermon.

The centrality of the sermon also serves to educate the congregant about Classical Reform. This is particularly necessary inasmuch as the Classical Reform position is not generally encountered in the mass media. Sermons devoted to current issues in the Jewish community serve the particular purpose of providing the congregant, as an adherent of a minority viewpoint, with the answers he requires if he is to reply to the detractors of Classical Reform.

In contrast with his colleagues, some of whom must preach twice each week instead of only once, Rabbi Isaacs devotes a major portion of his time to the preparation of sermons. Perhaps because they measure themselves against the traditional rabbinical role, other rabbis in Lakeville say that they do not strongly esteem the role of preacher.[9] They also say that they are skeptical about the efficacy of the sermon as an educational device. Rabbi Isaacs, however, feels that preaching is the most

---

* While some of those who worship at the other congregations may have great difficulty with affirming various aspects of traditional Jewish theology, it is only at the Einhorn Temple that the rejection of the idea of a personal God is conscious and persistent.

important and gratifying of his tasks. But, esteeming the role of preacher so highly, he feels no surcease from homiletical pressures. Instead of speaking from notes, Rabbi Isaacs attempts to deliver his sermon from memory. He begins his preparations on Monday morning and completes his final draft on Saturday night. The sermon is promptly mimeographed and distributed. A special point is made of supplying copies to the teaching staff, for their pedagogic responsibilities preclude attendance at the service. The teachers are expected to familiarize themselves with the sermons and to utilize them as source material for interpreting the ideals of Classical Reform to their students. The sermons also serve to provide the teachers with guidance on problems of current concern which are not reflected in their textbooks.

Another distinctive feature is the place of the Torah service, which is traditionally of central importance at Sabbath worship. At Einhorn, however, it is subordinate. Its abbreviated character is partly a result of the fact that only the briefest of excerpts from the portion of the week is read. Also, the portion is not read from the *Sefer Torah;* the ark (which contains only a single *Sefer Torah*) is not opened except on the High Holidays and the Festivals.* Rabbi Isaacs feels that opening the ark each week and taking out the *Sefer Torah* would lead to veneration of an object and belief in its magical qualities and would thus increase superstition. Furthermore, many of the elements traditionally associated with the Sabbath service are excluded. This includes the institution of *Aliyot* † as well as of petitions asking for blessing on those about to be married, on the newborn and their mothers, and on the sick.

The prayer book for the weekly service is a mimeographed booklet, rather than a printed volume. One distinguishing feature is the absence of Hebrew script: the few Hebrew prayers that are included are reproduced in transliteration.‡ Hebrew has also been discarded in the musical portions of the service, for all hymns are sung in English. Only Western musical modes are employed. Works by classical composers such as Beethoven, Haydn, and Mozart and by American composers whose

* *Sefer Torah:* the Torah scroll of parchment on which are written the Five Books of Moses. The most sacred religious object in Judaism, it is removed from the ark for the Torah service each Sabbath morning.

† Plural of *Aliyah:* liturgically, the ascent to the Torah. The individual—traditionally the male age 13 or over—is called up to the lectern during the Torah service to read a portion of the Torah, or to have the portion read by a surrogate, and to recite the appropriate blessings.

‡ Any Hebrew which is utilized during the service appears forced, especially since Rabbi Isaacs seems ill at ease in the language.

works are commonly encountered in Protestant hymnals form the basis of the Temple's music.

Whether because of adherence to traditional norms or out of a desire to increase interest on the part of the laity, other temples in the community place considerable emphasis on participation of the worshiper in the religious services. At periodic intervals, laymen conduct the entire proceedings, and no service is held without some lay participation. The Einhorn Sabbath service, on the other hand, is characterized by little if any lay participation. Officials believe that the conduct of the service is a rabbinical responsibility. They also stress that other congregations utilize lay participation as a device to stimulate attendance and interest; they feel that their worshipers come out of sincere interest rather than because they have been given a role to perform. In summary, all these features taken together—the rabbinically centered service,[10] the primacy of the sermon, the diminished importance of the Torah service, the absence of Hebrew, the Westernized music—give the Sunday morning service at the Einhorn Temple a character that is recognizably different from the Sabbath services conducted at the other synagogues of Lakeville.

Surprisingly enough, Einhorn holds an additional Sabbath service each week: a Friday afternoon vesper service. This service leads a fugitive existence, but nevertheless is held regularly. Since the service points to the persistence of the feeling that Saturday is the Jewish Sabbath and Sunday the Christian Sabbath, it contradicts the ideology which the group espouses.[11] As a consequence, no regular announcement is made; unlike other activities, the vesper service is not listed in the Temple bulletin. According to Rabbi Isaacs, there is very little interest in the vesper service, and thus there would be no point in giving it publicity. While attendance is discouraged, from one to eight persons come, all of them women.[12]

The leadership of the Temple are somewhat sensitive about the shift to the Christian Sabbath * and have consequently deviated on occasion from the practice of secrecy. When charged with making no provision for prayer on the traditional Sabbath, they cite the existence of the vesper service. Rabbi Isaacs' description of the service is explicit on this point:

> As for Sabbath services, we do hold a vesper service at 5:30 on Friday. Very few people come. The maximum number is eight; sometimes only

---

* The Sunday morning service is thus designated in the Temple bulletin as the "Weekly Worship Service," rather than the "Sabbath Service."

one person, Evelyn Weil, comes. We use the Union Prayer Book,* but sometimes we don't have any formal service, only a meditation period. I'm not trying to attract a crowd; frankly I don't care how many people attend. But the congregation can reply to those who say that we have no observance of the Sabbath. They can say that we do have something on Friday night.

Rabbi Isaacs has wrestled with the problem of which Sabbath to observe. As a religious professional, he has undoubtedly felt more severe conflicts on this score than the great majority of his congregants. Rabbi Isaacs' aim has been to achieve a clean break with the traditional Jewish Sabbath, but he confesses that he has not been entirely successful:

> I have not quite decided what to say about Friday night. I don't want services to be held that evening, but I don't deny that because of my background and training Friday night is different. My feeling, however, is that Friday night is vestigial and should be done away with. As for candles, we don't light them in my home; we would feel self-conscious about doing so. But if someone feels that it is pleasant to light candles, they ought to do so.

On the Festivals of Sukkot, Pesach, and Shavuot, there is no ambiguity about which calendar to follow: services are held on Sunday, regardless of the day of the week on which the holidays fall. On the High Holidays, however, the opposite procedure is followed: the occasion is celebrated in conformity with the Hebrew calendar. Why the exception? It is apparent that the High Holidays have retained a hold on exceedingly wide segments of the Jewish group, and presumably the members of the Einhorn Temple share in this attachment to some degree. Furthermore, the appeal of the High Holidays to such wide segments of American Jewry makes a calendric deviation exceedingly difficult; it would place the Einhorn group in an even more sectarian role than they presently occupy. Finally, there is the fact that, to some degree at least, the general community is geared to noting the observance of the High Holidays according to the Hebrew calendar.[13]

While the celebration of the High Holidays on the days prescribed by tradition has created no strain at Einhorn, the holidays themselves have posed one very difficult problem. This is the lack of a Classical Reform prayer book for Rosh Hashanah and Yom Kippur. The various editions of the High Holiday prayer book issued by the early Classical

---

* The prayer book issued by the Central Conference of American Rabbis and the Union of American Hebrew Congregations.

Reform rabbis are now long out of print, and neither contemporary spiritual leaders who sympathize with the Classical Reform position nor the American Council for Judaism has published such volumes.

Since the Einhorn leadership have no enthusiasm for publishing a prayer book, they have been compelled to use the Union Prayer Book. To make the volume more acceptable, a plan was devised providing for the deletion of those passages most clearly Neo-Reform in emphasis as well as for the addition of supplementary prayers of a Classical Reform variety. Although satisfying in theory, the procedure proved to be unworkable. Worshipers had no access to the marked copy of the Union Prayer Book which the rabbi had prepared. Becoming confused by the deletions and additions emanating from the pulpit, worshipers found it impossible to follow the service in their own prayer books. It thus became necessary to discontinue the practice, and at the present time the Union Prayer Book is utilized as is; its Neo-Reform heresies are overlooked.

PROBLEMS OF BUILDING AND PROGRAM

Both the religious school and the Sabbath, Festival, and Holiday services of the Einhorn Temple are held in a commodious and recently built public school located in the community. The Einhorn group have been highly satisfied with their accommodations, and due to the cooperation of the school board the Temple has been spared the nomadic existence which was characteristic of its predecessor, the Wise Temple.

The Einhorn Temple is, curiously, a store-front synagogue. It has no building of its own. Rather, it maintains an office on a business street. Although the premises which it occupies have been altered, the commercial purpose for which they were originally intended is still evident. And in spite of careful remodeling, the setting seems more suitable for a struggling Pentecostal sect than for a congregation whose roster includes important businessmen and well-established professionals. Situated adjacent to such enterprises as groceries, drug stores, and dry-cleaning establishments, the tone of the Temple's headquarters is out of keeping with the *éclat* suggested by the comfortable residences of its leaders and by the broad lawns and spacious patios that surround their homes. Like the Wise Temple of an earlier period, Einhorn's facilities are substandard.

Officials of the Einhorn Temple are aware of the incongruity between their station in life and the physical plant of their Temple. Nevertheless, they are determined to resist erecting a suitable building. They have remained adamant precisely during the period when one wit said that American Jewry has become afflicted with an "edifice complex."

Is the hesitancy about erecting an appropriate building similar to the reaction of the founding fathers of the Wise Temple? Some of the same elements are undoubtedly present. But perhaps the most obvious contrast is that while the earlier group in the main felt that resistance to erecting a building was a matter of expediency, the Einhorn group feel that it is a matter of principle. In the 1920's, residents seemed to have feared an increase in Jewish visibility; they were loath to make a formal declaration of the existence of a Jewish community; and they may have unconsciously wished to disappear as a group. But in contrast to the leaders of the Einhorn Temple, they did not have a principled objection to erecting a building.

The leaders of Einhorn are firmly committed to the principle of continuing to use public facilities. When questioned, they present a variety of reasons for their viewpoint. They feel that the establishment of a building would involve them in compromises. They believe that once a drive for funds was inaugurated, they would of necessity have to moderate their views so as to appeal to as wide a group of supporters as possible. Furthermore, they believe that the cost of maintaining a suitable structure would necessitate an expansion of the membership, with the result that individuals of dubious loyalty to Classical Reform would have to be invited to become members. They fear that such individuals might gain control of the institution and that the end result could be a repetition of the history of Wise Temple.

Since the economic standing of the membership is high, the group is quite capable of financing the construction and maintenance of a very adequate building. One of the reasons which they adduce would seem more determinative than the financial excuse: namely, that if a building were erected, the program of the congregation, as distinct from its membership, would have to expand. They fear that they would become victims of a variation on Parkinson's Law: activities would inevitably increase in order that the new space be utilized. Since there is no desire to expand religious activities (as, for example, increasing the frequency of services), such expansion would inevitably involve adding leisure-time activities to the congregation's program. Such activities would constitute a violation of the principle that Jews should associate with other Jews only in a religious context.

It is self-evident to the leadership that Gentiles would not desire to participate in Temple-sponsored activities, even if they were conducted along non-sectarian lines. The leadership therefore reasons that a building would have the effect of both formalizing the existing separation between Jew and Gentile and eventually magnifying it. Here we come to the heart of the matter. The leadership of the Einhorn Temple does not view a building as something normal—that just as a family requires a home, so does a congregation. Rather, they see it as a device that would sabotage the very ideals for which the congregation stands. In essence, they feel it would spell the defeat of Classical Reform's objective of providing a type of Jewish religious life that is compatible with full integration into the life of the community.

So strongly is this feeling held that except for the rabbi, the leadership of the Temple has been insensitive to the possible violation of church–state separation implicit in the use of public facilities. That delicate situation has been overlooked also by the school authorities, who have made every effort to accommodate the Temple. For example, they have allocated storage space, thus obviating the necessity for the Temple to remove its property from school premises each week. Among the items which the Temple stores at the school are the Ark and the *Sefer Torah.**

The original understanding of the authorities was that accommodations were to be provided on a temporary basis. It was their assumption that as soon as the institution was established on a solid footing, it would acquire its own property. Lately the authorities have been growing restive; they have started to prod the group into making other arrangements. While the school officials (almost all of them Gentile) were not interviewed about the problem, we may assume that they are at a loss to understand just why their tenants, so obviously well endowed financially, have continued each year to request a renewal of their lease.

While to the observer the refusal to build can be viewed less in terms of ideology and more in terms of ambiguity about Jewish identity, to the leadership of the Temple their principled objections received practical confirmation when a request was made to form a youth group. Although realizing that such a group would not devote itself either to worship or to religious study, the officers of the Temple, after much discussion, reluctantly concluded that they had no alternative but to accede to the request.

The youth group came about as a result of pressure exerted by the parents of recent confirmants. The parents pointed out that after Con-

---

* Each Sunday morning, the principal of the school, or one of his assistants, is present in order to patrol the premises and see to it that school property is safeguarded.

firmation their children had no connection with the Temple. What concerned them was not the resulting absence of institutional loyalties on the part of their children, or even the effect which noninvolvement might have on the home observance or synagogue attendance of their offspring.* Rather, they were motivated by the fear of assimilation. Specifically, since their children had no relationship with Jewish young people other than what might occur by chance in clique groups formed on the basis of neighborhood or school contacts, they believed that their children might easily become involved romantically with Gentiles.

The parents did not base their request on this ground, however. Rather, they argued that all the churches in Lakeville sponsored clubs for young people and that it was only their children who were deprived of such a facility. They stressed that a youth group would not promote segregation, but would only provide a service already available to Christians in the community. The Temple pleaded lack of facilities, but the parents replied that they were agreeable to an improvised meeting place. Although the parents won their point, the Temple's leadership underlined that their decision constituted a concession which should not be construed as a precedent for the formation of additional auxiliaries and leisure-time groups which would serve other age grades of the congregational family.

The grudging acceptance of a youth group has meant that its program has been as minimal as possible. Meetings are held only during the school year and then at monthly intervals; even this schedule has been lightened on occasion. Little Jewish content is featured; programs stress such activities as bowling, talks by Lakeville civic officials about community problems, and exchange meetings with church groups, especially with the youth group of the local Episcopalian Church. While from the point of view of religious ideology contact with a more liberal Protestant denomination might be preferable, status considerations have pointed toward interacting with Episcopalians. Although, on the face of it, such interfaith gatherings may be said to vitiate the purposes that motivated parents to agitate for the establishment of a youth group, this is probably not the case in actual practice. Since the encounter is structured on the basis of group affiliation, the meetings may result more in Episcopalian meeting Jew rather than in boy of one faith meeting girl of another. In any case, when exchanging visits the youth group of the Einhorn Temple has confined itself to Christian groups; there have been no exchanges with the teen-age clubs of the Wise Temple or the Schechter Synagogue.

* Accordingly, they did not request that post-Confirmation classes be initiated or that special youth services be instituted.

PROBLEMS OF INSTITUTIONAL SURVIVAL

The Einhorn Temple sponsors only one additional activity: a course for adults on the Prophets. The course meets for fifteen sessions each year, with attendance averaging between thirty and forty persons each session.

Aside from membership on the board of directors, there is very little opportunity for lay activity. This results in part from the lack of affiliated groups as well as the absence of a network of lay committees. In contrast to Wise and Schechter, where there are numerous temple committees—each charged with supervising a particular activity or advising the board of directors of the congregation about a particular problem—there are only two general Temple committees at Einhorn: the school committee and the religious affairs committee. Only the former is really active. In addition, there is a woman's activity committee which arranges for the coffee hour on Sunday morning.

Is an institution of the Einhorn type viable? While the congregation is no longer rapidly expanding, it has shown no signs of a decline. The religious school is the keystone of the institution and is the essential reason for the Temple's strength. Since membership in the congregation is a requirement for registration in the school, the enrollment of a sizable group of members is assured.

In terms of institutional viability, it might be claimed that the minimalism of the congregation's program does not encourage a commitment strong enough to guarantee organizational survival. However, minimal commitment is the very essence of the appeal of the Einhorn Temple, and at least from the short-range point of view is highly functional. No pressing demands are made on the average member for his time, money, or energy; he is not coerced into uncongenial loyalties and affirmations; he is not urged to increase his religious observance; no appeal is made to him to strengthen his religious commitment because of the need of upholding the efforts of the religious school in its task of socializing his child into the Jewish heritage.

The minimalism of Einhorn is illustrated by Rabbi Isaacs' discussion of Passover with the children of the religious school. The rabbi avoided any implication that a Seder is a *sine qua non* or any assumption that his audience would take part in the ritual. He began his explanation of the symbolism of the holiday by saying, "If you have a Seder, you will see that. . . ." Similarly, in a sermon the previous December, Rabbi Isaacs stressed that the observance of Christmas is an individual matter. He stated that he was indifferent to the Christmas-tree issue; the decision to have or not to have a tree was an individual problem. Each family, he maintained, was free to proceed in a manner which best suited its particular needs and predilections. Rabbi Isaacs' approach is apparently very close to that of many of his members. One of the Temple's inner circle—a man who feels that he has much greater objectivity than his peers—stated, "Our congregation has two assets, one the school and the other the personality and popularity of Rabbi Isaacs. Ed [Rabbi Isaacs] is a good image of a rabbi for the people who belong. He shares the same liberal interests, and his Freudian views evoke a real response."

At the same time that there is no effort on the part of the rabbi to coerce the congregant, there is no effort on the part of the congregant to coerce the rabbi. Rabbi Isaacs has an arrangement with the congregation permitting him to be away from Lakeville several months each year on private business. There has been no attempt to modify this arrangement and thus to increase his opportunities for ministering to the membership. The minimalist orientation of the leadership undoubtedly makes them agreeable to this unusual arrangement.

A peculiar aspect of the minimalism of the Einhorn Temple is that it exists alongside an image—strongly held by the leadership, at least —that Einhorn Temple stands for a radical program of Jewish religious reconstruction. Viewing themselves as the sole authentic religious voice of American Jewry, they look upon other Jews as compromisers who, having tasted the forbidden fruit of Jewish sacramentalism and found it good, have thereby corrupted the purity of the Jewish tradition. Only the Einhorn Temple and a handful of comparable institutions in the nation have remained faithful to Judaism's unique contribution to mankind: the message of the Prophets. Accordingly, the leaders say that Einhorn's approach is necessarily unpopular: the proponents of Prophetic Judaism have always suffered at the hands of less sensitive religious spirits. How can the religious revolutionary, they ask, be appreciated by those who represent the religious *status quo?*

Inasmuch as Einhorn's minimalism does not call for a transvaluation of values or for alienation from the secular culture, it at once becomes apparent that their stance is much more conservative than they assume it to be. A clue is contained in the congregation's "Statement of Principles," where the contribution of the Prophets is hailed as the most significant event in Jewish history:

The Old Testament Prophets wrote the most significant pages in the development of Judaism. They first conceived and articulated a religion dependent upon inner, moral strength, rather than upon land, nation or ritual. . . . Through the majestic spiritual contributions of the Prophets Judaism transcended the destruction of the Hebrew nation and we are Jews today because we accept this Prophetic faith.

But the statement also goes on to say:

. . . we shall observe [those] practices, customs and ceremonies which shall be meaningful for us because they symbolize in effective and beautiful form the principles of our faith, *compatible with our lives as Americans* [emphasis supplied].

This final clause is the clue to the conservatism of the approach that Einhorn espouses. Stressing integration into the culture, rather than alienation from it, the statement implies the observance of only those aspects of the suprasocial system which are deemed compatible with such integration. In the final analysis, the approach is contrary to the Prophetic tradition inasmuch as it reconciles, rather than heightens, the tension between religion and culture. Preaching integration into the secular life of the community, the Classical Reformism of the Einhorn Temple can be seen as protecting the individual from the radical demands of religion.[14]

Whatever the distance between the overt radicalism of the congregation's ideology and its covert conservatism, the Temple meets the needs of the Jew raised in the tradition of Classical Reform. In probing feelings about congregational affiliation, we find that Einhorn members more frequently than members of other congregations cite the religious approach of the institution as the reason for satisfaction with their affiliation. For example, while only 11 per cent of members of Wise cite the religious approach of their institution as its most satisfying feature, 44 per cent of the members of the Einhorn Temple do so. As we might expect, some of those who are particularly attracted on this basis are former members of the Wise Temple. A very prosperous sales executive of German descent and a member of the fourth generation who "grew up" at the Wise Temple describes his feelings as follows:

Before this congregation formed, we grew apart from Wise. Now I feel I am back in a congregation which contains my views on Judaism.

The same feeling is experienced by more recent arrivals in the community. A forty-year-old woman of German descent who had been active in Holdheim Temple before she and her sales-manager husband moved to Lakeville feels that Einhorn is "the closest to the type of temple we've always had." She explains her attraction to the Temple in the following terms:

Einhorn is ideologically what I like, and people in it are my type. They're intelligent about religion, with no hocus-pocus.

Occasionally we find instances of former Wise members who feel that Einhorn is too anti-Zionist. A third-generation owner of a prosperous manufacturing business who was confirmed at the Wise Temple represents this minority viewpoint among longtime residents of Lakeville who have switched to Einhorn. He is of East European rather than German descent and sees his present affiliation as "the lesser of two evils" because

I was dissatisfied with Wise's tendency toward Conservatism, but I don't like Einhorn's connection with the American Council for Judaism.

Einhorn numbers among its families many nonobservant individuals who view the Temple solely as a means of exposing their children to minimal religious education. Thus a fourth-generation mother of two children who attend Einhorn's religious school regards her religiosity in the following terms:

You have a very unreligious person in front of you. I get nothing out of it. I go so my daughter will go.

Another fourth-generation mother of a daughter whose recent Confirmation was the occasion for the family's sole attendance at services during the year replied in the same vein, "It means strictly nothing to me. I'm not even slightly religious." The attitudes of at least a segment of the membership are candidly and succinctly summarized by a committed but critical fourth-generation woman who is a member of the Temple's board of directors and who was reared in the Classical Reform tradition:

I think most members of the congregation don't want to be Jewish but want to give their children more than they had, and this is closest to nothing they can dream up.

If Einhorn's minimalism, as well as the deep alienation of so many of its members from Jewish tradition, is no threat to institutional survival, it is nevertheless apparent that the congregation is not as homogeneous as its leadership likes to think. The attachment of a significant segment of the membership to Classical Reform is weak; such individuals have been attracted to the institution because of the religious school.

While the Einhorn Temple has promulgated a "Statement of Principles," it has no real way of screening uncommitted individuals. True, the "Statement" is more than was possessed by the oldtimers at Wise, but the Classical Reformers of the Einhorn Temple have not instituted a series of creedal requirements to which the novice must give assent before he is accepted for membership. The ideological proclivities of new and old members are thus not subject to review, and the interest of parents in Lakeville in giving their children some type of Jewish schooling means that the Temple continues to draw support from a public wider than those who have a record of loyalty to Classical Reform.

The group which is uncommitted to Classical Reform is not presently represented in the leadership of the institution to any significant extent. Their views are rarely made known, but when they have spoken out they have centered their criticism on the Temple's anti-Zionism. Unconcerned with the problem of perpetuating Classical Reform in all its particulars and apathetic to the threat which the Temple's leadership feels is posed to the security of American Jewry by the Zionist movement, they view the leaders as zealots who use their position to promote a political cause. They charge the congregational leaders with mixing religion and politics —the same complaint that the Temple's leaders have made against their antagonists in the Jewish community. Thus, while the leaders of the Temple have accused other Jews of mixing Zionism and religion, some of their followers at Einhorn have thus accused *them* of mixing *anti-*Zionism and religion. Stating that they have no objection to anyone's belonging to the Council if he so wishes, the uncommitted group say that the Council has entirely too much influence over the Temple. They emphasize that the Council is a political organization and must be kept at arm's length by a religious institution such as the Einhorn Temple.

The uncommitted fail to understand how the Zionist issue can arouse the passion of the Temple's leadership. Nonideological in approach, they wonder why the Temple seems to involve itself in controversial questions and why the rabbi takes such an extreme position on so many issues. For example, they see no reason why the Temple should not be in the main stream of American Reform Judaism and proceed to join the Union of American Hebrew Congregations. They suggest that if criticism is called for, it would be more responsible to criticize from within Reform Judaism than from without. But the leadership are resistant to joining the Union, fearing that the move would be interpreted as a compromise with Neo-Reform, that it would strengthen the hand of the uncommitted within the Temple, and that it might presage the end of one of the country's last bastions of Classical Reform Judaism.

If the problem of the Schechter Synagogue is how to reconcile traditionalism and modernism, the problem of Einhorn is whether, given its extreme integrationist orientation, the next generation will feel strongly enough about minority group identity to continue with Classical Reform Judaism. To remain Jewish, there must be an element of uniqueness— even in a pluralist America where structural uniqueness far exceeds cultural uniqueness. To some members of Einhorn, it is not at all clear what that uniqueness is. And if there is ambiguity in the present generation, it may increase in the next.

A recent sermon by Rabbi Isaacs on the subject of "Reform Judaism and Unitarianism—Their Similarities and Their Differences" is symptomatic of the problem. Speaking from his Classical Reform stance, Rabbi Isaacs said that Unitarianism and Reform Judaism are "two closely related religious expressions. So closely related that it is far simpler to find their similarities than their differences." The differences that Rabbi Isaacs pointed to were: (1) the varying approach of the two faiths to the centrality of Jesus and (2) Unitarianism's espousal of what he termed Jesus' "[impossibly high] morality, this ethical pinnacle that has condemned man throughout the centuries to continuing failure."

We must regard as an open question whether the children and grandchildren of Einhorn members will aspire to what Rabbi Isaacs feels is a more demanding morality; whether they will be satisfied with what he feels is Judaism's more realistic morality; or whether, moralism aside, they will seek to find their place in a fourth community which is neither Catholic, Protestant, nor Jewish.

The Samuel Hirsch Temple

GROWTH AND DEVELOPMENT

The Samuel Hirsch Temple, established in the 1950's, has its roots in the Samuel Adler Temple, one of Lake City's well-known Reform synagogues. In the 1940's, the Adler Temple chose Rabbi Abraham Lubin as its spiritual leader. Although Neo-Reform in orientation, Rabbi Lubin stressed the importance of a prophetic Judaism. He combined this orientation with an emphasis on Zionism and Jewish peoplehood. Furthermore, he involved himself in a variety of liberal and leftist causes. Not only was his blend of these elements unique but his "style" was exceptional. His spoken and written word was more sophisticated than that of most of his colleagues, and his interest in the arts indicated a higher than average brow level.

As a consequence of his exceptional qualities as well as of the relatively high level of sophistication of residents of the neighborhood in which the congregation was located, Rabbi Lubin began to attract an unusual type of member to the Adler Temple. These were individuals who found the sermons delivered by other Reform rabbis uninteresting and the services conducted in other temples unsatisfying. While they frequently worked at the same occupations as those in other congregations, they were exceptional in that they had received their education at colleges and universities of distinctly superior academic standing. As a consequence, these newer members of the Adler Temple tended to be doctors and lawyers, wholesalers and retailers, whose cultural horizon was above the average. Furthermore, a group of individuals joined the Temple who made their living in unusual fields—they were musicians, writers, professors, psychiatrists. But whether in women's wear or in classical music, in modest or prosperous circumstances, the new members were political liberals. Indeed, one observer made the claim that the decay in liberal and radical politics which occurred during and after World War II helped motivate their affiliation. In any case, under the leadership of Rabbi Lubin the Adler Temple came to view itself as exceptional. It came to look upon other synagogues in Lake City—including the Holdheim Temple—as staid and backward religious institutions.

When Negroes began to move into the area, the Temple was confronted with the difficult decision of whether or not to relocate. Other congregations would have chosen to move and would have done so without guilt feelings. But at Adler the problem was an immensely complicated one: the decision to leave the neighborhood would mean that congregants were unfaithful to the liberalism which they and their rabbi professed. After a succession of agonizing appraisals, the Temple resolved to remain in what was fast becoming an interracial neighborhood and might soon become a Negro ghetto.

The Temple made the decision to remain, but this did not prevent some of its members from moving to the Heights suburbs, including Lakeville. While the leadership of the Temple disapproved of families who left their community in order to settle in an all-white area, confronted with a declining congregation they felt it necessary to retain the loyalty of as many members as possible. Thus they countenanced the opening of a branch in Lakeville. Services were held under the leadership of Rabbi Lubin or his assistant, and religious-school classes were started.

The group soon began to undergo the same process as did those members of the Holdheim Temple who had moved to Lakeville several decades earlier. In the present instance, the problem of forming an independent congregation was complicated by the fact that Adler members had an even stronger attachment to Rabbi Lubin than did the Holdheim group to their rabbi. Rabbi Lubin was also in good health and had many years before retirement. The group in Lakeville decided to induce the rabbi to leave his post and to become their spiritual leader, and to this end they decided to form an independent congregation, which they named the Samuel Hirsch Temple. They assumed that the old neighborhood would turn into a Negro ghetto and that in due course their congregation would become the successor to the Adler Temple.

After prolonged indecisiveness, Rabbi Lubin declined their offer. The Hirsch group was disheartened. But while some members resigned, others continued feeling that neither Wise nor Einhorn met their needs. They decided to persist in the plan to form a new congregation. Appointing an interim rabbi, they proceeded to scour the country for a junior edition of Rabbi Lubin. They found so many candidates unsuited to their requirements that the infant institution became an object of wry comment in rabbinical circles. Finally they settled upon Rabbi Samuel Aaron. A youngish man, Rabbi Aaron had been devoting the major part of his time to graduate studies—some thought in preparation for a teaching career. Rabbi Aaron was a person of wide culture who possessed considerable facility of expression. He blended great seriousness about intellectual matters with a somewhat casual attitude toward the proprieties. He was the very opposite of a "stuffed shirt." He was attracted to the Hirsch Temple because so many of its leaders were people who were not ordinarily active in a synagogue. They, in turn, were attracted to him because he was the type of person who was not ordinarily a rabbi.

SERVICES AND SCHOOL

In spite of the lack of a building and a smaller membership than Wise, Schechter, or Einhorn, the Samuel Hirsch Temple has a nucleus of very devoted members plus a peripheral group with some measure of loyalty. Although it requires additional financial support, the Temple does not want to grow very large. It wishes to base itself on a comparatively small and therefore select membership. Most of the group feel that their institution offers them something they cannot find at any other temple. They are particularly critical of the Wise Temple, with its huge membership and its multitude of activities. While some still yearn for Rabbi Lubin, many feel that Rabbi Aaron is distinguished by unique qualities of heart and mind and will be capable of fulfilling their special requirements.

The Temple holds its Sabbath service on Friday evening; it does not have an adult service on Saturday morning. Services presently take place in a public hall which has about it an air of shabby gentility. The services are closely supervised by a worship committee. The officers, feeling that the membership of the Temple would not be responsive to the usual type of Reform service, have given the committee unusual responsibilities. In consultation with the rabbi, the worship committee was charged with creating an entirely new type of Jewish religious service. It is the consensus that while the ritual they prepared may need some further revision, it is much superior to, and far more satisfying than, the ritual followed by other Reform congregations.

Early in its deliberations, the worship committee made the decision to discard the Union Prayer Book. The feeling of uniqueness which is so constant a theme at the Hirsch Temple made it impossible to utilize the standard Reform liturgy; it appears that only Rabbi Aaron is aware that the service which the committee composed and had mimeographed follows the Union Prayer Book rather closely. Nevertheless, Hirsch's "Order of Worship" booklet serves the purpose of affirming to the membership their image of the Temple as a "thinking man's congregation."

Although the "Order of Worship" follows the liturgy used in other Reform congregations more closely than the worship committee would care to admit, some unusual features are included in the service. Each week a different member is charged with writing a "creative prayer." The prayer is presented at the service by the author. A second member is charged with presenting an excerpt from a book he has recently read. While Rabbi Lubin allowed the selection to be chosen from world literature, Rabbi Aaron insists that it be Jewish. His stipulation is not narrowly construed, however; an excerpt from Kafka, for example, is quite acceptable. But even when the readings are of a more traditional character, they fall into definable patterns, the most popular source being the literature of Hasidism.

Considerable emphasis is placed on the reading of the Torah portion. The appropriate blessings are recited in Hebrew by those who participate in the Torah service. Rabbi Aaron reads part of the portion of the week from the *Sefer Torah*, fluently translating as he finishes each line. This practice is followed on the theory that the worshiper must comprehend what is being read and should not be exposed to long passages of material in a language he does not understand.

While Rabbi Aaron's sermon forms an important part of the Sabbath service, it is felt that congregants as well as the rabbi have the right and responsibility to air their views. The worship committee's regulations provide that twice each month the rabbi's sermon is to be replaced by a panel discussion led by members of the congregation, one such panel to be a commentary on a recent sermon. In actual practice, the ideal of equal time for rabbi and congregation is not adhered to; because of the difficulty of organizing the panels, Rabbi Aaron speaks more frequently than provided for in the plan of the worship committee. Nevertheless, the procedure serves to bolster the image of the Hirsch Temple as an institution in which the rabbi serves congregants who are his equal in intellectual power and spiritual sensitivity.

Most of Rabbi Aaron's sermon topics deal with religious problems. His approach is neither Classical Reform nor Neo-Reform. It is, in a sense, Post-Reform; he draws upon existentialism and crisis theology, combining them with certain traditional Jewish themes which are outside the sacramental framework. While there has been some criticism of his choice of topics as well as his religious approach, even those who are unsympathetic have been attracted by his wide knowledge, high intelligence, and quick wit. Rabbi Aaron found that on one sermon topic there was no controversy:

> The largest Friday evening attendance since I came to the Temple was when I spoke about Freud. I used the Jones biography as a starting point. I was not alone in doing this; I notice that all the rabbis in Lakeville have devoted at least one sermon to the same topic. Mine was very well received; I cannot say that some of my other sermons elicited the same degree of enthusiasm. Practically everyone agreed with what I had to say about Freud. Even those who did not were delighted that I had chosen to preach on this subject.

One of the most distinctive features of the service is its note of informality. Hirsch's informality is not, however, similar to that of the average Orthodox service: there is no conversation among the worshipers, no moving about, no praying at one's own speed and in one's own style. Rather it is a type of suburban informality which expresses a belief in casualness as a way of life; it is a casualness which demonstrates that the individual knows the proprieties, but is superior to them.

The most obvious aspect of such informality is the manner in which Rabbi Aaron and the choir are dressed. Both appear in street clothes, rather than in robes. The absence of robes would appear to be a studied attempt to achieve informality and a desire not to distinguish between those who worship in the congregation and those who function as professionals in front of the congregation.

An excellent example of the informality esteemed at the Temple is an incident observed one Friday evening. The service centered around the dedication of a *Sefer Torah,* with both the husband and wife who donated the *Sefer* participating in the service. Toward the conclusion of the ceremony, Rabbi Aaron thanked the husband and turned to the wife, whom he had known for only a few months. Without self-consciousness, he kissed and embraced her. Instead of disapproval, the worshipers reacted most positively; their satisfaction with the rabbi's conduct was apparent. His act was interpreted as a spontaneous show of affection which would have been repressed in a more staid religious institution.

Informality, casualness, and humor pervade many aspects of the Temple's program. Writing in the bulletin, Rabbi Aaron gave a sensitive interpretation of this approach:

> Freud was impressed by the Jew's ability to laugh at his own most treasured habits and convictions. Nothing for him seemed to be sacred. But the point is that nothing was sacred in appearance only because everything was sacred in reality. To the modern epigone of Puritanism, the humorous is equated with the secular. But the Jew knew no secular. His laughter, particularly his laughter at himself, was a way of trying to see life from another side. It was a curb to his pride; it made even his chosenness a prank.
>
> I often feel that the most "religious" moment of our own service comes when our president makes the announcements. Because here, pre-eminently, the human, the humorous, and the humanitarian come into our terribly serious service. And these are what true religiosity is about. The man who loves God loves himself, too. But he knows that sometimes he is a clown.

Like those of the other congregations of Lakeville, the religious school of the Hirsch Temple is a highly important focus of the congregational program. A public-school building is rented each week. The school meets on Saturday morning, rather than on Sunday morning. While Hebrew instruction is available, the emphasis is on Confirmation. The ceremony of Bar Mitzvah, performed on Friday evening, is disapproved of by Rabbi Aaron. He would like to dispense with it. The school is the fastest-growing part of the congregation and is supervised by an active temple committee, the majority of whose members are women. Some of them have had considerable experience in secular education. Rather than use volunteer teachers, the Temple employs professionals, most of whom live in Lake City.

ADULT EDUCATION

Some of the members of the Hirsch Temple believe that the most un-usual feature of the congregation is its program of adult Jewish educa-tion, rather than its Friday evening service. The objective of the con-gregation is to involve each member in study—an objective to which none of the other congregations aspire. According to a statement prepared by Rabbi Aaron:

> Believing that no Jew can be a good Jew who does not know the meaning of his religion, we are especially convinced that we ourselves must study. Our technique emphasizes discussion rather than lecture, and in place of pontifical pronouncement we assert the need for each member of our congregation to confront our sacred texts and tradition for himself. We believe that this can lead only to good for us and for liberal Judaism in America.

It is difficult to trace the origin of this emphasis. Did it originate in the conception that the adult, sending his child to religious school, must impose a similar obligation on himself? Is there a fear that without adult education the training given in the religious school will result in the child's outdistancing his parents intellectually? Does it constitute a realization that while the member's secular education is on a high level, his Jewish knowledge is elementary in scope, and that if this discrepancy is not eliminated the member can only be an ill-educated and uncultured Jew? Is it merely the aspiration to distinguish oneself from those of lesser refinement and sensibility? Or is it that the Hirsch member, wishing to make a Jewish affirmation, cannot do so on the level of religious feeling, belief, or ritual and therefore chooses study as the only Jewish value to which he can commit himself? Or is the emphasis on study a result of adherence to the traditional Jewish notion that religious learn-ing is one of the highest forms of piety and is in effect a form of com-munion with God?

Whatever the motivation of the adult education program or the extent of participation by the membership, it is quite clear that the ideal of study is not only endorsed by the leadership of the Temple but one of the crucial marks by which the congregation distinguishes itself from other temples. Each week one of two groups meets; each group alter-nates in meeting on the same evening every other week. One is the Bible Seminar, which is attended by about fifty individuals. The second, with only about twenty attendants, is devoted to current affairs but is as likely to discuss questions such as problems of being Jewish as to consider issues of national concern. In both groups, the emphasis is on participation, rather than on attending a lecture by the rabbi or some other expert. Members are required to prepare papers, which are for the purpose of providing the group with background information. As is implied in Rabbi Aaron's statement, the Hirsch Temple avoids what many other congregations feature: the sponsorship of public lectures by well-known personalities.

In actual fact, the study groups sponsored by the Hirsch Temple are not unique. More unusual is the emphasis on study and discussion which pervades several other activities of the congregation. Thus, Temple committees stress the analysis and systematic investigation of whatever problem they are concerned with; they write position papers and various kinds of reports. Furthermore, the board of directors does not wish to limit itself to the usual kind of congregational business. While it holds a business meeting once a month, it also conducts periodic luncheon meetings at a Lake City hotel where discussion of congregational affairs is set aside in favor of analyzing the principles the Temple should espouse.

CONGREGATIONAL PROBLEMS

The Hirsch Temple prides itself on the fact that it has no affiliated organizations. It does not have a principled objection to these organizations, as is the case at Einhorn. Rather, the attitude at the Temple is that such organizations involve activities which are unworthy of serious men and women. But there is a feeling among some in the congregation that Hirsch's intellectuality has been carried too far. When the annual meeting of the congregation was opened for discussion, an observer reported:

> The first question was about the need for more social activities. The man who asked the question said that the congregation could well use a sisterhood, a men's club, and perhaps a couple's club. Part of the financial problem of the congregation, he added, would be solved by these groups. The questioner also said that there were certain people in the congregation who did not attend the study groups and thus did not get to know their fellow members. His implication was that Hirsch should become a more "normal" congregation.
>
> The chairman stated that the problem would be taken under advisement. He implied that such a demand was not new. He stated that the congregation did not want to have all these auxiliaries and thus be like the other congregations.

The same approach is apparent in a letter to the editor written by one of the women in the congregation and appearing in the Temple bulletin:

> The Rabbi said recently that the people who join Hirsch do so because of those who are already in it. I believe that this is true. And yet, although our main motivation in belonging to Hirsch is a desire to be associated with one another, it seems there are too few who feel they really *belong*. New members complain that we are cold and that they do not feel welcome among us; some old members say that they often feel lonely at services and at the Oneg Shabbat which follows. And who wants to go where he will be lonely?
>
> I don't think we are really unwilling to make friends. I think the situation is to blame: we have organized our activities in such a way as to make friendship difficult instead of easy. We act as though the object of each activity were strictly limited to the purpose in hand, such as worship, or study, and as if friendship were a relatively unimportant by-product. In fact it is most important—even essential. We are an association, and our success, our very existence, requires that our members be bound together by affection and common interests.
>
> I suggest that we include a social aspect in all our present activities, and that we introduce other, purely social, activities. For example, we could have a group formed to discuss various matters of Jewish interest, or we could have social clubs, or parties, or all three.
>
> We will be far more willing to give our congregation not only money, but time and work and loyalty, which are really parts of ourselves, when we know each other well, and feel at home together.

The problem is not immediate, inasmuch as the congregation is small and a certain proportion of the membership necessarily become acquainted. But if the congregation grows, as it must, the Temple will be confronted with the necessity of sponsoring activities that will afford increased opportunities for interaction.

Hirsch's desire for intellectuality has ramified effects. While Rabbi Aaron emphasizes the importance of prayer, for some the unique approach of the Temple means that prayer is unimportant. Although there has been no attempt to reduce the frequency of services, some who come have made it known that what they are primarily seeking is an intellectual experience. A woman member of the board of directors who formerly belonged to Adler Temple commented,

> Some people come only for intellectual stimulation and would like to cut out prayer service. I wouldn't want prayer eliminated because it sets a mood. It's necessary for spiritual attainment.

Just as the congregation would prefer to avoid sponsoring social activities out of concern for intellectuality, so it would prefer to avoid erecting a building. Rabbi Aaron feels that a building would produce a host of new problems and that such problems would detract from the quest for greater intellectual and spiritual understanding. He feels that it is possible to have a loyal congregation without having an edifice. He and many others would prefer to continue using homes for the study groups, public facilities for the religious school, a community hall for services, and rooms in an office building for congregational head-quarters.* The small group which favors a building raised the issue at the annual meeting. One proponent said, "I would like to know where I'm going when I leave my house."

The congregation cannot grow much beyond its present size unless it has a building, and in order to meet its growing budget it must increase in size. It is already more similar to other congregations than it would care to admit. It has yet to confront the fact that the congregational form of organization imposes certain routines upon any institution. Further-more, it is unclear whether its intellectual approach is truly serious. For some it obviously is. Thus, a fourth-generation mother of three young children, who lacked contact with Jewish life in childhood and is a room mother at the Sunday School, defines her search in the following terms:

> I'm in the process of developing my religious views. I felt rather lost and don't want this to happen to my children. I want them to have a Jewish identity and feeling of belongingness. So I'm exploring and trying to find the right kind of religious affiliation in Judaism. I feel like a tree which needs roots, so then I can feel free to move about.

With others, we cannot be so sure. A relatively observant middle-aged woman who was an apathetic member of the Schechter Synagogue for a decade recently joined Hirsch and now attends services regularly. Her enthusiasm for her new affiliation is apparent, but we cannot be certain that her search for Jewish values will be a continuing enterprise:

> There's an intellectual approach at Hirsch that we like. I like their values. They are not materialistic. And they are searching for the truth.

While Hirsch's approach has a certain precedent in tradition, it has yet to confront Judaism's sacramental emphasis. And it is still not clear

---

* The Temple leadership are worried about school facilities. They hope that their members who serve on the local school board will be able to influence the authorities, should the present arrangements come under fire as a violation of the separation of church and state.

whether the congregation can offer its membership a pattern to live by. For the moment, this is not a problem as more families join and discover a congregation whose serious concern with intellectual search and apparent lack of dogmatism are "different" and attractive. Wives seem to be more drawn to the approach than their husbands. There is the example of the woman who participates actively in a writers' group and "can't stand PTA meetings. I can't bear large groups of women. I get frantic while they decide what kind of cookies to serve." She is full of admiration for what she found when the family joined the Temple:

> They're a young, vigorous group. They're trying to make a Reformed Judaism work.

But until the congregation's approach is tested by time, its emphasis on the searching intellect will exercise a strong attraction for those who are not dogmatically either Classical Reform or Neo-Reform and feel that the membership and program of the other congregations in the community cannot engage their sympathy and attention. In the interim, it will be difficult to control the contempt which the intellectually oriented members of Hirsch feel toward what they conceive of as the unenlightened members and the crass spiritual leaders of the other congregations. Even Rabbi Aaron has become worried about the chauvinism of his congregants and their denigration of outsiders:

> This month and next I am meeting more or less officially with each of the four other synagogues of the Heights. I have already been privileged to share celebrations and problems with their rabbis and their membership. My impression is that they are dedicated, each in its own way, to the same ideals that we cherish. I could not nor would I wish to defend every one of their projects, nor claim that I have not seen among them anything I should rather not see. But I believe that they are sincerely working for the cause I consider my own.
>
> Therefore I am troubled by the bitterness some of our people feel toward one or another of these congregations. . . . I am shocked by the excessive hostilities shown by many who know these synagogues better than I do, but cannot temper their scorn. I am pained by the venom with which rabbis and lay leaders among our people are sometimes discussed by people otherwise temperate and friendly.
>
> Our congregation will not be great because another one is vulgar. We are not nourished by another's illness, nor builded by another's failure. No man loves his family because it is better than someone else's, nor his wife because his neighbor's is a shrew. Almost the opposite is true. The happily married couple looks for happiness in other homes. The really

loyal American is not the violent enemy of any other nation, but its friend. The good man does not dwell on other's sins, but searches his own heart.

I pray that as we are more truly moved by our faith and its ethical imperatives, we may learn to find in our sister synagogues not enemies, but friends whose help we need and for whom we shall wish only good.

The Max Lilienthal Temple

HISTORY

The Max Lilienthal Temple is the newest congregation in Lakeville. It is composed almost entirely of young families who arrived in the community well after World War II. The oldest member of the Temple is a man in his sixties; he is considered the "grandfather" of the group. The Lilienthal Temple is unique in that it is the single Reform congregation in Lakeville which has not been an outgrowth of a congregation in Lake City. Only a small proportion of its members were actively involved with a synagogue before they became suburbanites.

Composed largely of families of East European descent, the Lilienthal Temple thinks of itself, and is thought of by the other congregations, as occupying the bottom of the economic ladder in the community. However, a number of members of the congregation come from prosperous families. They will eventually inherit all or part of the medium-sized family businesses in which they work and which are presently controlled by their fathers and uncles. But the most notable factor about the Lilienthal Temple is the brow level of even its more prosperous members: the level is modest by Lakeville standards. While many of the members of Lilienthal are college graduates, few are alumni of leading private universities. In the main, they are from junior colleges and municipal and state universities. Some graduated from evening colleges.

The group which organized the congregation felt that none of the existing institutions met their needs. The Solomon Schechter Synagogue was unappealing because it was Conservative. The Einhorn Temple was not acceptable because of its Classical Reform emphasis. While the Neo-Reformism of the Wise Temple was acceptable, the group felt ill at ease in such a big and rich congregation. Lacking an advanced brow level, a first-class education, a particular talent, or ample financial resources, it was clear that at Wise one would be only a name on an addressograph plate. And while the Hirsch Temple was small enough, the

intellectual aspirations of this group produced unease. A second-generation East European wife of a member of the Lilienthal board, who is also
a Sunday School teacher at the Temple, summarized the distinctive character of the membership:

> As a group, the people are nice. It's the sort of group that doesn't belong
> —doesn't quite fit into any other group.

Lilienthal is a marginal congregation; enrollment is less than two hundred families. While the Wise Temple claims that it is interested in helping the struggling institution, its assistance has not gone much beyond
donating a *Sefer Torah* and some surplus religious articles. Lilienthal has
remained a small congregation in spite of the fact that it has solicited
members more aggressively than any of the others. The Temple sub-
scribes to a "welcomer" service set up to provide merchants in the
community with lists of new residents. Representatives of the institution
call on recent arrivals. The Temple also sponsors attractions for prospective members, such as barbecues and "meet-the-rabbi" gatherings.

Since the Lilienthal program consists of the same basic ingredients as
the other institutions, its limited appeal would appear to be due to the
modest status level occupied by its membership. Not only has it experienced difficulty in interesting new residents but it has made little head-
way among members of existing congregations. While some members of
the Wise Temple complain about the size and impersonality of their
congregation, few have been attracted to a group characterized by high
intimacy. And although some members of Hirsch Temple, as we have
seen, complain about the intellectuality and the lack of social activities
of their congregation, they also have not been attracted to a temple which
stresses the warm heart rather than the cool mind and is convinced that
life is with people.

At one point, the Lilienthal group became discouraged by the lack of
growth and the resulting financial problems. They decided to explore the
possibility of amalgamating with another congregation. The only possible
choice was Hirsch: it was a rather small congregation and was not committed to Classical Reform. After several discussions had been held and
a joint religious service conducted, the Hirsch group broke off the
negotiations. Rabbi Aaron, who says that he was in favor of the merger,
states that the Lilienthal group pleaded for the amalgamation and were
even agreeable to giving up their identity instead of merging on a *quid
pro quo* basis. He feels that one of the reasons that the Hirsch people
resisted the proposal was their feeling that the Lilienthal group were their

social inferiors. The distance between them is apparent in the description given by a woman prominent at the Lilienthal Temple who described what occurred when the joint service was held:

> I felt that the Hirsch people were very reserved; they did not try to be the least bit friendly. After the service, I offered to help with the refreshments, and I was given a curt reply to the effect that my help was not needed. Also, someone from Hirsch passed a remark that: "We just don't seem to know the same people."

After this fiasco, the Lilienthal group decided to persevere. The feeling of its nucleus of highly devoted members is that if the congregation can sustain itself for several more years it will become a successful institution.

THE RABBI AND THE CONGREGATIONAL PROGRAM

Lilienthal's largest single asset is that it has a rabbi: Joshua Cohen. His presence gives the institution a certain equivalence with the other congregations. Rabbi Cohen is a friendly person who is quite uninhibited in his manner. He comes from an Orthodox background and was trained at a yeshivah before he entered Hebrew Union College, the Reform seminary. The rabbi, who has served the congregation for only a short period, feels that the group has possibilities. He was touched by the warmth of his reception:

> This congregation is different from most others. In fact, the members come close to observing the Christian tradition of rendering personal service. For example, part of my house was painted by some of the men in the congregation. Our youth group worked on the grounds. When we arrived here, people came to the airport to meet us; they had a meal waiting for us at the house. People stopped in during the first few days and left food.

Like Einhorn and Hirsch, the Lilienthal Temple rents the auditorium of a public-school building for its weekly service. This is held on Friday evening; no service is held on Saturday morning. The Union Prayer Book is used without alteration. The order of service most closely approaches the Neo-Reformism of Wise, but since attendance averages fifty persons, the atmosphere is considerably more intimate. The spirit of intimacy and camaraderie is even more intense during the long social hour that follows the service. Almost everyone stays for this pleasant period and the refreshments which accompany it. According to an observer:

> The service takes place in the auditorium of one of the schools—a large room which does not lend itself easily to holding a service. Everything is

very much improvised. One comes in through the regular school hall, placing wraps in a coat rack in one of the corridors. The ushers at the door hand the worshiper a prayer book. The service is conducted by the rabbi from the stage. There is a professional cantor. A piano accompanies the singing.

The service seems very traditional for a Reform service. Rabbi Cohen did not wear the usual type of stole-*tallit* worn by many other American Reform rabbis, but rather used a regular *tallit*. He read a considerable number of the prayers in the Union Prayer Book in Hebrew and also read a sizable amount of the portion of the week in Hebrew. His Hebrew was exceedingly fluent.

There was a good deal of social interaction among the worshipers after the service. Most of them obviously knew the others and seemed happy to see one another. A man was celebrating a birthday, and a special cake had been baked in his honor: I have never seen this in any other congregation in Lakeville. The event was a kind of personal *simchah* being celebrated in an extended family setting. The refreshments served at the social hour were the most "Jewish" refreshments that I have tasted at any temple in Lakeville. There was a good deal of sponge cake and marble cake, and the pastries were two or three times the size of those served at the Hirsch Temple. The refreshments were abundant, and everybody seemed to enjoy partaking of them.

The Temple rents space in a public-school building on Sunday morning for its religious school. In spite of the modest size of the membership, the school is crowded: the great majority of the families are young and have at least one child enrolled there. All the teachers are members of the congregation, serving without pay. However, there is no emphasis, as at the Einhorn Temple, on ideological conformity. Rather, the teaching staff is drawn from the Temple membership because of economic reasons: the school budget can sustain only a single paid official, a principal. Most of the teachers are women, of whom many taught in the public-school system before resigning because of their family responsibilities. The level of Jewish knowledge of the teaching staff varies considerably. Utilizing volunteers, the Temple has not been able to insist on rigid qualifications. In addition to the Sunday School, a midweek Hebrew class is available. The curriculum culminates in Bar Mitzvah, which is performed on Friday evening, since there is no Saturday morning service.

In contrast to the Hirsch Temple, which makes much of its adult education program, the Lilienthal Temple places little emphasis on this activity. Rabbi Cohen recently organized a study group and agreed to their choice of the Bible as the subject matter. He expressed his reservations, however:

> This interest in the Bible is Protestant; its motivations are not Jewish. Jews have not been interested in the Bible *per se*, but only in the Bible through later legal documents. I've told the group that we Jews don't just read the Bible; we read it in connection with Talmud. These groups do become sort of Protestant with their stress on the Bible.

A good deal of importance is given to synagogue affiliates. The Temple sponsors a Sisterhood and a Men's Club, both of which are fairly active organizations. The bowling league sponsored by the Men's Club is particularly successful. With over one hundred men enrolled, the group is more than half as large as the congregation itself. In addition to other objectives, the affiliates seek to raise funds for the congregation. The Temple also sponsors a club for teen-agers.

In spite of fiscal problems, the leadership of the institution is actively engaged in making plans for a building. There is no resistance to the plan on the grounds which have prevented the two other congregations from erecting synagogue buildings. Most of the members feel that a congregation should have its own home; whatever hesitancy exists centers on fears about fiscal costs. The feeling of the leadership is that a building is necessary not only for the present congregation but in order to attract new members. The officers do not feel that the Temple can afford to erect its own structure. Rather, they are seeking to locate a large old residence which can be renovated. They have not yet raised a fund which would serve as a down payment, but they feel that as soon as a suitable structure is located the membership will rise to the occasion.

They may well succeed at their objective. While some upwardly mobile individuals may leave the congregation others may join, and in any case interpersonal relationships among the members are strong. In fact, interpersonal relations—a sociable climate and congenial personal attributes of members—emerge as a leading source of gratification at Lilienthal in response to our question about satisfaction with temple affiliation. Typical of the feeling of the membership is that of a newcomer to Lakeville who works for a produce firm and is active on the Temple's board. He has a college education, earns an income of less than $10,000 per year, and is very satisfied with his affiliation:

> We were looking for a group as a point of identification. I like the people at Lilienthal as a whole. They're young, dynamic, in the same socioeconomic strata.

The Effort to Establish an Orthodox Synagogue

While Lakeville lacks a congregation representing one of the three branches of American Judaism, an attempt was made to establish an Orthodox institution in the community. This abortive effort is the single instance in Lakeville where an attempt to develop a congregation resulted in failure. The lack of appeal of Orthodoxy, in contrast to the success of Reform and Conservatism, is another bit of evidence concerning the religious temper of the Lakeville Jew.

Unlike other congregations in the community, the entire initiative for establishing an Orthodox synagogue came from a single individual. Isaac Katz, an accountant and investor in Lake City, moved into Lakeville after World War II. Katz had long been active in Jewish life, especially in Orthodox circles. His rapid rise was related to the scarcity of youthful, prosperous, and relatively acculturated individuals who retained an Orthodox viewpoint.

In Lake City, Katz had served as the president of an Orthodox congregation and as a board member of various Orthodox educational and charitable institutions. He had also served as president of the federation of Orthodox congregations of Lake City. By the time he reached his middle years, he had held most of the leadership positions available in the Orthodox community. Katz did not, however, attempt to shift from the local scene to the national scene. Nor did he seek to establish himself as a leader of the overall Jewish community of Lake City. Rather, he took on the self-appointed task of establishing Lakeville's first Orthodox congregation.

Katz explained his interest on the basis that Orthodoxy would not long survive if it did not follow the movement of the Jewish population and locate in areas where influential Jews were settling. However, when he decided to build a home on a piece of property he owned in Lakeville (he had hesitated to build on the site for some years, but on the other hand had resisted selling the land), it is doubtful that his decision was dictated solely by a desire to extend the influence of Orthodoxy. He had made no thoroughgoing assessment of the most strategic place in the metropolitan area to locate a new Orthodox synagogue. Rather, it appears that it was his personal interest in making his residence in the statusful suburb of Lakeville, rather than an objective assessment of the possibilities for opening a new Orthodox institution, which prompted his decision to build a home in the community.

One of the significant aspects of Katz's decision is that his Orthodoxy did not prevent him from coming to Lakeville. The fact is that the type of Orthodoxy which he followed did not alienate him from the life styles practiced by his non-Orthodox fellow accountants and by the businessmen whom they served. While Katz was quite observant of the *mitzvot,* in other respects his attitudes and behavior did not deviate radically from those of his peers. Lakeville became irresistible to him, despite the fact that its country clubs served food he would not eat, its residents espoused religious principles he would not accept, and its system of Jewish education did not include the type of facilities he required for his children.

Katz was clear in his own mind that moving to Lakeville constituted no disloyalty to Orthodoxy. He defended his decision by insisting that although he would find it more comfortable to live elsewhere, he deemed it his duty to settle in Lakeville and thereby bring Orthodoxy to a community from which it had been absent. He constantly reiterated that because of the prominence and prosperity of its residents, Lakeville was vitally important to the future of his movement.

Katz built himself a very commodious house. Well equipped for entertaining, his residence stood out among the more modest houses that surrounded it; his home was located in one of the newer areas of the community where middle-priced dwellings were being built. Beyond meeting only the needs of his own family, the house was designed with an eye toward using it as a hub from which Orthodox influence would radiate. When this happened, Katz was sure that his friends in Lake City would understand the wisdom of his removal to Lakeville.

Katz saw his synagogue as starting in the traditional way: individuals who lived in the neighborhood would come together for prayer, form themselves into a *minyan,* and eventually incorporate and erect a synagogue building. Reasoning that the High Holidays would provide the strongest impetus for the formation of a *minyan,* he resolved to hold services in his home on Rosh Hashanah and Yom Kippur. He engaged a rabbi from Lake City, secured *Sifrei Torah,* and purchased a supply of other religious articles.* He proceeded to canvass his neighbors in addition to running an advertisement in a local newspaper. He got in touch with a number of wealthy local residents who had served with him on the boards of Orthodox institutions in Lake City or had made substantial contributions to such institutions. He also contacted a number of Lakeville residents who were the scions of prominent Lake City

---

* *Sifrei Torah,* plural of *Sefer Torah.* See p. 139.

Orthodox families. He made it clear to everyone that attendance at the High Holiday services did not involve any long-range commitment or financial obligation.

A total of about twenty-five couples came to the services. The traditional *Machzor* * was used. However, fully Orthodox procedures were not implemented: although men and women were separated, no partition was erected. Katz had hoped that at the conclusion of the holiday the group would spontaneously suggest that they continue to stay together and hold services each Saturday morning. When this did not occur, Katz sought to keep the group together by different means. He turned from prayer to the other major activity which traditionally takes place on synagogue premises: religious study. He proceeded to form a study circle and invited a rabbi to come out to Lakeville at regular intervals to lead the group. Determined to make the study circle as attractive as possible, he avoided choosing a traditional legal text as the basis for the sessions. Instead, he selected the most non-halachic portion of the Mishnah: *Pirke Avot.*†

By the time spring arrived, only five or six people were coming to the study group on a regular basis. Katz was deeply troubled by the indifference. He discovered that local residents who could be counted on to support Orthodox institutions in Lake City were uninterested in forming an Orthodox synagogue in Lakeville. He also found that the scions of prominent Orthodox families were not only uninterested in his project but in some cases actually hostile: they wished to integrate into the regnant patterns of Jewishness in Lakeville, rather than to follow in the footsteps of their parents. Most of the supporters of Orthodox institutions as well as the offspring of prominent Orthodox families belonged to the Solomon Schechter Synagogue and were satisfied with their affiliation. In respect to his neighbors, Katz found that they were not partisans of the cause he espoused: many of those who had attended the High Holiday services or a meeting or two of the study group came more out of curiosity than conviction. They could not see themselves as founders of an Orthodox synagogue. The more traditional and the prosperous among them leaned toward the Solomon Schechter Synagogue, while others thought they might join the Max Lilienthal Temple.

Katz persisted in spite of the fact that he could not discover a real

---

* *Machzor:* the prayer book used on the High Holidays.
† *Pirke Avot,* often translated as *The Sayings of the Fathers,* is traditionally studied during the late spring and summer. There is, of course, no bar to utilizing it during the fall and winter.

public to which he might appeal. Again he resolved to sponsor High Holiday services. In the hope of achieving better results, he decided to vary his formula and rented a hall for the services. According to traditional norms, a residence was a perfectly appropriate place for religious services, but Katz felt that individuals might be more interested in attending if the services were held in a public place. Believing that his publicity of the previous year had been inadequate, he stepped up his advertising campaign. His ads described the services as "traditional." He said, "I was afraid that if I said 'Orthodox,' people would tie it up with a dirty place, men with long beards, and Yiddish."

In spite of the time and money lavished on the services, they were more poorly attended the second year than the first. This time no one came out of curiosity; the community had been informed via the grapevine as to what Katz was about. Attendance was so poor that at times the services were in danger of being suspended because of the lack of a *minyan;* several times the call had to go out for additional worshipers.

When Katz attempted to continue the study group after the High Holidays, he found that the results were no better than before. He decided to persist, however, and reasoned that if individuals were not interested in prayer or study they might be attracted by social events. Katz noted that the desire to meet congenial people had attracted individuals to other congregations, and he reasoned that this might be the impetus needed to establish an Orthodox synagogue. Thus he arranged a series of cocktail parties and barbecues at his home. But his food and liquor failed to attract. In Lake City, an invitation to the Katz home was not to be despised: he was a prosperous Orthodox Jew, a professional man rather than a businessman, acculturated even if European-born. In Lakeville, however, his prosperity was less important; there were many who exceeded him in wealth. His professional status meant little; others were in higher-status professions and had received their education at universities more eminent than the school from which he had graduated. But most important of all, the social skills which had sufficed in Lake City were inadequate in Lakeville; Katz could not compete with his fellow suburbanites. He lacked sophistication and grace; he was not an expert raconteur; he was not widely traveled. He was not even an unpolished diamond whose very robustness would attract a following. Except for his affinity for Orthodoxy, he was unexceptional.

After the failure of the cocktail parties and barbecues, Katz made one further attempt to hold High Holiday services. When this also failed, he conceded that his dream of establishing an Orthodox synagogue in Lakeville was doomed. Should he leave the community or should he remain and become a member of the Solomon Schechter Synagogue? He felt that since he had tried so hard, he could adopt the latter alternative with a clear conscience. He would seek to influence the Solomon Schechter Synagogue to adopt more traditional ways. However, rather than requesting a membership application, he sought a personal invitation to join from the leadership of the institution, for he reasoned that he was not an average citizen.

No such invitation was forthcoming. The leadership of the Schechter Synagogue resented Katz's desire to establish an Orthodox institution; they interpreted his efforts as a move which would bring dissension into Lakeville by splitting the ranks of the traditionally minded. Not requiring Katz's financial assistance and suspicious of encouraging an opinionated individual who might bring discord into their ranks, they turned a deaf ear to his hints that he would join if solicited.

The lack of response from the Conservative group, the complaints of his children, the dissatisfaction of his wife, who did not feel welcome in the community, and the continuing requests from Orthodox institutions soliciting his support finally convinced Katz that it might be best to move. With great reluctance, he placed his house on the market. A buyer would not be easy to find: a family willing to pay his price would need a home geared to entertaining large numbers and would have to overlook the fact that the house was not located in one of the more desirable neighborhoods of Lakeville.

The Membership of the Five Synagogues: Similarities and Differences

We see in Lakeville an end to the simple correlation between class position, level of acculturation, and degree of religious traditionalism which prevailed at the turn of the century in the central city. At that time, the Jewish religious community was bifurcated into the affluent and acculturated Reform temple and the poor, immigrant, Orthodox synagogue whose constituency was drawn from families coming from the same European town, province, or country. Acculturation and prosperity in all segments of the Jewish community, the pervasive impact of secularization, and the shift of the Reform movement from Classical

Reform toward a moderately traditional orientation have transformed this correlation, at least in Lakeville, into a more complex and ambiguous relationship. As a consequence, Lakeville has not one but four Reform temples, which differ in many social and religious characteristics. Nor are the members of the single Conservative synagogue clearly the least affluent or unacculturated or consistently the most observant in religious behavior, despite their synagogue's formal identity as the most traditionalistic institution in Lakeville.

In each of the five synagogues, there is variation in religious observance and attitudes, in intergroup orientation, and in such social characteristics as age, descent, generation, and income. Yet in spite of considerable overlapping, each synagogue is distinctive in one or more characteristics. The distinctions that emerge may seem marginal to an outsider, but they are often crucial to those who already belong and to those who are considering joining. Having alluded to some of these distinctions in a qualitative way when analyzing the history and program of each of the synagogues, we may now do so in quantitative terms.

THE WISE MEMBERSHIP AND THE SCHECHTER MEMBERSHIP

The members of the two largest synagogues in Lakeville—the Isaac Mayer Wise Temple and the Solomon Schechter Synagogue—differ noticeably in religious ideology and practice and to some extent in social characteristics as well. Almost all members of Schechter view themselves as "Conservative," while almost all those affiliated with Wise think of themselves as "Reform." While 54 per cent of Schechter members base themselves on a sacramentalist conception of religiosity, only 34 per cent of Wise members follow this approach (see Table 4–1).* Furthermore, Schechter members exceed Wise members in home observance by a wide margin (5.4 versus 2.8 mean observances), although by a narrower margin in synagogue attendance (5.4 versus 4.2 mean score). Schechter members are considerably more interested in Jewish culture than Wise members.

These divergencies are paralleled by differences in intergroup orientation. Schechter members are less integration-minded [15] than Wise members, and they devote less time to non-sectarian groups and activities. In both of these aspects of intergroup orientation, Schechter members are

---

* Most of the statistics cited in the following pages are to be found in Table 4–1.

at one end of the spectrum, while Wise members approach the average for the community.

In respect to income, the Wise Temple has a substantial share of the wealthier families of Lakeville; the gap in income between Wise members and Schechter members is quite noticeable ($24,620 versus $17,620). Accordingly, more of Wise than Schechter members live in the highest-status residential areas, while about half of the membership of both temples reside in medium-status areas.[16] In educational level, however, the profile of the two congregations is very similar: about half of the membership of each have completed college. Furthermore, differences in life cycle are not overly striking, for both institutions have a wide representation of younger and older families. Wise, however, has more families in the later phase of the cycle, reflecting in part the fact that it was the first synagogue in Lakeville. In both institutions, second-generation East Europeans comprise the largest group, but the early history of the Wise Temple is reflected by the fact that there are third- and fourth-generation Germans who belong to the institution. Whatever the descent group, the proportion of Schechter members who are fourth-generation Jews is minuscule.

THE SMALLER REFORM TEMPLES

Members of the three smaller Reform temples overwhelmingly identify themselves as "Reform," just as do the members of the Wise Temple. That this label has some significance is made apparent by the fact that the Conservative membership of Schechter exceeds that of any of the Reform congregations in the emphasis placed on sacramentalism as the criterion of religiosity. However, members of the Lilienthal Temple equal Schechter members in frequency of attendance at religious services (5.3 versus 5.4 mean score) as well as in their interest in Jewish culture. While Lilienthal members do not match Schechter members in home observance, they are by far the most observant among the Reform group. The membership of this Temple is distinguished by its resemblance to the Conservative group. Thus Lilienthal members have a higher level of home observance and synagogue attendance than Wise members and exceed them in interest in Jewish culture. Their "right-wing" Reform Judaism has the effect of placing the membership of the Wise Temple in a middle-of-the-road position.

Lilienthal members also devote less time to non-sectarian groups and activities than Wise members and are less integration-minded. The con-

TABLE 4–1. SELECTED RELIGIOUS AND SOCIAL CHARACTERISTICS OF SYNAGOGUE MEMBERS

Religious Attitudes and Practices	Solomon Schechter Synagogue	Isaac Mayer Wise Temple	Max Lilien- thal Temple	Samuel Hirsch Temple	David Einhorn Temple
In evaluating own religiosity, per cent feel adequate in					
Sacramentalism	54	34	35	22	15
Moralism	24	31	43	39	36
Religious feeling	22	19	13	9	23
Belief in God	13	14	30	35	21
Home observances (mean)	5.4	2.8	3.9	2.7	1.2
Per cent nonobservant	3	13	—	4	31
Synagogue attendance (mean)	5.4	4.2	5.3	4.3	4.0
Per cent never attend Sabbath services	17	24	4	13	31
Per cent have a great or moderate interest in Jewish culture	60	37	57	48	23
Intergroup Orientation					
Per cent high integration-mindedness score (6+)	9	40	21	56	78
Per cent spend half or more time in nonsectarian groups and activities	28	42	31	94	54

Life-Cycle Phase—Per Cent

Pre-school or early-school	25	17	65	44	12
Peak-school	54	46	35	39	82
Late-school or post-school	21	37	—	17	6

Descent and Generation—Per Cent

German, 3rd and 4th generation	—	15	4	9	41
Mixed descent, 3rd and 4th generation	4	8	8	13	23
East European, 2nd generation	47	40	26	26	5
East European, 3rd generation	21	15	35	22	13
Any descent, 4th generation	1	11	17	39	51

Socio-Economic Status

Family income—per cent

Under $15,000	37	21	77	32	18
$15,000–$29,999	44	42	14	45	36
$30,000 or more	19	37	9	23	46
Median	$17,620	$24,620	$11,667	$18,334	$27,840

Residential Status—per cent in

High-status areas	23	41	13	32	55
Medium-status areas	49	46	13	45	39
Low-status areas	28	13	74	23	6
Per cent "upper" or "upper-middle" class identification	50	64	22	66	83
Per cent completed college	53	51	61	70	49
N	(78)	(108)	(23)	(23)	(39)

trast between Lilienthal members and those of Lakeville's largest and most prominent Reform congregation are heightened when social characteristics are considered. Lilienthal has a higher percentage of younger parents than Wise (it is, in fact, the most youthful of all the congregations). While second-generation East Europeans are the predominant group at Wise, at Lilienthal the third-generation East European group outnumbers the second. The contrasts between the two congregations in income and social status are very wide. With a median income of only $11,667, Lilienthal families are the least affluent group in the community. Lilienthal has a very high concentration of members (74 per cent) residing in the lowest-status residential areas. Furthermore, only 22 per cent of those affiliated with the congregation consider themselves upper or upper-middle class. Many social characteristics of the membership of this institution will change as the group grows older, but what is particularly apparent at present is that these social characteristics are in decided contrast to their educational attainment, for some 61 per cent of Lilienthal membership are college graduates. (Their favorable educational position is, of course, partly traceable to the fact that they are so young.) But in spite of their high educational status, it is extremely doubtful that the gap at Lilienthal between education and income, or education and social status, will be entirely closed in the years ahead.

Turning to another of the smaller Reform congregations, we notice that the members of the Hirsch Temple are similar to Wise members in home observance and synagogue attendance and have only slightly greater interest in Jewish culture. Their conception of religiosity is different, however: fewer base themselves on sacramentalism. This congregation exceeds all others in the percentage who feel that belief in God is central to the concept of religiosity. The distinctive approach of Hirsch is additionally apparent when we consider their intergroup orientation. They are more integration-minded than are members of the Wise Temple, but their sharpest deviation from that congregation is the overwhelming proportion of the membership (94 per cent) who devote more time to nonsectarian activities than to Jewish activities.

Hirsch members are predominantly third- and fourth-generation, and their origins are not limited to a single descent group. They are typically in the early and middle phases of the family cycle. While they are less affluent than the members of the Wise Temple ($18,334 versus $24,620 average income), a full 32 per cent live in high-status areas, and only 23 per cent live in low-status areas. Whatever their degree of economic inferiority in comparison with Wise, they have a clear superiority in educational attainment: 70 per cent have completed college or beyond.* Together with other social characteristics, such attainment undoubtedly explains why a full 66 per cent consider themselves members of the upper or upper-middle class, a figure which slightly exceeds the proportion at the more prosperous Wise Temple.

Turning to the Einhorn Temple, we notice that the predominant attitude of their membership is consistent with the position of Classical Reform: fewer here value sacramentalism than in any of the other congregations. In addition, behavior conforms with attitude: the Einhorn Temple ranks lowest in home observance. In fact, a full 31 per cent of the Einhorn members observe no rituals. However, while the Temple's level of synagogue attendance is also lowest, it is not much lower than that of Wise members.

Einhorn members are apparently consistent with the position of their Temple's leadership in another aspect: the unacceptability of ethnic and other non-religious expressions of Jewishness. A full 78 per cent score high on the integration scale, and they are by far the most integration-minded of all the congregations. Interestingly enough, however, their behavior does not match their convictions; only 54 per cent spend half or more of their time in non-sectarian activities. This is in contrast to the situation at the Hirsch Temple, where the membership is less non-sectarian in attitude, but more non-sectarian in behavior.

The Einhorn Temple has the largest group of third- and fourth-generation German Jews: 41 per cent versus 15 per cent at the Wise Temple. Another 23 per cent are members of third and fourth generations of mixed descent—larger than at any other temple. There are very few second-generation East Europeans at Einhorn, although a noticeable but still quite small group of third-generation families of this descent group belong to the institution. The Einhorn Temple is further distinguished by the fact that it is the only synagogue in Lakeville where a majority of the membership is fourth-generation. In sum, advanced generation and German descent give the Einhorn Temple the appearance of a semi-exclusivist religious institution.

The distinctiveness of the Einhorn group is also apparent in respect to income. The membership has the highest income of all the congregations ($27,840 versus $24,620 for Wise), and age differences foreshadow continued and perhaps even greater fiscal superiority in the years to come. While there are few very young families at Einhorn, in only 6 per cent

* It will be recalled that many Hirsch members attended the "better" colleges.

of the families are all the children over 14. Present income will be increased as its membership ages. Present superiority and potentially greater affluence combine with other factors such as generation and are reflected in a variety of ways. Einhorn has the largest percentage of members who reside in high-status areas (55 per cent versus 41 per cent for Wise) and the largest proportion who see themselves as upper or upper-middle class (83 per cent versus 64 per cent for Wise). All of this occurs in spite of the fact that Einhorn has the lowest level of educational attainment in the community: only 49 per cent of its members have completed college.

Since all but one of the synagogues in Lakeville are Reform, the predictions of those who have suggested that division in American-Jewish religious life is being reduced and that a common "American Synagogue" is emerging would seem to be borne out. And yet beneath the label of "Reform" we have noticed considerable diversity. Some of this diversity is based on differences in religious outlook, some in social and economic stratification, some in intergroup attitudes and behavior, and some in the newer area of cultural taste and style of life. While some of these differences are strongly interrelated, it is difficult in the compass of our study to trace what is cause and what is effect.

As we have seen, once a Jew in Lakeville decides to affiliate with a synagogue, a variety of institutions is available to him. So great is this variety that it often facilitates the initial decision to affiliate. Whatever the five synagogues serving Lakeville have in common (and they actually have a great deal in common), diverse religious and social characteristics do distinguish their memberships. This diversity allows the prospective member to discover a synagogue suited to his personal predilections and situation. Diversity thus permits the incorporation of the largest possible number of families into the community's religious structure. Prospective members who might overwise reject a standard pattern of worship or find uncongenial a given group of synagogue members may be attracted to alternative settings and become enthusiastic adherents, or at least marginal members. However, while diversity maximizes the possibility of incorporating individuals into the religious life of the community, it also means that the individual need not undergo a transformation of values when he joins a synagogue. Since the individual will encounter so many others who are like-minded in the synagogue of his choice, once he integrates himself into the congregation he will not necessarily be forced into a confrontation with the radical demands of his faith.

5

THE SYNAGOGUES OF LAKEVILLE: AFFILIATION AND INVOLVEMENT

The synagogue has always occupied a central position in the Jewish community. But in contrast to the German or East European villages from which our respondents' ancestors came, in Lakeville the synagogue emerges more as a private than a public facility. While in theory the synagogue is open to all, in actual fact for the individual to relate himself meaningfully to a synagogue he must "affiliate"; a Lakeville Jew becomes part of a synagogue only as a conscious act. While the Jew's ethnic-religious identity is recognized as entitling him to synagogue membership, it does not in and of itself make him a member. Rather, acts such as submitting a membership application, remitting dues, and in some cases paying a building assessment change one's status from "unaffiliated" to "affiliated." The individual is now entitled to the privileges of membership.

The synagogue in America has taken on the character of a voluntary association. It vies with other associations, both inside and outside the Jewish community, for affiliation and involvement. The associational nature of the modern synagogue has become even more apparent as "denominational" lines have developed. And as we have seen, synagogues of the same "denomination" in Lakeville compete with one another for support. In any case, each synagogue is the equal of all others; each one constitutes a corporate body controlled by its own members, rather than by any local, regional, or national body.

The voluntaristic character of American-Jewish religious life and the independence of individual religious institutions has not inhibited the synagogue's development into a leading suburban Jewish institution; if anything, it has enhanced such development. However, while the synagogue has continued to function as the repository of sacred values, it has done so with a significant shift of emphasis. Of the three traditional functions historically associated with the synagogue—house of prayer, house of study, and house of assembly—prayer was a staple of the traditional synagogue program. Private prayer was assumed in the German or East European village, but corporate prayer was highly important: according to Jewish norms, it was preferable to private prayer on many occasions, and on others it was mandatory. The Jew existed to render honor to God in prayer; the synagogue was the Jew's second home, and there he repaired for corporate worship. Connected with prayer was religious study, which in theory was carried on in the home on an individual basis but in any case took place on both an individual and a group basis in the synagogue.

Responsibility for the religious education of the young was shared by the home and the community; it did not take place on synagogue premises. However, in the American environment, and particularly in the contemporary suburb, the education of the child has become a preeminent function of the synagogue. The transmission of the community's sacred values to the young and their development of a sense of Jewish identity are increasingly viewed as a responsibility of the synagogue and have become major spurs for affiliation.

Involvement in a Lakeville synagogue may be expressed in any or all of three ways, each sanctioned by tradition: worship, participation in adult religious study, or social interaction with peers. Unlike the traditional synagogue, however, in Lakeville such interaction does not flow naturally out of, or have its origin in, worship and study activities. Rather, interaction (or to use the term more current in the community, "involvement") originates in activities that are more frankly social and recreational in nature.

In this chapter we shall trace the relationship between life cycle and synagogue affiliation and focus on how the act of affiliation is motivated by the desire of parents to socialize their children into a Jewish identity. We shall also analyze the involvement of Lakeville Jews in synagogue activities, relating such involvement to worship and study as well as other aspects of religiosity.

Affiliation and the Life Cycle

Although nearly all Jews in Lakeville affiliate with a synagogue at some point in their lives, most wait until their children reach school age. Only a small minority join in the early phase of the family's life cycle: a mere 19 per cent of families in which all the children are under school age belong to a synagogue (see Table 5–1). The affiliation rate triples to 56 per cent in the early-school phase and spurts to 87 per cent when there is a child in the peak years of religious education.

The steep rise in membership which takes place during the first three phases of the family's life cycle occurs in all descent and generation groups. However, at the peak-school phase somewhat more families of

T A B L E   5 – 1 . SYNAGOGUE AFFILIATION BY FAMILY LIFE CYCLE, GENERATION, AND DESCENT

	Life-Cycle Phase		
Per cent members among	Pre-School	Early-School	Peak-School
All families	19	56	87
N	(68)	(103)	(162)
Third and fourth-plus generation of German descent	*	62	78
N	(*)	(13)	(23)
Third and fourth-plus generation of mixed descent	27	46	80
N	(11)	(13)	(15)
Second generation of East European descent	25	54	89
N	(16)	(35)	(54)
Third generation of East European descent	19	58	96
N	(26)	(24)	(27)

* Too few cases.

East European origin are synagogue members than are those of German or mixed descent: about four in five of the latter belong, compared to about nine in ten of the former. The third-generation East European group has the highest proportion of affiliated families and experiences the steepest spurt: affiliation reaches 96 per cent from a low of 19 per cent, or a fivefold increase.

THE PRE-SCHOOL PHASE: DELAY

The low rate of affiliation in the pre-school phase of the life cycle does not stem from financial problems or from an unfamiliarity with the community. The more affluent families remain unaffiliated just as frequently as the less affluent; those who have lived in the community three years or more affiliate no more frequently than those who have resided in Lakeville one or two years (see Table 5–2). In the pre-school phase of the life cycle, affiliation is noticeable only among observant families: about half of the more observant families are affiliated, compared to only one in twenty of the minimally and nonobservant families.

TABLE 5–2. Families in Pre-school Phase: Synagogue Affiliation by Level of Home Observance, by Family Income, and by Length of Residence in Lakeville

Per Cent Members among Families					
Who practice		N			
No observances	5	(20)			
1–2 observances	4	(25)			
3–4 observances	50	(10)			
5+ observances	46	(13)			
With income		N	Who lived in community		N
Less than $10,000	20	(15)	1–2 years	19	(32)
$10,000–$14,999	18	(28)	3–4 years	17	(23)
$15,000+	21	(24)	5+ years	23	(13)

Nevertheless, nearly all non-members are potential joiners and indicate an intention to affiliate. Even those few who raise objections to organized religion leave the door open. The chief reason given for delay is that the children are not yet ready for religious education. A third-generation father of East European descent who has two girls aged 2 and 4 and is in comfortable financial circumstances admits that "I haven't been pushed into joining yet by my children; they're not old enough." "My child is so young I haven't even thought about it, but we do plan on joining," says a third-generation woman who has taught Sunday School and is the parent of a two-year-old boy. Some indicate specific plans regarding when they will join as well as the institution they have selected. A mother of a four-year-old, who is already an active clubwoman although she has lived in Lakeville less than two years, states that the family "expects to join in the next three or four years definitely." Another mother whose oldest child is 5 and who observes no rituals in the home "intends to join next year when Johnny will go to Sunday School." "Chances are we'll join Schechter," says a minimally observant mother of two pre-schoolers, who is already active in the institution's affiliated groups but is waiting for her eldest to reach Sunday School age. An unobservant second-generation physician of East European descent knows only that "we will probably join a Reformed temple" when his four-year-old reaches school age.

Some non-members in the pre-school phase complain about the high cost of affiliation, but only because they do not expect to receive full value from their membership until their children are ready to use the congregation's educational facilities. An active clubwoman whose child is a year and a half old explains, "It costs $100 a year. For two services it's not worth it. When our child is old enough we may join." A father whose first-born is a three-year-old, whose income is over $15,000, and who is considering joining a temple which has a higher membership fee states flatly, "$175 is too high."

Although most families in the pre-school phase postpone their synagogue affiliation until the start of the child's religious schooling, it is already an issue of which they are aware. Affiliation is their leading religious question. It is experienced more frequently than problems of ritualism; the subject of synagogue affiliation concerns a total of 55 per cent of non-members who have been troubled by a question of a religious nature.[1] "Joining a temple and which one—the pros and cons. That's the biggest question," remarks a young wife of an affluent broker with an eighteen-month-old child in response to our query about religious problems. "Should we join a synagogue—and which?" is the major religious problem of a mother who has not attended religious services in recent years but who believes that "it's important for the children." In highly atypical families, the issue erupts into family controversy. A mother of two pre-schoolers, a self-described atheist whose in-laws belong to the Schechter Synagogue, reports on an "argument with my mother-in-law about joining a temple." She quickly adds her own opinion: "I think it's so hypocritical when people who aren't interested themselves send their children to Sunday School."

THE EARLY-SCHOOL PHASE:
A SENSE OF URGENCY

The surge in synagogue membership during the early-school phase affects a wide range of families, especially the least observant. As a consequence, the gap in affiliation in the pre-school phase between the more observant and less observant families narrows somewhat. While almost none of the minimally or nonobservant families join in the pre-school phase, nearly one-half of such families affiliate in the early-school phase. Three-fourths of the most observant families are now members, compared to about one-half in the previous phase. Joining bears no relationship to the value attached to the act: those who believe that a synagogue affiliation is irrelevant to being a "good Jew" are almost as likely to join as those who believe it desirable or essential (see Table 5–3).

Since synagogue membership, although urgent, is not quite so pressing

TABLE 5–3. FAMILIES IN EARLY-SCHOOL PHASE: SYNAGOGUE AFFILIATION BY LEVEL OF HOME OBSERVANCE, BY VALUE OF SYNAGOGUE-BELONGING, BY FAMILY INCOME, AND BY LENGTH OF RESIDENCE IN LAKEVILLE

Per Cent Members among Families					
Who practice		N	Who believe that to be a "good Jew" belonging to synagogue		N
No observances	45	(11)	Is essential	59	(22)
1–2 observances	48	(42)	Is desirable	57	(56)
3–4 observances	58	(26)	Makes no difference	52	(25)
5+ observances	75	(24)			
With income		N	Who lived in community		N
Less than $10,000	44	(16)	1–2 years	38	(39)
$10,000–$19,999	55	(53)	3–4 years	64	(33)
$20,000+	63	(33)	5+ years	71	(31)

as in later phases of the life cycle, and since religious observance is no longer as potent a factor in determining affiliation, social characteristics have an effect on the rate of affiliation. The more affluent families thus surge ahead: 63 per cent of those earning $20,000 or more join, compared to only 44 per cent of those making less than $10,000 per year. Those resident in the community only one or two years also lag behind: only 38 per cent of newcomers are affiliated, compared to 64 per cent of those who have been in the community three or four years and 71 per cent of those who have lived there longer.

The majority of the non-members are potential joiners who feel that their eldest child is still youthful enough to justify delay in enrollment. There is, however, a greater feeling of urgency about affiliation at this stage of the life cycle. Many report that their child is almost ready to start religious school. As a consequence, a greater number of parents have made tentative plans for affiliation and have settled on a specific synagogue. Some are still shopping, as, for example, a woman who is active in a popular Jewish welfare group and has lived in Lakeville for seven years. She plans on visiting the single congregation that she has not yet inspected and will then come to a decision: "I have just not found one I want to belong to. Next year when my son is 8 I will have to belong. I still have to go to Hirsch and see what I like." Even those whose comments lack a note of urgency—as do those of a young salesman of modest income who feels his six-year-old is "too young for Sunday School and we are in no rush to join"—are reasonably certain which temple they will choose. In his case, it is the Wise Temple.

Some of those who experience a sense of urgency are new to the community. A minimally observant father of an eight-year-old, who has lived in Lakeville only one year, states, "We just haven't gotten around to deciding which one to join. We will, though. By next year, he should go." Another newcomer, a father of a six-year-old, whose religious observance is moderate, describes his predicament and its resolution: "When we first moved in, we didn't know which temple to join. We went to various affairs [of the different synagogues] and have just decided to join Schechter next fall when our eldest daughter will start Sunday School."

THE PEAK-SCHOOL PHASE: WIDESPREAD AFFILIATION

The sense of urgency which is generated in the early-school phase develops momentum as the Bar Mitzvah and Confirmation years approach. Nearly all groups are carried along: as many as 81 per cent of those who exclude synagogue affiliation as a mark of a "good Jew" have joined, compared to 92 per cent of those who believe it essential (see Table 5–4). Nearly all the more observant families (those practicing three or more home rituals) have joined by now, and the rise in affiliation among the minimally observant (those practicing one to two home rituals) is sufficiently large to further narrow the gap between the two groups. Given the spurt in affiliation among both groups, a considerable spread is present between them and the nonobservant, for only nonobservers resist the trend to affiliation; their rate remains stable. About half of nonobservers remain unaffiliated even in the peak-school phase.

TABLE 5–4. FAMILIES IN PEAK-SCHOOL PHASE: SYNAGOGUE AFFILIATION BY LEVEL OF HOME OBSERVANCE, BY VALUE OF SYNAGOGUE-BELONGING, BY FAMILY INCOME, AND BY LENGTH OF RESIDENCE IN LAKEVILLE

Per Cent Members among Families					
Who practice		N	Who believe that to be a "good Jew" belonging to synagogue		N
No observances	53	(19)	Is essential	92	(49)
1–2 observances	81	(64)	Is desirable	86	(65)
3–4 observances	97	(36)	Makes no difference	81	(47)
5+ observances	100	(43)			
With income		N	Who lived in community		N
Less than $15,000	87	(37)	1–2 years	72	(29)
$15,000–$29,999	84	(80)	3–4 years	94	(35)
$30,000+	93	(43)	5–8 years	88	(52)
			9+ years	89	(46)

For most, however, the pressing need to join a temple not only bypasses ideological considerations but also overcomes objective circumstances. Almost nine out of ten of the families with an income of less than $15,000 join, compared to only a little more than nine out of ten of those with an income of $30,000 or more. Even the few families whose income is less than $10,000 affiliate. In addition, unfamiliarity with the community is no longer so large an obstacle to affiliation. Although somewhat fewer recent arrivals join than older residents, a considerable number of newcomers (72 per cent) find an affiliation. This is almost double the rate among early-school-phase newcomers.

Parental status and the consequent sense of responsibility for Jewish continuity is readily acknowledged as a reason for affiliation, especially by those who are religiously alienated. Two-thirds of the members with little or no home observance say that parenthood has led to increased interest and involvement in Jewish life, and of these more than three-fourths cite their synagogue affiliation (see Table 5–5). This is equally true among the members in the early-school phase. Furthermore, about two-thirds in the peak-school phase who believe that synagogue membership is irrelevant to being a "good Jew" experience increased Jewish interests, and of these more than four in five specifically cite their synagogue involvement. By way of contrast, a greater percentage of the more observant members and of those who believe that affiliation is an important Jewish value feel that they would have been at least as involved in Jewish life if they had no children. Even if they do acknowledge increased Jewish interests, they mention their synagogue involvement less often and cite other forms of Jewish commitment. In sum, more than half of the religiously alienated members, contrasted with about one-third of the more committed members, acknowledge that their synagogue affiliation or participation symbolizes an expanded interest in Jewish life —one which is generated by their desire to expose their children to Jewish education and to give them a Jewish identity.

"We would not be members of a temple if not for the children," states a minimally observant mother of a recent Bar Mitzvah, who joined the Schechter Synagogue within a year after moving to Lakeville, despite a relatively modest income. A second-generation father of three children, belonging to the same synagogue, who is slightly more active in congregational affairs and slightly more observant than the previous respondent, states, "I had to join a congregation in order for the children to be able to go to Hebrew school." A nonobservant fourth-generation wife of German descent—the mother of an eleven-year-old—who is married to a second-generation man of East European descent, states with some sarcasm that the family "joined Einhorn to get my daughter to become more religious than I am." Another minimally observant mother of two young teen-agers—both herself and her lawyer-husband being of East European descent—joined Einhorn because as "our children grew up they wondered why they didn't go to Sunday School."

Some parents—usually those who are more observant—attribute their greater activity and involvement in the synagogue (in contrast to their

TABLE 5–5. CHILD-ORIENTED INTEREST IN JEWISH LIFE AND IN SYNAGOGUE INVOLVEMENT, BY LEVEL OF HOME OBSERVANCE AND BY VALUE OF SYNAGOGUE-BELONGING: AMONG SYNAGOGUE MEMBERS IN EARLY-SCHOOL AND IN PEAK-SCHOOL PHASE

	Life-Cycle Phase					
	Early-School		Peak-School			
	Observances		Observances		Synagogue Belonging*	
	3+	0–2	3+	0–2	Valued	Devalued
Per cent say that if had no children interest and involvement in Jewish life would be						
Less	53	68	54	66	56	68
As much	47	28	41	33	40	29
More	—	4	5	1	4	3
N (TOTAL MEMBERS)	(32)	(25)	(76)	(61)	(99)	(38)
Of those admitting less interest, per cent cite their synagogue affiliation and participation as example of greater interest	59	76	66	78	67	81
N (TOTAL SAYING LESS INTEREST)	(17)	(17)	(41)	(40)	(55)	(26)

* Comparison of those who believe synagogue-belonging is essential or desirable for a "good Jew" with those who feel it makes no difference. Data for early-school phase omitted because of too few cases.

affiliation) to their status as parents. A fairly observant woman who has resided in Lakeville only two years but who is already highly active in the PTA of the Wise Temple relates, "My interest has become stronger because of my children. I became active in Temple work because I feel every child should have a knowledge of his nationality and background." And an Orthodox-reared and still observant father who belongs to the Schechter Synagogue, and whose two sons will soon celebrate their Bar Mitzvah, states: "I would belong anyway . . . but I might not participate as much."

We must conclude, then, that in a significant number of cases the presence of children is connected with the decision to join a synagogue. The synagogue is viewed by parents as the central symbol of Jewish life. Given the frequency of parental alienation from worship and study, the child comes to constitute a major link to the religious institution. But, as we shall see, many parents—even if initially attracted to the synagogue because of their desire for the Jewish socialization of their children—develop a less time-bound conception of synagogue affiliation.

Appropriately, the aspect of the synagogue's program most directly concerned with children—its school and youth activities—emerges as a major consideration in the parents' overall evaluation of how satisfied they are with their affiliation. In earlier phases of the life cycle, this feature is subordinated to several others, including the synagogue's religious orientation; but at the peak-school phase, this aspect is more determinative of satisfaction than any other. In evaluating their affiliation, half of the parents in the peak-school phase give consideration to what the synagogue does for their children. Moreover, most of these parents focus on such activities as the primary or sole factor, thereby subordinating or excluding other characteristics and features of the institution. The less observant members, as well as the members who dismiss affiliation as necessary for being a "good Jew," not only mention educational and youth activities more often but concentrate on them more frequently: over seven in ten of the former and about two-thirds of the latter who cite this aspect of the program give it greater consideration than other features of the synagogue. Furthermore, such a child-oriented focus results more often in unqualified satisfaction with the synagogue of one's choice. Equal consideration of other features of synagogue life results in a more critical evaluation: 39 per cent of those in the peak-school phase who emphasize child-centered features are "very satisfied" with their affiliation, compared to 25 per cent of those who give this aspect no greater consideration than other aspects.

This child-oriented and highly satisfied focus is perhaps best exemplified by a mother of four children, ranging from the pre-school to the early adolescent years, who is affiliated with the Schechter Synagogue. Her belief that a "good Jew" need not belong to a synagogue is consistent with her minimal home practices and almost complete nonattendance at synagogue services:

> We are very satisfied in relationship to what Schechter offers our children. We have our own habits and social patterns, but we use the Synagogue for the children's needs, and it does satisfy their needs. They use the camp, the youth group, the school—everything they offer our children take advantage of.

A blunter version is offered by an affluent salesman whose family size, affiliation, and religious orientation parallel those of the previous respondent: "I like Schechter. It gives my boy a good Hebrew education. And they've left me alone—I've never been inside." A businessman with a similar religious orientation, whose daughter attends the same religious school, states, "We joined for the kids. The kids like it, so we are satisfied. We feel no need for religion." And a minimally observant woman active in youth-welfare groups, particularly one devoted to the improvement of mental health, says of her Wise affiliation, "It's the only temple that satisfies my need, which is basically a Sunday School for the children."

But a majority of those who base their feelings on the religious school and youth activities qualify their approval of the synagogue of their choice. This is not always because of criticisms of the institution; more frequently it is because the parent feels that while his children are benefitting, he is not. The respondents whom we quoted earlier are very satisfied with their affiliation because the synagogue has not required a commitment on their part to worship, to study, or to participate in social activities. There are more sensitive spirits, however, who would like greater involvement, but cannot achieve it; their meager Jewish background or religious remoteness prevents them from receiving more than limited satisfaction from their affiliation. A second-generation mother of three children enrolled in the religious school of Schechter Synagogue, whose lack of observance and extreme unsophistication about Jewish life are coupled with a positive attitude to Jewish education, states, "We know very little about Hebrew or religion and can't appreciate the service and can't learn from it. The children will benefit by it." And an accountant with a similar orientation to Jewish religion and culture, whose father was a tailor and who was reared in an immigrant home, regrets his lack of Jewish education. He feels only "somewhat satisfied" in respect to his affiliation because "you only get out of it what you put in. If I were active at Wise, I wouldn't feel so strange. My only justification for membership is the good Sunday and Hebrew schools for the children."

There are also a small but significant number among those who do not seek religious or social involvement on a personal basis who are dissatisfied with their affiliation because the school program does not produce the desired effect of giving their children a firm and positive Jewish identity. Such parents, of course, trace responsibility for failure to the school, rather than to their own orientation to Jewishness and the effect it may have on their children. Thus a professional man who combines an interest in Jewish culture, especially in Jewish music, with a pronounced dislike for religious institutions and an avoidance of religious rituals states, "My purpose in affiliating at Wise was only to get my son to the religious school so he could be bar mitzvahed. But the school is not satisfactory. Both he and my daughter are completely bored with it all over."

We see from all these respondents that whatever the level of satisfaction with their synagogue or the motive for joining a congregation, there is a strong tendency among peak-school-phase parents to view their affiliation in terms of their children. Some of these respondents are estranged or ambivalent in their own personal relationship to the synagogue. Nevertheless, the step they have taken by enrolling their children in a temple religious school indicates that they are not apathetic about Jewish continuity. And in those instances where a respondent feels that the synagogue has failed him in respect to Jewish continuity, he receives little gratification from his affiliation; he does not consider that he has failed the synagogue.

THE POST-SCHOOL PHASE:
CONTINUED AFFILIATION AND THE
RISE OF DISAFFILIATION

Although the child is the key to the high rate of synagogue membership in the peak-school phase, this factor can no longer play a significant role after Bar Mitzvah or Confirmation. Decreased emphasis on this motive is already apparent among member families who still have at least one child of high-school age; when all children are of age 18 or over, child-centered themes are almost completely irrelevant. After the peak-school phase, parents no longer think about or discuss questions regarding Jewish education for their children. Families in the advanced phases of the life cycle no longer consider the educational and youth program in evaluating the extent of satisfaction with their affiliation: the group doing so drops from about half to about one in four and finally to hardly more than one in ten (see Table 5–6). Furthermore, only a minority still attribute their own general interest and involvement in Jewish life to their children: the three in five in the peak phase who stated they would have been less interested if they had no children declines to two in five and finally to one in four. Yet despite the virtual disappearance of the earlier basis for synagogue affiliation, the great majority of families in the most advanced phase of the life cycle continue to belong to a synagogue.

TABLE 5–6. CHILD-ORIENTED INTEREST IN RELIGIOUS QUESTIONS, IN EVALUATION OF SYNAGOGUE AFFILIATION, AND IN JEWISH LIFE, BY LATER PHASES OF FAMILY LIFE CYCLE: AMONG SYNAGOGUE MEMBERS

	Life-Cycle Phase		
	Peak-School	Late-School	Post-School
Per cent			
Have thought about or discussed questions of religious education in past year	23	5	—
Consider educational and youth programs in evaluating their affiliation	48	25	13
Would be less interested and involved in Jewish life if they had no children	59	40	25
N	(140)	(20)	(48)

Although there is no stampede from affiliation, there is an overall reduction in membership among families all of whose children are beyond high-school age: 72 per cent of such families are affiliated. The dropout group, however, is differentiated by descent and generation. Although the rise in membership in earlier phases of the life cycle was fairly uniform across generation and descent lines, the dropouts are concentrated among third- and fourth-generation German Jews (see Table 5–7). The extent of affiliation in this group decreases from 78 per cent to 57 per cent, while second-generation East Europeans and others experience only a slight decline, reducing from almost nine in ten to almost eight in ten. As many as 33 per cent of the advanced-generation German group become former synagogue members, compared to only 12 to 18 per cent among second-generation East Europeans and others.[2]

TABLE 5−7. SYNAGOGUE AFFILIATION AND DISAFFILIATION BY LATER PHASES OF FAMILY LIFE CYCLE, GENERATION, AND DESCENT

| | *Life-Cycle Phase* | | |
Per cent members among	Peak-School	Late-School	Post-School
All families	87	91	72
N	(162)	(22)	(67)
Third and fourth-plus gen-eration of German descent	78	*	57
N	(23)	(*)	(21)
Second generation of East European descent	89	*	79
N	(54)	(*)	(24)
All others †	87	*	77
N	(85)	(*)	(22)
Per cent ex-members among			
All families	7	5	21
N	(162)	(22)	(67)
Third and fourth-plus gener-ation of German descent	17	*	33
N	(23)	(*)	(21)
Second generation of East European descent	7	*	12
N	(54)	(*)	(24)
All others †	6	*	18
N	(85)	(*)	(22)

* Too few cases.
† There are too few cases for separate analysis in each of the other generation-descent groups, especially in the post-school phase.

The general decline in membership in the post-school phase is further due to a steep drop in the rate of affiliation among the most religiously alienated segment of the community. In the main, even moderately ob-servant persons retain their membership, not to speak of those who rate high in observance (see Table 5–8). Among those who celebrate few or no home rituals, however, synagogue membership drops from 75 per cent to 56 per cent, and among the minority who hardly ever or never attend a synagogue service there is an even sharper decrease: the already low rate of 64 per cent drops to 36 per cent.

TABLE 5–8. SYNAGOGUE AFFILIATION BY LATER PHASES OF FAMILY LIFE CYCLE AND LEVEL OF RELIGIOUS OBSERVANCE

		Life-Cycle Phase	
Per cent members among families whose level of		Peak-School	Post-School
Home observance is			
High or moderate (3+)		99	96
	N	(79)	(26)
Low (0–2)		75	56
	N	(83)	(41)
Synagogue attendance is			
High (5+)		99	95
	N	(71)	(21)
Moderate (3–4)		88	83
	N	(49)	(24)
Low (0–2)		64	36
	N	(42)	(22)

Many of these former members who streamed to the synagogue in an earlier phase of the life cycle despite their own estrangement from religious activity remained on the fringes of synagogue life. They retained their membership only as long as required by their child's schooling. They make explicit that their lack of religiosity made continued affiliation meaningless. A third-generation banker of German descent who is completely estranged from Jewish religious life and whose social life centers around the Wildacres Country Club explains why he severed his ten-year membership at the Wise Temple: "I never was a temple-goer. I never really participated or belonged to any groups in the Temple." An attorney of similar social origin, very active in civic groups but with only residual ties to Jewish life, resigned after five years in the same temple "since I never went and have no belief in any deism," hastening to add that his "parents and grandparents were not churchgoers [sic]."

Among families whose relationship to Jewish religious life is highly attenuated and whose children are all past Bar Mitzvah or Confirmation age, discontent or even mere displeasure with a particular aspect of synagogue life can easily result in disaffiliation and *in failure to join another synagogue*. A fourth-generation wife of an affluent businessman states that the family severed its ten-year membership at Wise just after their youngest child turned eighteen because "the Conservative trend in the Temple" conflicted with their own Classical Reform background. According to a wealthy and sophisticated fourth-generation woman who is a leader in school and civic affairs and is devoted to Rabbi Abraham Lubin, the family's resignation occurred when the Adler Temple group on the Heights decided to form the Hirsch Temple and found themselves unable to lure Rabbi Lubin to Lakeville: "We decided that as long as we were not temple-goers, we would discontinue our affiliation." A New York–reared wife of a traveling salesman, comfortable, but not wealthy, permitted the family's membership at the Lilienthal Temple to lapse after less than a year. No rituals are observed in the home. Asked about her childhood memories in respect to Jewishness, the woman relates:

> We never had Seders or anything like that. My mother, may God rest her soul, was a very modern woman, and when holidays came around we had a family dinner, and we enjoyed it very much without all the rigmarole that goes with religious dinners.

Her children were mature by the time the family settled in Lakeville:

> When we first moved here, we joined Lilienthal because we thought it would be a good way to meet people, but we quit because my husband travels so much that he was never able to go to the services or any of the doings there, and I couldn't go alone. I went to one service on a Friday night, and I didn't see anyone there that I would even want to get acquainted with.

With the exception of such religiously alienated persons, a high proportion of those in the most advanced phase of the life cycle maintain their membership. If—as the substantial annual membership fee as well as building-fund assessments would seem to suggest—continued affiliation represents something more than drift, inertia, or the prolongation of a habit difficult to break, we must conclude that the child-oriented interest in affiliation in the earlier phases of the life cycle becomes transmuted. As we have seen, such an orientation was actually based on the parent's personal sense of responsibility for Jewish continuity, a self-image which appears to have grown rather than waned with the passage of time. The mere fact of sustained affiliation suggests an increasingly direct expression of a sense of belonging to the Jewish community and of a recognition of the synagogue as a central institution in Jewish life—a belongingness and a recognition which in earlier phases were expressed in great part through, and in behalf of, the child.

We find that those groups who maintain their synagogue membership as they move from the peak-school phase into the post-school phase also become more firm believers in the intrinsic value of the synagogue—in its function as a house of worship as well as a central institution of Jewish life. Thus, as second-generation East Europeans grow older, they become even more convinced that in order to be a "good Jew" one should belong to a synagogue, attend on the High Holidays, and even come to services on the Sabbath. Two out of three in the post-school phase, compared to two out of five in the peak phase, believe synagogue membership is essential to being a "good Jew," while the proportion who feel that it makes no difference declines from almost one in three to one in six. The proportion expressing the essentiality of High Holiday attendance rises from about one-third to more than half; the indifferent group decreases from more than one in four to one in eight. And even the proportion who believe that attendance on the Sabbath is essential increases from one in fifty to one in eight, while the indifferent drop markedly from about one-half to about three in ten (see Table 5–9). A similar shift, except for the item of weekly services, occurs among other descent and generation groups. The exception is the advanced-generation Germans: they deviate very sharply from the pattern observable among second-generation East Europeans. As the advanced-generation Germans move from peak-school to post-school phase, their commitment to the essentiality or even the desirability of each of our three types of synagogue-connected religious behavior consistently declines, while the extent of indifference sharply rises. Only 13 per cent in the peak-school phase are indifferent about the value of synagogue-belonging and High Holiday attendance, but as many as 42 per cent and 61 per cent, respectively, in the post-school phase hold this attitude. Even the relatively large 43 per cent group in the earlier phase who are indifferent about Sabbath attendance increases to 76 per cent in the post-school phase.

The value of belonging to a synagogue, of attending services on the High Holidays, and of worshiping on the Sabbath, whether affirmed as essential or as merely desirable, is independently related to retention of synagogue membership in the post-school phase of the life cycle.[3] Whatever one's descent or generation, those who continue to esteem the synagogue along these lines maintain their membership as they move from the peak-school to the post-school phase. This principle applies to advanced-

TABLE 5-9. INTRINSIC VALUE OF SYNAGOGUE BY LATER PHASES OF FAMILY LIFE CYCLE, GENERATION, AND DESCENT

	Second-Generation East Europeans		Third- and Fourth-Plus-Generation Germans		All Others	
	Life Cycle		Life Cycle		Life Cycle	
	Peak-School	Post-School	Peak-School	Post-School	Peak-School	Post-School
Per cent believe that to be a "good Jew"						
Synagogue-belonging						
Is essential	41	66	35	29	22	50
Is desirable	28	17	52	29	46	36
Makes no difference	31	17	13	42	32	14
Attending High Holiday services						
Is essential	35	54	17	10	19	32
Is desirable	37	33	70	29	45	45
Makes no difference	28	13	13	61	36	23
Attending Sabbath services						
Is essential	2	13	4	—	6	9
Is desirable	46	58	53	24	47	41
Makes no difference	52	29	43	76	47	50
N	(54)	(24)	(23)	(21)	(85)	(22)

generation German Jews as well, but, as we have just seen, because relatively few among this group retain such values their overall level of affiliation declines. Since those who are indifferent to the synagogue experience sharp decreases in membership in the post-school phase,[4] even the indifferent second-generation East Europeans drop their affiliation, moving from about four-fifths who are affiliated in the peak-school phase to as low as one-third in the post-school phase. But because many of this group indicate an enhanced appreciation of the synagogue's intrinsic function as they became older, their overall level of affiliation is generally maintained even after the years of child rearing have passed.

In the light of extensive religious alienation among advanced-generation Germans, we wonder how long Jewish identification will continue in this group. In the previous chapter, we suggested a coming crisis among those reared and confirmed at the Einhorn Temple; these are precisely the young people whose parents are more frequently than not third- and fourth-generation German Jews. In our present perspective, the question occurs as to whether the parent who himself is already highly acculturated, who joins a religious institution only out of a desire for his child's Jewish identity, and who does not develop any abiding personal or ideological links with the synagogue (or with any other Jewish institution or area of activity) will be succeeded by a child who will conform to the same pattern. Or will the child neglect to join a temple when *he* becomes a parent, be apathetic to giving his offspring a Jewish identity, and even encourage, overtly or covertly, his child's shift to another identity?

Involvement in the Synagogue

If many Lakeville Jews are affiliated and even continue their membership when their children are grown, we must next confront the question of the basis and extent of synagogue involvement. The two institutions in the community whose members are most removed from Jewish sacramentalism and culture—Einhorn and Hirsch—are from a special point of view closest to traditional norms: they stress that worship or study is the heart of the synagogue program and should be the sole basis for institutional involvement. However, it is true that in their denigration of activities that emphasize social interaction they betray a kind of untraditional extremism. In the case of Hirsch, such involvement is considered not only low-brow but a deflection from worthy spiritual or intellectual goals. In the case of Einhorn, it is considered subversive: social involvement means that Jews associate on an ethnic basis and thus embrace an un-American principle of social organization.

The two major congregations in Lakeville (Wise and Schechter) as well as one of the smaller congregations (Lilienthal) have no objection to involvement that is primarily social or institutional. They not only feel that social and institutional activities have value in themselves but also acknowledge, whether directly or indirectly, that the synagogue is an ethnic association. As such, it can grow as a result of increased interaction between Jew and Jew. Furthermore, these synagogues feel that such interaction represents a contribution to Jewish survival.

Wise, Schechter, and Lilienthal also seem to recognize that the encouragement of many levels and types of interaction among the members of a voluntary association enhances its viability. Holding that social interaction is necessary for institutional maintenance, these synagogues do not feel that such interaction is thereby rendered unworthy or subversive. The way in which these institutions are structured also suggests that they believe that involvement in synagogue-centered leisure-time activities is a way of ultimately increasing participation in the two classical functions of synagogue life: religious worship and adult study.

In evaluating these differing approaches to synagogue involvement, we shall gain perspective if we review certain facts about Jewish religious behavior in Lakeville and if we analyze such facts against the backdrop of Gentile religious behavior in the community. We are familiar with the fact that 66 per cent of Lakeville Jews are affiliated with a synagogue. We also recall that very few come to religious services on any regular basis—that a mere 6 per cent of Lakeville Jews attend weekly. Not only is this figure perilously low, considering the emphasis placed on Sabbath worship in Jewish tradition, but it is also in stark contrast to the behavior of Lakeville's Gentiles: 22 per cent of Protestants and 73 per cent of Catholics attend a religious service weekly (see Table 5–10). Thus Jews and Gentiles do, indeed, go their separate ways on their respective Sabbaths, but while in the overwhelming majority of cases the Jewish path leads past the house of worship, this is not so with the Catholics. As for the Protestants, who are especially important since they comprise 64 per cent of Lakeville's Gentile population, a significant minority attend.[5] Protestants and Jews also diverge in respect to less regular attendance at services: while only 26 per cent of the Jews attend once a month or more, 58 per cent of the Protestants do so. But in spite of

TABLE 5–10. AFFILIATION, ATTENDANCE AT SERVICES, AND INVOLVEMENT IN SYNAGOGUE OR CHURCH, BY RELIGIOUS GROUP

	Jews	Protestants	Catholics
Per cent			
Synagogue (church) members	66	66	94
Attend services each week	6	22	73
Attend services once a month or more	26	58	91
Members of synagogue (church)-affiliated groups	36	24	45
Spend time weekly in synagogue (church) activities	33	42	37

the magnitude of such divergence in devotional behavior, the percentage of Protestants who consider themselves church members is exactly the same as the proportion of Jews who consider themselves synagogue members.[6]

Since Jews belong but do not attend, how then can they integrate into the synagogue? Inasmuch as religious study is not an important focus of activity, it is apparent that if Wise, Schechter, and Lilienthal were to base themselves on the devotional proclivities of the Lakeville Jew, or even on his desire for Jewish education for his child, they would be far different types of institution. They would hardly be viable in their present form. What these congregations have done is to create activities around social and institutional interests and simultaneously to implement the traditional program of religious worship and study. Thus we find in Table 5–10 that while few Jews in Lakeville engage in worship on a weekly basis (or study, for that matter), a significant proportion engage in some synagogue activity.* While Lakeville Jews have relatively tenuous ties to the synagogue on the basis of their worship or adult study activities, almost as large a proportion of them engage in institutional activity on a regular basis as do the more devotionally oriented Protestant and Catholic groups. In spite of absenting themselves from services, then, Lakeville Jews are only slightly less active in synagogue activities than are Gentiles in church activities: 33 per cent of all Jews in the community

---

* While Einhorn and Hirsch do not permit formally organized social activity, they do create a certain amount of interaction around institutional concerns. This is particularly the case with Hirsch, some of whose congregational and committee meetings are very "clubby" indeed.

spend some time each week in synagogue activities, while 37 per cent of the Catholics and 42 per cent of the Protestants do so in church activities. Thus, although the great majority of Lakeville Jews are not involved weekly in worship or adult study, a significant minority do give some time each week to synagogue activities.

Part of the time so devoted is spent with synagogue-affiliated organizations, as with the afternoon meetings of the sisterhood, the evening meetings of the men's club, or in committee work for these organizations. Some 36 per cent of all Lakeville Jews are members of such synagogue-affiliated organizations. And as we notice in Table 5–10, the proportion of Jews who belong is greater than the proportion of Protestants who are affiliated with church-related groups.[7] In addition to the synagogue affiliates, there are, particularly at Wise and Schechter, various special-interest groups that meet on a regular basis. And in each of these institutions (as well as to some extent at Lilienthal) there is an elaborate structure of synagogue committees: buildings and grounds, ways and means, legal, ushering, social action, hospitality, interfaith, publicity and public relations, and many more, including a committee on committees. In theory, there is a committee for every member, whatever his talent or taste; the objective is to involve each family in committee activity.[8]

ACTIVITY AND SATISFACTION

As we should expect, the more active the member, the greater the likelihood that he will be satisfied with his affiliation. Thus more than half of the highly active express unqualified satisfaction, compared to more than two in five of the less active members and only about a third of the inactive. Among the various reasons given for general satisfaction, the one that differentiates active from inactive members is favorable interpersonal and social relations (see Table 5–11).[9] It is the highly active group for whom such relations are a prominent feature; the difference between them and the less active is considerable. About three in five of the most active members mention such reasons, compared to about one-third of the less active and one in five of the inactive members. This pattern applies not only to the more superficial, external types of relationships, such as those based on congenial attributes of other members or of the social climate of the institution, but also to deeper ties of identification and belonging.

A highly observant professional man who is a member of the board of directors of the Schechter Synagogue and a leader in its Men's Club finds

TABLE 5–11.   SOCIAL SATISFACTION WITH AFFILIATION
BY LEVEL OF ACTIVITY OF
SYNAGOGUE MEMBERS

	Activity: Hours per Week		
	2+	1	0
Per cent			
Very satisfied	54	42	34
Somewhat satisfied	26	35	34
Not satisfied	20	23	32
N	(61)	(64)	(155)
Per cent mention			
Favorable interpersonal-social relations *	59	33	21
Personal identification, feeling of belonging	34	11	4
Favorable membership characteristics	40	24	19
N (TOTAL SATISFIED)	(49)	(49)	(105)

* Is less than total of subtypes because some give both types of responses.

that the institution is "a means of meeting people, and I enjoy it." An older and less observant man, an electrical contractor, belongs to the same synagogue and is active in its Men's Club; he uses his contacts in the building trades to the Synagogue's advantage. And each year he helps to erect the congregation's *sukkah*.* He reports, "I like the people I meet over there. Most of them are nice people. We have common interests." "Like the people" and "nice people" are recurrent phrases in these responses. A magazine distributor who is on the board of the Lilienthal Temple is satisfied with his affiliation because the Temple is "comprised of people close to us in age and income bracket, which is desirable for us." According to the moderately observant young mother who is active in the experimental theater group at Wise and very satisfied with her affiliation, the congenial social climate at the Temple makes the individual "feel at home."

This sense of satisfaction in meeting and sharing with peers shades imperceptibly into a more intense feeling of belonging, a pervasive sense of personal identification with the congregation. A leader of the Sisterhood at Schechter whose accountant husband is a member of the congre-

* *Sukkah:* temporary booth erected for the Festival of Sukkot in which meals are customarily eaten.

gation's board of directors responds as follows: "We have never been as happy in any synagogue as we are here. The people are warm, and we feel like we are part of the congregation." An officer of the Sisterhood at the Wise Temple, whose husband is also active at the institution, states, "I'm a very integral part of the Temple; I get the answers to all my needs." One of the strongest expressions of satisfaction comes from a leader of the Men's Club at the Schechter Synagogue who was pleasantly surprised at the reception accorded him when he moved to Lakeville and joined the Synagogue: "It's the first synagogue I've belonged to that I feel I'm a part of. The rabbi calls me Al. The president calls me Al. It never happened before."

Satisfaction is also intense among veteran members who have continued to be active over a long period of time. A very wealthy businessman of German descent who has remained prominent at the Wise Temple in spite of the departure of many of his friends states, "I've been part of building the Temple. I like the fact that I've grown up with it." A businessman who helped Schechter grow from a struggling group of devoted members into a firmly established institution has also remained active in his synagogue. He reacts in the following terms:

I'm a part of Schechter. When you give to an institution, you enjoy it. I started with it. I saw it grow. A good portion of our social life stems from the synagogue.

ACTIVITY AND RELIGIOSITY

Given this picture of activity in synagogue affairs and satisfaction with institutional affiliation, we wonder whether involvement constitutes more a defense against the radical demands of religion rather than a mechanism for reinforcing religious interests. We wonder, for example, whether activity means a de-emphasis of attendance at services and adult study. Does it signify complacency about religious values? Does it detract from concern with religious problems and issues? Furthermore, what is the religious background of people who become active in synagogue life?

In regard to attendance at worship, we find that while only 8 per cent of the inactive are located in the top attendance group, 29 per cent of the active and 42 per cent of the highly active—an unusually large proportion—are in this category (see Table 5–12).[10] As many as 28 per cent of the inactive never or rarely attend, contrasted to only 2 per cent of the very active people. The inactive synagogue member, then, comes to services only on the High Holidays and on one or two Sabbaths during the year, while the active member tends to be a praying member.

TABLE 5–12. LEVEL OF SYNAGOGUE ATTENDANCE BY LEVEL OF ACTIVITY OF SYNAGOGUE MEMBERS

Per cent at following attendance level	*Activity: Hours per Week*		
	2+	1	0
High 7–9	42	29	8
5–6	40	37	19
3–4	16	27	45
1–2	2	5	21
Low 0	—	2	7
N	(62)	(66)	(157)

The same general relationship obtains in respect to adult Jewish study. While only 17 per cent of the inactive have joined a study group or have attended lectures during the past year, 44 per cent of those who are active and 58 per cent of those who are very active have done so. The active also surpass the inactive in Hebrew study. The only modification of the picture is that those who are very active do not attend study groups or lectures with greater regularity than those who are only somewhat active (see Table 5–13).[11] We find, then, that the member who is not involved in institutional affairs or does not use the synagogue as a house of assembly does not generally utilize it either as a house of prayer or as a house of study.

TABLE 5–13. PARTICIPATION IN JEWISH STUDY BY LEVEL OF ACTIVITY OF SYNAGOGUE MEMBERS

Per cent attended Jewish study group or lecture in past year	*Activity: Hours per Week*		
	2+	1	0
Any	58	44	17
Regularly	27	26	11
Occasionally	31	18	6
Per cent did something to keep up Hebrew knowledge	21	12	6
N	(62)	(66)	(157)

Not only does the uninvolved member abstain from using the synagogue for traditional purposes but he assigns a diminished role to the synagogue as a religious—and even as a Jewish—institution. The inactive member more often devalues the importance of institutional belongingness and devotional standards: compared to the active member, he more frequently believes that a "good Jew" need not be affiliated with a synagogue or attend services on the High Holidays and the Sabbath. As many as one-third of the inactive are apathetic to attendance at High Holiday services, and more than one-fourth are indifferent to synagogue affiliation (see Table 5–14). Furthermore, inactive members feel more alienated from religion generally. About two in five of them—twice as many as the active members—consider themselves only somewhat or not at all religious.

TABLE 5–14. EVALUATION OF OWN RELIGIOSITY AND INTRINSIC VALUE OF SYNAGOGUE, BY LEVEL OF ACTIVITY OF SYNAGOGUE MEMBERS

	Activity: Hours per Week		
Per cent consider themselves	2+	1	0
Very or moderately religious	81	76	59
Somewhat or not at all religious	19	24	41
Per cent believe that to be a "good Jew"			
Synagogue-belonging			
Is essential or desirable	92	83	73
Makes no difference	8	17	27
Attending High Holiday services			
Is essential or desirable	89	78	67
Makes no difference	11	22	33
Attending Sabbath services			
Is essential or desirable	74	60	45
Makes no difference	26	40	55
N	(62)	(66)	(157)

Among members who are parents of school-age children, the religious alienation of the inactive is underscored by their more child-oriented approach to the synagogue. Although the parents of school-age children are more active than those members whose children are grown, their active involvement is generally less motivated by child-centered considerations than is the affiliation of their peers who remain inactive. In both the early-school and peak-school phases, it is the inactive parents who more often believe that their interest and involvement in Jewish life as well as their synagogue affiliation were spurred by their parental status and who more often appraise their affiliation on the basis of the synagogue's school and youth program.

If active members can be distinguished from inactive ones by a more traditional and less child-centered approach to the synagogue—and by a stronger religious self-image—they also possess a more traditional background. Thus the observance of religious rituals in the home is associated with involvement.[12] Among families with school-age children, those who rank high in observance are noticeably more involved: more than three-fourths spend some time in synagogue activities, contrasted with one-third to one-half of those at lower levels of observance (see Table 5–15). However, in the post-school phase—the phase of the life cycle that witnesses a general decline in synagogue activity—observance ceases to nurture activity.

TABLE 5–15. ACTIVITY OF SYNAGOGUE MEMBERS BY LEVEL OF HOME OBSERVANCE AND FAMILY LIFE CYCLE

Per cent spend time each week in synagogue activities during	*Number of Observances*		
	5+	3–4	0–2
Early-school phase	78	47	36
N	(18)	(15)	(25)
Peak-school phase	77	34	34
N	(43)	(35)	(62)
Post-school phase		28	26
N		(25)	(23)

Furthermore, among members with school-age children the factor of religious observance is more important in stimulating synagogue involvement than is the presence or absence of a child-centered orientation to the synagogue. Because religiously alienated members tend to attribute their synagogue involvement to their parental status, it is important to control this element (see Table 5–16). When we introduce this control, we find that whether or not involvement derives from child-centered motives, the more observant member is found to be consistently more active. This occurs among those who acknowledge their children's influence as well as among those who do not admit such motives. On the other hand, when level of observance is taken into account, child-centered motives have little relation to activity: parents who attribute their involvement to their children are generally no less active than those denying such influence. Only among the relatively few less observant members in the early-school phase is activity diminished.

TABLE 5–16. ACTIVITY OF SYNAGOGUE MEMBERS BY LEVEL OF HOME OBSERVANCE, CHILD-ORIENTED INTEREST IN SYNAGOGUE INVOLVEMENT, AND FAMILY LIFE CYCLE

	Synagogue Involvement			
	Attributed to Having Children		Not Attributed to Having Children	
Per cent spend time each week in synagogue activities during	Observances		Observances	
	3+	0–2	3+	0–2
Early-school phase	60	24	64	50
N	(10)	(13)	(22)	(12)
Peak-school phase	52	39	59	30
N	(27)	(31)	(49)	(30)

As a consequence of his deeper involvement in synagogue group life, the more observant member can be stimulated into thought and discussion on a variety of religious issues and questions. But it is not his traditionalist orientation alone that encourages such interest; it is rather that his involvement affords access to groups and persons with similar concerns. Among equally observant members, whether they are only at a moderate level (three to four practices) or at a higher level (five or more rituals), religious questions were raised more often during the previous year by those who are active in synagogue activities.

The religious concerns of synagogue members who are active as well as observant embrace not only ceremonial and ritual problems but also general queries about the nature of Judaism as well as ultimate questions of belief. The frequency with which such general questions are mentioned ranges upward from about one in four to about two in five among the most active members and downward from about one in four to about one in eight among the inactive members (see Table 5–17). Questions about the relationship between religion and morality, although rarely raised, tend also to be of greater concern to the active.*

TABLE 5–17. CONCERN WITH RELIGIOUS QUESTIONS BY LEVEL OF ACTIVITY AND OF HOME OBSERVANCE OF SYNAGOGUE MEMBERS

	Number of Observances					
	5+			3–4		
	Activity: Hours Per Week			Activity: Hours Per Week		
Per cent concerned during past year with questions about	2+	1	0	2+	1	0
Any religious problem	90	92	67	85	79	76
Rituals and ceremonials	33	24	21	31	14	19
General nature of Judaism	36	32	15	31	21	17
Belief and theology	24	24	12	38	50	26
Morality	15	16	3	15	—	2
N	(33)	(25)	(33)	(13)	(14)	(42)

More often than not, the active members' formulations of such questions evince a measure of authenticity and reflection. The wife of a lawyer, who with her husband is an active worker at the Schechter Synagogue, has been troubled by the "sincerity of observing *kashrut* in the home," despite her own extensive observance of the dietary laws. In this connection, she has consulted *Basic Judaism* by Milton Steinberg. A highly active and observant Reform Jew who is a member of the Wise Temple cites a recent discussion with a friend who is active in a Reform temple "where you can have your choice of wearing hats or not." The problem on which their discussion centered was "how much ritual to observe and what direction to take in religion."

This man suggests one of the questions with which active members tend to be concerned: the differences within American Judaism, especially between Reform and Conservative Judaism. The problem forms

* Satisfaction with social relations in the synagogue does not subvert religious concerns. Among the observant and active members, those who voice such satisfaction have been no less concerned with these various types of religious questions than those who do not mention such satisfaction. Thus the "happy" integrated synagogue member is not diverted from religious issues.

the matrix for discussions of "all kinds of questions" in one fairly observant family in which both spouses are highly active at the Lilienthal Temple. The wife identifies herself as "Conservative Reform" because of her very traditional upbringing; her husband, who is in the communications industry, leans toward a more radical position. A partner in an electrical appliance business who is also an active member of the Lilienthal Temple has been considering "how a Reformed Jew fits within the pattern of Judaism." A very affluent businessman who has been active for many years in the leadership of the Wise Temple has been concerned with the "old, old question: is Judaism a religion or a nationality?"

Such questions may lead to probing the problem of the relationship between religion and morality. An articulate woman who is highly active at the Schechter Synagogue has been concerned with the question of "what is a 'good Jew' " because it involves the whole basic concept. She asks, "Is it being a good Jew or being a good human being?" She cites *Pirke Avot* as her relevant reading. A similar problem has occurred to another woman, who serves as a room mother at the religious school of the Wise Temple. She formulates it in the following terms: "Whether to follow Judaism as a religion or to follow right from wrong."

Involvement in synagogue group life does not inhibit active members from pursuing more traditional theological questions. "The existence of God or of a Divine Being" has been the single most important religious question confronting a veteran Hadassah leader who has recently become active in the bowling league of the Wise Temple Sisterhood. An officer of the same temple has been bothered by the concept of revelation. He was troubled by a rabbi "who said one must accept the physical revelation of God to Moses." And a leader of the PTA in the same temple, a third-generation woman of East European descent who has not had the advantage of a formal Jewish education, has been concerned with revelation from a different vantage point. She has found "many logical fallacies in the various books of the Bible."

Such thought and discussion about religious issues, as we have noted, occur particularly among more observant members who become involved in synagogue activity. The minimally observant or nonobservant members who take their place in congregational life have about the same level of concern with most religious questions as their inactive peers. Their levels of religious concern are not inconsiderable, however, and approximate those of the more observant but inactive members.

Those less observant but active members who focus on issues of religious observance often betray an ambivalence and impatience that contrast markedly with the concerns of the more observant. A young wife of an engineer, who is active as a room mother in the religious school of the Hirsch Temple and in her home observes the single ceremony of lighting the *menorah,* is skeptical about "whether it's good to have a lot of ritual in religion." And the wife of a lawyer, who is an enthusiastic and active member of the Einhorn Temple, has been concerned with recent developments in the Reform movement:

> I can't understand this sudden return to form and ritual. This sudden clinging to safe religion is like a sorority pin. When I went to college, I was so happy I was accepted by a sorority who told me what to wear and whom to date. Now the congregation sets up all the regulations: how to pray, what to do on Friday nights.

Only rarely do such concerns indicate reflection and perceptiveness, as in the case of a descendant of an old German-Jewish family who, despite his "virtually non-religious background," attends Sabbath services quite regularly and devotes much time to the Wise Temple as well as to other Jewish groups. He has been troubled about "the meaning of prayer: why people do or don't pray; the reasons for greater or less religious observance." His reading, while centered in books written by Reform authors, has ranged from Solomon B. Freehof's *The Responsa Literature* to the works of the Jewish historian Jacob R. Marcus.

Thus our findings indicate that no assumption can be sustained to the effect that involvement in social and institutional aspects of synagogue life subverts concern with religious values or fosters apathy in respect to worship and study.[13] Our findings also tend to deflate the image of the alienated Jew who is repelled by the thick ethnicity of his less sensitive peers, but can be attracted to a synagogue which would concentrate on responding to his religious doubts. If the image of the Jew questing for religious values has validity—an image which has marked some of the literature on the religious revival in suburbia—it applies in greater force to the more observant, active, and extroverted synagogue members—those most integrated into the institutional life of the congregation.

Lakeville has a wide variety of congregations, each making a lesser or greater appeal to a distinctive segment of the Jewish community. Each is in some measure satisfied with the efficacy of its approach to Judaism. Nevertheless, none of the synagogues in the community seems to have the magic formula for converting religiously alienated Jews into believing and practicing Jews.

THE INACTIVES

Since inactive synagogue members constitute a group of significant size, they call for a more detailed profile. Just as interpersonal relationships are an important aspect of the active member's satisfaction with his affiliation, so do they play a part in the less favorable attitudes of inactive members. We recall from Table 5–11 that only a small minority of the inactive felt any satisfaction with these social relationships. The leading source of the inactives' discontent with their synagogue is unsatisfactory interpersonal relationships. (This complaint is volunteered by 44 per cent of the inactive but by only half as many of the active.) The bulk of the dissatisfied inactive lack a feeling of personal identification with their synagogue; they experience a void between themselves and the congregation. Furthermore, inactive members are distinguished by diffuse feelings of alienation and apathy rather than by specific criticisms of their fellow members: they do not complain any more frequently than do active members about uncongenial or repellent characteristics of members of the synagogue of their choice. Feelings of unsatisfactory personal relationships and of institutional alienation reinforce the marginal member's position at the fringe of synagogue life and thereby serve to insulate him further from exposure to the active member's religious concerns.

Some of the inactive who feel apathetic or estranged have apparently become disenchanted with their affiliation as a consequence of an unsuccessful attempt to establish social relationships with other members. Such inactives do not reject synagogue life generally, but rather feel alienated only from their own particular congregation. This tendency is underlined by the fact that such individuals are likely to be moderately observant in their religious practice, rather than unobservant.

One such respondent is a former teacher, active in various mental health groups, who is very dissatisfied with her affiliation with the Lilienthal Temple: "I am not happy there. I don't feel part of the group. . . . This makes me sad because a temple had been part of my life as a child, but not in Lakeville." Another example is a woman who is also interested in promoting better mental health and is married to a prosperous manufacturer. She is dissatisfied with the family's affiliation at the Wise Temple because the synagogue is "way too big and monstrous; there's no close feeling of belonging to a group. It's like a factory." Because of the multiplicity of congregations in Lakeville, this type of inactive member can sometimes find a suitable affiliation. Thus a formerly inactive and dissatisfied member of the Wise Temple is now an active and satisfied member of the Hirsch Temple. This woman, the well-educated wife of a professional man, reacted to Wise as follows:

> The size was undesirable. We couldn't have a personal relationship or feeling of belongingness or being wanted. My husband had the feeling that Rabbi Greenberg is sincere, has ability and mind, but he got no emotional response from him. We didn't get what we wanted. Certainly not from two shifts on the High Holidays. We'd rather be a big fish in a little pond. In a meeting of the parents of the Confirmation class, they tried to steam-roller the ideas of the rabbi through.

She enjoys the people at Hirsch, is enthusiastic about Rabbi Aaron, and feels the congregation has "a certain tradition of intellectual curiosity and social consciousness" which matches her own proclivities.

The majority of the inactive, however, have not shifted from one congregation to another with good results. Nor have they ever attempted to establish personal relationships with their fellow members. Indeed, their problem is not that of finding a synagogue which is of the right size or of locating like-minded people among its membership. Rather, they are alienated from the Jewish religion and from Jewish religious life. They are total or near-total abstainers from religious observance. Their attitude to synagogue affiliation ranges from apathy and indifference to hostility.

"I have no feeling. We're not temple-goers. We just belong," reports a longtime member of the Wise Temple who is married to a prominent business executive. This woman spends a great deal of her time working for the League of Women Voters and other non-sectarian groups. "It means strictly nothing to me," says a mother with a Christian Science upbringing about the Einhorn Temple, where her children are attending religious school. Another woman, active in the National Conference of Christians and Jews and married to a department store executive, blames her husband for making the family join the Einhorn Temple after being inactive members of the Wise Temple for many years: "I have no feelings. No, nothing at all. My husband just wanted to have someone to say a few words over him to bury him. That's the only reason for joining." A somewhat more hostile attitude is revealed by a childless, middle-aged businessman who is a newcomer to Lakeville and claims that he joined the Wise Temple at his wife's insistence. Never affiliated previously, he opines: "Temples mean nothing to me. I would prefer to watch prize fights Friday evening. All temples are a hodgepodge of internal politics." And a woman with a professional career, who suspended her consuming occupational interests when Adlai Stevenson ran for the presidency ("I worked on the telephone squad day after day; I felt we had the opportunity to have a really great person as President"), has her children enrolled in the religious school of the Wise Temple. Hostile to religious institutions, she confines her organizational memberships to non-sectarian groups: "I don't like organized religion. It separates people more than it brings them together."

While some of these respondents appear to have turned to non-sectarian associations and values as a result of religious apathy or hostility, in actual fact there is only a small and inconsistent difference between the inactive and highly active with respect to their level of integration-mindedness (see Table 5–18). The difference is found only at the

TABLE 5–18. LEVEL OF INTEGRATION-MINDEDNESS BY LEVEL OF ACTIVITY OF SYNAGOGUE MEMBERS

Per cent whose integration-mindedness score is	Activity: Hours per Week		
	2+	1	0
High (7–9)	10	20	20
Intermediate (4–6)	67	62	56
Low (1–3)	23	18	24
N	(62)	(66)	(157)

higher levels of the scale; there is no difference at lower levels of integration-mindedness. This virtual parity in integration-mindedness occurs in part because there are available to inactive synagogue members alternative ethnic associations espousing a variety of approaches to Jewishness. Since many of our respondents belong to at least one such association, the role of the Jewish voluntary association requires detailed study; it is possible that such associations fill the institutional void created by the alienation of the inactive from synagogue life. But before turning to the study of the Jewish voluntary association, we must first analyze the relationship of the Lakeville Jew to Israel.

6

THE LAKEVILLE
JEW AND ISRAEL

The Zionist idea was born out of the social changes of nine-teenth-century Europe: the development of nationalism, the emancipa-tion of the Jews, the secularization of wide segments of Jewry, the disillusionment with the promise of eventual liberty, equality, and fra-ternity between Jew and Christian. The Zionist movement was dominated by those who rejected assimilation and at the same time lacked faith in normative Judaism: some had left behind the traditional way of life of their childhood while others did not have such an upbringing. And what-ever their religious background or ideological proclivities, they could find no satisfaction in a "liberal" Judaism. For most leaders of the move-ment, then, Zionism was a secularist form of Jewishness.

To study whether our respondents share the Zionist idea—whether they are Zionists, non-Zionists, or anti-Zionists and on what basis—would be an interesting exercise. However, the establishment of the State of Israel has profoundly affected older ideological formulations. Further-more, the Jews of Lakeville constitute a unique generation. Most are old enough to remember the era when Zionism was only an idea; they have witnessed the establishment of the State of Israel and thus have seen the transformation of Zionism from aspiration to reality.

The central problem with which we shall concern ourselves in this chapter is not so much that of discovering whether the Lakeville Jew is a Zionist as that of analyzing how he feels about Israel and ascertaining what role Israel plays in his life. Since we have noted that many Jews in Lakeville have broken their bonds with Jewish sacramentalism, we wonder whether Israel functions as a substitute focus for Jewishness. Does Israel have its own involvements and obligations, all serving as functional equivalents for the traditional *mitzvot?*

Feeling and Concern

We utilized several approaches to gain insight into the feelings of our respondents toward Israel. One was to suggest a reversal of the great event of 1948 when Israel became a state: "If the Arab nations should succeed in carrying out their threat to destroy Israel, would you feel a very deep, some, or no personal sense of loss?" This question was followed by a probe: "Why do you say that?" Some 90 per cent of our respondents told us that they would feel a sense of loss; of these, 65 per cent answered that they would feel a "very deep" sense of loss, while the remainder of 25 per cent said that they would experience "some" sense of loss. A total of 10 per cent of our respondents said that they would feel no sense of loss at the destruction of the State of Israel.

Some seven in ten of those who would experience a sense of loss react in this manner because of their feeling of Jewish identity (see Table 6–1). Perhaps the best expression of this approach is found in the response of a businessman who was active at the Wise Temple for many years and now serves as a trustee of the Jewish fraternity to which he belonged in college. He would experience a sense of loss because "I feel a sense of identity with every Jew in the world—something deep and something compulsive in me." The same basic approach is evident in the answer of another businessman who is also a member of the Wise Temple and whose main community activity is the support of cancer research. He would experience a sense of loss "because basically I am Jewish. . . . Being a Jew, you can't help but feel for other Jews." These respondents and others, constituting about a third of those who would experience a sense of loss, express the idea that all Jews are brothers and are responsible for one another.

TABLE 6–1.   REASONS FOR FEELING A PERSONAL SENSE
OF LOSS IF ISRAEL WERE DESTROYED

Per cent express		
Feelings of Jewish identity: *	70	
"All Jews are brothers"		31
"Israel is the Jewish homeland"		13
"Israel is a personal haven"		1
"Israel is a haven for Jews"		28
"Proud of Israel's achievements"		30
Humanitarianism and feelings of Jewish identity	19	
Humanitarianism alone	11	
N (TOTAL FEEL A PERSONAL SENSE OF LOSS)	(388)	

* Specific reasons add to more than 70 per cent because more than one reason is possible.

A considerably smaller number respond by explaining their potential sense of loss on the basis of Israel's constituting the Jewish national homeland. Thus a housewife who is active at the Hirsch Temple as well as in the Lakeville chapter of the League of Women Voters states, "I always felt Israel was the established homeland for the Jewish people." Probably because of the place of religion in American society as well as the importance of the Land of Israel in Jewish tradition, a salesman, who now belongs only to his trade association but states that he will affiliate with a synagogue when his children reach school age, reacts to the homeland conception in somewhat different terms:

> I would feel a loss in tradition, although it'll never kill Judaism in any respect. But as the Vatican is the hub of the Catholic wheel, Israel can bring the light as far as Judaism is concerned.

Very few of our respondents state that the reason for their feeling of loss would be the destruction of a place of refuge for *themselves*. An example of this minuscule group is a woman who is an officer of the Lakeville chapter of a national Jewish welfare group, who was reared by highly Orthodox parents but is herself not very observant, and who has affiliated with the Schechter Synagogue primarily so that her daughter may attend its Sunday School:

> I like to feel there is some place I can go if there should be any trouble. I don't feel that there is any safety in the world for a minority group. We have democratic ideals, but who knows about the future? We've had an example in Germany. . . .

Much more common is the reaction that an Arab victory would mean the destruction of a country which has served and will serve as a haven for refugee Jews. Almost three in ten of those who would feel a sense of loss express this idea. These respondents do not view Israel as a reception center for secure American Jews. The wife of a prominent physician —a woman who is active in a variety of endeavors both in the Jewish and general community—typifies this response:

> I've felt Israel is the answer for European Jews after World War II. I'd like to help them get set there and be comfortable and have a place where they can live unpersecuted.

The wife of a sales representative—a woman active in the local chapter of a Jewish welfare group—makes explicit the difference between a personal haven and one for persecuted Jews:

> Israel is a country desperately needed for deprived Jews of the world. It's for the underprivileged and deprived who can't live as citizens in countries they had lived in. But it's not necessary for the Jews of this country.

An equally substantial group reply in terms of their pride in and identification with Israel's achievements; they say that they would feel a sense of loss because these advances would be wiped out. A manufacturer's wife, a passive member of the Schechter Synagogue but an active member of various Jewish welfare groups, responds,

> They are the people of our heritage, and everything they built would be destroyed—all their work gone to waste.

So widespread is this feeling that a man who is a partner in a public relations firm would feel a sense of loss at Israel's destruction, in spite of the fact that he is affiliated with and active in the Einhorn Temple. He has great admiration for the Israelis, but his Classical Reform proclivities are demonstrated by the fact that he describes them as "coreligionists":

> They are fellow coreligionists who have struggled hard. They have done wonderful things. They're wonderful people; I'd hate to have anything happen to them.

Those who respond in terms of the achievements of the State of Israel are not mere admirers of achievement; even if they esteem other countries which have made progress in spite of heavy odds, they have a particular concern with Israel. Other respondents, however—about a fifth of those who would feel a sense of loss—are troubled by the fact that they hold an ethnocentric bias. They are concerned about the strength of their Jewish feelings, and they seek to balance such feelings by viewing Israel through the non-sectarian lens of humanitarianism or Americanism. Thus an office worker who belongs to Lilienthal Temple and is active in Democratic Party affairs speaks of Israel in the framework of American political interests, apparently out of a need to balance his deep Jewish feelings:

> I have strong feelings regarding Israel. I'm a Jew, and it represents a Biblical prediction of the return. It's the only democratic and liberal state in the Middle East—the only one this country could call upon or depend upon in the Middle East. It's my birthright.

Another example is a prosperous salesman of German descent who is affiliated with the Einhorn Temple. He has lived in Lakeville for about a decade and feels that the most important problem facing the community is the influx of Jewish residents. But while he reacts in terms of a general humanitarianism, he has enough insight to realize that he would not be similarly concerned about the loss of sovereignty of other small nations:

> I'd give you the same answer if the Russians were successful in eliminating Greece. I don't believe any country should destroy another. I'd feel a little stronger about Israel; countries *have* been destroyed and eliminated. I'd feel worse about Israel because I feel a sympathy and limited ownership there.

The response of a woman who is a more recent resident and married to an affluent machinery manufacturer is significant in this connection. The family is affiliated with the Wise Temple, and the woman is strongly antagonistic to members of the Einhorn Temple because "they bury their Jewishness in Americanism" and "try so hard to be 200 per cent Americans." But in spite of holding such attitudes, she senses a need to balance her feelings of Jewish identity with her general commitments. Stating that she would have a deep sense of loss if Israel were destroyed, she adds,

> I'd feel the same over any country that was destroyed. Because of the same religion in Israel as mine, I'd feel closer to it.

Our smallest group of respondents, totaling about one in ten of those who would feel a sense of loss, are those who state that their attitude to Israel's demise would entail no special feeling of association with the country. Such respondents are humanitarians first: they would be equally concerned with the fate of any small, democratic nation. A highly successful middle-aged attorney of East European descent, a member of the Hirsch Temple who is very satisfied with his affiliation, says that he would:

> feel a deep sense of personal loss whenever a democratic nation is submerged. There's no emotional kinship with Palestine.

Then there is the case of a woman who is new to the community. The wife of an executive in the textile industry and the mother of a pre-schooler, she is not yet affiliated with a temple, but has joined the League of Women Voters and has been most favorably impressed with the organization. While she says that she would feel a deep sense of loss, she maintains that her feelings stem solely from a humanitarian impulse:

> . . . I feel the same way about the satellite countries being overrun. I don't like to see this happen to any human beings living in any country, not because it is Israel or because they are Jews.

The orientation of the 10 per cent who say that they would feel no personal sense of loss at Israel's destruction is not very different from that held by such respondents. They also reject any suggestion of having a special feeling of identification with Israel. The wife of a manufacturer of lighting fixtures, who is an inactive member of the Wise Temple and a very active member of the parent–teacher associations at the schools which her children attend, told us,

> I as an individual would feel no personal sense of loss—same if it happened to India—but I wouldn't like it. I'd feel badly for anyone.

A mother who was confirmed at the Holdheim Temple and works at a local bank because she is now in straitened circumstances formulated her reaction in the following terms:

> I can't associate myself with Israel as my national homeland. I would feel an impersonal sense of loss because of sorrows that go with the people who worked so hard to settle in a barren land. . . . I have great admira tion for the common man who settled that land.

Another member of the group which would feel no sense of loss presents a more ideological response. She is a newcomer to Lakeville who is married to an up-and-coming salesman. Highly acculturated, this woman believes strongly that her pre-school children should be given the tree and presents which her Reform parents denied her at Christmastime:

I'd feel badly, but no personal loss. I don't believe in a homeland for a religion. I can't see the point of a native American segregating himself because of a religion.

The Presumed Effect on American-Jewish Status

The desire to raise the status and improve the security of Jewry was a key motivation in the efforts which culminated in the establishment of the State of Israel. In addition to providing for those who would come to the Jewish homeland because of a "positive" motivation, Zionism stressed the provision of a place of refuge for all Jews who were affected by anti-Semitic persecution. And by virtue of the fact that there would be a Jewish homeland, Zionism stressed that the relationship between Jews and non-Jews would be normalized. Such normalization would mean a radical improvement in Jewish–Gentile relationships.

The presumed salutary effect of the establishment of a Jewish state is not so clear for American Jews as it has been for those in certain other countries. Thus Israel has not had to function as a place of refuge for American Jewry as it did for German Jewry. On the other hand, it has generally not served to make the Jewish position untenable, although such a development, unforeseen by Zionism's founders, has occurred in some Arab countries. In any case, although there has been some research on how the position of the American Jew has been affected by the establishment of the State, little of this has reached the Jewish public. The impact of Israel on the status of American Jews, then, is a presumed effect. The subject is sufficiently ambiguous so that a query in this area is not so much a test of information as an additional avenue to the study of feelings about Israel.

Accordingly, we asked our respondents: "Do you think that the existence of the State of Israel has had any effect on the status and security of American Jews?" Those who gave a positive response were probed: "Has it been a beneficial or a harmful effect?" as well as "Why do you feel this way?" Some 66 per cent feel that the existence of the State has had an effect on American Jewry, while 33 per cent feel that it has not had any effect.[1]

Among those who believe that Israel has had an effect, the majority—some 66 per cent—feel that the effect has been beneficial. On the other hand, 19 per cent feel that Israel's effect has been harmful, while some 14 per cent believe that the effect of Israel has been both beneficial and harmful.[2] We find that estimates of Israel's impact on the situation of American Jewry are not independently arrived at, but rather are a function of feelings toward Israel. Thus Israel is seen as a threat to American Jewry by 68 per cent of those who would feel no sense of loss if it were destroyed. On the other hand, 78 per cent of those with a very deep sense of loss feel that Israel has had a beneficial effect on the status and security of American Jewry. Those with lukewarm feelings toward Israel are more inclined than other respondents to feel that Israel has had beneficial as well as harmful effects (see Table 6–2).

TABLE 6–2. PRESUMED EFFECT OF ISRAEL ON AMERICAN JEWS BY FEELING TOWARD ISRAEL

Per cent who believe Israel's effect on the status and security of American Jews is	Personal Sense of Loss if Israel Destroyed		
	Very Deep	Some	None
Beneficial	78	46	16
Both	9	31	16
Harmful	13	23	68
N (TOTAL BELIEVE ISRAEL HAS ANY EFFECT)	(201)	(62)	(19)

Since the status and security of American Jews are also determined by the Gentile majority, the question we put to our respondents elicited some estimate of the reaction of non-Jews. Such estimates are colored by the situation of the Lakeville Jew as a member of a minority which is in the process of solidifying a newly won position in American life. Some respondents believe Israel has improved their chances for solidifying that position, some are uncertain, and others are convinced that Israel has harmed their chances.

We find that those who believe that Israel is a threat to American Jews more often perceive of Gentiles, rather than Jews, as the group that is directly affected by Israel. They see Israel as endangering the position of American Jewry because it upsets the relationship between America's Jewish minority and its Gentile majority. On the other hand, those who believe that Israel is a boon to American–Jewish status and security perceive that Jews more often than Gentiles are directly affected by Israel's existence. Many in this group also mention intergroup relationships. Of course, when they do, they view the position of the American

Jew as enhanced rather than diminished by virtue of the effect that Israel has on the non-Jew.

The hopes as well as the anxieties that are invested in Israel illustrate the diverse ways in which our respondents grapple with their position in American society. A frequent concern expressed by the minority who view Israel as a threat is the "dual loyalty" charge; they fear that Israel's existence and actions can cause American Jews to be—or appear to be—in conflict with their allegiance to the United States. A businessman with a professional degree who was raised in a Gentile neighborhood and believes that Lakeville is becoming too Jewish ("they're moving out here in hordes") feels that

> the State of Israel has become too important. Most Gentiles feel the State of Israel is where all Jews believe in above any other place.

A woman who is the spouse of a very prosperous businessman and an active room mother in the public school which her son attends feels that

> Zionists bombard Presidents with their demands and give the impression of speaking for all of Jewry. Jews resent it. Non-Jews certainly resent it because Israel is a country separate and apart, and we shouldn't think of it first.

Other respondents who feel that Israel is a threat to the status and security of American Jewry stress the country's sensitive geographical and political position. Viewing Israel as a highly visible "trouble spot," they feel that Israeli foreign policy can conflict with United States foreign policy, thus exposing American Jews to unfavorable public notice and ultimately increasing anti-Semitism. One segment of this group believes that American Jews can become scapegoats for Israel's faults, as, for example, the lawyer who is affiliated with the Hirsch Temple but finds his most satisfying affiliation with the local chapter of the Council on Foreign Relations:

> The average non-Jew believes Israel causes trouble, and this spills over to the belief that Jews cause trouble.

Although he is careful to hedge his statement, a man who teaches in the public-school system of a neighboring suburb expresses the fear that Israel's existence can encourage a move to expel Jews from the United States:

> Some people who might have tended that way anyway would now say, "You have a country; now go there."

Unlike the small group which feels that Israel tends to pose serious problems for American Jewry's status and security, a large number of those who feel the country is a boon rather than a threat view Israel as a Jewish homeland and a symbol of Jewish identity. Some of those who feel that Israel has had a positive impact point to it as a factor in strengthening religious and ethnic consciousness and associational ties among American Jews. A graduate of a fashionable New England women's college who is very satisfied with her children's Sunday School at Wise Temple and attends services more regularly than did her parents believes that Israel has stimulated an awareness of Jewishness:

> Israel made a lot of Jews re-examine themselves and become conscious of being Jews and send their children to temples.

Many more of those who view Israel's impact in a positive vein feel that it has been an essential element in furthering the integration of American Jewry. They do not believe that a Jewish homeland places any strain on the political loyalties of American Jews. Rather, they see Israel as placing American Jews even more firmly in the main stream of the American tradition by supplying them, at long last, with a homeland. These respondents tend to cite the experience of other ethnic groups as a model. A young wife and mother who is very satisfied with her affiliation with the Lilienthal Temple and gives much of her leisure time to this institution as well as to other Jewish groups states,

> Like all Norwegians belong to Norway, all the Jews should belong to Israel. We need a country to originate from, to belong to.

A real estate broker's wife, active in one of Lakeville's Jewish welfare organizations, emphasizes much the same idea:

> . . . every person should have a flag or a country that they can call their own. Israel has given the American Jew a place in the world.

A manufacturer's wife views the impact of Israel—particularly Jewish support for Israel—as improving the relationship between Jew and Gentile:

> The fact that there is a homeland helps the prestige of the Jew in the United States. He gains the respect of non-Jews by showing how much he cares and does for his own people. By helping and sending money to the Jews of Israel, *he* feels better for it.

Some of those who consider Israel to be a boon do so because they view its existence as serving to relieve feelings of insecurity which derive from the Jew's position as a member of a minority with a long history of persecution. They do not make as sharp a distinction between Israel as a haven of refuge for disadvantaged Jews and American Jews as was evident in responses to our question on feelings of loss if Israel were destroyed. Such respondents voice a sense of security deriving from the belief that Israel is available to all Jews who must seek refuge from persecution. A mother who is active at the Lilienthal Temple states,

> Israel is a last resort. In the event of open conflict, a Jew has a place to go and be accepted.

A doctor's wife, the mother of two grown sons, who was formerly active in community affairs but is now more interested in her flower garden, feels that the American Jew has experienced a heightened feeling of security since Israel was established:

> There's a security in knowing that Israel is there. If there were any difficulties here for Jewish people, it's a secure feeling to know that they could go there and be made comfortable.

Finally, some who feel that Israel constitutes a boon view its favorable effect in terms of changing the image of the Jew held by the Gentile. Unlike those who feel threatened by Israel's impact on the Gentile, such respondents believe that Israeli achievements have had a salutary effect on anti-Jewish stereotypy. They believe that the image of the Jew which Israel projects is that of the fighter and frontiersman, and they feel that the projection of such an image is bound to have beneficial results. A prosperous accountant, who is a satisfied but inactive member of the Schechter Synagogue, typifies this kind of response:

> I think in the non-Jewish community people become aware that Jews have guts and stand up and fight—that the Jew is a *man,* not just a merchant.

An engineer who grew up in a non-Jewish neighborhood and works for a large manufacturing firm advances much the same view:

> The American Jew has acquired more status because Jewish people showed themselves to be pioneers, soldiers, farmers—things that people didn't know they could do. [Israel shows] they have *guts*. And now Gentiles take a different look at their Jewish neighbors.

A prosperous lawyer who is a member of a Jewish intergroup relations agency as well as the National Conference of Christians and Jews presents a more measured response:

> Well, I think Gentiles admired what the Israelis did. I think we got something *we* didn't deserve from it—it spilled over to us.

Support and Involvement

While a large majority of Lakeville Jews are pro-Israel in feeling and concern, the question occurs as to their sentiments in respect to two other important dimensions of the relationship of the American Jew to Israel: support and involvement. We asked our respondents for their stand on six different kinds of support which American Jews can render Israel: raising money, encouraging their children to immigrate, belonging to Zionist organizations, seeking to influence United States foreign policy in favor of Israel, giving Israeli financial needs priority over local causes, and participating personally in the building of Israel through immigrating and becoming an Israeli citizen. We find that almost all our respondents approve of raising money, while almost none of them believe that American Jews are obliged to go to Israel themselves or to encourage their children to do so (see Table 6–3). Not only do very few believe in individual or familial participation in the upbuilding of the State, but only 14 per cent approve of giving Israeli financial needs priority over local Jewish causes.

TABLE 6–3. TYPES OF SUPPORT OF ISRAEL

Per cent approve following types of help by American Jews for the Jews of Israel	
Raise money for Israel	91
Seek to influence U.S. foreign policy in favor of Israel	63
Belong to Zionist organizations	31
Give Israeli financial needs priority over local Jewish causes	14
Encourage their children to immigrate to Israel	1
Participate personally in the building of Israel through becoming a citizen of Israel	1

It would thus seem that Israel is cast in the role of just another Jewish philanthropy. This is not really the case, however, inasmuch as 63 per cent approve of influencing American foreign policy in favor of Israel. The majority of Lakeville Jews thus go beyond financial assistance and see Israel as a political cause which American Jews should support as well as an object of benevolence. Nevertheless, fewer approve of using

Jewish influence than approve of raising money. And there is even greater disagreement in regard to the means for involvement in the political process: only 31 per cent favor affiliation with Zionist organizations. Thus, while willing to take a political stand in connection with their Jewish identity, the majority of our respondents do not favor Zionist organizations as the vehicle for exercising such influence. Zionist organizations are viewed as agencies whose sole concern is with Israel; the majority of our respondents reject the necessity of adherence to a specialized pro-Israel association.

The frequencies with which various types of assistance are favored follow the pattern of a cumulative scale, rather than one of discrete or alternative actions.[3] Thus a person approving the less favored types of aid tends to endorse the more popular actions as well. Table 6–4 indicates the varying limits of action favored in behalf of Israel and the proportion of persons favoring each limit. We find that only 7 per cent reject all types of support, 28 per cent favor an exclusively philanthropic role by restricting Jewish support to financial contributions,

TABLE 6-4. LEVELS OF SUPPORT OF ISRAEL

Per cent approve following	
None	7
Raise money only	28
Raise money, influence U.S. policy	32
Raise money, influence U.S. policy, and additional action	33

some 32 per cent also favor an ethnic political role by including efforts to influence foreign policy, and another 33 per cent support raising money, using influence, and taking one or more additional actions.*

Feeling and concern about Israel are, of course, reflected in the response to our question on support for Israel. While 43 per cent of those who would feel a deep sense of loss if Israel were destroyed approve of American Jews giving money, using influence, and proceeding with additional action, only 2 per cent of those who say that they would feel no personal loss in Israel's demise would render similar support (see Table 6–5). A sharper and more significant cleavage between the two poles of feeling

---

* Such action is generally affiliation with a Zionist organization. Secondarily, it means giving Israel financial priority over local causes.

centers about the issue of using political influence in Israel's behalf. As many as 78 per cent of those who would experience a deep sense of loss favor using such influence, contrasted with only 26 per cent of those who would have no special feeling of loss. Yet most of those who say they have no personal sense of loss do not want to prevent Jewish philanthropic aid: only one-fourth advocate such a policy. At the other extreme, we find that a surprising one-fifth of those who claim they would feel a very deep sense of loss favor limiting Jewish support of Israel to the raising of funds.

TABLE 6–5. LEVEL OF SUPPORT OF ISRAEL BY FEELING TOWARD ISRAEL

	Personal Sense of Loss if Israel Destroyed		
Per cent approve following	Very Deep	Some	None
Raise money, influence U.S. policy, and additional action	43	20	2
Raise money, influence U.S. policy	35	28	24
Raise money only	20	41	48
None	2	11	26
N	(281)	(107)	(42)

Much the same relationship is apparent in respect to the beliefs about Israel's effect on the status and security of the American Jew. Some 52 per cent of those who view the country as a boon advocate raising money, using influence, and taking additional action, while only 6 per cent of those who feel that Israel's effect on the status of American Jewry is harmful do so (see Table 6–6). However, these two groups pull even further apart on the issue of using influence than do those who are at opposite poles in respect to a feeling of loss. While 85 per cent of those who believe Israel constitutes a beneficial force for American Jewry favor a political role, only 23 per cent of those who fear the country's impact are willing to go as far. Yet most of these fearful persons feel secure in a philanthropic role, and less than one-fifth would refuse all support.

The picture that emerges, then, is that varying degrees of personal identification with Israel and opposed views about the country's impact on American Jewry become translated into certain levels of support. The most significant cleavage centers about the issue of an ethnic polit-

TABLE 6–6. LEVEL OF SUPPORT OF ISRAEL BY PRESUMED EFFECT OF ISRAEL ON AMERICAN JEWS

	Israel's Presumed Effect on American Jewish Status and Security		
Per cent approve following	Beneficial	Both	Harmful
Raise money, influence U.S. policy, and additional action	52	25	6
Raise money, influence U.S. policy	33	25	17
Raise money only	14	40	58
None	1	10	19
N	(189)	(41)	(53)

ical role versus an exclusively philanthropic role. It is apparent, however, that just as the majority of our respondents are not religious traditionalists, so they are not Zionist traditionalists. In fact, an analogy with the Jewish religion is quite apt. Thus the great bulk of Lakeville Jews accept the legitimacy of a Jewish religious identification, but perilously few rate high in respect to home observance and synagogue attendance. Similarly, most are pro-Israel in sentiment, but only a minority are willing to advocate that Jews practice a high level of commitment.

However we evaluate the levels of concern, feeling, and support, when we examine the character of Jewish life and institutions in Lakeville we find that it is not permeated with Israel. While it is true that there is some pro-Israel activity in the synagogues, in various Jewish organizations, and in philanthropic work, such activity tends to be episodic; involvement based on intense and continuing ties with Israel is limited. Only 13 per cent of our respondents rate themselves as having more than a "poor" knowledge of Hebrew. Only 8 per cent have attempted to study the language or have done something else to keep up their Hebrew knowledge in recent years. Furthermore, while almost all our respondents find that at least some attention is paid to Israel in their "contacts with fellow Jews and Jewish organizations," only 2 per cent have attended study groups, courses, or lectures concerning Israel in the past year, and only 8 per cent have tuned to a radio or television program dealing with Israel in the past three months.

One growing avenue of contact is travel to Israel. We do not know how many of our respondents have visited Israel one or more times and what meaning such trips have had for them. Undoubtedly, travel is becoming a significant aspect of contact with Israel; since many Lakeville Jews have the means and the desire to travel, the percentage of those visiting Israel will surely rise. But whether such contact will have a pervasive influence on the level of involvement with Israel remains to be seen.

Another aspect of contact is recordings of Israeli music as well as Israeli souvenirs and objects. Some 43 per cent of our respondents say that Israeli souvenirs and objects can be found in their homes. Such objects were generally purchased in gift shops run by the synagogues, at a Jewish bookstore, or at a department store, rather than on a trip to Israel. By way of contrast, only 18 per cent of the parents of our respondents had such objects in their homes during our respondents' childhood years. The difference is, of course, connected not so much with contrasting levels of sentiment as with the growth of Israel and of new channels of distribution for Israeli products. While we do not have data on exactly what sentiment is attached to such objects, we do know that they are found in the Lakeville home as frequently as or even more frequently than certain basic religious objects. For example, while 43 per cent have an Israeli-made object, in only 39 per cent of the households are Sabbath candlesticks to be found.

In respect to institutional involvement, a mere 17 per cent of our respondents are affiliated with Jewish organizations whose major focus is the State of Israel. Most such memberships are concentrated in Zionist organizations; others are in "Friends of Israel" types of groups such as the American Technion Society. In any case, affiliation with an Israel-oriented organization does not necessarily reflect an ideological commitment to Zionism or to Israel; conversely, the lack of such an affiliation does not necessarily reflect an absence of commitment. What it does reflect in part is the different organizational styles of men and women.* In spite of the fact that there is no attitudinal cleavage between the sexes, 26 per cent of the women belong to Zionist organizations, in contrast to only 4 per cent of the men.

The association to which virtually all of these belong is Hadassah. This organization is known for its efforts in advancing health and welfare in Israel, rather than for political or ideological work. In fact, the majority of our respondents who belong to Zionist organizations are not

* See below, pp. 255–259.

ideologists. Rather, they affiliate with such a group on the basis of their feelings of Jewish identity and solidarity as well as their desire for Jewish association. Thus we find that only 10 per cent of the women who are affiliated with a Zionist organization believe that to be a good Jew it is "essential" to support Zionism. As many as 41 per cent of such women believe that "it makes no difference" in being a good Jew whether one is or is not a Zionist.

The success of Hadassah in Lakeville (and concomitantly the lack of success of more politically oriented Zionist groups) serves to highlight the lack of Zionist traditionalism among our respondents. It also illustrates that the relationship of the Lakeville Jew to Israel flows more out of Jewish identity than out of Zionist ideology. But the example of Hadassah also demonstrates how precarious it is to base a general Jewish association even on involvement in Israeli philanthropy; it shows that such an organization can be superseded by another organization serving the same needs for identity, solidarity, and association.

This shift has already occurred in Lakeville: while Hadassah is the largest and strongest non-synagogue Jewish women's organization of the nation at large, in Lakeville it has been superseded by Women's ORT (Organization for Rehabilitation through Training), which enrolls some 40 per cent of all Jewish women in the community. After World War II, ORT grew from a minuscule chapter to a network of active groups, each meeting in a different area of Lakeville. Its rate of recruitment among recent Jewish residents is much higher than that of Hadassah, and ORT is thus not only the largest but the fastest-growing Jewish organization in the community.

While ORT carries on some philanthropic activity in Israel, its operations, centering on vocational training and rehabilitation, are world-wide. Although it is vaguely pro-Israel, it does not require even the nominal ideological commitment advanced by Hadassah. It also avoids involvement in political efforts in support of Israel. On the one hand, it is not so intellectual as Hadassah (it does not sponsor study groups or programs of serious Jewish content), and on the other hand, it is not so money-oriented. Its fiscal sights are set on a lower level; ORT does not make the same financial demands on its members in terms either of personal giving or of raising money from others. In sum, this group has not required a Zionist program or even a concentration on Israel to expand from a minor voluntary association to Lakeville's most popular Jewish organization.

Influences on Pro-Israel Support

We have already noticed that there is a good deal of variation in concern, feeling, support, and involvement with Israel among Lakeville Jews. What are the factors, we wonder, associated with a pro-Israel position? For example, how is such a position affected by intergroup orientation? And is a pro-Israel position strengthened by involvement in synagogue affairs, by religious observance, and by one's orientation to religion? Since we began our analysis of the Lakeville Jew and Israel by asking whether Israel serves as a substitute for an older sacramentalism, we shall turn first to the area of religion.[4]

RELIGIOUS OBSERVANCE AND INVOLVEMENT

Although modern Israel actualized long-held religious yearnings, the Zionist movement from which it originated was predominantly secularist and nationalist in emphasis. Furthermore, Zionism encountered strong opposition both from those who were extremely Orthodox and those who were extremely Reform. The latter saw in Zionism a counter-ideology to Classical Reform's religio-ethical conception of Jewish life,* while the former viewed Zionism as a secularist revolt proceeding out of lack of faith and lack of satisfaction with a way of life sanctioned by generations of pious Jews. If Zionism involved a reconstruction of Jewish existence—counterposing a national homeland for the old "homeland" of the synagogue—how strongly, if at all at the present time, is pro-Israel sentiment rooted in religious involvement?

We find that involvement in synagogue life is clearly related to pro-Israel support. Thus, 49 per cent of the highly involved favor raising money, influencing American foreign policy, and taking additional action, compared to only 26 per cent of those with no synagogue connection (see Table 6–7).[5]

We also find that attendance at religious services is associated with

---

* As we have seen, Classical Reform is represented in Lakeville by the Einhorn Temple, some of whose leaders reflect the anti-Zionist ideology of the American Council for Judaism. Since this institution is oriented in a negative direction toward Israel, we shall analyze the sentiments of its membership separately. Accordingly, members of the Einhorn Temple are excluded from the tabulations that follow (Tables 6–7 to 6–14).

TABLE 6–7. LEVEL OF SUPPORT OF ISRAEL BY
INVOLVEMENT IN SYNAGOGUE LIFE

	Synagogue Involvement Score			
	High 3	2	1	Low 0
Per cent approve following				
Raise money, influence U.S. policy, and additional action	49	42	32	26
Raise money, influence U.S. policy	32	34	34	36
Raise money only	17	18	31	33
None	2	6	3	5
N	(82)	(95)	(93)	(123)

pro-Israel support (see Table 6–8). While 48 per cent of the most frequent attenders favor the highest category of support, only 21 per cent of nonattenders advocate similar actions.

Finally, we discover that home observance is even more strongly associated with pro-Israel support (see Table 6–9). While only 10 per cent of the nonobservant favor our highest category of support, 60 per cent of the more observant group do so. Furthermore, those who neglect home observance evince even less support than those who abstain from attendance at services. In sum, the Lakeville Jew who is more religiously observant or more involved in synagogue life is more committed to Israel.

We find, furthermore, that religious observance increases the level of

TABLE 6–8. LEVEL OF SUPPORT OF ISRAEL BY
LEVEL OF SYNAGOGUE ATTENDANCE

	Attendance Score			
	High 5+	3–4	1–2	Low 0
Per cent approve following				
Raise money, influence U.S. policy, and additional action	48	36	27	21
Raise money, influence U.S. policy	31	37	33	33
Raise money only	18	21	36	40
None	3	6	4	6
N	(127)	(144)	(70)	(52)

TABLE 6–9. LEVEL OF SUPPORT OF ISRAEL BY
LEVEL OF HOME OBSERVANCE

	Number Observances		
Per cent approve following	5+	1–4	0
Raise money, influence U.S. policy, and additional action	60	33	10
Raise money, influence U.S. policy	25	37	37
Raise money only	13	25	44
None	2	5	9
N	(105)	(218)	(70)

pro-Israel sentiment among the unaffiliated just as it does among those who belong to synagogues. Our data also show that synagogue membership in itself has little relation to pro-Israel sentiment. Thus, given a similar level of observance, the amount of pro-Israel support among synagogue members is generally about equal to or only slightly greater than that of non-members. In fact, the relatively few synagogue members who eschew all home observance tend toward a considerably lower level of support than non-members who fail to observe Jewish rituals.

Does the superior effect of religious observance in contrast to that of mere synagogue membership signify that involvement in a synagogue has no additional influence on pro-Israel support when religious observance is controlled? We find that such involvement results in an increased level of support only if there is little or no religious observance. Not only is the increase noticeable but the support level approaches or equals that prevailing among the more observant. Observant members who are relatively uninvolved in synagogue life favor as high a level of support as do those who are more involved.

Among persons who have not joined a synagogue, it is participation in religious observance that helps maintain higher levels of pro-Israel support. But among synagogue members with low observance, high involvement in synagogue life is a substitute form of religious commitment and results in a high level of support for Israel. On the other hand, among those synagogue members whose religious commitment is expressed in religious observance at home or at the synagogue, a lesser degree of synagogue involvement does not depress their relatively high level of support for Israel. In sum, pro-Israel sentiment is sustained by some form of religious commitment. And commitment to Israel does not generally function as a substitute for Jewish observance, devotionalism, or involvement in synagogue affairs. Rather, for the Lakeville Jew pro-Israel sentiment goes hand in hand with religious commitment. Nothing could be more paradoxical to many founders of the Zionist movement and to many of those whose efforts led to the establishment of the State.

These relationships do not hold true at the Einhorn Temple, however. We find that Einhorn members are a special group: they not only rank lower than members of all other synagogues in respect to level of pro-Israel support but even score lower than respondents who are not affiliated with a synagogue. One-fourth of Einhorn members would not render Israel any support, in contrast to less than one in twenty-five in any of the other synagogues. Another half would favor fund-raising, but avoid any other type of assistance by American Jews. Furthermore, Einhorn is the lone synagogue in Lakeville in which both leaders and veteran members favor lower levels of support for Israel than newer or more passive members. Only those who are inactive or have been affiliated merely for one or two years approach the levels of pro-Israel support encountered among the low-ranking groups in some of the other synagogues.

The sentiments of Einhorn members in respect to Israel are part and parcel of their Classical Reform approach. Their conception of Jewish identity is affiliation with a religious creed, and consequently their Jewishness is shorn of ethnic and cultural aspects. Thus almost 70 per cent of Einhorn members responded to our question "What is a Jew?" in *exclusively* religio-ethical terms, stating that a Jew is a person who believes in the Jewish religion or who follows its moral teachings. This compares with less than 40 per cent among other respondents. Furthermore, those Einhorn members who defined a Jew in purely religio-ethical terms evinced considerably less support for Israel than members who also included ethnic elements in their definition. But even those using an ethnic definition had lower levels of Israel support than similarly oriented respondents who belonged to other temples or were unaffiliated.

In sum, the adherence to an exclusively religio-ethical conception of Judaism among Einhorn members neutralizes the effect of Jewish religious commitment on pro-Israel sentiment. In contrast to others in Lakeville, the Einhorn member who is active in synagogue life, attends services, or observes Jewish rituals in his home is no more pro-Israel than his peers who are religiously quiescent.

JEWISH ORGANIZATIONAL INVOLVEMENT

In addition to religious involvement, it is reasonable to suppose that individuals who are active in Jewish communal life outside the synagogue would have a higher level of pro-Israel sentiment than those who are inactive. Participating in the life of the group, organizational actives should approve of a higher level of support for Israel—as a pervasive symbol of Jewish identity, solidarity, and ethnicity—than those who stand outside of organized group life.

We find that such participation is inconsistently related to pro-Israel support (see Table 6–10).[6] The more active participants in Jewish organizations differ in support level from those less actively involved only at one

TABLE 6–10. LEVEL OF SUPPORT OF ISRAEL BY INVOLVEMENT IN JEWISH ORGANIZATIONS

Per cent approve following	Jewish Organizational Involvement Score				
	High 4	3	2	1	Low 0
Raise money, influence U.S. policy, and additional action	58	47	40	27	31
Raise money, influence U.S. policy	16	38	31	33	38
Raise money only	26	12	23	33	27
None	—	3	6	7	4
N	(31)	(66)	(70)	(112)	(112)

level: a more frequent approval of pro-Israel actions in addition to political aid. Less active participators tend to avoid such additional actions and more often limit support to political aid. Thus there is little difference on the issue of a political versus an exclusively philanthropic role: a greater degree of involvement in Jewish groups does not always result in more political support; for example, those least involved favor using political influence almost as often as those at the highest level of involvement. The inconsistency in the overall relationship is a result of including those who are affiliated with Zionists or Israeli-focused organizations. When such persons are excluded, we find that greater involvement in Jewish organizations does result in consistently stronger political support.

We also find that any pro-Israel support that is engendered by greater participation in Jewish organizations presupposes a relatively high level of involvement in religious life. Thus when synagogue involvement is low, participation in Jewish organizations does not result in a higher level of pro-Israel sentiment (see Table 6–11). Similarly, involvement in

TABLE 6–11. LEVEL OF SUPPORT OF ISRAEL BY INVOLVEMENT IN JEWISH ORGANIZATIONS AND INVOLVEMENT IN SYNAGOGUE LIFE

Per cent approve influencing U.S. policy or additional action, and whose involvement in synagogue life is	Jewish Organizational Involvement Score	
	High (2–4)	Low (0–1)
High (2–3)	84	69
N	(101)	(76)
Low (0–1)	66	62
N	(66)	(148)

Jewish organizations has no effect on pro-Israel support when home observance or synagogue attendance is low. Only when observance or attendance is high does organizational involvement affect the level of support for Israel. But even these residual effects of participation in Jewish organizations become somewhat attenuated when members of Zionist or "Friends of Israel" organizations are excluded. However, both home observance and synagogue attendance markedly affect the level of pro-Israel support, regardless of the degree of involvement in Jewish organizations. Thus while the two forms of Jewish commitment—religious and ethnic—appear to have interacting influences on pro-Israel sentiment, the effects of the latter depend almost entirely on the former. In sum, while all the components of commitment to Jewish life promote favorable sentiment toward a general ethnic symbol such as the State of Israel, such sentiment is evoked most effectively by even a moderate level of religious observance, somewhat less effectively by participation in synagogue life, and least effectively by participation in Jewish organizations.

The fact that involvement in religious traditionalism, rather than participation in non-synagogue Jewish organizations, is closely connected with the holding of a pro-Israel position is ironic; as we have noted, the founders of modern Israel were in many cases individuals who had been deeply touched by secularism and had revolted from the passivity engendered by adherence to traditional Jewish religion. But we see that in Lakeville the sentiments and ties that underlie support for Israel are reinforced within the framework of a suburban Jewish community where synagogues are a highly prominent feature of the Jewish landscape and religion is the mark of Jewish distinctiveness. In the next chapter, we shall analyze in greater depth the meaning of Jewish organizational affiliation; but at this point it is sufficient to point out that such affiliation and activity, although based on ethnicity, does not transform feelings of ethnic identity into overriding support for the State of Israel independently of adherence to religious traditions and institutions.

INTERGROUP ORIENTATION

Another potential influence on pro-Israel sentiment is the relationship with the non-Jew. It is possible that Jewish commitments are not so crucial a determinant of pro-Israel sentiment as the degree of integration into the organizations, institutions, and values of the general community. It is reasonable to suppose that those with strong ties to the general community should feel minimal loyalty to an ethnic symbol such as the State of Israel. It is also reasonable to suppose that those who have weaker ties to the larger community—whether because they feel alienated from Gentiles, find greater responsiveness and community of interest with fellow Jews, have long-standing Jewish associations, or for some other reason—should possess stronger in-group ties and therefore should evince a higher level of pro-Israel sentiment.

This approach oversimplifies the problem, however. It neglects the increasing variation of both intergroup and intragroup orientations among acculturated American Jews. Specifically, it ignores the integrationist Jew with high intragroup commitments as well as the Jew who is not a strong integrationist, but nevertheless has few intragroup commitments. Therefore, we must examine the problem of whether Jewish isolation or alienation from intergroup relationships results in greater pro-Israel sentiment, regardless of the level of commitment to Jewish institutions and groups. If ties to Jewish groups and institutions are minimal, is such intergroup alienation a residual source of pro-Israel sentiment? And if Jewish group commitments are high, does an integrationist orientation nevertheless diminish pro-Israel sentiment?

The concept of integration-mindedness [7] subsumes various facets of behavior and values which indicate the extent of the Jew's involvement in organizations and styles of life of the general community and his preferences regarding such integration. Little or no integration-mindedness can be conceived as a tendency to alienation or isolation from such relationships.[8]

Table 6–12 indicates that such alienation (denoted by a lower integration-mindedness score) is highly associated with support for Israel. While none in the extreme integrationist group are found in the highest category of pro-Israel support, over half of the most alienated are located there.[9]

TABLE 6–12. LEVEL OF SUPPORT OF ISRAEL BY LEVEL OF INTEGRATION-MINDEDNESS

Per cent approve following	*Integration-Mindedness Score*						
	High 8–9	7	6	5	4	3	Low 1–2
Raise money, influence U.S. policy, and additional action	—	12	24	38	48	50	53
Raise money, influence U.S policy	43	29	35	32	35	35	33
Raise money only	38	47	35	26	17	12	12
None	19	12	6	4	—	3	2
N	(21)	(42)	(69)	(83)	(76)	(60)	(42)

We also find that feelings experienced in situations of social contact with Gentiles have little influence on pro-Israel sentiment: those who experience greater feelings of discomfort in relations with non-Jews exhibit only a slightly higher level of support for Israel. Furthermore, discomforting experiences bear considerably less relationship to pro-Israel sentiment than does one's orientation to Gentiles. Thus, among integrationists as well as among the more alienated, those who experience greater discomfort with non-Jews barely differ with respect to Israel from those who do not experience intergroup discomfort. But an alienated orientation results in significantly greater support independently of intergroup experience (see Table 6–13). Thus it is more the Jew's posture regarding intergroup relationships which is associated with his sentiments about Israel than it is the degree of anxiety or tension he experiences in his actual relationships with Gentiles.

However, the posture toward intergroup relationships does not uniformly affect the level of pro-Israel sentiment when the factor of Jewish

TABLE 6–13. LEVEL OF SUPPORT OF ISRAEL BY
DISCOMFORT WITH GENTILES AND
LEVEL OF INTEGRATION-MINDEDNESS

Per cent approve influencing U.S. policy or additional action, and whose integration-mindedness score is		More uncomfortable with non-Jews than with Jews	
		Yes	No
High (5+)		62	55
	N	(103)	(110)
Low (1–4)		89	78
	N	(90)	(88)

commitment is taken into account. While the alienated exhibit greater support for Israel if they are at lower levels of commitment to Jewish life (whether their commitment is manifested by involvement in Jewish organizations or synagogue groups, in home observance, or in attendance at services), at the highest levels of activity, attendance, and observance, the sentiments of integrationists are as pro-Israel, or almost as pro-Israel, as those of the alienated. For example, among those highly involved in synagogue life, virtually as many of the integrationists as of the alienated—about four in five in each group—approve the use of political influence or additional action. Among those at the highest level of home observance, such support is favored by as many of the integrationists (88 per cent, compared with 85 per cent), while among those whose observance level is moderately high, integrationists are only slightly less pro-Israel (75 per cent, compared to 86 per cent). However, among those less active in the synagogue or less observant at home, the proportions of the integration-minded who favor such support range downward from 64 per cent, in contrast to more than four in five (81 to 87 per cent) among the alienated (see Table 6–14). When religio-ethnic ties are weak or moderate, the expansion of pro-Israel sentiment is related to alienating attitudes and behavior. Nevertheless, strong ties to Judaism and Jewishness are able to nourish a high level of pro-Israel sentiment even when integrationist commitments are high; given firm ties to Jewish life, such commitments do not significantly diminish pro-Israel sentiment.

The impact of an alienated intergroup orientation on pro-Israel sentiment is strongest among those with the weakest Jewish ties. Thus, the

TABLE 6-14. LEVEL OF SUPPORT OF ISRAEL BY LEVEL OF INTEGRATION-MINDEDNESS AND INVOLVEMENT IN JEWISH LIFE

		Integration-Mindedness Score	
Per cent approve influencing U.S. policy or additional action, and whose involvement in synagogue life is		High (5+)	Low (1–4)
High (3)		77	83
	N	(40)	(42)
Moderate (2)		64	87
	N	(47)	(48)
Low (1)		52	85
	N	(55)	(38)
None		48	82
	N	(73)	(50)
and whose home observance is			
High (6+)		88	85
	N	(24)	(42)
Moderately high (4–5)		75	86
	N	(33)	(38)
Moderately low (2–3)		60	86
	N	(67)	(51)
Low (0–1)		43	81
	N	(91)	(47)

more attenuated the ties, the greater the margin of difference in pro-Israel support between the integrationist and the alienated. Despite their meager commitment to Jewish life, not only do the less integration-minded respondents demonstrate greater pro-Israel sentiment but their level of support approaches that of the most Jewishly committed. Attenuated ties to Jewish voluntary associations or to Jewish religious life, then, do not automatically lead to diminished pro-Israel sentiment so long as the orientation to Gentiles and to thoroughgoing integration into the general society is lukewarm or negative.

We thus see that a relatively high level of commitment to Judaism and Jewishness, especially in respect to religious practice and synagogue life, is one basis for pro-Israel sentiment and that this influence is not affected by an integrationist orientation to the wider community. Moreover, an integrationist stance is compatible with a firm attachment to Israel when it is accompanied by a strong Jewish commitment. Only when religio-ethnic supports diminish do integrationist commitments radically reduce the level of pro-Israel sentiment. But even if such supports dissolve, pro-Israel sentiment is still sustained among those who are alienated from the Gentile world.

The fact that pro-Israel sentiment is manifested by Jews who are marginal religiously and institutionally but also minimize or reject inter-action with Gentiles and with Gentile life styles suggests an ethnic soli-darity based primarily on informal group ties. Association in homoge-neous Jewish friendship groups is, indeed, frequently encountered among alienated Jews with very low levels of Jewish activity. Thus, among those at the lowest level of home observance, over half of the alienated have an exclusively Jewish set of close friends, compared to only three in ten of the integrationists. The alienated also have more of a history of ex-posure to ethnically homogeneous social environments than do the inte-grationists, specifically in respect to the neighborhood in which they spent their childhood and the clique associations they had as teen-agers. We shall have occasion to study the overall significance of informal group ties in a later chapter.

GENERATION

An integrationist orientation often reflects an extremely high level of acculturation. Such acculturation, usually connected with the number of generations in the United States, is generally thought to be associated with a reduction in ethnic sentiment. If so, it should be reflected in pro-Israel sentiment, which should decline in each successive generation.

We do, indeed, encounter such a situation in respect to the level of support for Israel, but the decline is limited within each descent group.[10] Thus support for Israel declines with successive generations among Ger-man Jews, but only a small minority in the fourth generation—less than one-fifth—would not favor any aid by American Jews; most favor exclu-sively philanthropic support (see Table 6–15). Thus almost three-fourths of fourth-generation Germans would either limit aid to philanthropy or refuse support; by way of contrast, the same proportion of first- and second-generation Germans [11] are willing to render assistance on the political level with or without the additional actions specified in our highest category of support. Adherence to this highest category of sup-port drops sharply in the third generation. Among East Europeans, there is also a noticeable lessening of sentiment in the third generation

TABLE 6–15. LEVEL OF SUPPORT OF ISRAEL BY GENERATION AND DESCENT

	Generation of							
	German Descent			Mixed Descent			East European Descent	
Per cent approve following	First & Second	Third	Fourth Plus	First & Second	Third	Fourth Plus	First & Second	Third
Raise money, influence U.S. policy, and additional action	43	12	—	30	26	10	51	29
Raise money, influence U.S. policy	28	31	28	35	26	40	30	41
Raise money only	24	42	54	35	39	30	17	28
None	5	15	18	—	9	20	2	2
N	(21)	(26)	(39)	(17)	(23)	(20)	(165)	(85)

favoring such additional support; but the decline in overall political support in this generation is not a sizable one and suggests that in this descent group pro-Israel sentiment is being stabilized at this level of support.

Although the influence of descent persists within each generation—for example, in the third generation East Europeans favor more pro-Israel actions than do those of German or mixed descent—there are signs that it plays a diminishing role among our more youthful respondents. Thus younger Germans and East Europeans tend to differ from their older counterparts of the same generation and also show signs of converging toward a similar position. For example, younger Germans of either the third or fourth generation favor a higher level of pro-Israel support than older Germans, who tend to confine themselves to an exclusively philanthropic role. Similarly, younger East Europeans of the second or third generation veer away from supporting our highest category of pro-Israel actions, which are favored by their older counterparts.

These changes indicate that in both descent groups more of the older respondents appear to be bound by traditions that were influential in the immediate past. Thus older Germans adhere to the tenets of a Classical Reform Judaism which rejected traditional ethnic and religious components in Judaism and Jewish life. They are ambivalent about any identification with Jews other than on narrowly construed religious grounds. Older East Europeans, on the other hand, appear to retain the strong sense of Jewish peoplehood that is associated with their Orthodox or Conservative religious backgrounds.[12] While historically this sentiment has not always been explicitly Zionist (several decades ago among some groups of East European Jews it was, in fact, non-Zionist or even anti-Zionist), it makes the older East Europeans highly concerned about Jews overseas, willing to act in uninhibited fashion in their behalf and specifically to favor a greater range of actions to assure the growth and development of the State of Israel. These contrasting religio-ethnic outlooks find fewer adherents among younger respondents, and consequently there is more bunching in the middle rather than at the polar positions on our measure of pro-Israel support. In terms of types of support for Israel, such a middle position is translated into a willingness to favor a political as well as a philanthropic role.

It is apparent from these findings that just as parental orientation has an influence on religious observance, so it is important in respect to attitudes toward Israel. However, we cannot analyze the influence of parental orientation directly, for we do not have data on the attitudes toward Zionism and Israel held by the parents of our respondents. But we know the religious orientation of the parental group, and thus we are able to approach the problem indirectly.*

We find that those respondents who feel that they are Conservative Jews are significantly more pro-Israel than those who consider themselves Reform (see Table 6–16). In fact, the level of pro-Israel sentiment among Reform Jews is about the same as it is among those who feel that they cannot identify themselves with any of the three main religious movements in American Jewish life.

TABLE 6–16. LEVEL OF SUPPORT OF ISRAEL BY RELIGIOUS ORIENTATION

	Religious Orientation		
Per cent approve following	Conservative *	Reform	None
Raise money, influence U.S. policy, and additional action	58	23	27
Raise money, influence U.S. policy	32	33	35
Raise money only	9	35	31
None	1	9	7
N	(121)	(266)	(45)

* Seven Orthodox cases included.

The influence of religious orientation on pro-Israel sentiment depends in considerable measure, however, on religious inheritance, rather than on present religious orientation. Thus, whatever the respondent's religious inclination, if his parents' orientation was Orthodox or Conservative he tends to favor considerable support for Israel. And if the orientation of his parents was Reform (or if his parents had no religious orientation), he tends to favor a very low level of pro-Israel support (see Table 6–17).[13] In this respect, Reform respondents of Conservative or Orthodox lineage bear less resemblance to their Reform peers who inherited their orientation than they do to Conservative respondents of Conservative or Orthodox lineage. In fact, those who inherit a Reform orientation most often favor the lower levels of support, even more than do those who follow their parents in claiming no religious orientation.

* As previously indicated in this chapter, religious orientation, especially in the parental generation, implied a distinctive set of attitudes about Jewish peoplehood and the desirability of a Jewish national homeland.

TABLE 6-17. LEVEL OF SUPPORT OF ISRAEL BY RESPONDENTS' AND PARENTS' RELIGIOUS ORIENTATION

	Religious Orientation						
Respondents	Conservative		Reform				None
Parents	Ortho-dox	Con-serva-tive	Ortho-dox	Con-serva-tive	Re-form	None	None
Per cent approve following							
Raise money, influence U.S. policy, and additional action	61	54	43	44	14	22	11
Raise money, influence U.S. policy	30	33	37	28	31	44	42
Raise money only	9	11	20	28	41	28	42
None	—	2	—	—	14	6	5
N	(70)	(46)	(35)	(46)	(167)	(18)	(19)

Inheritance of the parents' religious orientation thus has divergent effects on pro-Israel sentiment, with the widest differences occurring between Reform children of Reform parents and Conservative children of Conservative or Orthodox parents.

We find, furthermore, that parents' religious orientation affects the level of pro-Israel sentiment even among Reform respondents of the same generation. Conservative respondents in each generation generally approve a high level of support for Israel; the fact that the parents of some were Orthodox, rather than Conservative (as in the first- and second-generation group), produces few differences among them (see Table 6–18). However, among Reform respondents sharp differences in pro-Israel sentiment appear between those who inherit their orientation and those of Conservative or Orthodox background. Even in the first- and second-generation group, a Conservative or Orthodox childhood home results in a level of pro-Israel sentiment which approaches that of Conservative respondents, while an inherited Reform orientation produces a markedly lower level of support. In the third generation, Reform persons from Conservative background also have higher levels of pro-Israel sentiment than do those inheriting their Reform orientation, but the differences are not so large as those between Reform persons from Conservative homes and Conservative respondents generally. Thus first- and second-generation Reform respondents coming from more traditional homes appear to be influenced more by their background than by their peers who have inherited a Reform orientation; in the third generation, Reform persons reared in more traditional homes appear to be equally influenced by such peers.

Since the inheritance of a Reform orientation is correlated with minimal pro-Israel sentiment, it may be that the effect of successive generations in reducing pro-Israel sentiment is due in large measure to the fact that the more advanced generations inherit such an orientation more frequently than less advanced generations. We must thus confront the question of whether pro-Israel sentiment declines with successive generations of the same religious orientation.

Taking into account the individual's religious orientation as well as that of his parents, we find that the impact of generation becomes highly circumscribed. This can best be seen in Figure 6–1, which shows the level of support (in terms of median score values) according to each generation and for each combination of parent-and-respondent religious orientation for which data are available.[14] There are essentially three patterns of intergenerational change in religious identification between

TABLE 6-18. LEVEL OF SUPPORT OF ISRAEL BY RESPONDENTS' AND PARENTS' RELIGIOUS ORIENTATION AND GENERATION

Respondents	First and Second					Third			Fourth Plus
	Conservative		Reform			Conservative	Reform		Reform
Parents	Ortho-dox	Conserv-ative	Ortho-dox	Conserv-ative	Re-form	Conserv-ative	Conserv-ative	Re-form	Reform
Per cent approve following									
Raise money, influence U.S. policy, and additional action	61	50	45	54	23	61	31	14	5
Raise money, influence U.S. policy	31	38	38	23	23	28	31	34	30
Raise money only	8	8	17	23	45	11	38	39	47
None	—	4	—	—	9	—	—	13	18
N	(62)	(26)	(29)	(30)	(31)	(18)	(13)	(70)	(60)

the least advanced and most advanced generation: (1) an inherited Conservative or Orthodox orientation, (2) an inherited Reform orientation, (3) a change from Conservative or Orthodox to Reform orientation. Pro-Israel sentiment is at its highest level among those who inherit the more traditional orientation, even across several generations and including the most advanced (third) generation; it is at its lowest level among those

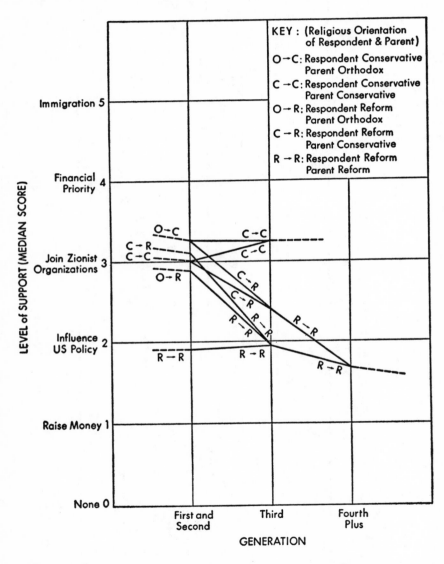

FIGURE 6-1. LEVEL OF SUPPORT OF ISRAEL BY GENERATION AND RESPONDENTS' AND PARENTS' RELIGIOUS ORIENTATION

who inherit a Reformist orientation, whether in the first or second generation or across several generations. Successive generations have little or no effect when either of these inheritance patterns has continued more than one generation. Successive generations lead to a marked decline in pro-Israel sentiment only during the process of change from a traditional to a Reformist orientation. Mere number of generations in the United States, then, does not reduce pro-Israel sentiment as much as does intergenerational change from an Orthodox or Conservative orientation to a Reform orientation.

Looking to the future, it appears that the brake imposed by East European descent on the decline in pro-Israel sentiment over the generations will become significant among those who inherit a Reform orientation; it should push their levels of pro-Israel sentiment higher than among the present inheritors of a Reform orientation. Descent from East European immigrant grandparents is an increasing trend among Reform inheritors in the third generation (half of this group is already of this origin), and our findings indicate that such persons approve of a higher level of support for Israel than Reform inheritors whose grandparents are of German or mixed origin. Although pro-Israel sentiment among respondents of East European descent declines during intergenerational change to a Reform orientation, it levels off at a higher plateau among succeeding generations of Reform inheritors. Thus in the third generation the higher floor of pro-Israel sentiment established by East European Reform inheritors is almost exactly like the level of persons who exchange the more traditional Conservative orientation of their East European–origin parents for a Reform identity. The latter, of course, have in turn considerably declined from the high levels maintained by those who inherited the more traditional orientation. Thus we may expect that overall the depressing effect on pro-Israel sentiment of generational changes to a Reform orientation will be even further circumscribed in subsequent generations of Reform inheritors.[15]

7

THE LAKEVILLE JEW
AND THE
JEWISH ORGANIZATION

The reader of the *Lakeville Bulletin,* the community's weekly newspaper, encounters evidence of the presence of Jews in the area in at least two ways. One is the religious columns of the paper, where the public is notified of the time and place of the services conducted in the various synagogues. The other is news stories reporting on the meetings of one or another Jewish organization. The uninformed reader who peruses these stories is perplexed; he soon becomes overwhelmed by the variety of Jewish organizations that meet in Lakeville and its environs. He finds that the names of some of them are so similar that it is difficult to distinguish between them. Their purposes present an even greater mystery: in many cases it is impossible to fathom the objectives of an agency from its name.

Other observers are also confounded. To those who look at Jewish life in historical perspective, or even to those whose only yardstick is utility and efficiency, it appears that what was once an integrated set of institutions expressing one or another facet of the Jewish sacred system has been replaced by a host of independent, competing, and secularized Jewish organizations. To such an observer, present-day Jewish organizations may appear as self-perpetuating interest groups seeking to justify their existence and to assure their continuity, whether or not they satisfy objective needs or project traditional Jewish values. And to an observer who is critical of Jewish "separatism," Jewish organizations may appear to be instrumentalities which serve to prevent the Jew from taking his proper place in the larger community.

Most Jews in Lakeville, however, see them in a different context. They feel that the agencies do "good work." They view them as important instrumentalities for improving Jewish and general welfare.[1] The perspective of the sociologist in respect to the agencies may differ altogether from the views of those who applaud or are critical. He may see them as a remarkable development which helps to mediate the crisis in Jewish identity experienced by those who find that they cannot give themselves fully either to the observance of the Jewish religion or to the development of the Jewish State.

The Jewish Organization in Perspective

In traditional Jewish society, the extended kinship group, together with the socially insulated Jewish town or neighborhood, formed a kind of circumscribed Jewish community in which face-to-face interaction unconsciously confirmed Jewish identity and expressed the Jewish way of life. In this setting, Jewish institutions performed specific functions required by the sacred system: sheltering the wayfarer, ministering to the sick, burying the dead, and many others. While serving the entire Jewish community, and in theory gathering funds from a very wide segment of the population, such agencies did not evolve into mass organizations: their activities were generally carried on by members of the elite. And since the focus of institutional activity was the performance of *mitzvot,* functions such as assuring Jewish identity or providing facilities for group interaction were secondary at best.

This kind of Jewish society no longer exists. One index of the fragmentation of traditional bonds is the marked attenuation of social interaction within the familial group. Such attenuation is, of course, a general social change hastened by such processes as social mobility and acculturation. But while the change represents a long-range development in the social order, the surprising thing is that even the present Lakeville generation has witnessed a measurable shift in familial interaction. When our respondents were children, 39 per cent of their parents spent more time socializing with relatives than with their friends. Only some 5 per cent of our respondents, however, spend more time with relatives than with their friends. And the children of our respondents will apparently be even less family-minded. While some 59 per cent of our respondents saw their cousins more than once a month when they were children and 46 per cent did so at least once each week, the comparable figures for the children of our respondents are 38 per cent and 22 per cent, respectively.

Social interaction has shifted away from the extended family at the same time that it has become detached from an ecological base. Not only does the interaction pattern of the Lakeville Jew extend far beyond the vicinity of his home but even those areas in Lakeville which are predominantly Jewish in population lack a distinctive Jewish character. And in any case, the neighborhood no longer fully performs its traditional function: even respondents who choose to make their residence in a predominantly Jewish area tend to have a strong desire to locate agreeable Gentile neighbors and to establish friendly relationships with them.

It is in the light of these changes that the significance of the Jewish organization must be understood: it partly fills the vacuum created by the erosion of the natural community of family and neighborhood.[2] Under contemporary conditions, then, affiliation and involvement in organizational life becomes a form of belonging to the Jewish community. As such, it is a way of affirming and validating one's Jewish identity. Under the circumstances, the importance of the organization derives not so much from its aims and accomplishments as from the contribution it makes to Jewish group survival. Indeed, the organization's accomplishments may lie more in the area of providing a mode of Jewish association and a way of leading a Jewish life in a predominantly non-Jewish society than in its strictly programmatic activities.

Membership and Involvement

We find that it is the exceptional Lakeville resident who does not have a Jewish institutional affiliation. Some 71 per cent of our respondents belong to a Jewish organization which is not sponsored by a synagogue, and if members of synagogue-related groups are included, this figure jumps to 78 per cent. Furthermore, if synagogue members who have no other Jewish affiliation are included, the total reaches 88 per cent. This figure of 88 per cent who have an affiliation with a Jewish voluntary association approximates the 91 per cent who belong to a non-sectarian association.[3]

Since the level of affiliation is not constant, but rather rises with each stage of the life cycle, these figures tend to understate the reach of Jewish voluntary associations. Thus in the most advanced phase of the life cycle 88 per cent are affiliated with at least one Jewish organization; if those who belong to a synagogue-sponsored group are included, the figure rises to 93 per cent (see Table 7–1). This accretion contrasts with the tendency of our respondents to drop their membership in non-sectarian associations in the most advanced phase. In fact, at this stage of the life cycle the slightly greater number affiliated with Jewish than with non-sectarian organizations represents a marked reversal of the pattern in the earlier phases.

TABLE 7–1. AFFILIATION WITH JEWISH AND NON-SECTARIAN ORGANIZATIONS BY FAMILY LIFE CYCLE

	Life-Cycle Phase				
Per cent members of	Pre-School	Early-School	Peak-School	Late-School	Post-School
Jewish organization *	62	64	72	86	88
Jewish organization (including synagogue-sponsored)	68	72	81	86	93
Non-sectarian organization	82	94	95	95	82
Two or more					
Jewish organizations *	34	26	45	78	61
Non-sectarian organizations	51	80	84	78	56
N	(68)	(103)	(162)	(22)	(67)

* Not sponsored by a synagogue.

Multiple memberships in Jewish organizations are common: some two in five belong to more than one association. And if synagogue-related groups are included, more than half hold a multiple affiliation. Multiple membership in non-synagogal Jewish groups reach their highest point just before the most advanced phase of the life cycle, somewhat later than do multiple memberships in non-sectarian groups. Another aspect of the appeal of these associations is that the older the respondent, the more important he feels it is to join a Jewish organization. While only 9 per cent of those at the earliest phase of the life cycle believe that it is essential to belong to a Jewish organization in order to be a good Jew, some 39 per cent of those in the most advanced phase of the life cycle feel this way.

In respect to involvement as distinct from membership, we find that for a significant number Jewish associational life is more than a dues-paying matter. If synagogue-related activity is included, more than half of our respondents (52 per cent) devote some time each week to Jewish institutional activity. Although a somewhat higher proportion are active in non-sectarian organizations (62 per cent), differences disappear when the more intensively involved are considered: some three out of ten spend over an hour each week in Jewish group activities, the same as the proportion involved at a similar level of activity in non-sectarian organizations. And at the most intensive level of activity (three or more hours per week), a slightly greater proportion of our respondents are involved in a Jewish activity.

What types of Jewish organizations appeal to Lakeville Jews? The answer to this question is complicated by the fact that there is no simple way of classifying Jewish organizations. While we shall employ conventional rubrics (such as health and welfare, social and recreational, cultural, educational, and community relations) it is apparent that they constitute only the roughest approximations of institutional functioning. Furthermore, some Jewish groups are multipurpose agencies. And while certain agencies confine their operations to Lake City, others are active in the country as a whole. The picture is further complicated by the wide spectrum of agencies that work overseas: some operate exclusively in Israel, some in Israel and elsewhere, and some only outside of Israel. Some agencies are comprehensive in approach, while others confine their operations to specific publics: college students at a local university, elderly persons in the metropolitan area, adolescent boys in the country as a whole, or aspiring musicians in Israel. Finally, some aid Jews exclusively, while others are oriented in a non-sectarian direction.

If synagogue-sponsored groups are excluded, we find that the types of organizational affiliations most prevalent among our respondents are groups devoted to health and welfare causes and to social and recreational purposes. Thus health and welfare groups enroll more than two of every five Lakeville Jewish adults (42 per cent). Among women, who tend to favor health and welfare causes, the most popular organizations are as follows: ORT (to which as many as 40 per cent of Lakeville women belong), Hadassah (which enrolls 26 per cent), and the National Council of Jewish Women (to which 18 per cent belong). Smaller numbers of women are involved in hospitals, assorted disease-research groups, homes for the aged, and youth work and vocational service agencies. Many such organizations limit their operations to the Lake City metropolitan area.

Some 45 per cent of Lakeville Jews are members of social and recreational groups.[4] Excluding the temple affiliates, to which about one-third of Lakeville Jews belong, the most popular social and recreational organization in the community is B'nai B'rith. It is by far the most popular agency among the men; some 37 per cent of all Lakeville men belong to a B'nai B'rith lodge. Another popular type of social and recreational organization among men is the Jewish country or city club, to which 25 per cent belong. A considerably smaller number of men are members of alumni groups of Jewish college fraternities.[5]

These levels of affiliation and involvement with Jewish organizations, especially with non-synagogue-sponsored groups, and the resulting emergence of a subcommunal structure find no parallel among Lakeville Protestants and Catholics. The contrast between Jews and Gentiles is particularly striking if we remember that there is a remarkable similarity between them in respect to involvement in religiously sponsored groups.* We find that among Gentiles membership in sectarian groups which are independent of church sponsorship is rare, as is membership in ethnically oriented agencies. The total number of non-Jews so enrolled comes to no more than 5 per cent, even if a liberal definition of sectarian is employed and if membership in such groups as the Young Men's Christian Association and Young Women's Christian Association is included. While a number of so-called non-sectarian organizations may actually function as sectarian organizations—although their sectarian purposes may be so elusive that even participants in the organization are unaware of them— there is still a substantial difference between the associational life of Jew and Gentile in Lakeville.[6]

The Differential Response of Men and Women

One of the most notable facts about organizational life in Lakeville is the greater involvement of women. As many as eight in ten women belong to at least one non-synagogue-connected Jewish organization, and about half belong to more than one (see Table 7–2). Only six in ten men

* See above, pp. 199–201.

are so affiliated, and only one-third hold a multiple affiliation. While more than four in ten of the women engage regularly in organizational activities and one-fourth are officeholders or board members, less than three in ten men are active, and only one in eight holds a similar position of responsibility. The sex gap becomes greater in the course of the life cycle, especially in respect to more intensive forms of involvement. While men and women in the earliest phase hardly differ with respect to multiple memberships and level of activity, at later stages women outdistance men in both respects. In the most advanced phase of the life cycle, three-fourths of the women have a multiple affiliation, in contrast to less than half of the men, and one in four women spend more than an hour a week in activities, compared to one in seven men.

TABLE 7-2. AFFILIATION AND ACTIVITY IN NON-SYNAGOGUE JEWISH ORGANIZATIONS BY SEX

	Men	Women
Per cent		
Members of following number of organizations		
0	38	21
1	30	28
2 or more	32	51
Spend time in activities (hours per week)		
0	71	58
1	15	18
2 or more	14	24
Hold leadership position *	12	25
N	(208)	(224)
Of members spend any time in activities	47	52
N	(129)	(177)

* Officers or board members.

Traditional sex roles have thus been upset in the field of communal activity. Instead of the man functioning as the active caretaker of communal needs and the woman taking responsibility only in the interstices of communal affairs, in Lakeville the woman is a full participant in communal activity. While women are less prominent in certain kinds of fund-raising—particularly drives which are organized on an occupational basis and those which solicit very substantial contributions—in certain other kinds of Jewish communal endeavor their influence is pervasive. The prominence of the woman in Jewish organizational life contrasts with the situation in the past, when the maintenance of such an important aspect of the social system as voluntary associations was a male responsibility.

The usual reasons cited for the new prominence of the woman are: (1) that the responsibilities of the man in business and professional life make it difficult for him to be active in communal affairs, (2) that the lack of such responsibilities on the part of the woman makes it easier for her to be active, and (3) that since the woman has a small family and is not gainfully employed, she is motivated to search for meaningful activity in fields of endeavor such as communal affairs. Are these perspectives— particularly the first and the second—valid? It is true that men are less active than women in all communal affairs, non-sectarian as well as Jewish. It is also obvious that involvement in organizations must find its place in the scarce leisure time available to the man. Furthermore, not only does the middle-class Jewish suburban woman have a more flexible schedule than the man (and presumably a greater amount of time) but to the extent that organizations are neighborhood- or community-based she is more strategically located; during the average day she has a greater opportunity to meet and confront her Jewish neighbors than does her spouse.

In reality, however, these are secondary considerations. For example, a significant proportion of Jewish men do not find occupational demands either so pressing or so engrossing as to prevent them from pursuing leisure-time interests. According to traditional norms, spare hours should be devoted both to religious study and to the assumption of communal responsibility, since such activities involve the performance of *mitzvot*. In Lakeville, however, men spend their leisure time, at least as often as do women, in a variety of activities which are personal, non-philan-thropic, and intended for amusement *—orientations foreign to tradi-tional Jewish culture and antithetical to the thrust of the Jewish sacred system. We are thus justified in concluding that changes in the area of values, rather than in the character of occupational life, are the strategic considerations.

Underlying the point about a value change is the finding that even when the Lakeville man becomes involved with a Jewish organization, he does not invariably turn to the affairs of the community either as an

* See Volume II, Chapter 6.

opportunity to perform *mitzvot* or as a relief from personal pursuits. Rather, a substantial number of men appear to seek in Jewish life a focal point for leisurely and pleasant association and consequently are attracted to expressive organizations—groups that appeal to the more private interests of individuals. A greater proportion of women, on the other hand, appear to seek involvement in instrumental organizations—groups that give them an opportunity to affect the lives of others. The evidence indicates that women are more commonly attracted to organizations with concrete and tangible goals than to those that only stress conviviality.

The greater organizational seriousness of women, then, is further evidence of a change in sex roles. According to traditional norms, males are the more serious sex—the sex whose horizon is not limited to the frivolous or the personal—and communal responsibility is uniquely the province of those whose life is devoted to the pursuit of the serious. But in Lakeville we find that it is the woman more than the man who desires transcendence, or at least who does so in the area of communal affairs. In the words of a young college-educated mother of two small children, who finds ORT to be her most satisfying affiliation, "I really have the feeling that this is the one thing I do that isn't for myself or for my children. It's really helping others." By way of contrast, the owner of a women's wear firm finds most satisfaction in the "social activities—the eating, drinking and swimming" of his elite club, while his only other membership in a Jewish organization is a lukewarm affiliation in Einhorn Temple. The club provides him with even more gratification than his active leadership of a Boy Scout troop composed of youngsters from a variety of religious backgrounds.

When women affiliate with a Jewish organization not connected with a synagogue, nine in ten of them choose the field of health and welfare. As many as 36 per cent of those in this kind of group find it to be their most satisfying affiliation. While about two in five of the women do join a social or recreational group, only 11 per cent of those with such a connection select it as their most satisfying affiliation. The orientation of the Lakeville male, on the other hand, is evident from the fact that when men affiliate with a Jewish association, fewer than one in five selects health or welfare, while as many as nine in ten join a group with a social or recreational purpose. More than one-fifth of the men who belong to a social group find it their most satisfying affiliation, and almost three in ten of those who belong to a city or country club choose that as their most satisfying organizational affiliation. This is surprising in the light of traditional Jewish norms, since such organizations exist less for the performance of *mitzvot* than for the pursuit of personal pleasure and leisurely association. Identification with traditional norms would dictate that even if the individual was highly pleased with such an affiliation, he would desire to portray himself as holding a more instrumental orientation. Thus he would avoid designating an expressive group as his most satisfying affiliation.

The Influence of Social Class

As we should expect, social class has a good deal of influence on affiliation and involvement. Only 14 per cent of men with incomes of over $30,000 per year lack an affiliation with a non-synagogue-connected Jewish organization, in contrast to 52 per cent of those who make less than $15,000; the comparable figures for women are 8 per cent versus 29 per cent. However, differences in level of activity are not as pronounced; in fact, among women the activity level of all income groups is approximately the same.

We find that more than half of the wealthy men hold multiple memberships, in contrast to about one-fourth of the men with modest incomes. The same holds true for as many as three-fourths of the wealthy women, as contrasted with less than half of the less affluent. But class position does not affect the tendencies of men and women to concentrate in social-recreational and health-welfare groups, respectively. Regardless of their income, almost all the men who join a Jewish organization select a social-recreational group, while almost all the women who affiliate choose a health-welfare group. But many of the wealthier men and women do join at least one other Jewish group in a category different from the one in which their basic affiliation is located. The wealthier men select health-welfare and community-relations groups, and the wealthier women social-recreational groups, and they join these groups more often than do less affluent persons of the same sex.

Particular organizations tend to draw differentially upon the various class segments, and men and women who differ in class position do not always belong to the same group within their respective major category of affiliation. Almost three-fourths of the less affluent men (those earning less than $15,000) who are affiliated with a non-synagogue group are members of B'nai B'rith, in contrast with less than half of the men whose income is over $30,000 (see Table 7–3). A majority of those in the highest income group are members of a Jewish country or city club, but only

TABLE 7–3. AFFILIATION WITH SELECTED NON-SYNAGOGUE
JEWISH ORGANIZATIONS BY SEX AND INCOME

	Income		
	Less than $15,000	$15,000–30,000	Over $30,000
Per cent of			
Men who are members of specific social-recreational organizations *			
B'nai B'rith lodges	72	64	48
Elite country and city clubs	6	16	43
Other country and city clubs	—	20	32
TOTAL MEN AFFILIATED WITH NON-SYNAGOGUE JEWISH OR-GANIZATIONS	(32)	(50)	(44)
Women who are members of specific health-welfare organizations *			
ORT	57	55	38
Hadassah	22	32	47
NCJW	22	16	36
General welfare campaign	3	14	26
Medical and health agencies	7	7	23
Character-building youth agencies	8	13	19
Social service agencies (non-youth)	7	14	17
TOTAL WOMEN AFFILIATED WITH NON-SYNAGOGUE JEWISH ORGANIZATIONS	(60)	(69)	(47)

* May add to more than 100 since more than one affiliation is possible.

about one in twenty of those in modest circumstances are so affiliated. As for the women, Hadassah has the greatest appeal to the wealthy; it attracts almost half of the most affluent women who have an organizational affiliation. ORT, on the other hand, draws heavily from those in modest circumstances. Nevertheless, while 57 per cent of the modestly situated affiliated women are members of ORT, as many as 38 per cent of wealthy women belong. The National Council of Jewish Women is somewhat more attractive to those who are in prosperous circumstances.

We conclude that while there is class stratification in the organizational life of Lakeville Jewry, it is manifested in most extreme form in the city and country clubs. While the instrumentally oriented health and welfare groups do not attract a perfect cross section of the community, in most of them the disproportionate representation of women of different class position is less than extreme. Three organizations in this category—ORT, Hadassah, and the National Council of Jewish Women—have the broadest appeal.

Some Functions of Jewish Organizational Involvement

A SECULAR ALTERNATIVE

For the religiously committed, involvement in Jewish organizational life outside the synagogue, particularly if it is strongly connected with the performance of *mitzvot* or *maasim tovim* (good deeds), is both a legitimate and necessary Jewish activity. For those who are less committed to the religious sphere, such involvement may provide a secular alternative—a means of expressing Jewish identity stripped of the encumbrances of religious interests and sanctions. The wide variety of Jewish organizations means that those whose bonds with Judaism as a religion are minimal need not thereby cut themselves off from associational ties to the Jewish community; indeed, some Jewish groups have a special attraction for the religiously alienated.

This function of Jewish organizations manifests itself in a variety of ways. For example, degree of religious commitment means little if any distinction in level of affiliation or even in the degree of involvement. This is particularly the case with the men. Thus the rate of organizational affiliation, of multiple affiliation, and of active participation among nonobservant men is comparable to that among observant men (see Table 7–4).[7] Also, affiliation among men hardly varies with whether or not they belong to a synagogue or are active in it; some 65 per cent of the religiously unaffiliated are members of at least one Jewish organization.[8]

Among the women, only those who are religiously unaffiliated or totally nonobservant have lower rates of organizational membership. Women who evince even a slight degree of religious commitment do not have a strikingly different rate of affiliation from those who are highly committed. Thus about three in five of the unobservant women belong to at least one Jewish group, in contrast to about four in five among the various categories of observant women. Nevertheless, multiple affiliation as well as level of activity generally increases with greater religious commitment, except that multiple membership is almost as frequent among nonobservers as among the highly observant.

TABLE 7-4. Affiliation and Activity in Non-Synagogue Jewish Organizations by Level of Home Observance and Sex

	Men				Women			
	Number of Observances				Number of Observances			
Per cent	0	1-2	3-4	5+	0	1-2	3-4	5+
Members of following number of organizations								
0	37	39	47	30	37	21	14	14
1	17	34	35	30	17	34	28	27
2 or more	46	27	18	40	46	45	58	59
Spend time in activities (hours per week)								
0	67	74	74	63	78	67	47	42
1	13	13	17	20	12	11	35	20
2 or more	20	13	9	17	10	22	18	38
N	(40)	(79)	(43)	(46)	(42)	(80)	(43)	(59)
Of members spend any time in activities	52	41	48	53	35	41	62	67
N	(25)	(49)	(23)	(32)	(26)	(63)	(37)	(51)

The religiously uncommitted, then, have a comparatively high rate of belonging. We find that they have an affinity for social and recreational organizations which avoid any instrumental or Jewish purpose. Thus, while at the highest level of observance almost nine out of ten men affiliated with a Jewish group belong to B'nai B'rith and almost none to an elite club, among the affiliated nonobservant men more than three-fourths belong to elite clubs, while less than a third are affiliated with B'nai B'rith.[9] In contrast to the country clubs, B'nai B'rith attempts to incorporate religious and ethnic values into its program of fraternalism.

Among women, there is considerable overlap between the mass-membership health and welfare groups and the sisterhoods: of sisterhood members who belong to a non-synagogue Jewish group,* almost three in five are affiliated with ORT, about half belong to Hadassah, and about one-third to NCJW. Women who are not members of sisterhoods join these groups in fewer numbers. In regard to the relationship between observance and affiliation, we find that some 78 per cent of the most observant women who are members of a Jewish group belong to ORT, some 45 per cent to Hadassah, and some 29 per cent to NCJW. Less observant women join these organizations, especially ORT and Hadassah, with declining frequency. However, nonobservant women, as well as women who do not belong to sisterhoods, are well represented in various locally oriented social service and character-building agencies, some of which serve a non-Jewish clientele as well as a Jewish public.

In summary, Jewish organizational involvement seems to provide a secular alternative for that segment of the population which lacks contact with religious values or institutions, but wishes to preserve a link to the Jewish community.

A JEWISH ALTERNATIVE FOR THE INTEGRATION-MINDED

If the proliferated structure of the Jewish community offers a form of Jewish association for the secular-minded, it also functions as a "Jewish alternative" in another sense: as a means of association for Jews interested in improving and extending relationships with non-Jews and furthering integration into the general community. Paradoxically, integrationist sentiment among Jews is mobilized and channeled within the framework of the ethnic community, rather than exclusively through non-

* Nine in ten sisterhood members belong to a non-synagogue Jewish organization.

sectarian groups. As a consequence, associational ties with the Jewish community can be retained and even strengthened at the same time that integration into the larger society is proclaimed.[10]

Thus we find that Jewish men and women who score high in integration-mindedness are affiliated with Jewish organizations just as frequently as their less integrationist peers (see Table 7–5). Among the men, integrationists are more active in Jewish organizations than those who are less integration-minded, while among the women, integrationists are only slightly less active.[11] This virtual parity in level of Jewish organizational involvement is not due to the possibly higher socio-economic status of integrationists; it prevails even when income is controlled.

TABLE 7–5. AFFILIATION AND ACTIVITY IN NON-SYNAGOGUE JEWISH ORGANIZATIONS BY LEVEL OF INTEGRATION-MINDEDNESS AND SEX

	Men		Women	
	Integration-Mindedness Score			
	High (6–9)	Low (1–5)	High (6–9)	Low (1–5)
Per cent				
Members of following number of organizations				
0	35	40	23	19
1	28	31	25	29
2 or more	37	29	52	52
Spend time in activities (hours per week)				
0	63	76	64	56
1	15	15	20	17
2 or more	22	9	16	27
N	(81)	(127)	(81)	(143)
Of members spend any time in activities	57	41	47	55
N	(53)	(76)	(62)	(115)

Furthermore, the affiliation profile of the integration-minded is just as distinctive as that of the secular-minded. Integrationist men favor community-relations groups and elite country and city clubs much more often than do their less integrationist peers, and they affiliate less often with B'nai B'rith lodges.[12] While the same number (42 per cent) of integrationist men belong to lodges as to elite clubs, this is largely because of the influence of the less affluent integrationists who cannot easily afford to join the clubs. Among the most affluent of our integrationist men, club membership outdistances lodge affiliation. By way of contrast, among equally affluent low integrationists, lodge membership is more common. The integrationist men who are less affluent but have more than a modest income also belong to the clubs more often than their less integrationist peers. The Jewish elite clubs, then, as an exclusive form of ethnic association, appear to be highly attractive to integrationists. The clubs allow the pursuit of activities and life styles which are characteristic of higher social strata in the general society, but without the necessity of shedding Jewish identity.[13]

The community-relations groups, on the other hand, appear to serve more frequently as a mode of affiliation for principled integrationists who desire to retain their Jewish identity. An example is a young, well-paid sales representative, a fourth-generation respondent who is still strongly identified with his Classical Reform origins. A very recent newcomer to Lakeville, he is looking for a temple affiliation which will approximate the "nice association with the temple groups" that he had in his previous community. When asked about his most satisfying membership in a voluntary association, he chose a Jewish community-relations group because "it represents a field that interests me. It works for better relations between Jews and Christians, for good brotherhood. It explains Jews to Christians."

The organizational profile among the integrationist women who belong to Jewish health and welfare groups approximates that found among the religiously alienated women: overrepresentation in local social service and youth agencies which are noted for having a "non-sectarian" orientation and underrepresentation in two mass-membership groups—ORT and Hadassah—whose philanthropic activities primarily benefit Jews.

A FRAMEWORK FOR SOCIAL RELATIONSHIPS

Whatever other functions Jewish groups perform, they provide their members with an opportunity to establish and develop social relationships with other Jews. Looked at from this perspective, the act of joining is a crucial step. But many do not join "spontaneously"; they are recruited. Organizational recruitment is sometimes done by friends, sometimes by neighbors, and sometimes by business contacts. A young credit manager for a wholesale firm which distributes electronic equipment joined B'nai B'rith, his most satisfying affiliation, primarily because "a business contact I have wanted me to join his lodge." Women are generally recruited into ORT by their neighbors. In the words of a mother of two pre-schoolers, who lives in a predominantly Jewish neighborhood and was recruited by someone on her block, "All the women in the neighborhood belong; you have to because of pressure." A fourth-generation woman of German-Jewish origin joined a small Jewish women's lodge group, her most satisfying affiliation, because she had been friendly with most of the members: "They are people I grew up with." In many such cases, join-ing a Jewish organization may serve to maintain and solidify prior rela-tionships with Jews. In other cases, joining a Jewish group may serve to shift the individual from relationships in the general community to new relationships in the Jewish community. But however the member is re-cruited, the organization provides the opportunity to develop new in-formal relationships with other Jews which in time may blossom into close friendships, as in the case of the owner of a drugstore who explains that when he joined B'nai B'rith as a newcomer in Lakeville, "I met peo-ple who live here." Subsequently, he continues, "I have adjusted to this community and . . . I feel I have a sense of belonging. It's a group of congenial fellows, some very close and some friendly." Thus, joining a Jewish organization can reinforce or initiate ties to a Jewish clique group.

Opportunities for initiating and maintaining informal social relation-ships are most apparent in groups that have a strong recreational aspect, such as the country clubs and lodges. Here the manifest purpose of insti-tutionally sponsored activities—whether golf, bowling, cards, or some other sport or game—is solely for the benefit of the members. Thus a retired manufacturer and longtime resident of the community is highly satisfied with his Jewish country club, one among several social clubs of which he is a member, because of his "association with people there." And a mother of three young children finds a great deal of satisfaction in her B'nai B'rith group, where she bowls and is otherwise quite active, because "the women are friendly and it gives me some social life."

Even the more instrumental Jewish groups, whose main goal is to help others or to affect conditions outside the group, often provide the basis for the cultivation of personal relationships. The wife of the owner of an advertising agency finds Hadassah her most satisfying affiliation both be-cause of "the work that it does" and because "I have many friends in it." A prosperous young businessman with two children, who is an officer of a Jewish child-care agency, finds what he terms the agency's "social" aspects just as satisfying as what he calls its "good purpose." A woman who belongs to many Jewish organizations and has made many friends in the process finds a local Brandeis University group her most satisfying affiliation because "I like the highly cultured, intelligent type of woman there. I enjoy them."

ORT is perhaps the best example of an instrumentally oriented group with a strong sociability function. Because its chapters operate in many of the local areas of the community, ORT can perform this function to a greater extent than any other instrumental Jewish group. Its method of recruitment appears to be particularly effective among young mothers who are tied down to the home. ORT is also attractive to newcomers to Lakeville who are seeking to make friends. "It's a neighborhood thing," explains a highly active leader of an ORT group, the young wife of a salesman with a relatively modest income. "The people I work with are friendly, warm," adds another highly satisfied ORT leader, a newcomer with older children, who devotes many hours each week to the organization, her only formal group affiliation. An insight into the reason for ORT's effectiveness among newcomers is given by one of its highly active leaders, a college-educated mother of three young children, who is also active in several non-sectarian groups. She is pleased with what she calls the "social factor" in ORT "which got me accepted in Lakeville." She goes on to explain, "It's divided into small groups, which makes it good for a shy person like myself."

So effective is Women's ORT as a setting for social activities and for developing personal relationships that its members frequently take great pains to define their interest in its welfare goals. One highly satisfied member, a mother with pre-school children, stresses, "It's not purely a social thing. It's helping the unfortunates. They rehabilitate displaced people." Most often, however, ORT's stated humanitarian goals and its almost equally obvious social advantages are coupled together as non-conflicting reasons for satisfaction with the organization. According to the mother of two school-age children, ". . . the goal, the motive, plus the women in it" are why she is so satisfied with ORT.

Not only do Jewish organizations provide a framework for social relationships, but it appears that they do so in a way that allows for greater directness, spontaneity, and personality fulfillment than is available in non-sectarian organizations. As a consequence, Jewish affiliation may prove to be highly satisfying to those who are not strongly Jewish in culture. Furthermore, Jewish affiliation can attract even those who have extensive contacts with Gentiles. A good example is a longtime Lakeville resident who owns a retail business in the community. He has very friendly relationships with non-Jews in the civic organizations in which he is active, but he finds that his most satisfying affiliation is with B'nai B'rith. He explains, "Rotary is not interesting any more. It's just business. B'nai B'rith members appeal to me. We bowl together, play baseball." An executive in an otherwise exclusively Gentile bank, who has very friendly contacts with non-Jewish bankers in his trade association and exchanges home visits with them, finds his Jewish country club to be his most satisfying affiliation because "it is the only one in which my activities and relationships are social." Another example is a third-generation businessman who is a partner in a national chain of women's wear stores and has many close contacts with Gentiles in the business world. He is even an American Legion member, an exceptional association for a Lakeville Jew. Nevertheless, his most gratifying affiliation is with his elite Jewish country club because of its "golf and social life—that's it." A fourth-generation German-Jewish wife of another affluent business executive, a woman who was raised as a Christian Scientist and has many Gentile friends, also finds her most satisfying affiliation to be an elite Jewish country club: "I enjoy playing golf and bowling and the other activities— going over for lunch, parties." A young third-generation East European housewife of more modest means, who is intensely active in several non-sectarian groups and engages in mutual home entertaining several times a year with the Gentile women in her Den Mother unit of the Cub Scouts, finds that ORT is her most satisfying activity because "it's socializing as well as participating."

In summary, whatever the formal purposes of the many diverse Jewish organizations, informal social contacts and the furthering of clique relationships are often key elements in their appeal. This appeal is minimized in non-sectarian organizations. Among the members of such organizations, it is the instrumental rather than the expressive groups that are more often chosen as the affiliation that provides the friendliest interfaith contacts. Social relationships are therefore developed indirectly, as a by-product of common interests and of involvement in the agency's goals.[14] By way of contrast, the Jewish organization, with its homogeneous membership and its frequently lukewarm demand for commitment to its goals, provides a more direct and spontaneous route to the rewards and satisfactions of social relationships. Finally, the ethnic organization offers none of the possible risks or embarrassments which are inherent in the encounter between Jew and Gentile.

8

THE FRIENDSHIP TIES OF
THE LAKEVILLE JEW

As we noticed in Chapter 7 the furthering of clique relationships is an important element in the appeal of the Jewish organization. In many cases, such associational-based relationships are just as meaningful to the individual, if not more meaningful, than the institutional activities in which he engages. But however significant, the Jewish organization is not by itself capable of filling the vacuum left in modern Jewish society by the erosion of the natural community of family and neighborhood. Friendship ties among Jews, which may develop out of involvement in an organization or quite separately, also help to compensate for such erosion.

The clique—or friendship group, as we shall call it—is characterized by strong affective bonds among its participants. It thus approximates the solidarity and cohesion of the older type of familial and neighborhood relationship even more than does the formal Jewish organization, especially in light of the fact that the ties in a friendship group develop in an almost unconscious manner and that they often endure over a long period of time.

Like any similar collectivity, the specifically Jewish friendship group exists for the satisfaction of personal needs and interests, rather than for advancing any special group purpose. Nevertheless, the Jewish friendship group may constitute an important influence in developing and solidifying in-group sentiment: by providing a mode of Jewish association in a predominantly non-Jewish society, it is capable of confirming Jewish identity and thus contributing to Jewish survival. The fact that the friendship group lacks many of the characteristics of an organization—a set time for meetings, the annual election of officers, a machinery which both advances the cause espoused by the agency and assures its perpetuation—is one of its greatest strengths; it can confirm and strengthen Jewish identity in a much more personal manner than an organization. Indeed, the overriding personalism of the friendship group is one of the most significant elements in its attractiveness.

In sum, the Jewish friendship group can work indirectly but nevertheless effectively to preserve group identity. It may constitute as great an influence, or an even greater influence, on the preservation of that identity than instrumentalities whose manifest purpose is the advancement of group survival.

The Character of Friendship Ties

Just as we viewed involvement with Jewish organizations against the backdrop of the erosion of the neighborhood and especially against the sharp decline in kinship interaction and solidarity, so must we evaluate the significance of friendship ties. When our respondents were growing up, 42 per cent of their parents spent more time socializing with friends than they did with relatives. On the other hand, as many as 88 per cent of our respondents spend more time socializing with friends than with relatives. A shift of this magnitude occurring within the space of a single generation carries with it the potentiality of fragmenting patterns of in-group interaction, for a high level of interaction with a family group minimizes the possibility of meaningful involvement with members of the out-group. The shift to a group which is self-selected rather than inherited may portend the end of in-group solidarity.

This potentiality is particularly high given the fact that Jews constitute a rather small segment of the population in the Lake City area. Even if adjustments are made for factors which strongly delimit the choice of friends—race, class, educational level, and the like—Gentiles still outnumber Jews by a substantial ratio. Furthermore, most of our respondents have spent extended periods of time—particularly during the period of their late adolescence and early adulthood—detached from traditional familial and neighborhood relationships. Frequently, Jews constituted a minority in such settings. New patterns of shared experiences in such settings may give rise to cross-ethnic friendships that might endure long after these experiences have passed.

One example of such a setting is the Armed Forces, in which many of our male respondents have served. A better example—because it encompasses a more like-minded population and also includes the great majority of our female respondents—is the college or university.[1] While the schools which our respondents attended had a much higher proportion of Jews than was true for the Armed Forces, in most cases they were in a decided minority on their particular campus. The state universities which our respondents attended drew on the varied segments of the population of the area in which they were situated; the private institutions of higher learning at the time generally chose their students on a variety of criteria which operated to select a so-called "balanced" student body. Furthermore, many respondents who attended colleges distant from their homes were almost completely dependent on the social life that they found in such campus situations. Taking into account, then, the shift from family to friends, as well as the exposure to environments where people of diverse backgrounds associate, what is the character of the friendship ties of the Lakeville Jew?

We find that such ties are predominantly—almost overwhelmingly—with other Jews. Some 42 per cent of our respondents report that their circle of close friends[2] is composed exclusively of Jews. Another 49 per cent say that their circle is composed of a majority of Jews. Only 7 per cent report that Gentiles constitute a majority in their circle of close friends or that their circle is equally divided between Jews and Gentiles.[3] The Jewish character of the friendship circle of the Lakeville resident is clearly revealed when we look more closely at the 49 per cent who say that their circle includes a minority of one or more Gentiles. We discover that approximately one-half of these respondents report that all or most of their Gentile friends are married to Jews.[4]

Perhaps the most remarkable aspect of this pattern of pervasive Jewish friendship ties is that in spite of being more acculturated than their parents and moving in a more mixed environment, our respondents make their close friendships with Jews virtually as often as did their parents. Thus, while 87 per cent of the parents had most or all of their close friendships with Jews, the same holds true for 89 per cent of our respond-

TABLE 8-1. PROPORTION OF CLOSE FRIENDS JEWISH AMONG
RESPONDENTS AND AMONG THEIR PARENTS

Per cent with following proportion of Jews among their close friends †	Parents *	Respondents
All (100%)	30 ⎫	42 ⎫
Almost all (91–99%)	31 ⎬ 87	10 ⎬ 89
Most (61–90%)	26 ⎭	37 ⎭
About half (41–60%)	5	6
Some (1–40%)	5	3
None (0%)	2	—
N.A., no close friend	1	2

* During the period when respondent was growing up.
† The proportions stated in percentages apply to respondents. These have been calculated from data supplied by respondents in answer to separate questions on the total number of their close friends and the total number of their close Gentile friends. These percentages are grouped in intervals which most approximate the descriptive categories used in the question applicable to the parents.

ents (see Table 8–1).[5] To realize the significance of this overlap between the generations, it is only necessary to recall the amount of disjunction in the area of religious behavior. And the continuity in friendship patterns between the generations is all the more remarkable, given such strong differences in the level of involvement with the family group.

Since friendship ties with Gentiles who are married to Jews are frequent enough to be of significance and will presumably bulk even larger in the future, a detailed analysis of them is required. The phenomenon suggests that a certain proportion of intermarried couples have found a place inside the Jewish group—that they have not assimilated into the non-Jewish world in a meaningful sense. Furthermore, we discover the startling fact that some of the spouses identified by our respondents as Gentile have actually been converted to Judaism. Of course, their categorization as Gentile indicates incomplete assimilation, this time into the Jewish group. Such categorization is also an aspect of the remarkable influence of ethnicity on our respondents—an influence which persists in spite of the prevalence of an extremely high level of acculturation.

While our respondents may not categorize all converts as Jewish, there is no question that they feel that such individuals, as well as non-Jews married to Jews, are quite different from the average Gentile. The distinction mentioned most frequently is that these intermarried Gentiles have adopted a Jewish identity and a Jewish way of life. In some instances, the attitudes and behavior of Gentile friends who are married to Jews are felt to be so typically Jewish that respondents are prompted to remark—as does a pharmacist's wife who is active in ORT—that their Gentile friend is "more Jewish than anyone else is." And according to a prosperous salesman whose only ethnic affiliation is with a local Jewish country club,

> This Gentile woman considers herself a Jew. We will kid her that: "We know you're not a Jew, so you don't have to bother acting like one." Yet in fact she does act like a Jew as much as the rest of us do.

A young and highly observant insurance broker, a member of the Schechter Synagogue who is quite active in B'nai B'rith, says of still another Gentile woman, "She has a warmth and attachment to things Jewish and follows its customs." And a lawyer's wife who is active only in non-sectarian groups and does not follow Jewish rituals in her own home details some of these customs and "things Jewish": "After her marriage this Italian girl started keeping a kosher house. She encourages her husband to go to temple and sends her kids to Jewish Sunday School."

Our respondents also emphasize that not only have such Gentiles become acculturated to Jewish ways, but they have become detached from Gentile clique groups. The insurance broker quoted above says of the Gentile woman whom he includes in his circle of close friends, "She primarily associates with Jews, and most of her friends are Jewish." An affluent salesman who does not feel entirely comfortable in the company of Gentiles nevertheless experiences no anxiety with his two close Gentile friends who are married to Jews: "[It is because] they move in a Jewish circle and are outside the pale of circle of their own kind." A further indication of the movement of such Gentile friends into Jewish clique relationships is the fact that when the most intimate of such friends is entertained, in seven out of ten cases most or all of the other persons present are Jewish.[6]

With respect to those whose friendship circle is predominantly Jewish but whose Gentile friend is not married to a fellow Jew, several types of relationships with such Gentiles are possible. For example, such a friend could be a detached Gentile who feels alienated from his peers and who as a consequence is willing, even eager, to join a Jewish clique group. Or the friend could be a Gentile who is well integrated with his traditional group and as a consequence may be eager to have the Jewish friend join *his* Gentile clique group. In the first instance, the character of the Jew's friendship ties would not be shifted, while in the second instance they could be strongly affected. There is also a third possibility, however: that the Gentile to whom the Jew is close is neither well attached to nor strongly alienated from his traditional group and that in any case this aspect is not a significant element in the relationship. Rather, for both Jew and Gentile their friendship is a very special relationship—a relationship which does not disturb their respective friendship ties. Tending to see each other alone, neither Jew nor Gentile becomes incorporated in the other's homogeneous friendship group.

While further analysis is needed to discover the character and dynamics of such relationships, what is presently apparent is that most Lakeville Jews who have such Gentile friends who are not married to Jews do not seem to be in the process of shifting their friendship circle. Instead of utilizing their contacts in the Gentile world to build a new pattern of friendship ties, they appear to pursue their interfaith relationship apart from their Jewish network. In summary, there tends to be no disruption of the predominantly Jewish friendship circle, even among those who have a Gentile friend who is not married to a Jew. Furthermore, Gentiles who are married to Jews may be incorporated into homogeneously Jewish cliques. The only marked deviation from the general pattern is the 7 per cent whose friendship ties are predominantly with Gentiles or are equally divided between Jews and Gentiles.

The Shift to a Homogeneous Friendship Circle

While the pattern of friendship ties of our respondents is so strongly Jewish as to duplicate the one prevalent in the parental generation, it was not always so. During adolescence, our respondents had many more Gentile friends than they do today. To be sure, in the majority of cases teenage friendship ties were predominantly with Jews. However, almost four in ten of our respondents report that in adolescence only half, or less than half, of their circle of close friends consisted of Jews (see Table 8–2). In actuality, the increased homogeneity of friendship ties is greater than these figures indicate, for, as we have noted, some of the present Gentile friends of our respondents have ties to Jewish life through marriage to a Jew.

While close friendships with Gentiles are much more exceptional today than they were in the past, adolescent patterns still retain their influence. Thus the greater the proportion of Jewish friends in adolescence,

TABLE 8-2. PROPORTION OF CLOSE FRIENDS JEWISH
DURING ADOLESCENCE AND TODAY

Per cent with following proportion of Jews among their close friends *	Adolescence	Today
All (100%)	14 ⎤	42 ⎤
Almost all (91-99%)	20 ⎬63	10 ⎬89
Most (61-90%)	29 ⎦	37 ⎦
About half (41-60%)	18	6
Some (1-40%)	15	3
None (0%)	4	—
N.A., no close friend	—	2

* The proportions stated in percentages apply to respondents as adults and were calculated and grouped as described in Table 8-1. The matched descriptive categories were used in the question referring to their teen-age period.

the greater the proportion today (see Table 8-3). However, the trend is toward a homogeneously Jewish pattern for all, even for those who had only some or no Jewish friends in adolescence, with those who had more Jewish friends to begin with having the highest proportion of all-Jewish friendships.

TABLE 8-3. PROPORTION OF CLOSE FRIENDS JEWISH
TODAY BY PROPORTION OF CLOSE FRIENDS
JEWISH DURING ADOLESCENCE

Per cent with following proportion of Jews among their close friends	Proportion of Close Teen-age Friends Jewish			
	All or Almost All	Most	About Half	Some or None
All	55	47	31	27
Most: Gentiles married to Jews	23	29	24	20
Most: Gentiles not married to Jews	21	23	37	31
Half or less	1	1	8	22
N	(149)	(123)	(78)	(81)

It appears that our respondents acquired and stabilized a relatively homogeneous pattern of close Jewish friendships while emerging from adolescence to adulthood, or at least before achieving parenthood. We find that throughout the parental phase of the life cycle, their sociability pattern remains stable: there is little difference between our younger and older respondents with respect to the ethnic composition of their friendship circles. Thus the friendship pattern acquired in the earliest phase of the parental life cycle remains constant through the mature years.

The trend to homogeneity in friendship behavior is comparable in some aspects to that which obtains in respect to religious behavior. Religious behavior is also at minimal levels during the adolescent and early adulthood years—transitional phases of the life cycle when the individual is in the process of loosening his bonds to his parental home, but has yet to establish his own household.* Nevertheless, the trend to homogeneity of association occurs earlier than the maximization of the religious aspect of Jewishness. Thus the intensification of Jewish association may constitute a kind of preview of the reintegration of the young Jew into a variety of other aspects of his Jewish identity.

What accounts for the increase in homogeneous friendship ties before the onset of parenthood as well as for their maintenance through the ensuing years? This question is deserving of extended research; we are only able to supply preliminary answers along one or two of many relevant dimensions.

If we focus on those whose present circle is composed exclusively of Jews, we find that in many cases they once had Gentile friends. These Gentile friendships were often formed in a mixed setting into which they had been thrust for a relatively limited period. When the situation terminated, their relationships with Gentiles ended. We cannot be certain why these friendships never deepened; all that we can say is that the relationship was not firm enough to withstand separation. A young woman who is very active in non-sectarian organizations recalls that when she attended a small women's college in the East, she had friends who were "Christians and Negroes. I went to their parties . . . and I also dated Gentile boys." While she describes her college chums as "old friends" and retains membership in her alumnae association, she has not seen her college friends in some years; she considers none of them to be her close friends today. A professional man recalls the peculiar quality of the relationships with his Gentile friends in the Army and later in dental school. In each instance, the friendships were terminated after his connection with the respective institution came to an end: "At the time, it's like being on a desert island. . . . But when it's over, you just break up." A young matron who had a mixed group of close friends as a teen-ager reports that

* See Chapters 3 and 5.

she also had mostly Gentile friends when she accompanied her husband during his military service. She sums up the situational nature of these relationships: "Of course, we broke up as we went from post to post. In making friends, I guess you take the path of least resistance, and these people were there."

Another relevant factor is that relationships with Gentiles did not receive the institutional, communal, or familial reinforcement that occurred with respect to relationships with Jews. Such reinforcement was apparently a factor which helped such relationships to endure long after the situation in which they developed had passed. Jewish friendships that have persisted since childhood and adolescence are especially instructive in this connection. We find cases where respondents trace their present homogeneous Jewish associations to the Jewish neighborhood of their childhood or even to their parents. For example, an executive in the entertainment industry who is somewhat active in Wise Temple soon lost contact with the close Gentile friends he made in adolescence. However, with respect to the Jewish friends he made during the same period, with some of whom he currently associates, he recalls, "Most of us came out of the same neighborhood; our communities were Jewish, and our families were heavily Jewish and traditional." Although as a teen-ager she had some Gentile boy friends, a young fourth-generation wife of a buyer—a woman who is active only in non-sectarian groups—says much the same thing about her Jewish circle: "Most of us grew up together. Our parents knew each other, and we are all Jewish." A sales executive who also has little attachment to Jewish religious or organizational life points out how his Jewish friendships were formed in the close world of the neighborhood in which he was raised in Lake City:

> Most of this circle [of friends] is an old-time relationship dating back to public school and Hebrew school where our activities kept us close together. Why should we bring newcomers into the group? One of the important things about it is that it's such an old group.

The tendency to homogeneity becomes particularly discernible in late adolescence. Some of the all-Jewish cliques formed during this period have no institutional connections, while others have as their locus formal organizations such as high-school or college fraternities and sororities. The wife of a prosperous salesman, who is equally active in Jewish and non-sectarian groups, traces her Jewish friendship circle to her sociability pattern as a teen-ager: "It all goes back to the local high-school sorority that was all Jewish." A minimally observant woman with a similar pattern of organizational involvement had many close Gentile friends as a teen-ager, including those of the opposite sex, but she lost these contacts after joining a Jewish sorority in college. She says of her Jewish clique, "We are a closed group from college. Most of us are sorority sisters or fraternity brothers. We've been together for years." The young owner of an automobile parts business, a minimally observant second-generation man who is not affiliated with any Jewish organization, relates how his clique group became increasingly Jewish as he grew from adolescence to adulthood:

> I was active in a high-school fraternity—all Jewish. Until high school, I had more non-Jewish friends than Jewish ones. Though I held on to the non-Jewish friends, they decreased in proportion; we weren't in the same fraternity and we did little or no double dating. . . . This pattern increased as I got older, dated, and got married.

This example is particularly instructive because it shows how such homogeneous ties facilitate "rating and dating" Jews of the opposite sex. It also demonstrates the relationship between a homogeneous friendship pattern and endogamy.[7] Should the youngster continue a pattern of mixed friendships as he grows toward late adolescence and early adulthood, the likelihood of an exogamous marital choice is increased. The period is so crucial that even those who are extremely integration-minded recognize its significance. It will be recalled that the high commitment to integration of the officials of the Einhorn Temple could not withstand the desire of parents to have their children marry Jews—a desire which necessarily involved some degree of segregation of their adolescents. The officials were forced into the recognition that the consistent implementation of their integrationist sentiments in respect to this age group would mean a clear-cut subversion of group survival.* The whole issue is stated concisely by an elderly and affluent business executive of German descent who recalls that as an adolescent he had an ethnically balanced group of close friends, but soon afterward his clique changed rapidly in a Jewish direction: "Intermarriage is frowned upon. Once out of high school, you relate with your own." Despite the fact that this man retains only a tenuous relation to Jewish religious or organizational life, all his close friends are Jewish.

While some of our respondents account for their homogeneous friendship pattern by highlighting factors that operated at an earlier period of their life, in the majority of cases it appears that present ties were formed

* See above, pp. 144–145.

during adulthood. Queried as to how they developed an all-Jewish circle, about half of our respondents feel that it results from the fact that Jews are more available and accessible to them. "There's more opportunity to make friends with Jews. We're with them a thousand times more: the Jews are around," explains a publisher who is somewhat active in Wise Temple and in a Jewish community-relations group. As a teen-ager, most of his close associations were with Gentiles, including a serious relationship with a Gentile girl. Such ties were dissolved, however, when he joined a Jewish fraternity at college. Another man who gives much the same type of response is a minimally observant advertising agency executive whose Jewish organizational affiliations are limited to a Jewish city club and to the Einhorn Temple. He grew up in a prestigious suburb on the Heights among predominantly Gentile friends, but he joined a Jewish fraternity at college. Today his close friends are all Jewish. He says, "I'm thrown into contact with [Jews] in many places and in many ways. It's easier. I don't feel the need to cultivate people. Proximity is the thing."

While many respondents allude to these Jewish associational opportunities in a general way, some specify the settings in which they occur: chiefly the neighborhood in which they live, the Jewish organization with which they are affiliated, and the synagogue in which they are active. "We all came into the neighborhood at around the same time about five years ago and have known each other as long," remarks a young second-generation mother of two children, who was reared in a small town on the West Coast where her close friendships were mainly with Gentiles. She has few ties to Jewish religious and organizational life. A physician's wife, a relative newcomer to the community, states that she "became friendly [with an all-Jewish friendship group] through organizations." She is a member of several Jewish women's groups, including the Sisterhood of Wise Temple. And a highly observant middle-aged owner of a men's clothing business states that he developed his friendships as a result of his activity in a Conservative synagogue in Lake City:

> I haven't had the occasion to mix with any [Gentiles] socially. I've never been in mixed community affairs. I developed a social life through the [X] Synagogue—the one place where I had causes plus friends and social activities.

While it is true that such associational opportunities are part of the situation in which individual Jews find themselves, in another fundamental sense they can be the outcome of individual preferences—the result of an attraction to fellow Jews and a desire for personal contact with them. It is apparent that because of this attraction many of our respondents place themselves in situations where it is Jews, rather than Gentiles, who are more available and accessible to them.

Jewish accessibility could, of course, be the result of nothing more than Gentile inaccessibility. This is not the picture which our respondents present, however. While one in ten of those who have a homogeneous Jewish friendship circle accounts for the pattern on the basis of exclusion by Gentiles, some four in ten say that it is a result of a preference for Jews. Some of these respondents consider such a preference to be self-evident, as does a moderately observant accountant who had some close Gentile friends as a teen-ager, but feels that "it's normal that Jewish people befriend other Jewish people." A college-educated and religiously unobservant wife of an executive in the construction industry, who also associated with Gentiles in adolescence, presents a more thoughtful formulation: "Today . . . Jews and Gentiles have much in common. But somehow a social barrier exists. Jews don't go seeking people different from themselves."

Other respondents emphasize that Jews are predisposed to social contact and intimate association with other Jews because of a common religio-ethnic heritage and a pervasive group identity. "It's because Jews go with Jews and Gentiles go with Gentiles. My background is so Jewish and my life is so Jewish that I'm happier surrounded by Jews," explains a young salesman's wife who is now active in Lilienthal Temple, although as an adolescent she had some close friends who were Gentile. "It's the identity, the background, the religion. It would be hard for a Gentile to be comfortable without these common bonds," elaborates an affluent lawyer and business executive who came to the United States from Russia when he was a youngster and is quite active in a variety of Jewish organizations. "There's a common notion of 'fate,' so we don't seek out non-Jews," is the concise reason given by a mother of three school-age children, who finds time for activity in several Jewish welfare groups despite her intense involvement in her local PTA group.

Some account for their preferences for Jewish social contacts by emphasizing life styles and manners which they believe are more commonly encountered among Jews. "There are cultural differences; we have common backgrounds, interests, and standards as Jews," is the general and somewhat cautious comment made by an affluent businessman, a member of Einhorn Temple, who did not receive a Jewish upbringing by his parents and claims to be entirely uninterested in religious matters. He considers none of the many Gentiles with whom he mixes socially to be a close friend. A more specific explanation is offered by a prosperous accountant highly active in a Jewish youth welfare group: "It's just our way of life—our parental background, our closer family and home ties, and our social tastes." He is no longer friendly with the Gentiles whom he met in college and in the Navy. And a young businessman who observes almost none of the traditional religious practices to which he was exposed in childhood mentions similar reasons to account for the fact that he lost contact with the non-Jewish friends he had before marriage:

> They went different paths because of differences in economics, education, and a different mode of living. The others bought homes earlier, but home-owning is only a recent thing for Jews.

Seeking out other Jews with whom one shares common attitudes and a way of life results in the strengthening of feelings of ethnic solidarity. Such solidarity, in turn, contributes to the formation of homogeneously Jewish cliques. "Jews seem to stick together. There's more security that way. It makes for a feeling of belonging," notes the wife of a prosperous businessman, whose intimate friends since childhood have been Jewish and is quite active in the PTA of the Wise Temple. A young salesman with a business degree who had some Gentile friends at college refers to "that family feeling" among Jews; his religious observance is minimal, but he is about to join the Schechter Synagogue. A fairly observant housewife who was close with several Gentile girls with whom she worked before marriage and is now active in the PTA and the Scouts summarizes the emotional basis of in-group solidarity in the following terms:

> My association with non-Jews has been good. But there's a warmth amongst Jews that couldn't be in a Gentile. A Gentile can't be as warm; he would have a different philosophy.

While this respondent and many others whose close friends are all Jewish account for their pattern by stressing the "positive" fact of attraction to Jews rather than such "negative" reasons as alienation, suspicion, or uncomfortableness with Gentiles, the possibility exists that their explanations contain an element of rationalization. In response to a direct query, we find that less than one in ten of those who have homogeneous Jewish friendship ties reports that either he or his friends would have an unfavorable reaction if a Gentile were to join the circle. On the other hand, we find respondents who, in trying to account for the fact that all their close friends are Jewish, are frank to admit that the presence of a Gentile would create strain. Thus a middle-aged housewife affiliated with a variety of Jewish groups, who recalls that half of her close friends during adolescence were Gentile, states,

> We have Gentile friends, but we'd never think of mixing them. It wouldn't work. We're very small drinkers. We like to have a nice dinner and play cards. We'd feel self-conscious, especially if they'd lose.

The presence of Gentiles would mean that conversation would have to be guarded. A woman who is highly active in the Schechter Synagogue as well as in ORT and is married to an attorney says of her Jewish clique, "They wouldn't be able to speak as freely about politics and religion if non-Jews were present." She is familiar with the ways of both groups, for as an adolescent she had close friends among Gentiles, and she still has Gentile acquaintances.

One matter about which respondents would feel inhibited is the use of Yiddish. While hardly any Lakeville family employs Yiddish as a household language, approximately three in four of our respondents use Yiddish expressions at least occasionally. The great majority who use these expressions do so in the company of family and close friends. Not only would a Gentile be unresponsive, but his presence would make some of our respondents self-conscious should they wish to use the language. The situation might become especially difficult if the conversation were to focus on non-Jews. A second-generation businessman who has only a few social contacts outside the Jewish group (he spends a social evening with his Gentile neighbors about once a month) explains the problem:

> You can have difficulty when you have a non-Jew in the group. You can't use Jewish words without having to tell him all the time what they mean. . . . And sometimes you might give a kibitz about Gentiles, and this would be embarrassing.

The pervasiveness of in-group humor is a related phenomenon. While some of this humor rests on the turn of a Yiddish phrase, more generally it deals with alleged peculiarities of Jewish life and temperament, whether they be virtues or foibles. Our respondents feel that such humor is inappropriate in a mixed group. "There are many people who feel that they have to watch their conversation [in the presence of Gentiles], and even telling Jewish jokes could make one uncomfortable," notes the young wife of the owner of an art supply business, a woman who is minimally involved in religious and organizational life.

We see, then, that the Lakeville Jew who has an all-Jewish circle explains his pattern of friendship ties in a variety of ways. What seems to characterize these respondents, and others as well, is that they feel more comfortable with Jews than with Gentiles—a feeling which they experience in spite of their high level of acculturation and their affirmation of the value of Jewish–Gentile integration. The sense of feeling comfortable with another person is, of course, a precondition for intimacy; it is difficult to establish a close and abiding relationship without such rapport.[8]

The varied responses of these Lakeville Jews who have homogeneous Jewish friendship ties not only are characterized by feelings of being at ease with Jews but also appear to involve a deep sense of kinship with other Jews. The composition of clique groups aside, if we take our respondents as a whole and compare their most friendly Gentile relationship with their most intimate Jewish one, we find that 76 per cent say that they are closer to their best Jewish friend and only 9 per cent say they are closer to their best Gentile friend. Some 14 per cent claim that they are as close to their best Gentile friend as they are to their best Jewish friend. Indeed, while our respondents generally refer to their best Gentile friend as a "friend," they frequently speak of their best Jewish friend as being like a "sister" or "brother." An active alumna of a leading Eastern women's college, who is also involved in several Jewish and non-sectarian groups, characterizes her relationship with her most intimate Gentile friend as "friendly" and finds the Gentile friend as stimulating as her closest Jewish friend: "They're both intellectually stimulating. Both are very good for my ego; I feel like a whole person when I'm with them." But she states that she has a "deeper relationship" with the Jewish friend. Her insightful characterization of the relationship with the Jewish friend is as follows: "It's like being [in] a family without the tension."

The Alienated Jew and the Homogeneous Friendship Circle

It is clear from the personal information which has been supplied about the respondents whom we have been quoting that some are apathetic to traditional Jewish concerns and affirmations. Since they are nevertheless involved in homogeneous friendship groups, it is apparent that the kind of group solidarity demonstrated by their "associational Jewishness" is not necessarily related to what may be described as more "positive" expressions of Jewish identity. Such solidarity can and does exist apart from any commitment to Jewish religious or organizational life and even apart from any affirmation of the concept of Jewish peoplehood as manifested in pro-Israel sentiment. While "associational Jewishness" may go hand in hand with strong Jewish attachments, the most significant fact is that associationalism is highly prevalent even among alienated Jews.

Thus we find that those who are uninvolved in religion and synagogue life have almost as Jewish a friendship circle as those who possess religious commitments. As many as six in ten of the unobservant, compared with about seven in ten of the most observant, claim that all their close friends are Jewish or are Gentiles married to Jews.[9] Barely more than one in ten of the unobservant claim that their circle of close friends is either ethnically balanced or predominantly Gentile. Furthermore, almost six in ten of those who lack an affiliation with a synagogue, although they have already reached that stage in the life cycle where the great majority join, report a homogeneously Jewish friendship circle.* This is not much different from the seven in ten among active synagogue members who have such a circle. Furthermore, only one in eight of the unaffiliated claim that Gentiles constitute half or more of their circle of close friends.

We find that even smaller differences in the character of friendship ties exist between the very small number who are completely estranged from Israel and the rest of our respondents who favor varying degrees of support for Israel. Thus some 62 per cent of those who would cut off all financial aid to Israel have a friendship circle that is homogeneously Jewish, compared with 67 per cent of those who not only favor such aid but support political efforts as well as other pro-Israel actions.

It is only in respect to involvement in Jewish organizations that the situation is different. While 73 per cent of those who are active in such organizations, whether they be less or more active, have homogeneous ties, only 56 per cent of the unaffiliated possess such friendship ties.[10] Furthermore, a larger percentage of the unaffiliated—although no more than 14 per cent—in contrast to the actives have a circle of close friends which is not predominantly Jewish or all-Jewish.[11] These findings highlight the function of the Jewish organization as a framework for social relationships; they suggest that the organization reinforces the tendency toward homogeneous friendship ties.

This pattern is accentuated among women (see Table 8–4). Among men, there is only a slight difference between the unaffiliated and the actives with respect to homogeneous friendship ties: while the unaffiliated less often report exclusively Jewish friends, more often they have a

* In this section, a homogeneously Jewish circle of friends refers to a collection of close friends which is either all Jewish or includes a minority of Gentiles who are all or mostly married to Jews. See footnote 4 as well as p. 271.

TABLE 8–4. Proportion of Close Friends Jewish by Sex and Involvement in Non-Synagogue Jewish Organizations

Per cent with following proportion of Jews among their close friends	Involvement in Jewish Organizations					
	Men			Women		
	Active Member	Inactive Member	Non-Member	Active Member	Inactive Member	Non-Member
All	55	37	43	44	41	28
Most: Gentiles married to Jews	15	24	23	31	30	17
Most: Gentiles not married to Jews	27	32	19	22	25	44
Half or less	3	7	15	3	4	11
N	(60)	(71)	(52)	(91)	(82)	(36)

minority of Gentile friends who are married to Jews. Among women, however, homogeneous Jewish cliques are found among as many as 75 per cent of the actives, but only among 45 per cent of the unaffiliated. It should be noted that the divergence between the sexes occurs chiefly among the unaffiliated; men and women who are active or nominal members resemble each other fairly closely with respect to their pattern of friendship ties. Thus while most unaffiliated men retain a homogeneously Jewish circle of friends, most unaffiliated women have one or more Gentile intimates who are married to Gentiles. It should be remembered, however, that an overwhelming majority of those of both sexes who are alienated from Jewish organizational life have their friendship ties primarily or exclusively with their fellow Jews.

One of the remarkable aspects of the friendship pattern of the Lakeville Jew is that it remains so Jewish despite the pervasiveness of integrationist sentiment.[12] Almost without exception, Lakeville Jews tend in the direction of integration, but an all-Jewish or predominantly Jewish friendship circle is even characteristic of more than nine in ten of those who score extremely high on our index of integration-mindedness (see Table 8–5). Such respondents do differ from others, however, in respect to the

TABLE 8–5. PROPORTION OF CLOSE FRIENDS JEWISH
BY LEVEL OF INTEGRATION-MINDEDNESS

Per cent with following proportion of Jews among their close friends	*Integration-Mindedness Score*						
	High 8–9	7	6	5	4	3	Low 1–2
All	33	44	33	46	44	50	50
Most: Gentiles married to Jews	10	25	22	26	31	21	25
Most: Gentiles not married to Jews	50	23	33	23	21	24	20
Half or less	7	8	12	5	4	5	5
N	(30)	(52)	(80)	(86)	(77)	(60)	(40)

ties which their minority of close Gentile friends have with Jewish life: as many as half of the integrationists, in contrast to only two or three in ten among the others, have Gentile friends who are not married to Jews.

Why does the Jew who is highly alienated or strongly integrationist-minded tend to make so many of his close friendships within the Jewish group? Some would answer this question in a suprasocial framework, viewing associational Jewishness as a kind of Jewish affirmation and stressing that it is characteristic of the "wondering Jew." According to this perspective, associational Jewishness expresses a desire to preserve a link with Jewish tradition with its basis in inspiration in God; the individual hesitates to sever his one remaining link with the group lest he foreclose all possibility of encounter with God.

The conventional sociological approach shies away from such a perspective. Instead, it highlights the function which Jewish friendship ties serve for the alienated. Accordingly, such ties may be seen as a buttress compensating for weak attachment to Jewish life. Thus the Jewish friendship circle might be viewed in the framework of the contribution it makes to Jewish survival.

The function of such ties aside, we are still left with the problem of explaining the persistence of a relatively homogeneous friendship pattern among strongly alienated and highly integrationist-minded Jews. Thoroughgoing research on this type of individual is necessary if we are to arrive at a definitive explanation for his puzzling behavior. However, our knowledge of the psychological orientation of the Lakeville Jew vis-à-vis the Gentile places us in a position to suggest an approach to such an explanation.

Earlier in this chapter, we described one aspect of the orientation of those whose friendship circle is composed entirely of Jews: their feeling of greater comfort with Jews than with Gentiles. Comfortableness may arise from a variety of sources. One is the belief that the style of life and values of the Jewish group are closer to one's own. Another is the fear that Gentiles hold negative attitudes about Jews. However, almost half of our respondents—among them many alienated and highly integrationist-minded individuals—claim that they are as comfortable with Gentiles as with Jews. But while they are sufficiently comfortable in more casual social contacts with members of the out-group to maintain a relationship, we suggest that their level of comfort drops sharply in more intimate social relationships. Thus we reason that their lack of ease in truly intimate relationships with Gentiles explains their peculiar pattern. While we have no direct evidence to support this conclusion, the indirect evidence is strong indeed. We find that the majority of Lakeville Jews see themselves as ambassadors to the Gentile world.[13] We also find that our alienated and integration-minded respondents are even somewhat more committed to this role than other Jews.

To specify this idea further, if the Lakeville ambassador performs his duties well, his lot, and that of his children as well as of Jews generally, will improve. If not, the relationship between the Jewish "world" and the Gentile "world" will deteriorate. It is apparent that the assumption of an ambassadorial role places a strain on the individual, for in his contacts with Gentiles he must constantly manipulate himself so that he may succeed in manipulating them. Such manipulative conduct is acceptable in a variety of secondary relationships, but inappropriate in the context of intimacy. Even strongly alienated and highly integrationist-minded respondents, then, find it difficult to establish and maintain the type of close contact with Gentiles which their ideological proclivities suggest. Like all people, they are most at ease in a psychological climate characterized by candor and trust, and it is precisely such a climate which favors the growth of intimate association. Thus, given their orientation to intergroup relations, they find it easier to develop such a climate with fellow Jews than with Gentiles.

Because the Lakeville Jew sees himself as a representative of the Jewish group, he feels that he shares responsibility for its public image. As a consequence, he tends to become extremely self-conscious in the presence of Gentiles, which is another way of saying that he becomes highly aware of being Jewish. Such a fixed attitude of group consciousness and responsibility encompasses the range of manners by which the Lakeville Jew attempts to alter and redeem the Gentile stereotype. "I have to be careful with my manners, my dress, my expressions," says a middle-aged lawyer. He is active only in non-sectarian organizations, but he claims no close Gentile friends. "I'm always on my guard as to whether I laugh too loud or my voice is too shrill," says a minimally observant woman whose close friends are all Jewish. "I feel that I have to count my words," says a chemist's wife who observes hardly any religious practices, but has a predominantly Jewish friendship circle.

One aspect of inhibition and self-consciousness is the fear of the Jew that in the encounter with the Gentile he may be regarded stereotypically and not appreciated as an individual; in the eyes of the Gentile, he will be a Jew first and an individual a poor second. Thus an unobservant businessman who believes it "fitting and proper" to have a Christmas tree each year, but confines his organizational life to a Jewish city and country club and his clique participation to Jewish friends, observes about Gentiles, "You have to be on guard and careful about subjects you discuss. I don't have the freedom of personality I have with Jews." This crucial aspect of psychological climate is described even more insightfully by a thoughtful young housewife who is a newcomer to Lakeville. A college graduate and the wife of a prosperous businessman, she is completely alienated from Jewish organizational and religious life and highly integration-minded. One of those respondents constituting the 7 per cent who do not have a predominantly or all-Jewish friendship circle, she has such a tenuous in-group connection that even the Jewish friend to whom she feels closest is intermarried. But with all that, this woman confesses, "I'm less comfortable with non-Jews because you feel that they think of you as a Jew. Jews don't really think of you as a Jew."

While the persistence of Jewish friendship ties among the alienated may contribute to Jewish survival, the pattern may not continue indefinitely. The ambassadorial function and the self-consciousness of the Jew in intergroup relationships is, among other things, related to the prevalence of prejudice and discrimination in the immediate past. Thus the involvement of the alienated in a Jewish clique structure not only grows out of the psychological situation which we have delineated but is also related to the fact that such cliques were reinforced by anti-Jewish sentiment and behavior on the campus, in public life, in business and professional affairs, and in club life. Some of this prejudice and discrimination was experienced personally, more was experienced through significant others, and even more was experienced vicariously through exposure to various channels of communication.

Since it is an unresolved question whether the old pattern of prejudice and discrimination will occur in the future (it has already declined sharply), the Jewish clique may represent a residual form of Jewishness, a "holding operation" preliminary to the assimilation of the individual—or of his offspring—into the majority community.[14] It may be assumed that even with the trend to a more open society, those who are less integration-minded—and who are closely attached to religion, the synagogue, Israel, and the network of Jewish organizations—will retain friendship ties with their Jewish peers. But at the very minimum, the trend to openness suggests that the remarkable discrepancy between the real and the ideal betrayed by the alienated will become ever more apparent. Those who are most firmly committed to the ideal of a mixed society and whose ties to Jewish life are extremely attenuated will be confronted more directly with the choice of transforming their associational life in accordance with their value system or of continuing to journey along the Jewish "Indian path" which they presently tread.

Even if they demur to affect any substantial change in clique behavior, it is questionable whether their offspring will tolerate—or find it necessary to abide—the same disparity between the real and the ideal. Presumably, the children of most alienated Jews will be no more firmly involved in traditional aspects of Jewishness, and it may also be assumed that they will be at least as integrationist-minded as their parents. The open society having been achieved, members of the younger generation may feel free to shed the ambassadorial role and with it their Jewish self-consciousness. At that juncture, close friendships with Gentiles might burgeon, many more Jews finding it psychologically possible to take their place as members of otherwise all-Gentile or predominantly Gentile cliques. Significant numbers might enter such cliques as the spouses of Gentiles, thus reversing the situation of the present Lakeville Jew whose friendship circle, as we have noticed, sometimes includes the Gentile spouse of a Jew.

These possibilities lead us to the problem of the Jewish identity of the next generation, which forms the subject matter of the following chapter.

9

THE LAKEVILLE JEW
LOOKS TO THE
NEXT GENERATION

"Moses received the Torah on Sinai, and handed it down to Joshua; Joshua to the elders; the elders to the prophets; and the prophets handed it down to the Men of the Great Assembly." So begins the first chapter of the tractate of the Mishnah known as *Pirke Avot,* the "Sayings of the Fathers."

It is apparent from all that we already know about the Jews of Lakeville that few are prepared to affirm in the full traditional sense this concept of *shalshelet hakabbalah,* the "chain of tradition." But it is equally apparent that despite the great latitudinarianism which prevails in Lakeville, the overwhelming majority desire to continue the chain of tradition in some form. In short, the Jew of Lakeville wants to transmit a Jewish identification to the next generation.

In the course of modern Jewish history it has not always been so. When in 1829 Abraham Mendelssohn discovered that his twenty-year-old son Felix was using the "Jewish" name Mendelssohn as well as the "Gentile" name Bartholdy, he became enraged, for he was afraid that his efforts at assimilation would come to nought. Fearing that his offspring—

the already-famous conductor and composer—would imperil what promised to be a brilliant future and might wreck the design which he had for his other children as well, he wrote to Felix in controlled fury:

> . . . I have to discuss with you a most serious matter. The suspicion has come to me that you have suppressed or neglected or allowed others to suppress or neglect the name which I have taken as the name of our family, the name Bartholdy. In the concert programs you have sent me, likewise in newspaper articles, your name is given as Mendelssohn. I can account for this only on the supposition that you have been the cause.
>
> Now, I am greatly dissatisfied about this. If you are to blame, you have committed a huge wrong.
>
> After all, a name is only a name, neither more nor less. Still, so long as you are under your father's jurisdiction, you have the plain and indisputable duty to be called by your father's name. Moreover it is your ineffaceable, as well as reasonable, duty to take for granted that, whatever your father does, he does on valid grounds and with due deliberation.
>
> On our journey to Paris [four years previously], you asked me the reasons why our name was changed. I gave you those reasons at length. If you have forgotten them, you could have asked me about them again. If my reasons seemed unconvincing, you should have countered with better reasons. . . .
>
> A Christian Mendelssohn is an impossibility. A Christian Mendelssohn the world would never recognize. Nor should there be a Christian Mendelssohn; for my father [Moses Mendelssohn] himself did not want to be a Christian. "Mendelssohn" does and always will stand for a Judaism in transition, when Judaism, just because it is seeking to transmute itself spiritually, clings to its ancient form all the more stubbornly and tenaciously. . . .
>
> The viewpoint, to which my father and then my own generation committed me, imposes on me other duties toward you, my children, and puts other means of discharging them into my hands. I have learnt and will not, until my dying breath, forget that, while truth is one and eternal, its forms are many and transient. That is why, as long as it was permitted by the government under which we lived [during the French occupation], I reared you without religion in any form. I wanted you to profess whatever your convictions might favor or, if you prefer, whatever expediency might dictate. But it was not so to be. I was obligated to do the choosing for you. Naturally, when you consider what scant value I placed on any form in particular, I felt no urge to choose the form known as Judaism, that most antiquated, distorted, and self-defeating form of all. Therefore I reared you as Christians, Christianity being the more purified form and the one most accepted by the majority of civilized people.

Eventually, I myself adopted Christianity, because I felt it my duty to do for myself that which I recognized as best for you. . . .

Here I must reproach myself for a weakness, even if a pardonable one. I should have done decisively and thoroughly that which I deemed right. I should have discarded the name Mendelssohn completely. I should have adhered to the new name exclusively. . . . My reason for not doing so was my long established habit of sparing those near to me and of forestalling perverted and venomous judgments. I did wrong. My purpose was merely to prepare for you a path of transition, making it easier for you that have no one to spare and nothing to care about. In Paris, when you, Felix, were about to step into the world and make a name for yourself, I deliberately had your cards engraved: Felix M. Bartholdy. You did not accept my way of thinking. Weakly enough I failed to persist. Now I only wish, though I neither expect nor deserve it, that my present intervention may not have arrived too late.

You can not, you must not carry the name Mendelssohn. Felix Mendelssohn Bartholdy is too long; it is unsuited for daily use. You must go by the name of Felix Bartholdy. A name is like a garment; it has to be appropriate for the time, the use, and the rank, if it is not to become a hindrance and a laughing stock. . . . I repeat: There can no more be a Christian Mendelssohn than there can be a Jewish Confucius. If Mendelssohn is your name, you are ipso facto a Jew. And this, if for no other reason than because it is contrary to fact, can be to you of no benefit.

Dear Felix, take this to heart and act accordingly.[1]

Abraham Mendelssohn would have preferred a world where there was neither Jew nor Christian, but one humanity. For a brief time during the Napoleonic period, it seemed to him that a new age was dawning: that all men would have equal rights and obligations. But with the triumph of reaction, his hopes were dashed; in disillusionment, he turned to Christianity. Whatever advice fathers in Lakeville are prepared to offer their children, it is doubtful whether any would repeat the message conveyed by this devoted paterfamilias—a member of a family which in some respects represented to the Jews of Berlin and its hinterland what the upper level of Lakeville Jews represents to the Jewry of Lake City. It would seem very strange to the Jews of Lakeville that paternal responsibility carries with it the obligation to assimilate or that filial devotion implies that children are duty-bound to further such assimilation. Indeed, most Lakeville parents feel quite the opposite: they believe that they are acting in their children's own best interest when they seek to create for them a Jewish identity, and they believe that dutiful children should accept such identity. Finally, those fathers and mothers who suspect that they are not fully living up to their parental responsibilities believe that their short-coming is not that they are too Jewish, but rather that they are not Jewish enough.

We do not know whether or not the children or grandchildren of our respondents will realize the plan which Abraham Mendelssohn had for his own descendants. If they should do so, it appears that Jewish identity will be lost through gradual attrition combined with intermarriage, rather than by wholesale conversion. But what we do know with certainty is that almost without exception Lakeville children who assimilate will be doing so against the wishes and hopes of their parents—wishes and hopes which endure even though they no longer convey the finality and the force of parental will characteristic of the pre-Emancipation Jewish community.

Transmitting Jewishness through Jewish Education

Almost all Lakeville parents say that they want to continue the chain of tradition. Responding to our query "How concerned are you, or have you been, with providing your children with an understanding or background in Jewish life?" a total of 93 per cent of the parents state that they have been either "very," "moderately," or "somewhat" concerned. Only 6 per cent say that they have "not been at all" concerned. A sizable proportion of these 6 per cent (as well as of the 1 per cent who did not answer the question) are the parents of pre-school children; most of them will undoubtedly become concerned when their children outgrow the nursery.

In response to a probe question inquiring into what the parent had done or was about to do in regard to his concern, we find that the over-whelming majority answer in terms of making provision for the Jewish education of their child. Parental answers are reflected in the statistics, for in point of fact it is the rare Jewish child in Lakeville who does not spend at least some time in a Jewish classroom: some 95 per cent of the families with at least one child age 10 or older have enrolled their off-spring in a Sunday or Hebrew school.* This figure of 95 per cent repre-sents a substantial increase, for only 83 per cent of the fathers in these families and 73 per cent of the mothers (for a total of 78 per cent) re-ceived some Jewish education.[2] We find that 96 per cent of the parents

---

* All data in this paragraph are based on such families.

who have been exposed to Jewish learning enroll their children, while a surprisingly high proportion—some 91 per cent—of parents who have not had any Jewish schooling do likewise. Part of the increase in the younger generation is accounted for by the abandonment of informal education as the prime means of socializing girls into Jewish culture. Lakeville represents a sharp departure from this age-old pattern of informal socialization, and thus we encounter the unusual situation in this community that the proportion of girls who are exposed to formal Jewish education is comparable with that of boys. Among those families where comparisons were possible, some 96 per cent of the girls have been taught in the Jewish classroom, in contrast to 94 per cent of the boys.[3]

It is not possible for us to compare the quality of the Jewish education received by the two generations or to estimate with any accuracy the influence of such education on the older generation in contrast to the younger. On the one hand, a somewhat higher proportion of the children have attended a Sunday school, which is the least intensive form of Jewish education. But on the other hand, a noticeable proportion of the parents received their education from private tutors. The majority of such tutors were untrained in pedagogical techniques; they were generally employed solely for the purpose of Bar Mitzvah preparation. While almost as many children as parents have been enrolled in Hebrew school, we find that the older generation attended for a greater number of hours per week than the younger generation. However, the number of years of attendance for all kinds of Jewish instruction appears to be on the increase. This reflects a diminishing tendency for children to receive an education which is exclusively geared to preparation for Bar Mitzvah or Confirmation. Thus we find that while 23 per cent of the fathers and 30 per cent of the mothers received only one to four years of schooling, a mere 16 per cent of the parents expect their children to receive such minimal schooling (see Table 9–1). We infer that parents are becoming accustomed to the greater number of years of Jewish schooling demanded by religious institutions and that they themselves are desirous of raising standards from what they were a generation ago.

While some children start their schooling at an earlier age than did their parents and thus are in a Jewish classroom for a larger number of years, on the whole Jewish education in Lakeville still generally terminates with Bar Mitzvah or Confirmation.[4] In both generations, these ceremonies are regarded as graduation exercises releasing the adolescent from the obligation of further Jewish study. Confirmation is the more prevalent of the two ceremonies among the younger generation. While

TABLE 9–1. NUMBER OF YEARS OF JEWISH EDUCATION EXPECTED OF CHILDREN AND RECEIVED BY PARENTS

Years	Expected of Children *	Received by † Fathers	Mothers
1–4	16%	23%	30%
5–6	25	19	19
7–8	30	35	22
9–10	24	13	16
11+	5	10	13
N	(293)	(175)	(171)

* Based on parents with at least one child exposed to Jewish education.
† Based on parent respondents who received a Jewish education.

less than three in ten of the fathers and less than half of the mothers were confirmed, almost three-fourths of the parents report that their children have been or are expected to be confirmed (see Table 9–2). Confirmation is more frequently performed for girls. Thus we find that for families in which information about the child's Confirmation can be distinguished by sex, only half of the sons, in contrast to four-fifths of the daughters, have been confirmed or will become candidates.

TABLE 9–2. CONFIRMATION AND BAR (BAT) MITZVAH AMONG CHILDREN AND PARENTS

	Confirmation	Bar Mitzvah	Bat Mitzvah
Per cent of parents who say that their children had or are expected to have ceremony	72	47	12
N *	(424)	(324)	(315)
Per cent of Fathers who had ceremony	29	53	†
N	(202)	(202)	
Mothers who had ceremony	47	†	‡
N	(222)		(222)

* N for Bar Mitzvah column refers to total respondents with at least one son; N for Bat Mitzvah column refers to total respondents with at least one daughter.
† Not applicable.
‡ Less than 0.5 per cent.

In respect to Bar Mitzvah, some 47 per cent of the parents of boys report that a son has had or will have this ceremony—about the same proportion that report a Confirmation.[5] But even more significant is the fact that this figure is very close to the 53 per cent of the fathers who had a Bar Mitzvah. The similarity is remarkable in view of the more traditional childhood background of the older generation. It is also apparent that the ceremony of Bar Mitzvah retains its hold in spite of the great popularity of Confirmation.

The newest ceremony marking the passage from childhood is Bat Mitzvah, a recent innovation for girls which is modeled on the Bar Mitzvah. Bat Mitzvah is not yet popular in any real sense, but it is making noticeable gains. Since almost none of the mothers had a Bat Mitzvah, the fact that in some 12 per cent of the eligible families a daughter has had or will have the ceremony is impressive. Furthermore, both Bar Mitzvah and Bat Mitzvah are retaining or even increasing their popularity. Thus, among younger parents—those whose children are all under 10 years of age—some 55 per cent who have sons are planning on a Bar Mitzvah and 17 per cent of those who have daughters are planning on a Bat Mitzvah.

The Jewishness of the Home

PARENTAL FEELINGS

The near-universal decision by parents to continue the chain of tradition through giving their children a Jewish education contrasts markedly with the restricted religious example they set in the home.[6] Yet the majority are satisfied with their example. When asked, "Do you believe the environment in your home is Jewish enough for your children, or is it too Jewish or not Jewish enough?" the majority—some 71 per cent—feel that the environment they provide is Jewish enough. There is, however, a substantial minority of 29 per cent who feel their home environment is deficient in Jewishness. Only a single respondent feels that his home is overly Jewish.[7]

Satisfaction with the extent of Jewishness in the home occurs among parents at all levels of religious observance: parents who observe few or no rituals are just about as satisfied as those who are strongly observant. In fact, a substantial group of our respondents—perhaps most of them, to a greater or lesser extent—present the following syndrome: minimal ritualism,[8] satisfaction with Jewishness of the home, enrolling their children in religious school, and a desire to have them confirmed or bar mitzvahed. Among the families with at least one child of age 10 or older, more than seven in ten of the parents who observe only two or one or no rituals are satisfied with their home environment. More than nine in ten of such parents have sent their children to a Jewish school, and over eight in ten have had or will have their children participate in the Confirmation or Bar Mitzvah ceremony.

Parents who hold to a pattern of minimal ritualism thus appear to rely primarily, and in some cases almost exclusively, on the religious school for the Jewish socialization of their children. This dependence on the Jewish school constitutes a radical departure from the traditional approach to the rearing of the Jewish child. In past eras, the effort of the school to transmit the culture (albeit to the male in particular) represented merely a continuation of efforts already initiated by the parents. But among Lakeville residents—so many of whom are at lower levels of observance and who in other ways do not provide a distinctive Jewish environment for their children—the function of socialization into Jewish culture has been separated from its traditional moorings in the family.

That minority among Lakeville Jews who feel that their home environment is deficient in Jewishness constitute a significant group. Such self-criticism, we find, bears no relationship to the individual's objective religious situation. We have already shown that the less observant are no more critical of themselves than the more observant. Nor is the standard of observance in the respondent's childhood home determinative. While self-criticism is expressed somewhat more often by less observant respondents who come from highly traditional homes (in contrast to more observant respondents coming from the same type of homes), it is voiced just as frequently by those who come from moderately or minimally traditional homes and continue the pattern in which they were reared.

We also find that nostalgia alone does not lead to a self-critical evaluation of the Jewishness of one's home. Thus parents who are either very or moderately sentimental about their childhood Jewish memories do not consider their homes to be Jewishly inadequate any more frequently than do those who are either slightly or not at all sentimental. The likelihood of a self-critical evaluation is increased, however, when nostalgia about one's Jewish childhood is linked to a belief that one's children's memories of Jewishness will be less pleasant than one's own. Self-criticism flows from a feeling that one's children are "missing out" on something. Thus, among parents who are highly sentimental about their Jewish childhood, there is a relationship between their estimate of their children's Jewish memories and their evaluation of the Jewishness of their homes. A self-critical evaluation occurs among as many as 45 per cent of nostalgic parents who believe their children will have less pleasant Jewish memories. In contrast, self-criticism occurs among only 18 per cent of nostalgic parents who think their children will have just as pleasant memories as they have and among only 26 per cent of such parents who feel that they will have more pleasant memories (see Table 9–3). But among

TABLE 9–3. ATTITUDE TO JEWISHNESS OF HOME BY ESTIMATE OF CHILDREN'S JEWISH MEMORIES AND ATTACHMENT TO JEWISHNESS OF CHILDHOOD HOME

Among parents very or moderately sentimental about their childhood Jewish memories	*Parents' Estimate of Their Children's Jewish Memories, Compared to Own Memories*		
	Less Pleasant	As Pleasant	More Pleasant
Per cent who believe that for their children their home environment is			
Jewish enough	55	82	74
Not Jewish enough	45	18	26
N	(91)	(61)	(34)
Among parents who are slightly or not at all sentimental about their childhood Jewish memories			
Per cent who believe that for their children their home environment is			
Jewish enough	64	72	69
Not Jewish enough	36	28	31
N	(22)	(39)	(51)

parents who feel little or no attachment to their childhood memories, there is no relationship between their forecast of their children's Jewish memories and their judgment about the Jewishness of their homes. The tendency, then, is for parents to find their homes insufficiently Jewish if their children's present Jewish experiences are contrasted with a warm Jewish past and are found wanting.[9]

Parents who believe that their children's remembrances of Jewish things past will not have a strong tinge of nostalgia appear to be realists;

Lakeville does not offer a very conducive setting for the development of warm memories of distinctively Jewish childhood experiences. Be that as it may, the fact that a sizable minority express self-critical attitudes suggests a desire to create a more Jewish home environment for their children. However, this desire to enrich the Jewish identity of their off-spring is frequently coupled with a feeling of helplessness about the possibility of achieving higher Jewish horizons. There is the case of a minimally observant advertising executive who is very nostalgic about the Orthodox home in which he was reared by East European immigrant parents. He is unhappy with the fact that his preadolescent daughters "are not being brought up in the same traditional life—it's not really a Jewish way of life." He believes that they would have "a better outlook if we gave them the Jewish life I was exposed to." However, he adds simply, "I can't."

When such parents specify what kind of Jewishness they have in mind, their focus is generally on religious observances. Thus a minimally observant businessman who believes that his two young sons "won't have some of the pleasant family experiences" to which he was exposed in the fairly observant household in which he was reared states in typical fashion, "We think we ought to light Friday night candles regularly, but we're lax about some of the things we talk about doing." And an extremely active ORT leader, who believes that her own very sentimental memories of a childhood spent in an Orthodox household will not be matched by that of her daughter, says ambivalently,

> We could have [Jewish] records or go to services Friday night or put up a *sukkah*. We don't because we're not that interested.

The laxness of those who experience a Jewish gap in their home life and their consequent failure to intensify the family's ritualism are surely associated with a lack of conviction about the suprasocial character of Jewish observances. But in addition to respondents who may lack conviction or some alternative justification for observance, there are other respondents who also experience ambivalence on the social level. To them, higher Jewish horizons seem discrepant with the way of life to which they have become accustomed. There is the example of a fairly observant mother, by Lakeville standards, who is very active in the Schechter Synagogue. She is highly nostalgic about her Jewish childhood and believes that her teen-agers' less pleasant memories will be due to a Jewish background "not as intense or delightful in influence." She told us that she had thought of enriching the home environment by hanging Jewish paintings in her living room. However, her ambivalence about the display of such art prevented her from making a purchase:

> I assume the responsibility. I just don't think I do enough. . . . I saw a picture of a rabbi and didn't buy it because of its content. I thought I didn't have the right room. . . . I should have bought it.

Whatever conflicts parents have in respect to increasing the level of Jewish religion and culture practiced in their homes, we should remember that they willingly expose their children to a much higher level of Jewishness in the school situation. It is possible to interpret such exposure in terms of a desire to immunize the child against assimilation: the parent is willing to take the chance that for a brief period the child may break out with a rash of Jewishness, but is confident that the rash will disappear, leaving behind immunity to assimilation. It is also possible to interpret such behavior in another context: while the parent feels incapable of achieving a higher Jewish horizon, he wishes his child to become a more traditional Jew than he is; he hopes that Jewish education will "take." If this perspective is adopted, exposure to a more Jewish regimen than is practiced in the home constitutes impressive evidence of the parent's lack of militancy about his own secularism as well as a feeling that his particular level of acculturation is not the only desirable one for the modern Jew.

THE REACTION OF THE CHILDREN

The reaction of Lakeville children to the Jewishness of their home is generally based on the models provided in their immediate environment, rather than on those in their grandparents' homes. On the whole, children are more satisfied with the Jewishness of their homes than are parents. Thus a total of 81 per cent of the parents report that their children feel that the Jewish environment of the home is "just about right," some 17 per cent say that their children feel it is "not Jewish enough," and only 2 per cent report that their children feel that the home is "too Jewish." * Parents who believe that their home is deficient in Jewishness are generally overruled by their children: some 70 per cent of such parents report that their children feel satisfied. However, a noticeable minority of such parents—some 28 per cent—say that their children agree with them about the poverty of Jewishness in the home.

---

* Based on families with at least one unmarried child of age 10 or older. These tabulations exclude some 3 per cent of parents in this category who did not answer the question. Most of them felt their children were still too young to have a reaction.

Most of the children who feel that their homes are deficient in Jewishness are from the less observant households—considerably more often than are the satisfied children. But regardless of the level of observance, parents' opinions are influential in determining children's evaluations (or at least parents prefer to think that their children agree with them). For example, among the minimally and nonobservant parents, 32 per cent of those who are critical of the Jewishness of their homes say that the children agree with them, while only 18 per cent of the satisfied parents report a critical reaction.

Like their parents, children who find their homes inadequate focus on the lack of religious observance. But children also tend to focus on the neglect of various customs which accompany ritual observances. A sales executive's wife who was reared by very observant immigrant parents and feels that her home is not Jewish enough (the only ritual observed is the lighting of candles on Hanukkah) reports that her ten-year-old son agrees with her. She says that the boy has complained "that on Friday night we don't go to services, don't light candles, and don't have chicken and soup." A dentist who is active in the Wise Temple and is highly observant by Lakeville standards reports that his adolescent son does not consider the home Jewish enough "because we don't have a white tablecloth [for Sabbath eve meals]." And a fourth-generation mother reports that her college-age children make an invidious comparison between their own home and that of their grandparents. This mother is a Hirsch Temple member who believes her own home is deficient in Jewishness and is very nostalgic about the home environment which her Reform, but comparatively traditional, parents created. She says,

> The children like me to do all the things my mother does. They love the holidays and wish I'd do the same things.

RELIGIOUS HARMONY IN THE HOME

These reactions aside, discontent with the level of Jewishness in the home is not a very conspicuous phenomenon among Lakeville parents or their children. The prevailing poverty of Jewishness is approved by a clear majority in both generations. Furthermore, the Lakeville home emerges as particularly harmonious in respect to Jewishness when parents compare it with their childhood home. In response to the question "Do you think that there is more agreement or less agreement between your outlook and interest in Jewish affairs and your children's than there was between yours and your father's (mother's) when you were a child?", some 37 per cent of our respondents report more agreement, and only 12 per cent report less agreement. The remainder—51 per cent—find no difference between the two situations.*

On balance, then, our respondents feel that there is greater consensus on Jewish issues between themselves and their children than prevailed in their own childhood home. Significantly, respondents who belong to more advanced generations report such agreement just as frequently as do those who belong to the second generation. The present consensus thus reflects more than the passing of the classic conflict between second-generation children and their immigrant parents. Rather, it rests in large part on the belief of our respondents, whatever their generational status, that they possess greater general competence in child rearing than did their parents and that they have successfully harnessed modern theories of child development to the goal of transmitting Jewish identity to the next generation. They claim, in short, to be more effective as Jewish parents.

The basic assumptions of the parents' image of themselves as possessing greater competence are as follows: the child is an individual with his own special needs; they as parents understand what these needs are; and finally, they as parents are capable of satisfying such needs. "I know my children better than my father did," explains a third-generation man of mixed descent whose minimal pattern of religious observance almost duplicates that of his childhood home, but feels that there is more agreement on Jewish matters in his own home than there was in his parental home. A teacher in the Lake City school system with a similar level of observance also reports more agreement with his two boys than he experienced as a child reared by Orthodox parents who were immigrants from Eastern Europe: ". . . we're more cognizant of the needs of children. I felt 'tolerated' [in my parental home] because I was there."

The attitude that the child is an individual with his own special needs has as its corollary the concept of autonomy: that the child is more than a mere extension of the parent and thus should not be expected to subordinate himself completely to parental wishes. But while the concept of autonomy promises freedom, it exists side by side with the requirement that the child be socialized: he must be taught to follow prescribed pat-

---

* Based on families with one or more children of age 10 or older. Some 3 per cent of the parents who did not answer the question are excluded from these tabulations. Most of those among the 51 per cent who volunteered additional comments indicated that there was relative harmony, rather than disagreement, in both home situations.

terns. The modern parent wishes the child to conform willingly, rather than as a result of coercion, and as a consequence the child must be motivated to do what his parents would like him to do. This often involves manipulation. The child comes to feel that he does something not because it is inspired by his parents but because he himself wants to do it. "We make things more pleasant religiously for our kids and they feel it's something they want to do," asserts a third-generation mother of two children attending Hebrew school at the Schechter Synagogue; her level of observance, while relatively high by Lakeville standards, is much reduced from what prevailed in her childhood home. A second-generation office manager with a similar religious history feels his parents were of the "old school with a tendency of 'you've got to.' I want to convince my son and get him to want to."

A related theme cited by some of those who believe that there is a higher level of consensus in their own home than there was in their parents' is that the present generation has greater concern with making the Jewish tradition comprehensible to their children. Thus a second-generation, moderately observant lawyer's wife, whose college-age daughters were both confirmed at Wise Temple, but who herself was never given any formal Jewish education by her Orthodox parents, recalls her childhood in the following terms:

> I think when we were young nothing was explained to the children. We didn't understand the rituals at home or in the *shul*. Today more understand them.

A woman reared in an East European immigrant home which she describes as Conservative and who recently resigned from the Schechter Synagogue to join the Hirsch Temple because of what she terms its "intellectual approach" believes that her greater agreement with her children, both now in their twenties, is due to "our efforts to explain more than my parents did to me." A minimally observant fourth-generation mother whose children attend the religious school at the same temple makes a much more serious and far less typical charge against her totally nonobservant parents. Not only did they fail to explain Judaism or provide her with a Jewish education but the mother had "ambivalent feelings about Jewishness, and so she couldn't give me anything in the way of understanding or evaluation."

Implicit in the claims of those parents who feel that they are more successful in making Judaism attractive and comprehensible to their children than were their parents is the belief that they have a higher level of interaction and communication with their offspring as regards both Jewish and general matters. Thus a second-generation professional man who is active in the Men's Club of Wise Temple, but is minimally observant, recalls the Orthodox home of his childhood in the following terms:

> My father and I never discussed [Jewish matters]. There was no relationship, no real basis for discussion. I *had* to do it.

The attitude is perhaps best summarized by a fairly observant owner of a hardware supply business, the father of two grown sons who were confirmed at the Wise Temple. While he feels that his East European immigrant parents were not very observant in comparison to others of their generation (he characterizes them as "between Reform and Conservative"), he implies that in their method of child rearing they were complete traditionalists. He discerns a marked contrast between the way he was brought up and the way in which he is raising his own children:

> I made a definite effort to inform my children and share with them. I was "enjoined" by my father, whereas I "joined" my children.

Religious permissiveness is the final factor mentioned by respondents who feel that they have achieved greater harmony on Jewish issues with their children. It is cited by approximately half of those who were reared in the most traditional homes. However, the relatively observant respondents who come from such homes claim that religious permissiveness is the basis for greater consensus with their children almost as often as do the less observant respondents who come from the same type of homes. In any case, all such respondents view the traditionalism which prevailed in their childhood home as a source of strain and conflict, and they see their present religious regimen as contributing to greater harmony. A minimally observant, second-generation mother of four children, who was reared in an Orthodox household, says typically, "We make no demands on our children. As a child, we were forced to follow what my parents were doing." More articulate is a second-generation mother of two grown sons, who is an active supporter of various Jewish welfare groups and a passive member of the Wise Temple. This woman, who was reared in an Orthodox household, attends services only on the High Holidays, and her home observance is confined to the lighting of candles on Hanukkah:

> It's been so easy for our children. There's been nothing that they had to do or had not to do. They could write or go to parties on Saturday. The only thing they had to do was to go to Sunday school.

A more observant lawyer who belongs to the Schechter Synagogue and feels that there was "too great importance attached to the rituals" observed in the Orthodox home of his immigrant parents attributes the parent–child consensus in his own home to the fact that "I've de-emphasized the ritual approach with the children and taken a more moderate approach."

In sum, Lakeville Jews view their goal of transmitting a Jewish identity to their children as fully compatible with the concepts of child rearing which they hold as modern parents. In fact, they believe that their modernity assists the achievement of this goal. They view their aim of transmitting Jewish identity as compatible with the achievement of harmonious family life and, indeed, as resting on the greater understanding which they feel characterizes the relationship between present-day parents and children. While some agree that in the course of adjusting to modernity traditional religious standards have been compromised, there is a tendency to view such changes as helping rather than hindering the effort to transmit Jewish identity.

Whether numbering themselves among the minority who feel that their homes should be more Jewish but find it very difficult to change or among the majority who feel satisfied with the level of Jewishness prevailing in their homes, Lakeville Jews are optimistic about the possibility of transmitting Jewish identity to the next generation. One problem, however, disturbs their feeling of satisfaction in respect to what they have achieved Jewishly and their optimism about their Jewish future. This is the threat of intermarriage.

The Threat of Intermarriage

PARENTAL FEELINGS

For the chain of tradition to be extended, the children of our respondents must establish a Jewish household when they become mature. This result ordinarily requires marriage to another Jew. But we find that in this regard a substantial proportion of Lakeville Jews are unsure of their children. Thus, in answer to the query "Do you think your child may marry a non-Jew?" some 36 per cent answered in the negative, 29 per cent said "possibly," another 29 per cent stated that they did not know, and 5 per cent said "yes." And when probed, even the 36 per cent who felt that their child would not marry a non-Jew indicated some degree of ambiguity.*

If many parents lack certainty that their children will act in traditional fashion, the fact of the matter is that they themselves are not always capable of experiencing the feelings that are prescribed by the old norms. In response to a query about what they would feel if an intermarriage occurred in their household ("How would you feel if your child were to marry a non-Jew? Would you feel very unhappy, somewhat unhappy, neither happy nor unhappy, somewhat happy, or very happy?"), only 29 per cent of our respondents choose the answer closest to Jewish tradition: "very unhappy." The largest proportion—43 per cent—say that they would feel "somewhat unhappy." A full 24 per cent say that they would be "neither happy nor unhappy." Only 2 per cent say that they would feel "somewhat happy" or "very happy."

What do these responses mean? Do they mean that Lakeville Jews would actually feel even greater unhappiness about an intermarriage, but are inhibited from expressing such an emotion because (*a*) they have an overwhelming fear of the possibility of an intermarriage, or (*b*) because they are so convinced of its coming prevalence that they have made an advance adjustment, or (*c*) because a strong emotion would be interpreted as an admission of an ethnocentric bias? Or should their answers be interpreted in yet a different context: as reflecting a lack of success in harmonizing the traditional goal of a Jewish marriage with what modernity has taught our respondents is the proper mode of marital choice in American society as well as the basis of marital happiness—individualistic choice and mutual love? Or do the answers simply reflect the modern parent's inability to control the courtship and marital decisions of his child? Or do they reflect something far deeper, such as ambiguity about the worthwhileness of Jewish survival? Should these responses, then, be interpreted as reflecting the fact that attitudes in this area are strongly in flux, just as are attitudes in respect to other aspects of Jewishness, and that as a consequence many Lakeville Jews cannot bring themselves to feel very unhappy about an intermarriage which might occur in their immediate family?

Since the problem of intermarriage is not the primary focus of our study, we do not have sufficient data to give authoritative treatment to

---

* Percentages in this section are based on respondents who have one or more unmarried children. We have, however, excluded the handful of families who have a child who is married to a Gentile.

each of these significant possibilities. We do find that—as we should expect—feelings about intermarriage and Jewish-Gentile integration are
related (see Table 9–4). The relationship is much less than perfect, however, for the majority of extreme integrationists would not be happy with
(or even indifferent to) an intermarriage, while half or more of the strongest nonintegrationists would not be very unhappy. We also find the same
type of situation in respect to synagogue involvement: there is a relationship between feelings about intermarriage and synagogue involvement,
but the relationship is not quite so strong as might be assumed. While one
in three of the parents who do not belong to a synagogue would be indif-

TABLE 9–4.   FEELING ABOUT INTERMARRIAGE BY LEVEL
OF INTEGRATION-MINDEDNESS

If child were to marry a non-Jew, per cent of parents would feel	*Integration-Mindedness Score*						
	High 8–9	7	6	5	4	3	Low 1–2
Very unhappy	10	11	25	32	33	42	49
Somewhat unhappy	52	37	36	49	52	42	38
Neither happy nor unhappy	28	46	36	19	14	16	13
Happy	10	6	3	—	1	—	—
N	(29)	(46)	(73)	(77)	(72)	(52)	(39)

ferent toward (or happy with) intermarriage, contrasted with only about
one in ten of those who are intensely involved in synagogue life, a large
proportion of the highly involved group—almost half—would be only
somewhat unhappy. It is true that there is a stronger relationship between
feelings about intermarriage and the observance of rituals. Almost half
of the nonobservant and more than one-third of the minimally observant
would not feel unhappy about such an eventuality, contrasted with only
one in twenty of the more observant group (five or more rituals). However, only half of the more observant express the traditional feeling of
intense unhappiness.

   If we make the assumption that the nonintegrationists and the religiously committed should be more unhappy than they say they would be,
we are justified in inferring that the question of intermarriage is such a
tender one that our respondents react in an inhibited manner. It also
appears that the Lakeville Jew feels under a certain constraint to present
himself as a reasonable man on the subject of intermarriage. But even

if we should claim that his sweet reasonableness is pure façade, a change of no mean significance has occurred. Not adhering to the old norms with regard to religion and culture, apparently the Lakeville Jew has left tradition behind in respect to his reaction to intermarriage as well.

When we relate feelings about intermarriage to generation and descent, we find that those who belong to the advanced generations are not always more receptive to intermarriage than are those who belong to more recent generations. This is particularly true among our respondents of East European origin, where the reaction of the third generation hardly varies from the second and first: only about one in five in each generation would be indifferent to an intermarriage in their own family and none would be happy with it (see Table 9–5). However, among those of German or mixed descent, we discover that there is less feeling against intermarriage in the advanced generations: somewhat more than half of the fourth generation would feel indifferent or even happy about their child's intermarriage, contrasted with much smaller proportions among the less advanced generations.

THE PARENTS' JUSTIFICATION FOR THEIR FEELINGS

How do respondents who would be either very unhappy or somewhat unhappy in the event of an intermarriage explain themselves? Our most striking finding is that relatively few justify their feelings on the basis of a concern with Jewish identity, Jewish survival, or the Jewish religion. In fact, only 14 per cent of those who oppose intermarriage explicitly base their reaction on such grounds.

One member of this small group responding in overtly survivalist terms is a moderately observant mother who was raised in an Orthodox home, graduated from college, and now divides her time between the ORT group in the predominantly Jewish neighborhood in which she lives and the Lakeville chapter of the League of Women Voters. While she would like her nine-year-old daughter, who attends the Hebrew school of the Schechter Synagogue, to have more contact with Gentiles, she maintains:

> I want her to stay within our group, just as I did and my husband did. It's a different culture, and a lot of things are involved. True, I've seen intermarriage work, but this person gave up Catholicism before she married a Jew. I'm broadminded, but in this area I'm not.

A concern for group survival is voiced more directly by an articulate engineer who identifies both his parents and himself with Conservative

TABLE 9–5. FEELING ABOUT INTERMARRIAGE BY GENERATION AND DESCENT

	Generation of							
If child were to marry a non-Jew, per cent of parents would feel:	German Descent		Mixed Descent			East European Descent		
	Third	Fourth Plus	Second	Third	Fourth Plus	First	Second	Third
Very unhappy	19	—	53	32	5	29	37	37
Somewhat unhappy	62	46	40	40	42	52	45	41
Neither happy nor unhappy	19	51	7	23	37	19	18	22
Happy	—	3	—	5	16	—	—	—
N	(16)	(35)	(15)	(22)	(19)	(21)	(128)	(81)

Judaism and plans to join a temple when his son is old enough for religious school. While he too would like more contact with Gentiles (he prefers a neighborhood with a small minority of Jews, and he feels that even a fifty–fifty ratio is "unhealthy"), he also maintains that intermarriage

> would mean breaking the chain. We are a unique group. To survive is necessary. No one likes to become a fossil, extinct. It's a matter of pride.

A member of the Hirsch Temple—a sophisticated fourth-generation mother who has become very friendly with several Gentiles whom she has met in a creative arts group—reacts as follows:

> I'm not an assimilationist, and an intermarriage means a loss. They slip away.

Most Lakeville Jews, however, explain their opposition to intermarriage in quite different terms. They stress that discord is inevitable in an interfaith marriage; they maintain that a Jewish-Gentile marriage is inherently an unstable union and therefore an unhealthy one. In fact, as many as nine out of ten of those who say that they would be unhappy with their child's marrying a non-Jew explain their feelings in these terms. Three aspects of the discord theme emerge from their answers. The primary one, advanced by seven out of ten, emphasizes disturbed relations between husband and wife. A secondary focus, mentioned by about three in ten, emphasizes difficulties which are created for the offspring of an interfaith union. A third aspect, mentioned by three in twenty, is the problematic relationship of the married couple to relatives, friends, and society at large.*

Those who emphasize the discord theme stress that marriage is "a matter of adjustment anyhow," as it is phrased by a minimally observant, second-generation woman who holds a post-graduate degree and is the mother of four children. As discord-oriented respondents see it, the process of marital adjustment is difficult under the best of conditions. "There are enough obstacles in married life to interfere with its success," states a woman highly satisfied with her membership in the Hirsch Temple and intensely active in non-sectarian civic groups. And a mother of three preadolescent boys, who has been very active in the Sisterhood of

---

* These proportions are based on the 72 per cent of our respondents who would feel unhappy if their child were to marry a non-Jew. The totals add up to more than the approximately nine out of ten who express the discord theme, since some express more than one aspect of the theme.

Wise Temple, puts it this way: "I think there's enough problems in marriage without bringing in others." In fact, parents tend to place so much stress on the difficulties of marital adjustment that a moderately observant father formerly active in the Wise Temple relates how he overreached himself:

> I told my older son that marriage is a hazardous business at best and explained the importance of mutual background, tastes, personality and so on. When I finished, he said, "Wow, Dad, I'll *never* get married to anyone."

Furthermore, those who stress the marital-discord theme look on interfaith difference as the crucial factor which tips the scale against connubial bliss. As we might expect, the specific formulation of this notion differs considerably from one "brow level" to another. An example of an unsophisticated response is that of a second-generation father who is highly observant and a loyal member of the Schechter Synagogue, where his son will soon become Bar Mitzvah. He confidently substantiates his argument that there is no possibility of happiness in intermarriage by citing his nephew's courtship experience with a Gentile girl as well as his own role in the affair:

> There are enough problems without creating any. My nephew kisses my feet for breaking up a marriage which was going to take place between him and a *shikse*. He hated me. Now he's ready to kiss my feet. He's really happily married.

A far different kind of response is volunteered by a father of two post-adolescent children, who is a loyal member of the Hirsch Temple and an active worker in a national interfaith organization. Circumspect in judgment and sophisticated in approach, he focuses on the connection between religious difference and marital discord in his own way:

> Marriage is a process of adjustment of personalities in which conflicting religious background is an obstacle if either is devoted to his religion and the other is anything but accepting.

Turning to those who stress the effect of an interfaith marriage on children, we find that they focus on the psychological aspect: the possibility that the child may grow up lacking a firm group identity and confused as to whether he is Jewish or Gentile. They do not mention that the child may be lost to the Jewish community. For example, a third-generation father who feels his home is not Jewish enough for his seven-year-old daughter, who is attending the Lilienthal Temple Sunday School, voices the fear that "the children [of an intermarriage] won't know where they belong and what they stand for." Another respondent, a woman who grew up in an all-Gentile neighborhood in a midwestern town and is now the fairly observant mother of three young daughters, goes so far as to suggest that the proper course for an intermarried couple is to remain childless:

> If I went into it, it would be with the understanding of having no children, because they would suffer. They would be neither Jewish nor Gentile.

Respondents who focus on the discord theme generally have at least one case history at hand to buttress their argument that the wages of intermarriage are unhappiness. Yet even as they recite their story and seek to advance their image of sweet reasonableness on the intermarriage problem, it does not require much insight to realize that they are far from being unbiased students of marital problems; they have not judiciously weighed the evidence and reluctantly come to the conclusion that an interfaith difference intrudes such a strong disharmonious element in marriage as to place an otherwise sound relationship in jeopardy. Rather, their advocacy of the view that interfaith marriage is a pathological relationship seems to be a safe way of expressing the desire to continue the chain of tradition while at the same time avoiding the appearance of ethnocentrism. Widely approving of the integration of the Jew into the general community, our respondents are under pressure to formulate a respectable alternative for their disinclination to sanction what is the ultimate in interfaith acceptance. Furthermore, they are apparently seeking to harmonize their desire for Jewish continuity with their belief that enlightened people have the right to freedom of marital choice. The notion that a Jewish-Gentile marriage is inherently unstable represents a resolution of this conflict; there is freedom to choose, but wisdom dictates that the choice be a fellow Jew.[10]

ROMANTIC LOVE AND INTERMARRIAGE

In our culture, romantic love is the sanction for contracting a marriage as well as the force which produces happiness in marriage. Romantic love is generally defined in universalistic terms—terms which submerge such particularistic values as the preservation of religious or ethnic identity. In fact, the most idealized kind of romantic love is often that which leaps across the barriers of class, religion, and ethnicity, bringing individuals together who would otherwise have no relationship with each other.

The pervasiveness of the romantic love ideal in American culture places the Lakeville Jew in a profound dilemma: he desires Jewish survival, but the culture which he internalizes believes in the rightness—even the imperative—of romantic love.

In order to gather data on this value conflict, we presented our respondents with a forced-choice situation in which the idea of romantic love was in opposition to the traditional norm of endogamy. Seeking to determine which value would take precedence, we asked our respondents to imagine that they had to choose for their child between a non-Jew with whom their offspring was in love and a Jew with whom the child was not in love.* We find that an overwhelming majority of Lakeville Jews— some 85 per cent—prefer the non-Jew and a mere 5 per cent choose the unloved Jew over the loved Gentile, while some 7 per cent could not make a decision.

Since the preference for the loved Gentile is so overwhelming, large majorities among all types of Lakeville Jews opt for exogamy. Thus more than eight out of ten of first- and second-generation East Europeans choose the Gentile, as do more than three-fourths of the religiously observant and the more active synagogue members and over eight out of ten of those scoring low in integration-mindedness. Even more significantly, those who strongly oppose intermarriage beat a retreat when confronted with the choice between a loveless intrafaith marriage and a love-based intermarriage; marriage with the non-Jew is preferred by as many as 70 per cent of those who would feel very unhappy if their child were to marry a non-Jew. Finally, under the conditions stipulated, some 64 per cent of our respondents who believe it essential that a "good Jew" marry within the group nevertheless choose marriage with a non-Jew.

Thus we see that romantic love is accepted as the basis of marriage, even when it conflicts with powerful traditional norms which aim to insure Jewish survival by restricting marital choice. Inasmuch as even those who strongly disapprove of intermarriage find themselves opting for romantic love, the pervasiveness of this value apparently constitutes the most significant potential threat to the Jewish defense against intermarriage. The widespread acceptance of romantic love is all the more striking when it is contrasted with the additional finding that other characteristics of a desirable marriage partner receive much less approval when they involve crossing religio-ethnic lines.[11] We presented our respondents with

* The exact formulation was as follows: "I'm going to ask you to imagine that you were choosing a husband or wife for your child. Would you prefer a non-Jew he (or she) was in love with, or a Jew he (or she) wasn't in love with?"

two additional forced-choice situations: "Would you prefer a non-Jew without any interest in organized religion or an Orthodox Jew who insisted on all the religious rituals?" and "Would you prefer a non-Jew in a professional occupation, such as law or medicine, or a Jew in a skilled trade such as carpentry?" [12] Since so few Lakeville Jews consider themselves Orthodox (and even those who do generally deviate widely from Orthodox standards), the prospect of marriage to an Orthodox Jew should be unattractive, to say the least. Nevertheless, a Gentile with no interest in organized religion is considered no more preferable than an Orthodox Jew: the Jew is selected by 43 per cent, and the Gentile by 44 per cent. Furthermore, class and status considerations in this wealthy and prestigious suburb figure even less importantly in an intermarriage than religious considerations. A non-Jewish doctor or lawyer is preferred by only 29 per cent of the parents, while his rival—the Jewish carpenter —is approved by 54 per cent.[13]

Both Jewish types—the Orthodox observer and the carpenter—are consistently preferred by large majorities among the less advanced generations, the more religiously committed, the least integration-minded, those who believe that endogamous marriage among Jews is essential, and those who would feel very unhappy if their child were to intermarry.[14] Only the advanced generations of German or mixed descent, the religiously alienated, the extremely integration-minded, those who believe that a good Jew need not marry within the faith, and those who would feel indifferent or happy if their child were to marry a Gentile prefer the non-Jewish professional and the non-religious Gentile.

INTERMARRIAGE AND PARENTAL ACTION

If many Lakeville parents are not fully capable of experiencing traditional emotions in respect to intermarriage, it is reasonable to assume that few are capable of acting in the traditional manner, such as refusing to acknowledge the marriage and disowning their errant child. In response to our queries on parental action ("If your child were to marry a non-Jew how do you think you would react? What would you do?"), we find that a mere 1 per cent would reject their child. Fully 93 per cent are prepared to accept the intermarriage and thus to retain their connections with their child; they would also attempt to build a meaningful relationship with his Gentile spouse.[15]

It thus appears that the broad consensus and harmonious relationship on Jewish issues between parents and children which we encountered earlier has a kind of hollowness about it. We see that the parent's feeling of identification with his child supersedes, if need be, his concern with his child's Jewishness. The same parent who is confident of his ability to create a firm Jewish identity for his child is unsure of his offspring in respect to marital choice, and in the event of intermarriage he would seek to maintain family unity on the basis determined by the child, even though such unity no longer assures the continuity of the chain of tradition.

An explicit rejection of the traditional reaction to intermarriage is apparent in the answers of some of our respondents. In the words of a religiously unobservant, second-generation woman whose son was recently confirmed at Wise Temple, "Would I throw him out? Absolutely not. He's still your child." "I would never disown my child. I'd make the best of it," is the response of a young housewife who was reared by Orthodox parents and is now a moderately observant, active member of the Schechter Synagogue. Neither of these parents would feel indifferent or happy if their child married a non-Jew.

In their rejection of the traditional model, many parents hope that they would have "enough sense," as some put it, to act in a reasonable manner. They wish that their deportment would endear them to their children, rather than provide grounds for a family rift. The most that the many parents can see themselves doing is clarifying the alternatives for their child. In doing so, they would play the role of responsible marital counselors whose only interest is the maximization of their clients' social adjustment and personal happiness. "I'd be as sensible as could be; before the marriage I would put the pros and cons before them. The final decision is not mine to make," explains a moderately observant young mother who is active in ORT. Whatever the actual dynamics of the Jewish family system, many parents are aware of and subject to the influence of the middle-class model of the proper parent–child relationship: the grown child is an autonomous individual who must be trusted to make his own decisions and his own mistakes.

In clarifying the alternatives for his child, the parent expects to lean heavily on the discord theme with which we are already familiar. But in the event that his clarification is not sufficiently persuasive, he is prepared to yield. Thus a businessman who is a member of the Einhorn Temple and the father of two young daughters says that he would try "to point out the pitfalls . . . and talk them out of it. But if they were dead set, I'd do all I could to help them." When clarifying alternatives, the typical Lakeville parent does not plan on stressing the problem of Jewish identity.

A professional man—otherwise a very devoted member of the board of the Lilienthal Temple—formulates his response in the following terms:

> I'd be mainly concerned about their happiness and compatibility rather than Jewishness. If you've done a good job in bringing up children, you must trust to their judgment. If you haven't, you can do nothing.

There are some respondents, however, whose attitude of reasonableness is not only for the purpose of retaining the affection of their child but also aimed at keeping him in the fold. Such respondents also hope that their friendly stance to the non-Jewish partner will be interpreted as an invitation to join the Jewish group. Sometimes this desire is conceived of in terms of exposing the Gentile spouse to Jews and their culture and thus gradually incorporating the individual into the ethnic community. In other cases, what the parent has in mind is a direct incorporation into the Jewish group through conversion. "I'd do everything in my power to welcome her into my group and smooth the way as much as possible," states a minimally observant, highly educated manufacturer of housewares whose nine-year-old son attends the religious school at Hirsch Temple. A young, moderately observant housewife with two pre-school boys, who is a fairly active member of the Wise Temple, would "certainly invite [the Gentile] to my home during the holidays. I'd try to educate her to Judaism." "I would try to influence the person to become a Jew," is the response of an engineer with a similar pattern of religious observance. And an active clubwoman—a second-generation mother whose pre-adolescent son attends the Wise Temple Sunday School—would accept her non-Jewish daughter-in-law in the hope that her grandchildren would be raised as Jews: "I would want her to become Jewish and bring up the kids as Jews."

One of the factors that prevent some parents from fulfilling traditional norms is their desire to be consistent with a liberal orientation to intergroup relations. Intermarriage is, after all, an aspect—and to some a crucial aspect—of intergroup relations. The high commitment of the Lakeville Jew to the improvement of such relations often makes it difficult for him to follow the model prescribed in Jewish tradition. "We've tried to teach non-prejudice and tolerance to the children, so we couldn't react too much," is the response of a highly educated woman who was reared by Orthodox East European immigrant parents; she sends her children to the school of the Schechter Synagogue, but is otherwise religiously inactive. A middle-aged third-generation professional man who belongs to the Hirsch Temple and is religiously observant by Lakeville standards is even more specific in declaring his commitment to intergroup understanding:

> I'd welcome my son's wife with open arms, whether white or black, Jew or Christian, Caucasian or Mongolian.

While this particular respondent may be as accepting as he claims, many of those who say that they are prepared to accept their child's intermarriage would do so without any feeling of enthusiasm. There is a sizable minority—36 per cent—who are frank to admit that their acceptance of an intermarriage in the family would be done with the greatest reluctance and, indeed, that the entire experience would be a traumatic one for them.[16] Such feelings are expressed more often by those who belong to less advanced generations, by those more highly committed to religious practices and institutions, and by those who are the least integration-minded. And while about nine in ten of those who would feel very unhappy if their child married a non-Jew make it clear that ultimately they would accept the marriage, more than half of such respondents indicate they would do so with reluctance and after a show of resistance. Progressively smaller proportions among those who would feel only somewhat or not at all unhappy would react in the same manner (see Table 9–6).

TABLE 9–6. PARENTAL ACTION IN CASE OF INTERMARRIAGE BY FEELING ABOUT INTERMARRIAGE

If child were to marry a non-Jew, per cent of parents would	Parents' Feeling if Child Married Non-Jew *		
	Very Unhappy	Somewhat Unhappy	Neither Happy nor Unhappy
Reject it	3	—	—
Accept it reluctantly	55	38	11
Accept it †	34	58	81
Action not specified	8	4	8
N	(116)	(170)	(93)

* "Happy" category omitted from table because of too few cases.
† Reluctance not indicated.

We do encounter instances of reluctant parents who are prepared to transform their attitude of resistance before marriage into wholehearted acceptance after marriage. An example is an affluent businessman of East European origin who is a member of the second generation and the father of an adolescent son and daughter. A highly active member of the Wise Temple, he would "be very disturbed at first—I'd try to talk him or her out of it—but I'd accept it completely and try to be as good a father-in-law as I could." In most such cases, however, resistance would be followed by less enthusiastic acquiescence. For example, a moderately observant second-generation mother of an eight-year-old daughter who attends the religious school of the Schechter Synagogue states, "I wouldn't like it and would do everything in my power to stop it, but I'd have to accept it."

It is clear that the reluctant parent is very unsure of his power. Clearly he is frustrated because he feels unable either to implement his values or to act normatively. The response of a third-generation woolen-goods salesman who often attends Sabbath services at the Schechter Synagogue with his wife, who is an active member of the Sisterhood, is instructive in this connection. Otherwise religiously unobservant, he says about the possibility of an intermarriage by his adolescent daughter, "I'd be madder than hops. I'd try every decent way of changing her mind, but I don't think I would succeed; there's nothing I could do." Many other such parents would be just as angry, but most would be fearful of displaying their anger. Their resigned acceptance of their child's intermarriage would be accompanied by a kind of silent suffering. A college-educated owner of a clothing store, a highly observant father of a son approaching his Bar Mitzvah at the Schechter Synagogue, says typically,

> I would make every effort to show him the error of his ways. Then I'd accept the situation, but I'd be brokenhearted.

"I'd accept it, but my heart would bleed," reports another observant businessman, a second-generation man of East European origin who is highly active in the same synagogue and the father of a preadolescent son.

In the case of some reluctant parents, their resigned acceptance and silent suffering are combined with a strong sense of guilt. A case in point is a young third-generation salesman who was raised in a highly traditional household but observes very few religious practices. The father of two small children, he states,

> I'd do everything in my power to make them see the light. Then if they did [marry non-Jews], I'd accept it. But I'd be disappointed; you'd almost blame yourself.

The poignancy of the situation of the reluctant parent is perhaps best illustrated by the reaction of a wealthy lawyer. The offspring of immigrants who arrived in the United States from Eastern Europe, he is the father of two young sons whom he is raising in what is an observant home by Lakeville standards. Highly successful in his profession and a prime example of the self-made man, he would be confronted—in the event of his child's intermarriage—with a case where his usual mastery of a situation might be of no avail:

> Initially I'd be very hurt. I'd do everything I could to discourage it before it happened. I'd convey to them the problem of whether their child would have a christening or a *Pidyon Haben*. But if it occurred, I'd have to make the best of a bad situation.

As he responded to our questions on intermarriage, his college-educated wife sat in tears at his side.

10

THE IMAGE OF THE GOOD
JEW IN LAKEVILLE

Much of our analysis thus far has been about behavior:
the kinds of synagogues the Lakeville Jew has established, what he does
in these institutions, what Jewish rituals he observes in his home, how
he acts in respect to Jewish voluntary associations, the type of social
relationships which he has with his fellow Jews. To conclude our study
of Jewish identity in Lakeville, we turn to a question which is entirely
attitudinal in nature: the conception of the "good Jew."

We assumed that our respondents had a conception of what qualities
were necessary for being a good Jew. The assumption seemed to us justified if only by virtue of the fact that exclamations may be heard in Lakeville such as: "X is not a very good Jew," "Y acts like a a good Jew
should act," "Z thinks he's a good Jew but as far as I'm concerned he's
not." Additionally, inasmuch as being Jewish in the modern world involves self-consciousness, we felt that whatever the *level* of Jewishness,
the *problem* of identity was central enough so that our respondents would
have a conception of the good Jew. In respect to the evaluation of their
answers, we assumed that there would be a strain toward self-legitima-

321

TABLE 10-1. THE IMAGE OF THE GOOD JEW

Item	Per Cent Who Believe That to Be a "Good Jew" the Item Is			
	Essential	Desirable	Makes No Difference	Essential Not to Do	N.A. D.K.
Accept his being a Jew and not try to hide it	85	13	2	—	—
Contribute to Jewish philanthropies	39	49	12	—	—
Support Israel	21	47	32	—	—
Support Zionism	7	23	59	9	2
Support all humanitarian causes	67	29	4	—	—
Belong to Jewish organizations	17	49	34	—	—
Belong to a synagogue or temple	31	44	25	1	—
Attend weekly services	4	46	49	—	—
Lead an ethical and moral life	93	6	1	—	—
Attend services on High Holidays	24	46	30	—	—
Observe the dietary laws	1	11	85	3	—
Be well versed in Jewish history and culture	17	73	10	—	—
Know the fundamentals of Judaism	48	48	4	—	—
Have mostly Jewish friends	1	10	81	8	—
Promote the use of Yiddish	1	6	69	24	—
Give Jewish candidates for political office preference	1	6	39	54	—
Gain respect of Christian neighbors	59	32	9	—	—
Promote civic betterment and improvement in the community	67	29	4	1	—
Work for equality for Negroes	44	39	16	1	—
Help the underprivileged improve their lot	58	37	5	—	—
Be a liberal on political and economic issues	31	32	35	2	—
Marry within the Jewish faith	23	51	26	—	—

tion: respondents would identify their own attitudes and behavior patterns as proper for a good Jew. But we assumed that there would be a tendency toward idealization as well: respondents would answer in terms of what the ideal Jew should be like as well as of the pattern of life which they—the real Jews—had adopted.

In order to study the image of the good Jew we provided our respondents with four alternatives:

In your opinion, for a Jew to be considered a good Jew, which of the following must he do? Which are desirable but not essential that he do? Which have no bearing on whether or not you consider him a good Jew? Which must he not do?

and asked them to respond to twenty-two items:

Accept his being a Jew and not try to hide it
Contribute to Jewish philanthropies
Support Israel
Support Zionism
Support all humanitarian causes
Belong to Jewish organizations
Belong to a synagogue or temple
Attend weekly services
Lead an ethical and moral life
Attend services on High Holidays
Observe the dietary laws
Be well versed in Jewish history and culture
Know the fundamentals of Judaism
Have mostly Jewish friends
Promote the use of Yiddish
Give Jewish candidates for political office preference
Gain respect of Christian neighbors
Promote civic betterment and improvement in the community
Work for equality for Negroes
Help the underprivileged improve their lot
Be a liberal on political and economic issues
Marry within the Jewish faith

Responses are presented in Table 10–1.

Turning first to an analysis of the "essential" category we find that the following items receive the highest ranking:

Lead an ethical and moral life	93%
Accept his being a Jew and not try to hide it	85%
Support all humanitarian causes	67%

Promote civic betterment and improvement in the community	67%
Gain respect of Christian neighbors	59%
Help the underprivileged improve their lot	58%
Know the fundamentals of Judaism	48%
Work for equality for Negroes	44%

This list of essential qualities for being considered a good Jew is indicative of how far conceptions in Lakeville deviate from past models of Jewish religious piety. The list also means that a Jewish nationalistic model is absent, as well as that a Jewish cultural model with roots in traditional Jewish life is missing.

At first glance the ideal of Jewishness predominating in Lakeville seems to be that of the practice of good citizenship and an upright life. To be a good Jew means to be an ethical individual; it also means to be kind, helpful, and interested in the welfare of neighbors, fellow Americans, and of humanity-at-large. But further examination leads to the conclusion that Lakeville's ideal of Jewishness is more than a sophisticated version of the Boy Scout who guides the frail old lady across a busy street. It is more than the practice of ethics. There is, for example, the aspect of Jewish self-acceptance: our respondents feel that in order to be a good Jew it is essential to freely and proudly acknowledge one's identity. Does this attitude, we wonder, result from the belief that Jewish existence is a great and wonderful mystery as well as a distinction and obligation which Gentiles are the poorer for not sharing? Or does it have its source in the belief that no honorable person would—either overtly or covertly—lay claim to being anything other than what he is? It is difficult to judge between these alternatives. All that we can say is that in other places and at other times in modern Jewish history it was not always so. Abraham Mendelssohn's letter *—characteristic of the mood of a segment of the Jews of his time—reminds us how much less of a premium can be placed on the affirmation of Jewish identity.

According to our respondents not only is it essential that the good Jew acknowledge his identity, but it is incumbent upon him to lead a life of moral excellence. Their conception appears to be that whatever else Judaism teaches, it teaches such excellence. The true test of being a good Jew is not loyalty to the old sacramentalism but the extent to which the individual actualizes moral ideals. We do not know whether our respondents consider Jewish ethical ideals as superior to those upheld by

* See pp. 292–293.

the religions which their neighbors practice, but it is apparent that they would reject the notion that such ideals are inferior.

Do our respondents, we wonder, locate the source of their belief in moral excellence in the ethic of Judaism, or do they draw upon the ethic common to all American faiths—an ethic which transcends specific religious traditions as it merges into the aspirations characteristic of secular American culture? Our conviction is that by-and-large Lakeville Jews locate the source of their ethic in Judaism, although if pressed they might say that other faiths now share the ethic which Judaism originally proclaimed. But it must also be stated that while the ethic identified by our respondents is certainly intrinsic to Judaism it appears that the motive power for their making such an identification comes from the general culture. Nevertheless, this is less significant than the fact that they identify the source of their ethic as a Jewish one. And we are again reminded that in other places and at other times in the modern history of the Jew it was not always so. Abraham Mendelssohn serves as an example that there have been Jews who felt that Judaism represents a necessary but outmoded stage in the evolution of man's religious thinking—their point of view was that Christianity is characterized by more lofty moral ideals than Judaism.

Some of our respondents introduce an important footnote to the conception of the ethical life as the keystone of being a good Jew: the attitude that the ethical life must not be limited to the personal. It must, rather, be social: the good Jew is a person who works to change the world as well as himself. Thus some feel that the Jew must work for equal rights for Negroes, a greater number believe in the essentiality of aiding the underprivileged, and even more believe that supporting humanitarian causes and working for the betterment of their community is required for being a good Jew.

Another significant theme is that gaining the respect of Gentiles is incumbent upon the good Jew. While it is to his self-interest to do so, more importantly he must make this effort on behalf of his fellow Jews. Gentiles will consider unacceptable behavior to be characteristic of the entire group. Thus the good Jew is under the obligation to conduct himself in an exemplary manner; each Jew represents the Jewish group and is obliged to act accordingly.

We are left with the item "Know the fundamentals of Judaism," which some 48 per cent of Lakeville respondents consider essential for being a good Jew. At first glance this would suggest the *mitzvah* of study, an exceedingly important emphasis in the Jewish sacred system. If accepted at face value this item might be considered as contradicting our earlier statements about the absence of traditionalism in Lakeville. We feel, however, that given the lack of importance accorded to other traditional patterns, agreement with this item does not necessarily mean attachment to the Jewish tradition of study as a form of worship. More likely what it suggests is that the intelligent and responsible individual has the obligation to know what he stands for; just as his identification as a citizen makes it obligatory to acquaint himself with American history and current affairs so identification as a Jew makes it obligatory to acquaint himself with the fundamentals of Judaism. In regard to the reflection of this attitude in the community it is apparent that while Jewish educational programs for adults in Lakeville are not so well attended as their sponsors desire, they are an accepted feature in all of the congregations. While the suprasocial impetus for attendance at such programs must not be denigrated, it appears that the image which the Lakeville Jew has of himself as an intelligent and responsible person is operating in respect to Jewish identity. Adult education flourishes in Lakeville; adult Jewish education is on the increase. Over all, the significant fact is that some apply the concept of intelligence and responsibility to their Jewish as well as to their general identity.

In summary, the essential qualifications for being a good Jew according to Lakeville residents are self-acceptance, moral excellence, good citizenship, and knowledge of Judaism. The acts which the good Jew is obliged to perform include advancing the general welfare, promoting social reform, and increasing intergroup amity.

Turning to the "desirable" category we find that the following items rank highest:

Be well versed in Jewish history and culture	73%
Marry within the Jewish faith	51%
Contribute to Jewish philanthropies	49%
Belong to Jewish organizations	49%
Know the fundamentals of Judaism	48%
Support Israel	47%
Attend weekly services	46%
Attend services on High Holidays	46%
Belong to a synagogue or temple	44%

In contrast to the essential category this list is more traditional: it includes items which relate to well-established religious, nationalistic, and cultural models. Thus, such items as attendance at services, support of Israel, and knowledge of Jewish history and culture are listed. A *mitzvah* such as contributing to Jewish philanthropies also occurs. In fact many of the items on the list constitute activities and attitudes ordinarily thought of as characteristic of "survivalist" Jews, such as belonging to a synagogue, joining a Jewish organization, and marrying within the Jewish group.

One of the items ("Know the fundamentals of Judaism") is found both on the desirable and on the essential list. But the significant point is that attitudes and actions directly connected with Jewish survival tend to be thought of more often as desirable rather than essential. It is of course true that if we combine desirable and essential ratings some of these items bulk large: "Contribute to Jewish philanthropies" then scores 88 per cent, "Belong to a synagogue or temple" 75 per cent, "Marry within the Jewish faith" 74 per cent, "Attend services on the High Holidays" 70 per cent, and "Support Israel" 68 per cent. While these are substantial percentages, they are generally exceeded by a wide margin when we reverse the procedure and add the desirable ratings to the items on the essential list: "Lead an ethical and moral life" then scores 99 per cent, "Accept his being a Jew and not try to hide it" 98 per cent, "Support all humanitarian causes" 96 per cent, "Know the fundamentals of Judaism" 96 per cent, "Promote civic betterment and improvement in the community" 96 per cent, "Help the underprivileged improve their lot" 95 per cent, and "Gain respect of Christian neighbors" 91 per cent. Only the item "Work for equality for Negroes" scores less than 90 per cent, inasmuch as some 16 per cent feel that such efforts make no difference in respect to being a good Jew. All of which is to say that in Lakeville there is greater unanimity in respect to what is essential rather than what is desirable, and if someone does not consider an item essential the chances are that he will consider it desirable. Items considered by some as desirable, on the other hand, will frequently be considered essential but some respondents may also consider them as making no difference in respect to being considered a good Jew.

Turning to the "makes no difference" category, we find that the item "Observe the dietary laws" scores highest. We are already well acquainted from Chapter 3 with the problem that observance of the dietary laws presents to the Jews of Lakeville. It is thus no surprise to find that some 85 per cent feel that such observance bears no relationship to being a good Jew; the group which believes that such observance is either essential or desirable constitutes a distinct minority. The next-highest item is "Have mostly Jewish friends," about which some 81 per cent feel indifferent. The third-ranking item is "Promote the use of Yiddish"; some 69 per cent feel that such promotion is irrelevant. This item is followed by "Support Zionism" with 59 per cent. The figure is in decided contrast to attitudes about supporting Israel, for most of our respondents believe that such support is either essential or desirable.

The great majority of our twenty-two items draw either an essential, desirable, or makes no difference response, and very few draw any substantial number of respondents who feel that to be considered a good Jew a given action must be proscribed. The exception is "Give Jewish candidates for political office preference." This idea is abhorrent to some 54 per cent of our respondents. Their answers could mean devotion to the concept of a political process free from the interest of pressure groups, a sophisticated political orientation where it is felt that Jewish interests can be as easily safeguarded by liberal Gentiles as by Jews, or a defensive reaction based on the fear that Jews will be charged with being more devoted to the advancement of their group than to the common good.

The next-highest item on the proscribed list—chosen by 24 per cent— is "Promote the use of Yiddish." The fact that a fair-sized minority react with vehemence to the idea of promoting Yiddish is significant. It suggests that some Lakeville Jews are highly insecure about Jewish status and acceptance. An interpretation of insecurity is strengthened by the fact that American Jews have the unquestioned right to promote the use of Yiddish, as well as the fact that the item gives no intimation that such promotion would be done through dubious or possible illegal means, or would involve the use of public funds or facilities.* Apparently the idea of promoting Yiddish conjures up an image of a Jewish community less acculturated and accepted than today's community. It may even suggest to some that present-day acceptance could be imperiled. The response to the item on the Yiddish language is especially significant inasmuch as there has never been a problem in the community over this issue, and very few residents belong to organizations which support the dissemination of the language. Furthermore no organizations exist which are explicitly anti-Yiddish. The response is doubly significant because attitudes in this area are uncontaminated by the operation of processes which ordinarily shape public opinion. This is very much in contrast with

---

* We have already noted that with the exception of the Schechter Synagogue religious institutions in Lakeville have avoided the question of the acceptability of using public facilities for the promotion of sectarian purposes.

Zionism—the Zionist question has been on the agenda of the Jewish community for many decades; pro-Zionist, non-Zionist, and anti-Zionist organizations vie for public support. In spite of efforts to shape Lakeville opinion in an anti-Zionist direction only 9 per cent feel that it is impossible for a good Jew to support Zionism.

How should our findings on the image of the good Jew be evaluated? Some would say that they indicate the hypocrisy of the Lakeville Jew. They would focus on such items as "Work for equality for Negroes" and point out that whereas a total of 83 per cent feel such work to be essential or desirable very few lend active support to organizations whose purpose is the advancement of civil rights. Furthermore, there has been no attempt to assist Negroes in purchasing homes in the community. Hypocrisy is not, however, the significant perspective for evaluating the gap between the image which our respondents have of the good Jew and the patterns which they follow in daily life. To stress hypocrisy is to be diverted from the most crucial aspect of these responses: the desire to retain Jewish identity and the simultaneous difficulty which the Lakeville Jew experiences in affirming actions which would help guarantee—or make more meaningful—that survival. Furthermore, it becomes clear that the actions and *mitzvot* which the Lakeville Jew affirms as most essential to being considered a good Jew are actions and *mitzvot* between man and man and that *mitzvot* between man and God assume a distinctly secondary place. Finally, the actions and *mitzvot* which the Lakeville Jew esteems most highly are found in the general culture. In sum, while the Lakeville Jew may be following certain Jewish sources when he formulates his ideals, the lack of distinctiveness inherent in his model of the good Jew is capable of eroding away group boundaries.

At the present moment the Lakeville Jew remains considerably more Jewish in action than in thought. Philanthropy is a good example of this dichotomy. Some 39 per cent consider that contributing to Jewish philanthropies is essential while 67 per cent believe that supporting all humanitarian causes is essential. To be sure almost all Lakeville Jews contribute to both Jewish and non-Jewish philanthropies, but the fact of the matter is that only 19 per cent give the bulk of their money to non-Jewish charities. While Jewish campaigns are better organized and set higher sights for givers, the philanthropic behavior of Lakeville Jews is not a result of greater efficiency of the Jewish fund-raising machinery. Rather it results from the Jews' feeling of identity. Leaving aside the fact that fund-raising techniques in the general community are becoming more sophisticated, the question which occurs is how long the present gap between action and thought in the area of philanthropic giving will survive. Will not a sectarianism which is unsupported ideologically wither away when social conditions change? Will future generations be prepared to live with the dichotomy which the Lakeville Jew abides: a universal humanitarianism as the prime value in combination with the practice of giving priority to Jewish causes? Will not future generations attempt to reassess Jewish anguish against the anguish of others, the importance of supporting Jewish institutions against the significance of other institutions? May they not conclude that their humanitarian aspirations dictate that they place the accent on the general rather than the Jewish?

If all of these questions come to mind with respect to philanthropy many more occur with respect to the item on having Jewish friends. One of the most significant responses in Table 10–1 is the 81 per cent who say that having mostly Jewish friends makes no difference to being a good Jew, while only 10 per cent consider it desirable to have mostly Jewish friends and a mere 1 per cent feel that it is essential. In actuality some 91 per cent of our respondents have an all-Jewish or predominantly Jewish friendship circle, and this pattern is crucial in explaining the cohesion of the Jewish community of Lakeville. Such cohesion, we realize, is supported by its members' social relationships rather than by their attachment to traditional religious, nationalistic, or cultural models. We reason, therefore, that until there is an increase in loyalty to more "positive" aspects of Jewishness, the cultivation and reinforcement of such Jewish social relationships will continue to be required in order to maintain group survival. The threat to such survival is that the Lakeville Jew lacks ideological commitment to his present pattern of friendship ties; he tends also to feel that a mixed neighborhood is desirable, that he should cultivate the friendship and esteem of Christian neighbors, and that he should not be parochial in his social attachments.

The pressure to change social relationships will not be overwhelming in the present generation of Lakeville adults, however. Relevant factors include the following: such relationships are already well structured, the rate of Jews leaving for less dense Jewish areas is small, and Lakeville itself gives every promise of becoming more—not less—Jewish in composition. But the pressure to change should increase in the next generation. The pressure could in fact become overwhelming as highly acculturated Lakeville youngsters—raised in a culture of equalitarianism and taught in a primary and secondary school system which reinforces equalitarian values—venture into colleges and university settings where today a kind of ethnic liberalism predominates. Particularly if they later practice their occupations in mixed settings those individuals who are products of the Lakeville environment should experience some difficulty in achieving strong Jewish identification. Will their socialization to traditional models and their attachment to Jewish identity—we wonder —be strong enough to assist them in building a viable life pattern which will combine both their Jewish and general identity and thus help to overcome the threat of assimilation?

In spite of the best of intentions, it is our conviction that only a minority of Lakeville parents have been able to provide their children with substantial materials for developing such a pattern. Of course each generation must achieve identity anew. Nevertheless each new generation is in part the product of its inheritance. The meager Jewishness to which the Lakeville youngster falls heir is perhaps the true *bête noire* of Jewish life in Lakeville. Lakeville makes available the abundant life; as we stressed at the beginning of our book, in many respects it is a model community which fulfills the American dream. But, at the same time it does not provide very rich Jewish experiences for the majority of those who are socialized in its fine homes, winding streets, excellent schools, pleasant beaches, tennis courts, and—let it be said—in its religious schools. Thus many of those who are the product of the Lakeville environment will be faced with the obverse of that which confronted their grandfathers, great-grandfathers, or even more remote ancestors when they arrived on American shores. While the resources of such ancestors— in terms of money, general education, and knowledge of the American way of life—were paltry, their Jewish resources—if not always considerable—were at least sufficient unto the day. Over the generations the families of present-day Lakeville Jews have increased their financial resources, their general level of education, and their mastery of the environment many times over. While some have multiplied their Jewish resources, many have dissipated them to a lesser or greater degree. It is indisputable that the majority of Lakeville Jews would like to conserve their Jewish resources. But unless an aggressive policy of growth is pursued the Jewish resources of a previous generation inevitably decline. The press of the general environment is so compelling that instead of being conserved the inheritance from earlier generations inevitably diminishes. In sum, the long-range viability of the pattern of Jewish adjustment characteristic of Lakeville is in question.

A prayer in the Rosh Hashanah liturgy speaks of the fact that some will die during the months ahead while others will live to greet another year, that some will prosper while others will not, that some will rise while others will be brought low. The Jew is counseled to repentance, prayer, and charity in order to avert the evil decree. If assimilation is an evil decree—as we think it is—the Jews of Lakeville have many favors to be thankful for: pluralistic America not only is permissive in respect to group survival but it also assists such survival in manifold ways. Yet in important ways it also threatens survival—in ways of which Isaac Mayer Wise did not dream and in modes more subtle than Solomon Schechter imagined.

At the beginning of this volume we quoted the opinion rendered by the rabbi of Slutsk in 1900. Now that we have concluded our analysis we realize how long is the road from Slutsk to Lakeville. And to understand how close we are to the year 2000 we need only realize that the individuals who will determine the character of group life in the twenty-first century have already been born, and that their socialization is already well under way. The burden of proof is on the Jews of Lakeville and on their counterparts in thousands of other American communities, for it is they who will determine whether the prediction which Jacob David Wilowsky made in the year 1900 will eventually come to pass.

11

LAKEVILLE:
A CHANGING SUBURB

Over the past two decades, Lakeville has retained and perhaps even enhanced its desirability as a residential community. The community has withstood the aging process. Lakeville stands in sharp contrast to Lake City, where in spite of urban renewal only a handful of neighborhoods have improved their ambience or even held their own. To be sure, Lakeville is more crowded than before; the open spaces of yesterday have been built up, and houses have been erected in places—adjacent to the sewage plant, for example—that were formerly deemed unacceptable. But such construction indicates how desirable a community Lakeville has become. Old settlers feel the lack of open space and complain that the quality of life is not what it was. But objective indicators show that Lakeville is at least as attractive a place to live as it was before.

Part of the attractiveness of Lakeville still resides in a public-school system which has always had the reputation of being among the best in the metropolitan area. Its public schools are still considered first-class. The busing controversy which traumatized many communities left Lakeville untouched.

Lakeville's recreational facilities, always considered excellent, have been expanded and are still meticulously maintained. Its many golf courses, both public and private, are among the best in the metropolitan area. Its beaches are restricted to town residents and are therefore relatively uncrowded. Other facilities include parks, baseball diamonds, outdoor swimming pools, boating facilities, a golf-driving range, tennis courts, playgrounds, and picnic areas. The conveniently located Lakeville Recreation Center includes everything from a gymnasium to a lapidary room. Several years ago six indoor tennis courts and four indoor racquetball courts were constructed. The newest facility is a year-round indoor ice skating rink. The program includes general skating, instructional lessons, and hockey. The rink also is available for rental for parties and special events.

Lakeville's unmatched recreational opportunities are complemented by a downtown business district which has remained viable. In other communities, business districts have decayed because of the pull of new shopping centers. Elaborate shopping centers are within easy driving distance of Lakeville, and a huge new shopping center was built on its outskirts. However, all of this did not sap the vitality of the community's old downtown area, which still attracts customers and presents a good appearance. The fact that Lakeville went "wet" several years ago has attracted a number of gourmet restaurants to the downtown area. In fact, one of these, Lake City's prime gathering place for the "beautiful people," is opening a branch in Lakeville's downtown area.

An important element in the preservation of the downtown area has been the emergence of Lakeville as a medical center. The key element was the expansion of the Lakeville Community Hospital. The hospital serves not only Lakeville but adjacent suburban communities as well. Once a small facility with limited capabilities, the present comprehensiveness of its services is suggested by the size of its attending staff, which includes approximately two hundred physicians and twenty oral surgeons. Its mobile intensive-care system is among the most advanced in the state. The Lakeville Hospital is equipped to handle every medical problem except open heart surgery or organ transplants. Prosperous local residents who formerly favored elite hospitals in Lake City now frequently use this local facility.

Most of the hospital's attending physicians and oral surgeons maintain offices in adjacent medical buildings. Furthermore, it is not unusual for medical doctors who reside in the community—whether they are general practitioners or specialists—to have offices in one of the medical buildings which now dot the community, thus saving themselves the time, expense, and trouble involved in travel to Lake City. Lakeville is also noted for its psychiatric services; in recent years, increasing numbers of psychiatrists residing in Lakeville or in the Heights have opened offices in Lakeville. Medicine has provided Lakeville with a growth industry which generates considerable income without creating problems such as pollution and encroachment on stable residential areas.

In addition to offering first-class recreational and medical facilities, Lakeville has expanded the cultural opportunities evident when the community was originally studied. Its center for the performing arts, noted for its first-rate musical and theatrical programs during the summer season, has retained its position as a national cultural resource. According to some professional music critics, the orchestra which makes its summer home at the festival is now the nation's most eminent symphonic ensemble.

The center for the performing arts has become much more variegated than before and has a longer season. In addition to the symphonic and chamber music programs for which it was widely known, the center now features jazz, blues, rock, and folk music concerts. Major dance companies are also featured. The center now runs art exhibits, thus including the visual as well as the performing arts. Lakeville's public library is also exceptional in the range of its holdings. The community's adult education program is still noted for the variety and quality of its courses. A new fine arts center has studio facilities for painting, sculpture, ceramics, and graphics, and the shows at its gallery are covered by the art critics of Lake City newspapers.

The class level in Lakeville has if anything been rising. In contrast to other communities, Lakeville has no problem in attracting or keeping upper-middle-class and upper-class residents. In fact, its problem is quite the opposite—that of affording living facilities for the working class and the lower-middle class, including those who help to operate its public services and medical facilities. The problem became so bothersome that the Lakeville Chamber of Commerce made a study and found that a majority of public employees, including teachers, post-office workers, policemen, and firemen, lived outside the community, largely because they could not afford to purchase a home or condominium in Lakeville. The Chamber also found that the number of homes or apartments available for rental was miniscule and that they were, in any case, beyond the means of public employees. The scarcity of housing has been such that although the law requires that policemen and firemen live within a prescribed distance of Lakeville, the regulation is not enforced. Lakeville is rising to the challenge, however, and is building public housing to accommodate low-income people, including workers at the hospital. It is also building some housing for senior citizens.

In sum, Lakeville's superiority as a residential community has been enhanced and stands in sharp contrast to the deterioration which is evident in many of the nation's older suburbs. Property values have risen sharply in the last few years. Lakeville has retained its desirability to such an extent that when we asked a Hebrew teacher employed by a local synagogue what Lakeville's leading community problem was, he replied: "Lakeville's worst problem is that it suffers from a superiority complex."

The Emergence of Lakeville as a Jewish Suburb

While Lakeville has done a first-class job of resisting deterioration, it is nevertheless a far different community today from what it was in the 1950's. The difference resides in the fact that Lakeville is no longer a community dominated by WASP's. In our original study, the Jews were in a minority. By the 1970's, they had become a majority.* This is remarkable considering that the Jewish population of the Lake City metropolitan area has declined noticeably in recent decades. Despite this decline, the attraction of Lakeville for middle- and upper-class Jews has been so strong that the area has grown in Jewish population. While some of the more elderly Jews have moved to the Sun Belt or to apartments outside of Lakeville, in the majority of cases their homes have been purchased by young Jews eager to reside in Lakeville and willing to pay a premium price for the opportunity.

The Jewish growth has also been made possible by the fact that White Christians have avoided moving into Lakeville. The exact date when the

* In 1975 the Jewish Federation of Lake City estimated the Jewish population as 17,000 out of a total population of 33,000. As we will see, Lakeville's mayor had a considerably higher estimate. The trend evident in 1975 has continued down to the present. It will be recalled that in 1957 there were approximately 8,000 Jews in Lakeville out of a total population of 25,000 (see p. 9).

"tipping point" was reached—that is, when the community became fixed in the public mind as a "Jewish" suburb,when Gentiles began to move away and new Gentile families moving in became fewer—is a project for historians. For our purpose it is enough to note that for some time now, when a Gentile family places their home on the market (assuming that it is located in a desirable residential area), in the majority of cases the home finds a Jewish buyer. Jewish-owned homes placed on the market have generally been purchased by Jewish buyers.

It is noteworthy that the change in the ethnic and religious composition of Lakeville has been a very gradual process. There has not been any panic selling on the part of Gentiles. If anything, Gentiles who have wished to move have been in no hurry to dispose of their property. They have been willing to remain until they could find a buyer willing to meet their price. Indeed, since the community has maintained its excellent facilities and its unique advantages and has even upgraded itself, there has been nothing to motivate panic selling on the part of Gentiles. While crime has increased, it has generally been in the category of home burglary and thus characteristic of many residential communities. In the case of Lakeville, the rise in home burglaries is a tribute to the wealth of its residents and to the standard of living which they enjoy. Street crime has never been a major problem.

In sum, Lakeville has had none of the conditions which would encourage rapid flight of Gentile residents. Nevertheless, at some time a tipping point was reached and Lakeville emerged as a "Jewish" rather than a "Gentile" suburb. Lakeville was in fact identified as a Jewish suburb well before the majority of the population was Jewish. Reaching the tipping point involved two processes: Gentiles avoiding moving into Lakeville and Gentile residents leaving in small but steady numbers.

Movement of Gentiles out of the community appears to have been motivated by the Jewish influx. By the mid-1960's, Lakeville had very few choice building sites available. When new homes were built, they were generally occupied by Jews. Furthermore, the removal of Gentile families occupying older homes was not balanced by an influx of Gentile families moving into Gentile-owned homes.

In the mid-1970's Joseph Manillo, an Italian Catholic who at the time was Lakeville's mayor and leading political figure, told us that he would be the last non-Jewish mayor of Lakeville. He viewed the situation as follows:

I would guess, being very conservative, that the figure today is somewhere between 70 and 75 percent Jewish. And I can't find any other figure. I cannot make it come out any other way. I can't find the other [Gentile] people. I would like to. But I have to say that, of the 33,000, we probably have somewhere in the vicinity of 23,000 people of Jewish descent.

Manillo was acutely aware of the Jewish influx. Each week he received the report of the Welcome Wagon organization which profiled the new residents. Among the items in the profile was religion:

Sometimes a person will say "no religion" or "none." But we know which direction they [the newcomers] are going in, and it's very heavily Jewish. Some weeks it could be 8 to 1, 7 to 2, or 6 to 2; 5 to 3 would be a good week.

Manillo's regret about the new Jewish dominance of Lakeville was just that—regret. He was no lover of WASP's. As a Catholic of working-class origin who was born in Lakeville and grew up there, he found that he was accepted more by Jews than by WASP's. Furthermore, he realized that he could never have achieved his post if the community had remained under WASP domination. Nevertheless, Manillo felt that there were no substantial intergroup relations problems in the community:

I don't think there's any anti-Semitism in the community because of its [Jewish influx]. There may be a slur against anybody. I get it myself. . . . I just think there's a resignation—that this is the way it is in Lakeville, and if you like it, fine, and if you don't, you don't have to stay.

And indeed, true to the Lakeville spirit of preserving community harmony, Gentile neighbors who left Lakeville had a ready battery of rational and inoffensive reasons to explain their removal: they wished to own a smaller house now that their children were grown, they preferred a community with more open space than was available in Lakeville, or they preferred an apartment or condominium where they would be freed from the burdensome responsibilities of home-maintenance. Nevertheless, it was noticeable that when two huge luxury high-rise apartment buildings were constructed on a choice lakefront location close to Lakeville, the majority of the apartments found Jewish rather than Gentile buyers. Gentile buyers tended to purchase in Gentile areas located some distance from Lakeville. This generally meant sacrificing the advantage of a location near the lakefront. Gentiles were willing to forgo the advantage.

Turning to Jewish attitudes and behavior, we should note that there was no organized attempt to make Lakeville a Jewish suburb. In traditional Jewish society the emergence of a Jewish area would be welcome. Not only would Jewish dominance insure greater safety of life and limb, but it would have the advantage of minimizing interaction with the out-group. However, Lakeville's Jews do not follow the pattern of attitudes found in traditional Jewish society. In fact, a significant segment favored the *status quo*—in effect a Gentile-dominated community. However, they could not bring themselves to take action which would insure continued Gentile dominance. Such action would have necessarily involved some form of exclusion of Jews, or at the very least the placing of the issue on the community's agenda. Both approaches were highly distasteful to established Jewish residents and were studiously avoided.

The continued influx of Jews is traceable to the fact that the elite of the Jewish community in the metropolitan area is not a miniscule proportion of the total Jewish population but rather is much larger than would be true for many other groups. As a result of the size of this elite, Lakeville had not exhausted its potential by the late 1950's.

Lakeville's emergence as a community where Jews constitute a majority rests upon a further fact: the willingness of some Jews to settle in a community where they are in the majority, or close to becoming one. There is little question that Jewish oldtimers in Lakeville preferred a community where Jews were a minority. But being such a large group, the Jewish elite has several strands of opinion, including one which has no objection to living in a community dominated by Jews. Thus, the fact that Lakeville is, in composition if not in ambience, increasingly like the older Jewish neighborhoods of Lake City as well as like several of the newer suburban areas did not deter some Jews. On the contrary, it increased their interest in moving to the community.

As Manillo put it, those who are unhappy with the changing composition of the community need not stay. Manillo told us that this applied to Jews as well as Gentiles—that over the years he had received calls from Jews as well as from Gentiles about the Jewish influx. He said that one of the Jews who had called him complained that "he was in a worse ghetto now than he had been when he lived in Lake City."

Those Jews who favored stabilizing the community and keeping Gentiles in the majority sought to have the office of mayor of Lakeville occupied by a Gentile. The tradition of retaining a Gentile mayor was supplemented by a further step—that of encouraging Gentiles to take leadership roles in community affairs. The hope was that the occupancy of leadership roles by Gentiles would alleviate Gentile anxieties and prevent the establishment of the image of Lakeville as a Jewish suburb.

There was one area of civic life, however, where Jews did not maintain a low profile. This· was the school board, or, more properly, the boards of the various school districts which include the schools of Lakeville and of some of the adjoining communities. The factors which made it difficult for Jews to restrain themselves from running for positions on the school boards include the following: their children constituted a substantial segment of the public-school population; they valued education; they had an affinity for public rather than private education; the Jewish level of education was higher than that of Gentiles; and of college- and university-educated residents, a higher proportion of Jews had attended first-quality institutions. Finally, Jewish familiarity with public education, both as professionals and volunteers, exceeded that of Gentiles. In sum, while care was taken to give Gentiles as much representation as possible on Lakeville's recreational commission, civic beautification commission, zoning commission, and similar bodies, the Jews did not cultivate the lowest possible profile in school affairs.

Control of local school boards had a special complication. As the proportion of middle- and upper-class WASP's was diminished by death and removals, and as this segment of the population aged, Lakeville became a community where the two leading components of the student body were Jews and Italians—or, more specifically, middle- and upper-class Jews and working-class and lower-middle-class Italians. An Italian area immediately outside of Lakeville was included in a local school district. The area, which had predated the Jewish influx, was founded by gardeners and construction workers who had helped to build and maintain the homes and gardens of the Gentile upper class. Although Italians slowly moved up the class ladder, the section remained Italian. Italian parents encouraged their children to remain in the area. Thus, the Italian section was a long-established area with firmly-rooted traditions.

While the Italian presence did not disturb elementary schools—each one of which tended to be responsive to local attitudes in respect to curriculum, ambience, and patterns of discipline—the situation was more complicated at the high school with its mixed student body. During the late 1950's and the '60's, much effort was invested in avoiding a confrontation between Italian and Jewish students at the high school as well as a showdown between their parents. Jews were interested in a high school which would produce students who could hold their own in competition with the products of the nation's best secondary schools—students who could score well on the SAT's and thus qualify for admittance to first-class private universities. Italians had no such ambitions, and they saw the high school as insensitive to the needs of the non-college bound or those who were going on to institutions of higher learning which were oriented vocationally rather than to the liberal arts. Jewish parents were also interested in curriculum innovation, whether in science, mathematics, social studies, or English. Italian parents were not similarly interested; they felt that the old methods were still acceptable.

The visibility of Jews in school affairs was more salutary than was realized, however. Dialogue was encouraged between and among students, parents, teachers, and administrators. While community rifts were not entirely bridged, they were placed under scrutiny, and human-relations programs were initiated to build contacts between diverse constituencies.

By the late 1970's, not only did Lakeville have a Jewish mayor but the low-profile pattern which Jews had established decades earlier had eroded away. While upper-class Protestants still lived in the community, they refused to take part in public affairs. As a long-time resident of German-Jewish background who has been active in civic affairs for several decades explained:

> The more involved Jews get, the more the Gentiles retire to their homes and just literally give up, except for a few that we call "show Catholics" and "show Protestants." There are maybe twenty of them, and they will get appointed to every single city-wide thing that goes on, because they'll do it—and they're very capable people. But the others won't even make an effort to come forth.

To all appearances, Lakeville is still the community which it was a few decades ago. During the Christmas season the stores and shopping areas are decorated in the fashion of the old Lakeville. Despite Jewish representation, the Chamber of Commerce still observes a venerable Lakeville tradition: the erection of Santa Claus House. But Gentiles both in Lakeville and in the Lake City metropolitan area know that Lakeville has changed; they identify the community as "Jewish" and thus as far different from the Lakeville of yesterday.

The Establishment of a Jewish Day School

Of all the new developments in the Jewish community, one stands out as pre-eminent: the establishment of a Jewish day school, the Solomon Schechter School of the Heights. A sizeable segment of the student body of the Schechter school comes from Lakeville. Many of the school's leading financial supporters also reside in Lakeville.

FACTORS LEADING TO THE ESTABLISHMENT OF THE SCHOOL

A proliferation of Jewish day schools took place in the United States in the 1940's and '50's. The movement was spearheaded by Orthodox Jews who felt that even the best supplementary school could not give their children the type of Jewish education they desired. Furthermore, they felt that attendance at even the most benign and sympathetic public school would have the effect of indoctrinating their children with non-Jewish culture, and thus undercut Jewish commitment. The only way to handle the problem of teaching general studies (i.e., non-Jewish culture), it was thought, would be to have them taught in the setting of a school which had a strong commitment to Jewish culture.

Lakeville appeared immune to the establishment of a Jewish day school. It had very few Orthodox Jews, and the effort made in the 1940's to establish an Orthodox synagogue had been a fiasco (see pp. 167–171). Jews in Lakeville did not feel that the public school stood for a value system different from the one they espoused, or fear that the value system of the public school would undercut their children's Jewish education. They were in fact proud of Lakeville's public-school system, with its reputation for educational leadership, and gratified that it had not been affected by the dilution of standards and the educational chaos which touched central-city schools during this period, and even some suburban school systems as well. Thus, it appeared that Lakeville would continue to rely upon supplementary schools as the basis for its system of Jewish education.

Lakeville, however, was not an island. The movements taking place in the nation-at-large inevitably had repercussions there. The growth of Orthodox day schools succeeded in placing the question of Jewish education high on the agenda of the Jewish community, necessitating a response by the Conservative movement. Conservative Judaism experienced contradictory pulls, however. On the one hand, there was no denying the superior knowledge of Jewish culture and of the Hebrew language achieved by day-school students. Thus, it became commonplace for Conservative rabbis and Jewish educators to enroll their children in day schools. On the other hand, it was felt that the public-school system was the keystone of American democracy and that it should be strengthened rather than further weakened.

The issue was resolved by the formula that the Conservative movement would continue to rely upon the supplementary system as its basic educational instrument. However, it would establish a network of Conservative day schools in the larger cities. Thus, for those Conservative parents who favored day-school education, there would be an alternative to Orthodox day schools. The theory was that while the supplementary school would educate the children of the Conservative masses, the Conservative day schools (named the Solomon Schechter schools) would educate future leaders, both lay and rabbinic, for the Conservative movement. No longer would Conservatism have to look to Orthodoxy for its rabbis; no longer would its laity be Jewishly illiterate—a leadership composed at best of individuals whose secular knowledge far exceeded their Jewish knowledge.

It was felt that the Schechter schools could in fact do what Orthodox schools could not do: integrate rather than compartmentalize the general curriculum and the Jewish curriculum. A frequently adduced example was the teaching of science and the understanding of the Book of Genesis; the Conservative schools would teach about fossils and at the same time present the Biblical story of creation in such a way that it would not contradict the findings of paleontology. The hope was that science would help to throw light on Judaism, and that Judaism, in turn, would help to humanize science.

The establishment of a day school on the Heights could not have taken place without these stirrings in the Conservative movement. Nevertheless, the pull of the public system of education was stronger in Lakeville than in most other communities. The factor which tipped the balance was dissatisfaction with the supplementary Jewish schools in Lakeville, especially the Hebrew school of the Schechter Synagogue.

The Schechter Synagogue had attempted to establish a first-class Hebrew school. Whether the problem was the principal, the faculty, the student body, or the suburban environment itself, the general consensus was that the school was less than first-rate. While many parents were not disturbed over the limited achievements of their children or worried by the lack of enthusiasm for attending Hebrew school, there was a minority who were ready to experiment with an alternative form of Jewish education—even one which would mean secession from the public-education system.

THE ESTABLISHMENT AND GROWTH OF THE SCHOOL

The Solomon Schechter School of the Heights was established in the early 1960's. It opened on a very small scale: the school consisted of a kindergarten and a first grade with a total of 21 children, quite a number of whom were the offspring of rabbis and Jewish educators. Classes were held in the building of one of the congregations in the area. Apparently, there was a market for a Conservative day school. Enrollment grew at a steady pace; the school was able to open at least one new grade each year. In a relatively short time, it had classes through the eighth grade.

The greatest problem proved to be that of finances, although the ideological issue of sectarianism and secession from public education was by no means absent. It was felt that should the school set its tuition at a figure which would fully reflect costs, the effect would be to discourage parents from enrolling their children.* Because most families had more than one child, parents would have to consider what the costs would be of sending a second or third child to the school before enrolling their first, especially since public education was an option.

Given its tuition policy and its small size, by the second year the Schechter school was running at a deficit. Furthermore, as the school grew the deficit increased; the opening of each additional grade and class added significantly to it. While the parents and friends of the school initiated a variety of annual fund-raising events, these events—even when they were very successful—were more helpful in supplying money for scholarships than in balancing the budget (the policy of the school was that enrollment *not* be restricted to those able to pay full tuition). It proved impossible to liquidate the school's debts; the best that could be done was to pay the interest on them.

---

* In addition to instructional costs, there was the burden of transportation costs. Relatively few students lived within walking distance of the school.

The logical place to look for support was the Bureau of Jewish Education of Lake City, which in turn was financed by the Jewish Federation of Lake City. Because the Federation subvented Orthodox day schools, the assumption was that similar funding would be provided for the Schechter school. However, the effort to gain Federation support involved a protracted struggle which embittered Schechter school supporters. The feeling was that the Federation favored the Orthodox schools, which had long cultivated strategic members of the Federation's board. Furthermore, the Federation seemed to engage in deliberate harassment when it asked the Schechter school for highly-detailed financial reports—reports which would necessitate hiring an accounting firm at a cost of many thousands of dollars. And even when professional help was obtained, the reports were criticized, since the school's bookkeeping during its earliest years left much to be desired—the emphasis was on growth and educational innovation rather than on record-keeping.

There are a variety of explanations for the miniscule appropriations which were forthcoming from the Federation. Many influential Federation board members were antagonistic to Jewish days schools but, as Schechter supporters noted, such individuals went along with appropriations for Orthodox day schools. The explanation for their behavior may be that, while they were willing to accept day-school education for Orthodox Jews, whom they saw as "unenlightened," they could not accept such education as appropriate for non-Orthodox Jews. A further factor may be that they viewed Jews who lived on the Heights as prosperous enough to afford day-school education; they could not accept that residents of the Heights—as distinct from those living in less-prestigious areas—had the right to community assistance for what many Federation board members viewed as a matter of personal choice rather than of social necessity.

The Schechter school's financial situation was so difficult that meeting each payroll became a crisis. The school was forced to resort to desperate measures to remain open, one of which was to utilize money deducted for Federal income tax. In due course, the Internal Revenue Service warned the school about the illegality of this practice, whereupon the Federation, fearful of a scandal, provided a loan to pay the amount.

In the struggle to get the Federation to provide a substantial subvention, the Schechter school threatened to have the students picket its headquarters—an event to which they said the media would be invited. After many threats, the submission of innumerable reports, and a host of stormy meetings, the Federation gave way and over a period of years increased the Schechter subvention to a level comparable to those given to Orthodox institutions. However, since the Schechter school had a smaller ratio of students per teacher, even with the increased subvention it did not always succeed in achieving a balanced budget.

Nevertheless, several events occurred which worked to the benefit of the school. The first was a gift which permitted the school to erect its own building. It no longer had to rely on renting synagogue facilities ill-suited to a full-time school. Construction of its own building gave the Schechter school an identity and a prominence which could not be achieved in rented quarters.

Of the rabbis in the area, Rabbi David Ginzberg of the Solomon Schechter Synagogue was the most firmly committed to the school; from the beginning he was instrumental in raising funds. It was Rabbi Ginzberg who succeeded in locating a potential donor for the school building. A close friend of the prospective donor, who was an ardent supporter of the school, then proceeded to have an architect prepare a rendering of the proposed building. The rendering, with the donor's name inscribed on it alongside his photograph, was unveiled for him in his wife's presence; he agreed to the sum requested. It was then easy enough to get a mortgage for the additional sum required to cover the full cost of the structure (built to accommodate 250 students) and its furnishings.

Somewhat surprisingly, the Yom Kippur War also worked to the advantage of the school. The causal connection between the War and the school is not clear to school officials, but after 1973 they noticed a rise in enrollment, a greater receptivity among long-standing friends of the school, and a manifestation of interest in the school in circles which had previously been indifferent. According to the president of the school:

> I think within the community there was a whole change in attitude to the school. The Yom Kippur War really awakened the feelings of a lot of people, and suddenly they began to be much more Jewishly conscious.

The school has also been helped by the religious policies it has adopted. Characteristically, the standards of religious observance at a Solomon Schechter school are much higher than those observed in the great majority of Conservative homes. But the Solomon Schechter School of the Heights, with children from Reform homes and from homes with no religious orientation, as well as from Conservative homes, has cultivated tolerance toward religious deviation. According to the school board's statement on "Religious Practices":

The school . . . shall constantly emphasize that the *mitzvot ma'asiyot*, the norms of traditional observances, are a necessary part of the fullest expression of Jewish life. An attitude of respect toward other, differing, approaches to religious observances shall be maintained, along with a sympathetic understanding of the varying home backgrounds that are represented by the student body.

Thus, the school has insisted that food brought into the building be kosher, but it has also sought to reduce guilt on the part of parents who do not observe the *mitzvot ma'asiyot* in the home. It has tried to minimize conflict between unobservant parents and children exposed at the school to the ideal norms of Conservative Judaism. The school board's official statement on this matter is as follows:

In teaching the concepts of Torah as they relate to the observance of Jewish living, the use of the term *averah* [sin] shall be limited to the breach of moral and ethical *mitzvot*. Ceremonial and ritual *mitzvot* shall generally be taught as expressions of piety, identity, and as the encompassing aspects of a more full Jewish expression.

The school also adopted a policy toward the religious participation of females that was well in advance of the consensus among Conservative Jews in the nation-at-large. This policy was very well received, however, and helped to give the institution a reputation for being progressive and pioneering. According to Morris Schwartz, the principal of the school:

We were the first Solomon Schechter school in the country that began to recognize that girls have a place in the scheme of things, and began to give them *aliyot*, and began to make them cantors, and rabbis, and readers of Torah, and all that sort of thing which is now becoming quite popular. When we did it, it wasn't popular.

The school's educational policies have been as astute as its religious policies. It recognized that it was dealing with parents who not only demanded the best for their children but also felt themselves to be experts on education. Morris Schwartz commented that 90 percent of the mothers of students are or have been teachers. His exaggeration is understandable given the volume of parental advice on curricular matters, school organization, and child psychology. In addition to this pressure from parents, the school has had to compete with the high-powered public-school systems of the Heights communities. The stance adopted by the Schechter school is one of openness to innovation; it promises that it will constantly monitor the latest advances in educational thinking and technique. According to the school's "Parent Handbook":

> A Day School is different from an afternoon Hebrew school. The Day School education encompasses the gamut of public school education. It must satisfy the requirements of the education set by the state. It, in fact, must go way beyond these requirements. The Day School has the responsibility to bring to its pupils the best thinking in education. Teachers must be knowledgeable using the most advanced techniques and approaches to learning and instruction. The Day School must keep its finger on the pulse of educational research. . . . The findings of a Piaget, of a Kohl, of a Goodman, etc. must become part of the educational thinking of the Day School personnel (both Judaic and general). To neglect all this is to deny the pupil the greatest opportunities for achievement and development both as a person and a Jew.

Finally, the school has protected itself from becoming a dumping ground for problem children. Its admissions procedures are designed to identify and weed out children who have potential behavior problems or learning disabilities. When children develop psychological or behavioral problems, the school makes every effort to bring to bear its own resources, as well as those available on the Heights, to solve them. Morris Schwartz is aware that the school will always have some problem children, despite all its screening efforts:

> The problems we have are the simple maladjustments which come either from overprotection or underprotection by parents. Or it will come from divorced parents, and we have quite a lot of those.

THE ATTACK UPON THE SCHOOL

By the mid-1970's, the Schechter school was an established institution. It had achieved an enrollment of over three hundred children, with a substantial waiting list, and succeeded in outgrowing a comparatively new building. While it did not succeed in liquidating its mortgage or its deficit, its finances had noticeably improved. The school regularly remitted withholding taxes to the IRS and was able to meet its payroll. In fact, the leading supporters of the school were thinking in terms of expansion—in particular, of the establishment of a high school and a Hebrew-speaking summer day-camp. And, most significantly of all, the prosperity and growth of the Schechter school were in marked contrast to what was occurring in the public-school system. Because of declining enrollments, the closing of several public schools in Lakeville and in adjoining communities was imminent.

Tragedy struck the Schechter school in 1975, on the second day of Rosh Hashanah. Sometime during the night, the school was broken into. School equipment was smashed, many windows were broken, furniture was destroyed, and large sections of the building were sprayed with paint from spray-cans. More importantly, innumerable swastikas were painted on the walls and floors, and the names of Nazi concentration camps sprayed on the walls. Names of individual students could also be discerned, followed by the words "will die." Other material on the walls included phrases such as "The Jews will die" and "We'll give you 24 hours." The anti-Semitic aspect was highlighted by the fact that the intruders had not taken any valuable objects from the building; equipment such as new electric typewriters and expensive microscopes was left untouched.

The immediate reaction was that the school had been attacked by a Nazi gang. However, the police discounted this theory, pointing out that the swastikas were drawn incorrectly and that damage was not systematic: many valuable objects which could have been destroyed were left untouched. Nor had the intruders brought any tools with them, using instead what was available in the building, and they had not desecrated the school's *Sifrei Torah*.

While the police conceded that the attack upon the school had an anti-Semitic aspect, they felt that if an organized anti-Semitic group was behind the incident, the interior of the building would have been systematically demolished rather than randomly vandalized. The detectives' study of fingerprints and footprints led them to the conclusion that three young men, probably teen-agers, were involved. They did not foreclose the possibility that one or all of the group might be Jewish—a Catholic school in the area had recently been vandalized and the culprits had been Catholic teen-agers.

The first reaction of the administration of the Schechter school was to call off classes until the damage was repaired. It was felt that the children would be traumatized by the scene. But Morris Schwartz, the principal, reconsidered. He decided to open the school and involve the children (together with a crew of professional painters, carpenters, and glaziers who were immediately hired) in the extensive cleanup and repairs which were necessary. According to a member of the school board:

> When Morris first saw it on Sunday, he said, "You know, we'll work through the night, and we'll call off school, and we'll get a cleaning service." He didn't want the children to come in here. And it was a good thing that he changed his mind. The kids reacted better than we did, much better. I think the little ones had no idea what was going on, but Morris called an assembly as soon as the kids came in Monday morning. He had everybody in the multi-purpose room, and he was beautiful. He let them cry because he cried too. He said, "You have to look at what a sick person has done." And after they were done crying, he said, "What do you think we should do now?" "What do you think would be the best thing for us to do now?" And the kids said, "Maybe we should just have our regular morning prayers."

After concluding the *shacharit* (morning) service, the children began the cleanup job:

> They went about cleaning up everything that they could do. They helped the crew of painters who were here painting. They really acted beautifully. It was a very positive thing. They understood it could happen. They're studying anti-Semitism. They weren't frightened by it. Only in the case where their parents were terrified were the kids terrified.

Although the incident immediately became known to the parents and to the local community, the Federation and the Anti-Defamation League insisted that no publicity be given to the incident in city-wide media. The rationale was that publicity would serve only to stimulate further attacks upon the school and upon other Jewish institutions. According to Morris Schwartz:

> They [the Federation and the ADL] felt, against my opinion, that it ought to be hushed up. "Why tell everybody where we are?" "Why raise a stink?" "If we let this be known we're only going to alert the rest of the anti-Semites." I said the anti-Semites know where we are, evidently. We don't have to let them know. It was even suggested that we take off the name Solomon Schechter from the buses. That I opposed and I said, "No, it's staying on." But the whole concept of hushing it up to me was a very amazing concept at this day and age, really.

The non-Jewish editor of the local community newspaper was particularly critical of the decision to prevent the incident from being brought to public attention. According to a Schechter school official:

He said, "You people remind me of the Jewish community in 1938. You have your head in the sand. This story is page 1, and if you cooperated, maybe what happened in '38 and '39 won't happen again."

The school agreed to the policy of the Federation, which emphasized designing a protective system to prevent a repetition of the incident. A force of four security guards was hired to patrol the building in two shifts from 6:00 P.M. to 7:00 A.M. The guards were a temporary measure until an expensive alarm system could be installed which would be connected to the local police station. During school hours, parents patrolled the corridors, and every visitor had to stop at the office to be identified and to receive a pass.

Morris Schwartz was sensitive to the deep sense of shock which the incident evoked among parents and supporters of the school, as well as among Jews living on the Heights:

> This is supposed to be the suburbs. It shows how ironic it is; we left the city for this. See, if this was the ghetto, I'd say what do you expect from the ghetto, right? We ran away from the ghetto. This is the Heights; things like this aren't supposed to happen here—it's quite ironic. It's not only ironic, but I think it's part of our whole environment in the United States today. It's a terribly, terribly violent environment.

The Isaac Mayer Wise Temple

There were five congregations in Lakeville during the 1950's: the Isaac Mayer Wise Temple, the David Einhorn Temple, the Samuel Hirsch Temple, the Max Lilienthal Temple, and the Solomon Schechter Synagogue. The first four were Reform and the fifth was Conservative.

Despite the existence of five congregations, there was a paucity of synagogue buildings. The Isaac Mayer Wise Temple had erected a building in the 1920's, but its location was inconspicuous, and by the 1950's, in view of the size and wealth of its membership, the structure was Lilliputian. The other building was that of the Solomon Schechter Synagogue, which had purchased an old mansion and added a school building and other facilities onto the original structure. At the time we completed our original study, the Schechter Synagogue was about to embark on a campaign to obtain funds for building a sanctuary.

None of the three other congregations had a building. They leased office space, and rented auditoriums and public-school buildings for their services and religious-school classes. In the case of the David Einhorn Temple and the Samuel Hirsch Temple, there were no financial reasons for not building ample synagogue structures. Only in the instance of the Max Lilienthal Temple could it be said that financial constraints operated. However, in the post-World War II era, many congregations whose treasuries were as limited as Lilienthal's had succeeded in erecting buildings. Just as the homeowner took out a mortgage, so did the synagogue.

The situation in the 1970's is quite different. All three congregations which lacked buildings have erected structures adequate to their needs. The Solomon Schechter Synagogue has a commodious sanctuary. And the Isaac Mayer Wise Temple has what local enthusiasts feel is the most outstanding synagogue structure in the United States. It is worthwhile to study what happened at the Wise Temple in some detail.

The Isaac Mayer Wise Temple was the pioneer congregation on the Heights (see pp. 98–119). It had a very large increase in membership in the immediate post-World War II era, and continued to grow to the point that, in the early 1960's, it became one of the largest Reform congregations in the nation. Some of its members felt that Wise was preeminent by virtue not only of its size but of its over-all program of services and activities, which included a religious school, a library and museum, and a lecture series. But even its most enthusiastic supporters did not claim that its facilities were superior. The building occupied by Wise had been constructed to serve about three hundred families. Although later enlarged, it remained for all practical purposes a small and inconspicuous structure, hardly comparable to the great edifices erected in the suburbs of major metropolitan centers in the years immediately after World War II.

Our earlier analysis ended at the point where the congregation was beginning to consider what it should do to accommodate a membership which numbered almost two thousand families. Should it make do with its facilities, build some additional facilities on a site adjoining its old location, or construct an entirely new physical plant?

The primary space-need of the congregation was that of accommodating the large numbers who attended Rosh Hashanah and Yom Kippur services. Attendance at Festival and Sabbath services was quite small, and worshipers could be accommodated in the Temple's sanctuary. The problem of finding room for High Holiday worshipers was solved by two steps: renting the auditorium of the local high school, and holding a double shift of services at both the Temple and the high school. The double shift necessarily involved some abbreviation of the services. It also meant that those leading the service, such as the rabbi and the cantor, had to repeat themselves and thereby had to assume the role of performer rather than worshiper.

There was no objection to these practices on the part of the vast majority of the congregation. If anything, the abbreviation of the service was thought of as a good thing. And there was no feeling about the religious and psychological implications of having the religious professionals repeat themselves. For many, the chief concern each Rosh Hashanah and Yom Kippur was the traffic and the parking problem.

There were some members of the congregation, however, who did feel that it would be more appropriate if all services were held on synagogue property—that attending services in a synagogue sanctuary was more uplifting than praying in a high-school auditorium. But the impetus to build new facilities did not become strong until the late 1950's, when it was rumored that school officials were unhappy with what seemed to be the indefinite continuation of the rental arrangement. The rumor had it that school officials had originally consented to the arrangement with the understanding that the congregation was going to enlarge its facilities as soon as it had raised the funds necessary to erect a new building.

The crucial figure in the discussions about what steps to take next was the rabbi of the Wise Temple, Rabbi David Greenberg. He disliked the use of the high-school auditorium, believing that a congregation of the size and wealth of the Wise Temple should be able to hold its services on its own precincts. He thought that the Wise Temple had outgrown its old building financially and psychologically, as well as physically. In sum, Rabbi Greenberg was convinced that the congregation needed a new home and at the very least should build a new sanctuary.

Rather than meet with school officials to ascertain the truth behind the rumors, Rabbi Greenberg proceeded to take the position that it was high time that the congregation built a structure worthy of the leadership position which—he maintained—the Wise Temple held in American Reform Judaism. When the sentiment was expressed that Wise should erect a building which would be unique—the finest Jewish sanctuary in the nation—Rabbi Greenberg strongly concurred.

BUILDING A JEWISH CATHEDRAL

It was obvious that the old location could not accommodate the type of structure envisioned. Thus, the building committee's first problem was to locate a suitable site. The committee's ambitions dictated that lake-front property be acquired. However, such sites were rare; few sizeable lake-front properties came on the market. After conferring with real estate brokers, the building committee proceeded to take the initiative. It located a particularly luxurious lake-front estate, which was owned and occupied by an elderly and eccentric millionaire, who was attended by a staff of servants and seldom ventured outside its walls. As it happened, the gentleman was Jewish. He was not, however, a member of Wise or of any other congregation. The committee sounded him out, suggesting that if he would donate his estate to the Temple, he would thereby be providing himself with an eternal memorial. The gentleman was not interested in a memorial. Nevertheless, after protracted negotiations, he reluctantly agreed to sell his estate at a substantial price.

After acquiring the property, the building committee proceeded to have the mansion demolished. Smaller buildings were also wrecked, so that no trace of the former occupant was left standing. What remained was a magnificent site, stretching from the shores of the lake to the boulevard that parallels the shoreline.

The next problem was the choice of an architect. The architectural firm which had built the original temple was still in business, headed by the son of the man who had designed the original building. The family had retained its affiliation with Wise and was one of the few founding families still represented in the congregation. Despite the fact that the firm was highly respected, the building committee decided to engage an architect from outside the congregation. The committee's view was that a local architect would be inadequate to the responsibility of designing a new sanctuary. If the Wise Temple was the nation's leading Reform congregation, it owed it to itself to engage the nation's leading architect. The reason presented to the congregation for going national was that there were quite a few noted architects in the congregation; the selection of any one would necessarily cause ill feeling among his peers.

The committee's problem now was to identify the nation's leading architect. As they were struggling with this question, a major news magazine came out with a cover story devoted to American architecture. The story featured the structures of ten architects reputed to be the best in the nation. The building committee proceeded to contact each person on the list. Members of the committee also traveled around the country to view some of the buildings which the ten had designed.

The field was narrowed down to two architects, one a Jew and the other a Gentile. The Jewish architect was interested in the project, but after deliberating with his associates he asked that his name be removed; his prior commitments were so heavy that he would not be able to turn his attention to the project for several years. The committee then designated Arthur Sero as its architect.

Sero, a non-Jew, had never designed a synagogue. This lack of experience made him even more attractive; the building he would design for the Wise Temple would be unique—Sero's only synagogue—since with his backlog of work he was unlikely to accept a commission for another. Any building designed by Sero would automatically gain public attention, but a synagogue by Sero would surely be featured in architectural and news magazines and occupy a conspicuous place in volumes devoted to his life and work.

Sero needed orientation. Rabbi Greenberg worked with him assiduously, teaching him something about Jewish history and liturgy and the function of Jewish houses of worship. In addition to these didactic sessions, Rabbi Greenberg prepared a list of books on Judaism for him to read. Sero discovered a whole world that he had been unaware of and became even more interested in the commission. Invited to attend services at the Wise Temple, he made a special point of attending on Yom Kippur, so as to experience the mood of the High Holidays.

It became obvious that, to fulfill its ambitions, the congregation would have to raise a considerably larger sum than originally envisioned. It seemed the better part of wisdom to engage a fund-raising firm. The goal was to raise a sum to cover the cost of the site and the building with its furnishings. However, not only did some members of the congregation give smaller sums than they had been assigned, but there were also some individuals who gave very little and were antagonistic to the whole plan, feeling that the old arrangement was satisfactory, that school officials could be influenced to continue the arrangement for the High Holidays, and that even if space were not available at the high school, there were other places on the Heights which could be rented. According to these members, there was no need for a new structure which would be empty except for two days each year. Despite such objections, the drive succeeded in raising a major proportion of the total cost, the remaining sum being obtained without difficulty by taking out a mortgage.

It was obvious that the money was going to be spent on a building of striking design, quite different from the innumerable synagogues built in the 1940's and '50's in suburban areas. Many of these had been designed by a handful of well-known Jewish architects who specialized in synagogue architecture. Their designs tended to be repetitive; Sero's design on the other hand, was novel, calling for a building of cathedral-like proportions yet in no way suggestive of a Christian house of worship.

While the cost as well as the novelty of Sero's design took some members of the Temple aback, nevertheless there was no organized opposition to Sero's plans. Armed with Sero's blueprints, the building committee engaged one of the nation's largest contracting firms and encouraged them to erect the building in record time. By utilizing innovative techniques which allowed construction to proceed even during the coldest days of winter, and by precasting parts of the structure on another site, the new sanctuary of the Wise Temple was opened in 1964.

The model shown to potential contributors had been impressive. However, the building was even more striking than the model. It was no higher than some of the wealthy Episcopalian and Methodist churches in the area, but it had the effect of being more massive. Its monumental quality inhered not only in its bulk but in the way Sero utilized the lake as a backdrop.

Sero's building has become an attraction for tourists as well as for residents of the Heights. Jewish visitors are almost invariably shown the building, and many civic and church groups have toured the premises. To meet the demand for tours, the Wise Temple has organized a group of volunteer guides, who explain the unique design of the building as well as the ceremonial objects it contains.

The original plan was to keep the old building and to use the new one only for the High Holidays and for special events. This did not prove feasible. The maintenance of two congregational homes was a fiscal burden, and it was difficult to administer a single institution located under two roofs, since the congregational budget did not provide for hiring duplicate staffs. The need to consolidate Temple activities soon became apparent. The obvious solution was to sell the old building, and since it had a considerable number of classrooms, it was purchased by a Catholic order which needed more space for its high school.

The consolidation has created as many problems as it has solved. Despite its size, Sero's building lacks many of the facilities of the old building. It has no chapel and no space adequate for the synagogue's library. (The Wise Library had a much larger collection of Jewish books than any other synagogue in the area and was used by the community-at-large as well as by the Temple's own members.) The Wise Temple owns a collection of Jewish ritual objects, and the new building lacks museum space. Classroom space is also at a premium, and even such elementary facilities as a kitchen are lacking. But one problem has disappeared: since the estate the congregation purchased was large, there is space for a sizeable parking lot. There are no longer any irate calls to the police from homeowners whose privacy is disturbed, as happened in the neighborhood where the old temple was located.

Despite the monumental size of the new building, it is not large enough to meet its original objective of accommodating at a single service all who come to worship on the High Holidays. Accordingly, the services are still abbreviated and the double-shift arrangement is still utilized. Further construction is needed. In the mid-1970's, a successful campaign was held to pay off the mortgage, but the feeling is that some time should elapse before a new building campaign is initiated.

Whatever the final cost of the new Temple proves to be, members of the congregation are very proud of it. It is too early to judge whether Sero's building will become a landmark in the annals of American architecture generally, and of synagogue architecture in particular. In any case, the response appears to be much stronger than the usual pride and enthusiasm engendered by a new facility. The building seems to have a meaning which goes beyond its physical aspects.

One need not be a student of architecture to notice that the new building is in many respects the antithesis of its predecessor. While the old building was unobtrusive, the new one cannot be ignored. The statement it conveys is that Jews no longer need to act as a fearful minority, afraid to display their wealth and achievements. By proclaiming the existence of the Jewish community to the community-at-large, the new building signifies that the Jews on the Heights have come out of the closet. The statement it makes is that Jews must now be accepted as equals. It suggests that the superordinate role of church over synagogue has come to an end.

Thus, the building functions to liberate the Jew from a feeling of inferiority. A symbol of a liberation achieved, it serves also as a stimulant toward liberation for those oldtime residents who wish to throw off the constraints of an earlier period when a low Jewish profile was the accepted style in intergroup relations.

As a symbol that the age of Jewish invisibility is over, the new Isaac Mayer Wise Temple serves the entire Jewish community. Other congregations in the area need not build a monumental structure, for while Sero's building is the property of a single congregation, it speaks to and for all the Jews who make their home in Lakeville and in the larger area known as the Heights.

THE CHOICE OF A NEW RABBI

Rabbi Greenberg, who pursued the idea of erecting the new sanctuary with single-minded devotion and interested himself in the planning of every detail of its exterior and interior, was not fated to enjoy it. Several years after the building was opened, the congregation indicated to him that it wanted a change of rabbinical leadership. Rabbi Greenberg did not contest the issue. He agreed to early retirement, and a financial settlement was arranged.

While Rabbi Greenberg had no stomach for public controversy about his retirement, he did want assurances that his associate rabbi—Rabbi Samuel Nathan—would be elected to his post. Rabbi Nathan would perpetuate the ideals which he stood for. Furthermore, in his view Rabbi Nathan had the right to the post by virtue of his long and devoted service. And if Nathan succeeded Greenberg, it would appear that a normal retirement was taking place, and that Rabbi Greenberg was graciously stepping aside so that his faithful assistant could have his own day in the sun.

Rabbi Greenberg's wishes did not receive the endorsement of many influential members of the congregation. A controversy ensued, at first known only to insiders, but inevitably becoming public knowledge. Those who agreed with Rabbi Greenberg maintained that it was only right that Rabbi Nathan should succeed him. Nathan not only had been Greenberg's loyal associate for many years but had turned down other pulpits and stayed on in the expectation that he would succeed his mentor. However, the dominant opinion was that while Rabbi Nathan was perfectly adequate as an associate rabbi, he did not have the qualities necessary to maintain the congregation's position as the pre-eminent

Reform temple in the nation. The dominant opinion held that there was nothing in writing which indicated that Rabbi Nathan had been promised that he would be named senior rabbi upon Rabbi Greenberg's retirement. If Rabbi Nathan had made that assumption, he was in error; if Rabbi Greenberg had promised him the post, Greenberg had exceeded his authority.

Rabbi Nathan did not actually claim that he had been promised the post. He reconstructed the sequence of events for us as follows:

> I was the associate rabbi of Wise and had been there for ten years. No promise had been made that I was to be the successor, but the understanding was that I was to be considered as one of the possible successors. I attended a meeting—rather two meetings—of the rabbinical selection committee, and I was told by a member of the committee that it was set up that I would not be the successor. It was all a charade, and I was not to be given the opportunity.

Presumably, Rabbi Nathan could have stayed on as the associate rabbi of the Wise Temple. However, he felt that the congregation's refusal to consider him for the post of senior rabbi left him little choice but to resign. With the support of Rabbi Greenberg and about forty members of the Wise Temple, he proceeded to establish a new congregation, the Bernard Felsenthal Temple.

While Rabbi Greenberg is in close touch with the Felsenthal Temple, his contact with Wise is minimal. He attends services there only occasionally. However, when he does he is accorded the honor of sitting on the platform, the *bimah*. The arrangement serves the function of a public display of harmony and is to the advantage of both parties. It suggests that Rabbi Greenberg was dealt with fairly and that the congregation recognizes its indebtedness to him and that, whatever his private feelings, he does not support any further dissension. His successor has seen to it that he is also accorded the respect of having his name appear in each issue of the Temple's bulletin, where he is identified as "Rabbi Emeritus." Thus, only those close to the situation know how bitter Rabbi Greenberg feels. However, after the initial period of hostilities, a truce was established, facilitated by the existence of the Felsenthal Temple, whose leadership was originally drawn from dissident members of Wise.

Just as the Wise Temple had scoured the nation for its greatest architect, so it sought to locate the nation's leading rabbi. Selecting a rabbi proved to be even more difficult than choosing an architect. There would be no point in selecting a nationally-known figure—such a rabbi would be near the age of retirement and thus could serve for only a limited number of years. The rabbinical selection committee had to choose from among the nation's younger Reform rabbis and to bet on which would become Reform Judaism's foremost spiritual leader a decade or two hence.

They chose Rabbi Daniel Resnick, a Midwesterner who had served as assistant rabbi and then as associate rabbi of a very prominent Eastern congregation. Rabbi Resnick had considerable experience in leading a prominent congregation, inasmuch as his senior rabbi had been involved with Jewish affairs on both a national and international level and thus was away a good deal of the time.

Rabbi Resnick is strikingly different from his predecessor. Whereas Rabbi Greenberg is tall and clean-shaven, Rabbi Resnick is bearded and rather short in stature. Whereas Rabbi Greenberg was always immaculately dressed in Ivy League clothing, Rabbi Resnick dresses with considerable informality except on "state" occasions. While he may wear corduroy slacks instead of faded and patched jeans, and his hiking boots may be less scuffed than those seen on the nation's Ivy League campuses, his appearance is that of a young faculty member who grew up in the 1960's and experienced the greening of America.

Rabbi Resnick manifests his countercultural tendencies in a variety of other ways. Instead of driving, he frequently comes to the Temple on a bicycle, not only because he hopes to improve the quality of the air, but also because that way he gets some fresh air for himself. When Rabbi Resnick does drive to the Temple, he parks in any available space; one of the first changes he insisted upon was that of abolishing the space reserved for the senior rabbi's car.

Actually, Rabbi Resnick represents two trends. The first is the informal life-style connected with the greening of America. The second is an intensified Jewishness. To be sure, Rabbi Greenberg helped to move the Wise Temple away from its Classical Reform beginnings and into the mainstream of Neo-Reform Judaism. However, Rabbi Resnick is more than Neo-Reform—his starting point is normative Judaism. Rabbi Resnick is seeking to bring the Neo-Reformism of the Wise Temple as close to normative Judaism as possible. He feels that the congregation was starved Jewishly under what he regards as Rabbi

Greenberg's timid leadership. He is convinced that the congregation is capable of digesting a much richer diet of Jewishness if it is offered to them in palatable form.

Rabbi Resnick has proceeded to make many innovations, all designed to increase traditionalism. He has introduced a considerable amount of Hebrew into the religious services and plans on steadily increasing it, thus making the service closer to the traditional mode. He builds a *sukkah* in his yard at home each year and advocates that members of his Temple do likewise. Rabbi Resnick believes strongly in the performance of ritual circumcision (*brit milah*) and has made his views known to the Temple's membership. Rabbi Greenberg, by contrast, would attend a *brit* if he were invited, but he never advocated the performance of Jewish ritual circumcision. Rabbi Resnick also advocates that members who did not have a Bar or Bat Mitzvah as children have one as adults. He has none of the reservations about Bar and Bat Mitzvah manifested by colleagues such as Rabbi Samuel Aaron of the Hirsch Temple, who was considered one of the more traditional Neo-Reform rabbis on the Heights (see p. 156).

The membership of the Isaac Mayer Wise Temple is considerably smaller than it was at its peak. The largest exodus was to the new congregation formed by Rabbi Nathan. But in an age when the number of giant congregations is on the decline, the situation of the Wise Temple is not exceptional. In fact, giant congregations of two thousand or more families have come into disesteem as cold and impersonal institutions, smacking more of corporations than synagogues. In any case, the Wise Temple has succeeded in stabilizing its membership somewhere between fourteen hundred and fifteen hundred families. Thus, it is still a major congregation and by far the largest in the Lakeville area.

Rabbi Resnick has an obvious appeal to the most intensely Jewish members of the congregation. They are not jarred by his countercultural style, since it is balanced by an intense Jewishness. He is equally attractive to those having a less intense Jewish identity, because he seems to be receptive to new ideas and not to be bound by the outworn formalities of an earlier age with its stiffness, hangups, and distinctions between upstairs and downstairs. In Rabbi Resnick's case, countercultural style is not threatening, so it can be accepted by both groups. Not only does he lead a conventional family life, but he does not advocate radical change in the general community. Unlike Rabbi Samuel Aaron of the

Hirsch Temple, who was the sworn enemy of the Jewish Establishment, Rabbi Resnick has not seen fit to issue any blanket condemnations of local or national Jewish institutions and their leaders.

How can the choice of Rabbi Resnick be explained? The answer seems to be that in the 1950's and '60's the problem which was uppermost in the minds of Lakeville parents of widely different Jewish convictions was whether their children would follow in their footsteps and take on a Jewish identity of any kind. The rising rate of intermarriage and the interest of young people in new life-styles suggested that Jewish survival could by no means be taken for granted. Such fears appear to have played a major part in the congregation's desire for a change in rabbinical leadership. Rabbi Greenberg's formal manner, beautifully-tailored clothing, striking appearance (more Gentile than Jewish), and contacts with Christian clergy and laity were highly appealing when the concerns of Jews on the Heights centered on their acceptance by the general community, but by the 1960's the problem had shifted to survival rather than acceptance. And the young were the key to survival.

The feeling of the lay leadership of the Wise Temple is that if anybody can turn the young on to Jewishness, it is Rabbi Resnick. Raised in a Zionist youth movement, he still retains a certain zest and looseness from his earlier years, when he sang Zionist songs around campfires in summer camps and dreamt of living in the Jewish Homeland.

Perhaps Rabbi Resnick's style and its contrast with that of the Temple's previous rabbis are best represented by the mural which covers one wall of the youth room. It portrays Hassidim dancing, garbed in traditional clothing such as the *streiml* and *kapote*, their faces stereotypically Jewish. The message of the mural is twofold: the Jewishness of the Heights has a long way to go before it can match what the Hassidim have achieved. Furthermore, better Judaism than involvement with such movements as Jews for Jesus, the Moonies, the Eastern cults, taking hard drugs or dropping out. In sum, even parents who cannot bring themselves to observe the more traditional Judaism Rabbi Resnick advocates think of him as a good influence upon the young.

It is significant that, while Rabbi Resnick (as well as the associate and assistant rabbis he selected) stands for intense Jewishness and for reforming Neo-Reform Judaism, he is not anti-Christian or antagonistic to Gentiles. He does not preach insularity. He is active in the general community and sees to it that his appearances before Christian groups are publicized in the Temple's bulletin. Rabbi Resnick maintains that despite the lack of support for Israel from Christians during crucial events in its history, it is poor strategy to sever relationships with Gentile groups. In his view, relationships with civic organizations, church groups, and clubs with a predominantly Gentile membership should be strengthened rather than allowed to atrophy.

Rabbi Resnick's message to the Gentiles appears to be the following: "You must accept me for what I am, for my differences as well as for my similarities. We Jews belong in Lakeville and on the Heights as much as you do. We have contributed a great deal to the community. You are better off for our having settled here." In a sense, his message parallels the message of the new sanctuary of the Isaac Mayer Wise Temple.

The Bernard Felsenthal Temple

During the first year of its existence, it was not apparent whether the Bernard Felsenthal Temple would live or die. However, by the beginning of the second year, it was clear that Felsenthal would survive. In fact, soon after its third year of existence the Temple would not accept any new members, because it had already reached the ceiling of 350 it had placed on the number of families who could join.

The ceiling has been strictly adhered to. For the past several years, applicants have been accepted only upon the death or resignation of a member. Felsenthal is proud of following a limited-membership policy because it implies that while the Wise Temple is interested in bigness and in increasing its power and the size of its treasury, the Felsenthal Temple is motivated by spiritual considerations. A further implication is that largeness is dehumanizing, and that in resisting the temptation to grow beyond 350 families, the Felsenthal Temple can do a better job of furthering the spiritual welfare of those it serves than can such giant institutions as the Wise Temple.

THE DEVELOPMENT OF A
CONGREGATIONAL PROGRAM

The Felsenthal Temple has lived happily with the constraints imposed by its limited size. For the first several years, it had no building and used rented quarters for its offices and activities. It also frequently held meetings, as well as some functions, in the homes of its members. The next step was to buy property. Felsenthal bought an old mansion, but not a particularly large or lavish one—Rabbi Nathan in fact characterizes it as "an old home which we remodeled on the inside so it would conform to the building code." Since the size of the building is limited, High Holiday services are held in a public-school auditorium. The Sunday morning sessions of the religious school are also held in a public school. The Friday evening service, which is the congregation's major weekly service, is held in a public facility as well.

The Temple's mansion is used for Saturday morning services, committee meetings, the youth program, the Hebrew school, and the adult education classes. The offices and library are also housed in the building. The facility is invariably referred to as the "Temple home" rather than "the Temple." As Rabbi Nathan put it: "the building is certainly not a temple, and I think the idea of a home is something that we like." When the building was dedicated, it was pointed out that the site was large enough for expansion. However, congregational officers went out of their way to make clear that Felsenthal did not contemplate building a sizeable sanctuary or a school building, that the congregation was satisfied with its modest physical plant and that, while it might add on several rooms at some future time, it would not proceed to tax its members as Wise did in order to build an imposing edifice. The implication again is clear: Felsenthal intends to spend its money on what is really important, namely, meeting the spiritual needs of its 350 families.

In a relatively small number of years, the Felsenthal Temple has developed a fairly complete congregational program. In addition to its Sabbath, Festival, and High Holiday services, it has services for other observances such as Yom Hashoah. Its Sunday School has grown rapidly and includes all grades from kindergarten to Confirmation. Its Hebrew school is large enough to sustain a considerable number of classes and produces students who qualify for Bar Mitzvah.

The congregation sponsors a considerable number of social and cultural events each year. These events substitute for a sisterhood and brotherhood, which the leadership of the congregation believes to be superfluous. The congregation mounts a youth program led by a professional group leader, and there is an adult education program which compares favorably with that of most of the other congregations in the area. While centered on the Heights, the program includes a monthly luncheon meeting held in the Lake City business district. At these meetings, the rabbi leads a discussion on a topic of Jewish or general interest.

The congregation runs a gift shop designed to make available gifts of Jewish significance, ceremonial objects for the home, and supplies needed for the celebration of the Jewish holidays. The congregation has sponsored a tour of Israel led by the rabbi and his wife. It has adopted a *refusnik*, a Russian Jew seeking to gain support for his right to emigrate from the Soviet Union and settle in Israel.

The congregation is also making provision for the dead and is in the process of opening a Felsenthal section at one of the local Jewish cemeteries. It keeps *Yahrzeit* records according to the English calendar, and reminders are sent to those who are obliged to say these yearly prayers for the dead.

Perhaps the most revealing aspect of the congregation's program is its annual scholar-in-residence program. The program involves a series of three lectures over a weekend. For the first several years, the program limited itself to talent available in the Lake City metropolitan area. However, the committee wanted to obtain a nationally-known speaker, and its ambitions culminated in an invitation to Elie Wiesel. Wiesel was hardly a new personality to the Heights, having lectured at many of the other synagogues in the area. But if Wiesel was old hat, the invitation indicated that the congregation felt it was ready to move up from the minor leagues to the majors—that it conceived of itself as the equal of any of the other synagogues in the area. Felsenthal's desire to have Wiesel and its push to establish itself as the equal of other congregations had been foreshadowed by an earlier invitation to lecture extended to Abram L. Sachar, chancellor of Brandeis University. While Sachar's style is very different from Wiesel's, he is an eminent personality widely known to the Jewish and non-Jewish public.

What has enabled the Felsenthal Temple to grow so rapidly? Demographic trends of course worked in its favor: there has been a steady influx of Jewish families into the Heights. Since in most cases these families arrived uncommitted to a particular religious institution, Felsenthal has had as good a chance to gain their affiliation as local synagogues with a longer history. These new arrivals have typically been young families with small children who, if they have even a mild level of Jewish identity, need a religious school. Felsenthal's religious school, having quickly achieved a reputation as a decent one, served to attract new members, since membership in the Temple was required for enrollment.

Felsenthal is somewhat less expensive than some of the other congregations in the area, as it does not require a new member to make a pledge toward the cost of the building and its renovation. And being a small congregation, it has put great emphasis on being hospitable and welcoming new families. While this is no longer necessary since the congregation can admit only a handful of new families each year, the tradition lives on.

The congregation stresses that it is the most democratic of all the synagogues in the Heights. As a recent president of the congregation put it in his annual message: "Adherence to a democratic spirit in the running of the affairs of the Temple is a basic concept of our congregation." Members of the congregation are permitted to attend board meetings, and it is customary that they be recognized by the chair should they wish to speak. The Wise Temple is viewed as an oligarchy in which a small clique of board members determine congregational policy.

While some leaders of both the Wise and Felsenthal Temples remember the distressing circumstances which gave rise to the new congregation, the founding of Felsenthal has actually been more advantageous than threatening to Wise and to the Jewish community as a whole. Families and individuals who would be unhappy at Wise, or who would not join Wise—intimidated by its size or unable to accept Rabbi Resnick's traditionalism—now have an alternative synagogue. There is also the matter of financial potency. While the membership of the Felsenthal Temple includes a number of very wealthy families, its image is one of moderate wealth. Thus, it is not threatening to those who are—by the standards of the Heights—in modest circumstances. Furthermore, while the Felsenthal Temple has its share of highly-educated families, its image is middle-brow rather than high-brow. Thus, it is not intimidating to those who lack degrees from Ivy-League-type colleges and universities. For example, no member of Felsenthal will be asked to compose an original prayer for High Holiday or Sabbath services, as is commonplace at the Samuel Hirsch Temple.

The most obvious remnant of the split which gave rise to the congregation is the refusal of the Felsenthal Temple to join the Union of American Hebrew Congregations. This refusal traces back to the feeling that the Union favored the Wise Temple in the dispute which gave rise to the establishment of the Felsenthal Temple. Given the congregation's localistic orientation, however, its lack of affiliation with its national body is not the handicap it might have been. There is also the fiscal advantage that the congregation is not obligated to pay dues to the Union.

THE ORIENTATION OF A MIDDLE-OF-THE-ROAD RELIGIOUS INSTITUTION

Rabbi Nathan is a considerable asset to the congregation and has played an important role in its rapid growth. He is pastoral in his approach and functions as a devoted leader of his flock. The fact that he does not aspire to national leadership or prominence—a characteristic which made him an unacceptable candidate for the post of senior rabbi at the Wise Temple—makes him very attractive to the members of Felsenthal. Even the interfaith work he does—work he places considerable emphasis on—is conducted almost exclusively in the Heights and surrounding communities. His efforts in the field of interfaith relations have been well received by the members of his Temple.

Rabbi Nathan is always available to his members. His only important outside interest is in encounter and therapy groups for married couples. This interest adds to his popularity, since it fits in very well with congregational life, which emphasizes the unity of the family. He has sparked the establishment of a "Family Life Committee" at Felsenthal that, given current anxieties about the future of the family, has gained considerable support. As Rabbi Nathan himself put it, the Family Life Committee is devoted "to a discussion of concerns that appear to be common to many members of our Temple."

Rabbi Nathan's localistic rather than cosmopolitan orientation is neatly complemented by his policy of following a middle-of-the-road approach. His proclivity to moderation in all things has been well received and is one of the hallmarks of the Felsenthal Temple. His policy on intermarriage illustrates the point.

On the one hand, Rabbi Nathan opposes intermarriage. Felsenthal's religious school, Confirmation ceremony, and youth activities are all designed to assure Jewish survival and encourage in-group marriage. However, Rabbi Nathan is willing to officiate at an intermarriage of a son or daughter of a Temple member. In fact, in the Temple's bulletin, intermarriages are accorded the same respect given to endogamous marriages: the parents are congratulated and given a *mazal tov* (best wishes).

Rabbi Nathan has made it clear that he will officiate at intermarriages only when the child of a Temple member is involved; he does not want to become known as a rabbi who is available to the general public as a performer of intermarriages. His policy has proven popular—parents have the assurance that if their child cannot be dissuaded from an inter-marriage, Rabbi Nathan will not desert them. Rather, he will cooperate by conducting a wedding to which they can invite family and friends with a minimum of embarrassment.

Another illustration of the congregation's moderate approach is the fact that its support for the Soviet *refusnik* bound for Israel has been balanced with help to a Jewish family from a South American country where the father had been incarcerated as a political prisoner. A special fund was established for the family to settle in Lake City, free medical service was provided by doctors who were members of the congregation, and the family were guests at the home of a Felsenthal member until they could be provided with a permanent home. Help was also given in locating jobs for both husband and wife. The question of whether the family should have settled in Israel rather than the United States was not considered.

Felsenthal has succeeded in carving out a niche for itself—no small accomplishment given the number of congregations in the area. Rabbi Nathan has formulated Felsenthal's position as follows:

> I think our congregation is unique in the area. In our immediate area we are the only small, middle-of-the-road Reform Jewish congregation. We are not leaning towards Classical Reform in any way. Our services are on Friday night and Saturday morning; we don't have Sunday morning services. We are pro-Israel. On the other hand, we are not anything like the Samuel Hirsch Temple which is—or anyhow used to be—highly ex-perimental in terms of worship and maybe other areas too. I think they are very controversial—which they like. I'm not deriding it in any way. We see ourselves more in the mainstream of Reform Judaism.

Rabbi Nathan's approach to Jewish ritual is also middle-of-the-road. He does not identify with Reform's left wing which derides ritual. On the other hand, he is antagonistic to the right wing of Reform Judaism which looks upon ritual as acts of sacredness. His emphasis is on the beauty and aesthetic appeal of ritual:

> . . . we're trying to help our members to see Shabbat in the home with the rituals not for the rituals' sake but because it's something that the family can become involved in; it is a beautiful thing. I compare it to

going to a symphony concert. One can live without going to a concert, but it adds to the dimension of life by going, and this is the same with the rituals of the Shabbat and then [attendance at] congregational services on Friday night.

Rabbi Nathan was raised in a strictly Orthodox home. He feels that Reform needs the warmth associated with traditional observances. However, he is strongly concerned that rituals be viewed as discretionary and not mandatory:

At some Friday night services we have had suppers preceding the service . . . and we sing *z'miros* (Sabbath songs) between the time the dinner closes and the time we have the actual service. So that we want to bring back this idea of warmth and participation. . . . Yet we are not heading towards the kind of movement that I think I see in Reform Judaism, of rigidity, of being told what one must do, or the reinstitution of rituals just for the sake of reinstituting rituals. We have our Saturday morning service and so on, but I'm not looking towards having that take the place of our Friday night service. I want to keep the Friday night service as a very important part of our program.

Dedicated as he is to what he conceives of as middle-of-the-road Reform, Rabbi Nathan feels that the current threat to Reform Judaism comes from the right rather than from the left. He is fearful that Reform may become too traditional and that the distinction between Reform and Conservative Judaism may erode away. He described his thinking in an article which appeared in the Felsenthal Temple bulletin:

A few months ago, a national Reform commission on liturgy met in our area. The repeated theme was a call for a return to *mitzvot* [religious obligations]. When asked to define what *mitzvot* were the ones to which we should return, the answer was "building a *sukkah*, lighting candles, holding *s'lichot* services, etc."

Early Reform placed greater stress on the rational than on the emotional areas of Judaism. This led to the charge that Reform was cold and impersonal. Now the trend is more toward including elements that early Reform had discarded. . . . It seems we are now in danger of becoming more obsessed with ritual than ethics. Ritual is important as long as we are aware of the values that the ritual symbolizes. . . . [However] Judaism's only purpose is to keep alive the messianic hope, and the obligation of every Jew is to bring that hope to fruition in all possible ways. That hope, expressed in the words of the prophets and the prayerbook, is for a world of honesty, justice, brotherhood, empathy, and above all else, *shalom*, peace.

By emphasizing that rituals should not become ends in themselves and that religion should stress moralism rather than sacramentalism, Rabbi Nathan's formula has considerable appeal. Its appeal is heightened by his familiarity with traditional Jewish culture (especially with Jewish folk culture) and his willingness to employ elements of that culture such as Sabbath *z'miros.* The special advantage of his position is that, by placing the emphasis upon the aesthetic appeal of tradition rather than upon its binding and suprasocial aspects, it permits those who fail to observe rituals in their homes, or who absent themselves from synagogue services, to consider themselves good Jews. They are not made to feel guilty; in Rabbi Nathan's view, they are only Jews who have yet to realize how Judaism could give their lives added dimension and richness.

In sum, Rabbi Nathan's pastoral personality and, more especially, his approach to Judaism appeal to a significant segment of the community. But we must ask the question of whether his approach will be attractive to the children of his followers. One of the objectives of the Felsenthal Temple when it established a ceiling of 350 families was that of enabling members to have a "maximum personal relationship with our Rabbi," as one of the congregation's yearbooks put it. The most important aspect of such a "maximum personal relationship" was that the rabbi get to know the children of members and influence them to internalize a Jewish identity. As we noted earlier, the fear that the younger generation might not take on such an identity was very important in Wise's choice of Rabbi Resnick. It is fair to say that the founders of the Felsenthal Temple were deeply affected, if not obsessed, by the same fear—that their children might not choose to follow in their footsteps.

The forty families who resigned from the Wise Temple and established the new congregation set down three objectives for their institution. The first is a standard one:

> The Bernard Felsenthal Temple aspires to express modern Jewish ideals and ideas while maintaining regard for Jewish tradition; to be relevant to Jews who take seriously the social as well as personal obligations inherent in the Jewish faith; and to conduct all of its affairs in a truly democratic spirit.

The second, however, is an objective which is seldom found in similar documents of congregations established in the 19th century, or even in the early decades of the 20th:

This congregation recognizes a special obligation to its youth who seek identities that in this time seem to elude them. We hope we can offer them something enduring to cling to and to live by, so that in their own faith—Judaism—they will find those identities.

The third objective, like the first, is standard:

It is our goal to stimulate in our adults, as in our children, such participation in local, national and world affairs as will contribute toward the fulfillment of the prophetic vision of a just society and a united mankind.

However important the first and third objectives may be, the founders of the Felsenthal Temple realize that its future hangs upon the achievement of the second goal. However attractive Rabbi Nathan's formulation of Judaism may be to them, the essential question is whether it will be appealing to their children. The fact that the founders recognize a "special obligation" to the youth of the congregation indicates that they are not at all certain that they will succeed in making their children into committed Jews. They can only hope that Rabbi Nathan's middle-of-the-road approach—which to them seems so sensible and so attractive —will find favor in the eyes of their offspring.

The Solomon Schechter Synagogue

In the period following our original study, the Solomon Schechter Synagogue (see pp. 120–133) continued to be as successful as before. As the only Conservative synagogue in the Lakeville area, it had a built-in appeal to those reared in traditional Jewish homes.

Under the leadership of Rabbi David Ginzberg, the synagogue completed its building program by erecting a sanctuary, built as planned in the front of the auditorium, thus allowing for both to be combined on the High Holidays and on other occasions when a large seating capacity was needed.

The completion of the building program also gave the congregation the opportunity to further its variegated program. The Schechter Synagogue sponsored a host of activities for all age groups and became an important center of Jewish life on the Heights. While attendance at services other than the High Holidays was quite low, there was a feeling of optimism and achievement. The synagogue's building program had been completed, and the congregation's facilities were in constant use.

THE COMING OF A NEW RABBI

When Rabbi Ginzberg decided to retire, there were extensive discussions about who his successor should be. The consensus was that the congregation required a spiritual leader who projected more religious depth than Rabbi Ginzberg. Although he was appreciated for his friendliness, his warmth to congregants, and his excellence as an organizer and fund-raiser, it was felt that the congregation needed a rabbi whose manner would be more polished and whose religious brow-level would be higher than that of Rabbi Ginzberg.

Rabbi Joseph Steinberg, the one chosen, was a very special kind of person. A third-generation American Jew, reared in a middle-class home by parents who were relatively uncommitted Reform Jews, he was given only a minimal Jewish education. But after experiencing a religious awakening, he resolved to become a rabbi and graduated from the Jewish Theological Seminary of America to become a Conservative rabbi of some note. He was chosen for the Schechter Synagogue post after having served as the assistant of one large congregation and as the rabbi of a second.

Rabbi Steinberg fascinated Schechter's rabbinical selection committee. He seemed removed from everyday affairs—a true man of the spirit. He was a master of the spoken word and had also published extensively. While the committee did not quite fathom Steinberg's consuming interest in Hassidism, they found his deep concern with religious questions refreshing.

For his part, Steinberg was strongly drawn to the Schechter Synagogue. He was impressed with the fact that it was the only Conservative congregation in the area. Furthermore, the financial standing of its membership suggested that he would have the resources to build a substantial religious and educational program. Steinberg believed that the American synagogue had made the mistake of being a department store catering to every whim and desire of the membership. He believed that while the Solomon Schechter Synagogue had followed the trend, it could be refashioned into a model religious institution which would set a standard for the rest of the nation. He accepted his new post in a spirit of great expectations.

Rabbi Steinberg was a believer in the wisdom of stressing the observance of a selected number of *mitzvot*. The *mitzvot* he concentrated on initially were the observance of the Sabbath and of Sukkot. As he saw it, building Sabbath observance would mean that the system of late Friday evening services, combined with a Saturday morning service, would have to be discontinued. Efforts would have to be concentrated on one service, and the obvious choice was the Saturday morning one. However, the discontinuance of the Friday evening service would involve shifting the Bat Mitzvah ceremony to Saturday morning. Rabbi Steinberg welcomed this change; not having been reared in Orthodoxy, he had no inhibitions about females participating in a religious service. While there was some opposition from the worshipers who attended the daily *minyan*, they were a small and uninfluential group.

Rabbi Steinberg prepared his Saturday morning sermons with great care. Timed to take exactly twenty minutes, they became the high point of the service. They were striking presentations filled with religious and ethical content. Bar and Bat Mitzvahs, which were performed each Saturday morning except during the summer, were de-emphasized. The Junior congregation was discontinued, permitting the family to worship together as a unit.

The Saturday morning service was a success. There was a noticeable increase in the number of regular worshipers, so that in a relatively short time the congregation did not have to rely upon those who came for the Bar or Bat Mitzvah. Furthermore, as the service took hold, the sanctuary was filled even during the summer. Large numbers stayed for the *kiddush* which was served each week.

A related development was the growth of a group who walked to and from synagogue on Saturday morning. While Rabbi Steinberg was not critical of those who drove to synagogue, he indicated that it was preferable to walk if one lived at a reasonable distance. A noticeable group of families began to follow his example of walking to and from services.

The Sukkot festival, which follows very closely after the High Holidays, was not observed by most Schechter members. Rabbi Steinberg, feeling that it was imperative to increase the observance of the festival, emphasized that Sukkot was an extension of the High Holidays. He focused on the importance of each congregant's building a *sukkah*, and directions, instruction, and assistance were given to those who were interested. There was a decided rise in *sukkah* building, and families competed with each other to build the most artistic and inviting one.

Trying always to multiply the observance of *mitzvot*, Rabbi Steinberg then turned to the festival of Shavuot. He instituted the tradition of *tikun layl shavuot*—an all-night prayer and study session. The program he instituted offered a variety of study sessions. Afterward, the entire group came together to hear a lecture by the scholar-in-residence, generally someone new to the congregation who served on the faculty of a university or rabbinical seminary. After the lecture, the study sessions were resumed. The *tikun* culminated in an early-morning service held outdoors on the beach. While attendance varied from year to year, the *tikun* soon became a Schechter tradition. The innovation was considered a success.

Rabbi Steinberg felt that the congregation's program of adult education was weak. Accordingly, classes were increased in number and made more substantial in content. Students were encouraged to purchase books for each course and to prepare assignments. Several courses were co-sponsored with the Hebrew college located in Lake City. While these courses did not carry credit, they were academic in tone.

Rabbi Steinberg also shifted the emphasis of the adult education program from forums in which a wide variety of speakers presented their views to a program which stressed scholars-in-residence, each of whom presented a minimum of three lectures. Elie Wiesel was by far the most popular of the scholars-in-residence; tickets had to be purchased far in advance for his lectures, which became what Rabbi Steinberg termed an "event." Wiesel was asked to return year after year; his subjects were announced long in advance and study sessions were held prior to his coming to familiarize his listeners with the material he would cover.

An attempt was made to institute a course called P.E.P. (Parent Education Program). The course was designed for parents of children in the early grades of the Hebrew school and the curriculum paralleled the material presented in the child's classroom. Rabbi Steinberg felt that Jewish education would have little success if it did not succeed also in involving the parent. Parental study would provide an example to the child and bridge the gap between home and synagogue.

Like many of his colleagues in the Conservative movement, Rabbi Steinberg was appalled at the dropout rate after Bar and Bat Mitzvah.

He stressed the importance of continuing Jewish education during the high school years, and when a regional high school for all the congregations in the area was established, the largest block of students came from the Schechter Synagogue. Particular emphasis was then placed on continuing to graduation; all students from Schechter who graduated were provided with a stipend to be used to supplement the cost of a trip to Israel.

The congregation prided itself on the extensive activities it sponsored for teen-agers, led by a professional youth director. The Sisterhood and the Men's Club also had active programs, the Jewish content of which Rabbi Steinberg sought to reinforce. A particularly successful group was the Couples Club. While too large to be a *havurah* (a group of like-minded families who meet together as a Jewish fellowship), the Couples Club, which had been started by Rabbi Ginzberg, developed along *havurah* lines. It met in homes and was responsible for its own direction. Its program included such features as the study of Jewish texts, retreats, trips, and Sabbath and holiday dinners.

Rabbi Steinberg believed that Schechter was indeed becoming a model synagogue. He thought that his emphasis on Sabbath morning worship was bearing fruit and that the congregation had the highest proportion in the Conservative movement of members who came to services on Saturday morning and families who built *sukkot*. In his estimation, the number of families which had introduced *kashrut* in the home exceeded that of any other Conservative synagogue in the nation. He felt that the program he had introduced was achieving the recognition it deserved when it was awarded citations from the United Synagogue of America, the national congregational union of the Conservative movement. In Rabbi Steinberg's view, the progress of the Schechter Synagogue proved that Judaism in America could be saved. What was needed was more rabbis who would insist on a challenging program of religious observance and study.

THE CONTROVERSY OVER RABBI STEINBERG

While it was generally conceded that many aspects of congregational life had burgeoned under Rabbi Steinberg's direction, Solomon Schechter was far from a unified congregation. Resignations were not uncommon, and a noticeable number were traceable to dissatisfaction with Rabbi

Steinberg. There were also members who did not resign but who felt deeply hurt or disappointed by Rabbi Steinberg and who made their feelings known. On the other hand, there were those who felt that Rabbi Steinberg was a man of great spirituality, that he exemplified what a rabbi should be.

The division of opinion was sharp enough so that, when Rabbi Steinberg's second contract came up for renewal, the board of directors decided to appoint a special "Rabbinic Liaison Committee" to advise them on whether or not it should be renewed. The committee held eleven full meetings, met with Rabbi Steinberg several times, interviewed past officers of the congregation, and received testimony from over a hundred of its members via letters, phone calls, and personal interviews.

On the plus side, the committee reported: "Positive achievements have taken place during Rabbi Steinberg's tenure at Solomon Schechter in terms of increased religious observance, commitment, and involvement of members in programs of Jewish content." The report further stated: "Many members came forward in praise of Rabbi Steinberg's accomplishments in the religious and spiritual areas, his inspiration towards commitment and his exemplary standards for Jewish living. Even most of his critics spoke highly of his performance in these areas."

The negative side of the committee's report stated: "Critical comments centered primarily on inadequate performance in the pastoral area, leadership of staff, the Rabbi's relationship to individual congregants, attention to the School and Youth groups and involvement with the general community. Most of the Rabbi's staunchest supporters voiced these criticisms as well."

When the committee confronted Rabbi Steinberg with these criticisms, he conceded that the congregation was not being adequately served in some areas. The reason, he felt, was lack of time, and he indicated his willingness to give more attention to the leadership and supervision of the professional staff and the pastoral needs of congregants; to having direct contact with the youth and their programs, the Hebrew school and its students (including periodic classroom visits),* and Bar and Bat

---

* The problem of the Hebrew school was compounded by dropping enrollment. While a decline in Hebrew school enrollment was a nationwide phenomenon in the 1970's and was bound to affect Lakeville, the community continud to attract some young families, and in theory enrollment should not have dropped with the rapidity it did. It was claimed by some that enrollment had been hurt by the establishment of the Solomon Schechter Day School. However, the general feeling was that the Hebrew school of the Schechter Synagogue needed to be made more attractive and to do a better job of pupil-retention as well as of pupil-recruitment.

Mitzvah candidates and their parents; and to increasing his involvement with the general community.

Although Rabbi Steinberg indicated that an assistant rabbi was called for, the committee did not make such a recommendation. Rather, the committee's report stated: "[We] pointed out to the Rabbi numerous complaints by congregants which had no relationship to lack of time, particularly in the area of personal relationships and rigidity in the application of ritual custom."

The committee recommended that Rabbi Steinberg's contract be renewed, but that it be limited to a term of three rather than five years (the "Guide to Congregational Standards" of the United Synagogue suggests a five-year term at second reelection). In the committee's view, this arrangement would give Rabbi Steinberg ample opportunity to demonstrate if he could satisfy his critics, while at the same time not committing the congregation for an unreasonable period of time. The recommendation of the committee was accepted by the board, and Rabbi Steinberg agreed to sign a three-year contract.

What was responsible for the ambivalent attitude to Rabbi Steinberg? Perhaps the best clue was supplied by Rabbi Steinberg himself when he wrote in an article:

American Jewish history, sometimes divided into three periods—Sefardim, Ashkenazim, and East-European—is better divided into two: pre-1933 and post-1933. The pre-1933 immigration was made up, for the most part, of the ne'er-do-wells, misfits, failures, the jobless, the *am-ha-aratzim.* . . .

The second period of American Jewish history begins in 1933, when Hitler forced the immigration of those who would otherwise have never come. Let me give several examples. The Lubavitcher Rebbe emigrated and was the prime mover of the day school movement which thrives today. The Satmar, Bobover and Klausenberger rebbes emigrated and brought Hassidic fervor. Rabbi Joseph Soloveitchik emigrated and became the principal force in bringing intellectual and halachic vigor to the younger Orthodox rabbinate. Rabbi Breuer emigrated and re-established Frankfurt Orthodoxy. Rabbi Abraham Heschel emigrated and opened hidden treasures of mind and spirit.

What is notable about the spiritual leaders selected by Rabbi Steinberg is that most of them did not function as congregational rabbis, and that those who had congregations headed synagogues far different from a contemporary Conservative one. Furthermore, none of them recognized the authority of lay leaders. The majority were Hassidic *rebbeim* accustomed to the deference of disciples who viewed them as charismatic leaders whose authority was not to be questioned. If such men were his models, Rabbi Steinberg was bound to alienate those congregants accustomed to interacting with the usual type of Conservative rabbi.

Given his model of what a rabbi should be, Rabbi Steinberg did not take criticism easily. He had no choice but to listen to the strictures of the committee, but it is doubtful that he accepted the assumption on which the committee based its report—namely, that while in the Conservative movement the rabbi is the ultimate authority in matters of religious procedure and doctrine, the ultimate control of the synagogue resides in the board of directors.

Rabbi Steinberg's problems were compounded by the fact that he had little interest in synagogue administration—in performing the many tasks necessary to keeping a large institution running smoothly. He experienced great difficulty in relating to key members of his staff—which included an education director, a sexton, a youth director, an executive director, and a cantor—and turnover was considerable.

The manner in which Rabbi Steinberg conducted *rites de passage* also tended to add to the criticism. Perhaps the prime example was the funeral. While Rabbi Steinberg delivered the eulogy at the funeral service, he did not accompany the family to the graveside, but rather sent the cantor. (Distances to the cemeteries of the Lake City area are great, and the travel time is considerable.) The problem was compounded when Rabbi Steinberg made *shivah* calls. Many bereaved congregants complained that he said very little to them and that they did not derive any comfort from his presence.

There was also criticism of Rabbi Steinberg's behavior when he conducted rituals of a joyous character. For example, he did not follow the custom of including a short address to the bride and groom in the wedding ceremony, with the result that some brides and grooms and, especially, their parents felt that it had an impersonal character.

Much the same problem existed with Bar and Bat Mitzvahs. Parents conceived of these as peak religious experiences; a positive experience, they felt, would be crucial in determining their children's Jewish identity. They wanted Rabbi Steinberg to meet with their children prior to the ceremony, establish a relationship with them, and use the occasion to forge a bond which would survive the vicissitudes of the teen-age period and early adulthood. Rabbi Steinberg, however, felt it was the job of other members of the staff to prepare the children for the ceremony, that the Bar and Bat Mitzvah had been given far too much significance, and that everything possible should be done to downgrade the importance attached to the ritual.

Rabbi Steinberg did make some superficial changes but, given his conception of the model rabbi, he could not institute the kinds of changes which the committee believed were called for. Hence, when his three-year contract came up for renewal, controversy was even sharper than before. Attempts were made to avoid confrontation; Rabbi Steinberg was told that majority sentiment was against him and that it would not be in his best interest to press for renewal.

Rabbi Steinberg, however, was convinced that the majority of the congregation was on his side. Having a very heavy emotional investment in the Schechter Synagogue, he was determined to fight for the renewal of his contract. The board proceded to vote on the matter, and the rabbi was defeated by a 4-1 majority. However, the rabbi and his supporters insisted that the issue be submitted to a general vote of the congregation at the annual election of officers. The official slate of officers was committed to the nonrenewal of the rabbi's contract; an opposition slate was formed committed to renewal.

A committee supporting Rabbi Steinberg was organized called the "Committee for the Preservation of the Solomon Schechter Synagogue." It mounted an extensive mail and telephone campaign to win support for the rabbi. Supporters told how Rabbi Steinberg had deeply affected their lives and given them a Jewish commitment they had not achieved previously.

The controversy left deep scars, splitting trusted business associates, old friends who had grown up together in Lake City, and newer friends who had met in Lakeville. It divided neighbors as well as the parents of young people who were close friends. News of it spread through the Jewish community and from there to the general community. Suspicion was so deep on both sides that it was decided to hire one of the nation's largest accounting firms to supervise the election.

The election proved that the majority of the congregation wanted a new rabbi. The opposition slate was defeated and the official slate voted in by a 2–1 majority. Almost fifteen hundred ballots had been cast, or a total of 84 per cent of those qualified to vote. With the possible exception of Yom Kippur, a greater proportion of the congregation had participated in this particular activity than in any other single event in the synagogue year.

The new administration was confident that the synagogue would survive the trauma, but they proceeded very cautiously in naming a new rabbi. They decided to leave the post vacant for a year and to utilize local resources while they conducted a nationwide search for a new rabbi. With extraordinary thoroughness they interviewed dozens of likely candidates. What they were after was a rabbi who would be able to bind up the wounds left by the controversy. But on a deeper level what they seemed to want was the best of all possible worlds—a man who would combine the openness, friendliness, and accepting quality of a David Ginzberg with the religiosity and fervent commitment of a Joseph Steinberg.

What of Rabbi Steinberg? He decided to stay in the community rather than leave. His followers established another Conservative congregation in the area, and he became their rabbi. They initially signed up 125 families, including a number of individuals wealthy enough to sustain a congregation if they were willing to make such a commitment. According to a report in a Lake City newspaper, "the new synagogue . . . is likely to be small. Its rabbi and its founders, however, are willing to test the notion that 'small is beautiful.' Not to be despised, they believe, is a community filled with the 'beauty of holiness.' "

This episode at the Schechter Synagogue highlights the fact that, in Lakeville, congregational problems still have the power to move people. Furthermore, it appears that in a community like Lakeville the choice of rabbi is crucial. Apparently, one's relationship to the rabbi is a very important part of one's Jewishness, and one's child's relationship to the rabbi even more crucial than one's own.

The David Einhorn Temple

The David Einhorn Temple (see pp. 133–151) is the Classical Reform Temple formed in response to the shift of the Isaac Mayer Wise Temple from Classical Reform to Neo-Reform. As a consequence, Einhorn's program and rituals came to be patterned on the Reform Judaism of the nineteenth century. Members of other congregations were highly critical of Einhorn; they tended to look upon it as an inauthentic institution which deviated so sharply from normative Jewish practice that it was not in any true sense a Jewish congregation.

Today the Einhorn Temple is quite different from what it once was. While it has retained some features which link it to its Classical Reform past, in many respects it resembles other Reform temples in the area. In fact, it regularly cooperates with neighboring congregations. Whatever criticisms are still made by those outside the congregation, Einhorn is now accepted by the local Jewish community. Furthermore, the congregation not only is part of the local scene but has affiliated with the Union of American Hebrew Congregations. While initially Einhorn did not advertise its affiliation, all its current bulletins and publicity do so, and officers of the congregation attend the national conventions of the Union as well as its regional and metropolitan conclaves.

Einhorn's is the story of a decision: whether to carry its doctrines to their logical conclusion—in which case it would have to cut itself off from the Jewish community—or to modify them and seek to position itself somewhere within the Jewish consensus. Einhorn chose the second alternative. To provide a definitive explanation of why the first alternative was rejected and how the second took hold is beyond our present scope; a separate study of large-scale proportions would be required. All we can say here is that despite the ambiguities in its Jewish identity and its alienation from Jewish tradition, when a choice had to be made the congregation declared its solidarity with the Jewish community.

It is evident even to the casual observer that the congregation has a very special history. The link with the past is most evident in Einhorn's schedule of services. The main service is still held on Sunday morning; the congregation has not shifted to the traditional Sabbath. However, the pride felt about holding services on Sunday morning has lessened. It is also noticeable that the emphasis is on the service and that the importance attached to the sermon has diminished. Rabbi Edward Isaacs, who was the spiritual leader of Einhorn when the original study was done, has long since departed. Rabbi Mark Gross, who was the rabbi when we returned to study the congregation, does not commit his sermon to memory, or spend the major portion of the week preparing it, or have it printed and distributed as was the case during Rabbi Isaacs' tenure. Rabbi Gross is emphatic in stressing that the Sunday morning service is not a Sabbath service:

The congregation knows full well that the Jewish Sabbath is Friday evening to Saturday evening and that the Sunday morning service is not a Sabbath service. I was very emphatic about that when I first came here. It's a weekday service, and worshiping any day of the week is very much a part of Judaism. I mean, our Orthodox brethren worship every day of the week. Therefore, our service on Sunday morning is a regular weekday service. It makes it very difficult because most of our beautiful liturgical music is geared towards the Sabbath, but I do not infuse any of that music on the Sunday morning service because I do not want to give the impression that that's the Sabbath.

In a sense, a compromise has been arrived at. Whatever his own feelings, Rabbi Gross has agreed to continue the Sunday morning service, although designating it as a weekday service. At the same time, the congregation has preserved its tradition of holding a Sunday morning service, and it is evident that this is the prime religious activity of the week.*

Another point of continuity with the past is that the festivals of Sukkot, Pesach, and Shavuot continued to be celebrated on Sunday rather than on the day they occur according to the Jewish calendar. They are celebrated, however, in a more traditional manner than before.

While continuity has been preserved in two crucial areas, there are obvious changes, the most obvious being that the congregation is now housed in its own building and its activities all take place on its own premises. During its early period, the congregation was very firm in its resolve not to build (see pp. 142–144). This position was connected with ambiguities in Jewish identification; it was felt that a building would formalize the separation between Jew and Christian in Lakeville and was incompatible with full integration into the life of the community. Attitudes began to change in the 1960's. The decision to build, which crystallized in the late 1960's, was a fateful one: it meant that the congregation was committing itself to becoming an integral part of the Jewish community. We cannot reconstruct the many agonizing dicussions which must have occurred between husbands and wives, between old friends, and between acquaintances—discussions which surely took place in a variety of settings such as at home, at golf and city clubs, at

---

* In view of the size of the congregation, attendance is comparable to that of other congregations in the area, and there is a group of worshipers who come on a regular basis. As before, the service is preceded by a coffee hour.

dinner parties, and of course at various Temple meetings. The intensity of feeling is suggested by an article which appeared in the Temple's bulletin on the occasion of the retirement of Rabbi George Klein, who was the predecessor of Rabbi Gross. The article states that the congregation "agonized over" the question of whether to build or not to build:

It was during Rabbi Klein's active ministry that we embarked upon, agonized over, and finally undertook our long-awaited building program. As our Rabbi and leader Rabbi Klein cooperated fully in this difficult venture, rallying enthusiasm and support for a project which he knew, perhaps better than we, was indispensable to the viability and growth of our institution. During the long series of home meetings in 1968 and 1969, when the building project was introduced to our members, and at every available opportunity Rabbi Klein was in the forefront of those explaining the need and generating the interest which made the final result so successful.

There was of course no sentiment for building a cathedral to compete with the Isaac Mayer Wise Temple. On the other hand, while the structure which was erected is modest, it is sufficient for the needs of the two-hundred-fifty-family congregation. Perhaps its most distinguishing feature is that it originally had no distinguishing feature: several years later it was "discovered" that the building had no Jewish symbol. To relieve this embarrassment, a sculpture was commissioned to be hung on the facade. According to the Temple bulletin, the sculpture was designed to "blend together the ritual object of the Menorah and the Judaic concept of the Torah as a Tree of Life."

The Einhorn building has always had one unique feature: a flagpole displaying the Stars and Stripes. This was part of the original design, and the flag is flown daily. None of the other synagogues in the community has such a display. Einhorn is located near a major highway, and the flag is evident to those who drive past. It constitutes a graphic example of the anxieties aroused by the decision to build. Apparently it reassures those who felt threatened—who feared that erecting a building was tantamount to disloyalty to the ideals for which the congregation stood and, furthermore, would undermine the status of Jews in the community-at-large.

Even with its new building, the Einhorn Temple remains a fairly small congregation. During its Classical Reform period, it suffered an exodus of those who felt that the congregation was too doctrinaire, that it had committed itself to an anti-Zionist posture more appropriate to an ideological organization such as the American Council of Judaism than a synagogue.

Einhorn realizes that it must recruit new families if it is to maintain itself. In its earlier days, the congregation was hesitant in soliciting members, concerned about the danger of accepting individuals who might not conform to its ideology. Now it has a membership committee, and members are encouraged to approach neighbors, business associates, and new residents who might be interested in joining a congregation. Efforts are made to orient new members to the congregation's ideology by acquainting them with Einhorn's "Statement of Principles" (see pp. 147–148).

As with American synagogues generally, Rosh Hashanah and Yom Kippur are the high points of Einhorn's religious year. Attendance is high for the evening service on Rosh Hashanah and for the Kol Nidre service on Yom Kippur; these services must be held in two shifts to accommodate all who wish to attend. However, on Rosh Hashanah morning and during the day on Yom Kippur a single shift suffices.

In addition to the High Holiday, Festival, and Sunday morning services, there is a brief "Sabbath Vesper Service" on Friday evening. There is no sermon, and music is confined to congregational singing without the assistance of a professional. It will be recalled that Rabbi Isaacs had a late Friday afternoon service which was conducted in a clandestine manner (see p. 140). The "Sabbath Vesper Service," on the other hand, is announced on the front page of each bulletin. In fact, during the summer the "Sabbath Vesper Service" is the congregation's only service inasmuch as Sunday morning services are concluded in May and resume in September. Attendance is generally poor, but Rabbi Gross has refused to become discouraged:

> Since I have been here, there has been a Friday evening service every Friday night. This service is the very fiber and heart of Judaism, but it's still a relatively new concept here at Einhorn. Attendance has been very small—many rabbis, I suppose, would call it discouraging. I have not. I would say that, since I've been here, maybe on half a dozen occasions I've struck out—that means I've had nobody but myself. On all other occasions we've had two couples, three, and as many as six or seven.

The Temple's religious school has undergone considerable change. Formerly, the school sought to indoctrinate the ideology of Classical

Reform Judaism rather than to provide a rudimentary knowledge of the Bible, Jewish history, and Jewish religious thought and practice. Teachers were carefully selected to reflect the ideological position of Classical Reform, and more especially its anti-Zionist stance. According to Rabbi Gross, teachers now come from a variety of backgrounds. Skill at teaching is the prime requirement. Teachers with anti-Zionist sentiments are not acceptable:

> All of our teachers are what I would call professional. By that I mean all of them, at one time or presently, are secular school teachers and hold teaching certificates. Their backgrounds vary from Conservative to Liberal Reform. Their ideologies vary from very-positively-pro-Israel to pro-Israel. . . . I would say that none of them on my staff at the present moment are what one would call anti-Israel. I wouldn't want that on my staff. Israel is an integral part of the total community of Jewry.

The sectarian stance has gradually eroded away and the emphasis is on exposing the students to the full range of Jewish life. According to Rabbi Gross:

> The kids are exposed to everything. I have one teacher who is teaching various aspects of Judaism, and who several weeks ago exposed the kids, not simply academically but in reality though it wasn't at the right time, to a Havdalah Service. I am trying in my Confirmation Class to expose the students to the breadth of Judaism, whether it be a Reform concept, a Classical Reform concept, a Conservative concept, or an Orthodox concept. It's part of the whole matrix of Judaism, and they should know what it is. They should have the total picture as to what it is so that they're comfortable within the Jewish community. If they walk into a traditional congregation they should have some idea as to what's going on—of what's happening when the Torah's read, *aliyot, kipah, tallit,* the hazzan, and all of the other things there.

Mid-week Hebrew classes, which meet for one hour per week, have also been introduced. Conversational Hebrew is avoided: the emphasis, congruent with the trend at Sunday morning services toward introducing additional prayers recited in Hebrew, is on what is called "Prayer Study Hebrew." However, the most remarkable aspect of the Hebrew program is that it has been the occasion for the introduction of a type of quasi-Bar Mitzvah. As stated in the bulletin, "After a three year period of study, a student may prepare for and participate in a Torah Service at one of our Sunday morning Services." This is called a "Ben Torah Service."

Originally, the Einhorn Temple had opposed the formation of a youth group. It reluctantly agreed only when the parents of post-Confirmants pointed out that their children had no connection with the Temple—a situation which presumably would ultimately lead to intermarriage. The current approach is quite different—the youth group is considered an integral part of the congregation's program, with a professional advisor and a program having a noticeable amount of Jewish content. The only remnant of the old ambiguity is the fact that the group has not joined the Reform movement's national association, the National Federation of Temple Youth.

The congregation does not sponsor its own program of adult Jewish education but has joined a number of other congregations in the area in presenting a cooperative one. The rabbi has a study group composed of about a dozen couples.

The Classical Reform ideology originally espoused at Einhorn precluded the formation of social groups. The principle was that Jewish association should be limited to worship and religious study. However, some years ago, in addition to the youth group a Sisterhood was formed. Called the "Women's Association," it offers social and cultural activities which parallel those of similar groups. Einhorn's group even includes an activity characteristic of such groups during the last decade: a weight-loss club. In 1975 the Women's Association presented its first theatrical, entitled "Marriage Makes the World Go Round." Although strictly an amateur effort, the show uncovered some talented writers and performers among the members of the Association. It generated a great deal of excitement, and attendance was larger than at any other congregational event with the exception of High Holiday services. The Couples Club, composed of younger women and their husbands, is another departure from the conceptions which animated the original founders.

The congregation does not have a committee devoted to pro-Israel activities. However, in times of emergency it has declared its solidarity with Israel; there was fund-raising during the Yom Kippur War. According to an article which appeared in the Temple bulletin in 1973:

> On the eve of Succos, over one hundred members of our Congregation gathered in the sanctuary to usher in the Festival of the Ingathering and, at the same time, express their concern for the plight of their fellow Jews in Israel. Every worshipper brought with him his hopes and prayers for a speedy end to the war raging in the Middle East. We found ourselves bound together by the invisible thread that has ever linked Jew to Jew.

. . . It is this binding force burning within the breast of every Jew that enabled us to share the bounties of our harvest with our brethren in Israel. To this date, we have joined hands and contributed over $36,000 to aid in the struggle for peace and freedom.

Perhaps of equal importance is the fact that pro-Israel activities of a general rather than an emergency nature are slowly being integrated into the Temple's program. For example, congregants are urged to celebrate Hamisha Asar B'Shevat by planting a tree in Israel, and the address of the local office of the Jewish National Fund is publicized in the Temple bulletin.

If measured against the most active synagogue programs in the Lakeville area, the Einhorn Temple's program of services, Jewish education, and club activities is minimal. However, measured against the congregation's own early history and the conceptions of its founders, the program is maximalist. Einhorn's membership in the Union of American Hebrew Congregations and its desire for legitimation as one of the congregations of Lakeville indicate that, while assimilation has proceeded on an individual basis, it has not occurred on an organized level. Furthermore, despite its distance from highly committed segments of the Jewish community, Einhorn has been affected by anxieties about Jewish survival. Its response has been to choose rabbis with much firmer convictions about the necessity of Jewish survival than Rabbi Isaacs evinced, and to support such rabbis as they have gradually moved the congregation away from the conceptions of Classical Reform Judaism.

The Kaufman Kohler Temple

Kaufman Kohler is one of the newer religious institutions on the Heights. The founders of Kohler were almost entirely German-Jewish in ancestry. Many were from families which had been affiliated with the Holdheim Temple in Lake City. When they settled on the Heights, they joined the Einhorn Temple but soon found themselves uncomfortable there. Rabbi Isaacs' ideological rigidity and lack of sympathy with anything which did not conform to his extreme interpretation of Classical Reform irritated them. They believed not only that Israel should be a place of refuge for those who wished to go there but also that they had a responsibility to maintain the right of Jews to an independent state. Thus, they were critical of Einhorn's lingering connection with the American Council for Judaism and of the anti-Zionism which that organization espoused.

The founders of Kohler considered themselves to be Reform Jews of the Classical variety, but they were unhappy in the highly-charged sectarian atmosphere of the Einhorn Temple. In 1969 they resolved to start their own congregation, in a more central location than Einhorn, so as to attract families from all parts of the Heights.

The most pressing problem was a Sunday School for the children. This had been one of their prime reasons for affiliating with Einhorn, and accordingly one was quickly organized. They also began to hold weekly religious services and, given their Classical Reform upbringing, they chose Sunday morning as the time. They engaged a retired rabbi to serve the congregation on a temporary basis, and utilized rented facilities while looking forward to the time when they would have their own building.

As the congregation grew, they felt ready to make long-term commitments. They selected Rabbi Albert Levine as their spiritual leader. Rabbi Levine was middle-aged and had served the same synagogue for most of his rabbinical career. The main attraction of the new post was the challenge it presented. His former congregation was a long-established one located in a small city where the Jewish population was very stable and where both Jews and Gentiles were set in their ways.

Rabbi Levine did not like labels such as "Classical Reform" or "Neo-Reform." He maintained that there was one entity—Reform Judaism. In his view, Reform Judaism changed over time and was capable of a variety of interpretations. He maintained, however, that the traditional Sabbath was one thing that could not be discarded, and while quite agreeable to a Sunday morning service, he insisted that there be a Friday evening service as well. The board was not enthusiastic but agreed to go along.

Rabbi Levine first turned his attention to the Sunday School. He found the curriculum weak, unchallenging, and overly centered on Bible stories, failing to convey a sense of the history of the Jewish people to the young. The revamped curriculum he proposed was accepted without dissension, and the school attracted new students each year and was soon a major undertaking.

The Friday evening service did not meet with the same enthusiastic reception. In fact, on some Sabbaths Rabbi Levine was the only worshiper. He informed the Temple's board of directors that if he was interested in personal prayer, he did not need to hold a service. He stressed that he had taken the position with the understanding that there would be a Friday evening service. The board agreed that they owed him the obligation to support the Friday evening service and promised that they would recruit at least a minimum number of worshipers.

The burgeoning activities and the growing membership of the congregation stimulated the need for permanent quarters. A successful building-fund campaign was held with some assistance from a professional fund-raiser. A mortgage was arranged to cover the balance as well as to provide funds until pledges which were to be paid in annual installments were fulfilled. Some financial difficulties were experienced as a result of the Yom Kippur War—congregants gave substantial amounts of cash to the local Federation for the emergency needs of Israel and consequently delayed payment of pledges. But the 375-family congregation managed to cope with the problem, and there was a heightened emphasis on fund-raising after 1973. Some older members looked back with nostalgia to the time when congregational expenses were minimal and budget surpluses common.

Considering its Classical Reform heritage, the Kohler Temple moved very rapidly into the mainstream of contemporary Reform Judaism. Although the Sunday morning service is the best-attended service of the week and Festival services are held on Sunday morning rather than on the date indicated by the Hebrew calendar, the congregation bears many similarities to the typical Reform congregation. Soon after Kohler was organized it joined the Union of American Hebrew Congregations, and it takes part in many Union activities.

Perhaps the best illustration of the mainstream trend of the Kohler Temple is its activities on behalf of Israel. While fund-raising for Israel at Einhorn during the Yom Kippur War was very low-key, at Kohler several rallies were held and their purpose was made explicit. In 1977 the congregation sponsored its first tour of Israel and participated in the march sponsored by the local Federation in observance of Israel Independence Day. The wide variety of trips, study tours, and service projects in Israel sponsored by the National Federation of Temple Youth is extensively publicized in the Temple's bulletin. The bulletin has also carried articles about the scholarships offered by the Federation to young people who want to spend a summer in Israel.

Another bit of evidence of the congregation's desire to integrate itself into mainline Reform as well as into the larger Jewish community is the relationship it has sought to establish with elderly Jews who still live in what was at one time a flourishing Jewish neighborhood in Lake City. The congregation has joined with other groups to provide them with assistance, bringing them to the Temple for luncheon and an afternoon of entertainment. Care is taken that only kosher food is served, and the menu also includes Jewish delicacies such as lox. One elderly woman commented that it had been several years since she had eaten lox; her budget did not permit the purchase of such expensive food.

For its own constituency, Kohler plans social events which have as their purpose both raising funds and increasing congregational cohesion. As the Temple has grown, what was once an almost exclusively German Jewish group has become a mixed congregation composed of East European Jews as well as German Jews. Despite such diversity, Kohler has not suffered the rifts experienced by the Isaac Mayer Wise Temple. The lack of polarization is perhaps best illustrated by a fund-raising event the congregation sponsored several years ago, "An Evening with Sam Levenson." The publicity stated: "Sam Levenson is a humorist in the purest sense of the word. His stories have their roots in experiences common to us all. His stories are about the family, about education, religion . . . things that touch all of us every day." Levenson grew up on the Lower East Side of New York City and is the offspring of foreign-born East European parents. Many of his stories trace back to his childhood. Despite their difference in upbringing, the old-line German Jewish element in the congregation supported the event.

The social groups at the congregation include a Sisterhood and a youth group. The youth group has its own lounge, and considerable effort goes into providing it with adequate facilities. There is also an emphasis on contact with other Jewish youth groups. For example, several years ago the youth group, with the help of adults in the congregation, acted as hosts for four days to a group of youngsters from a congregation in Mexico City.

The movement away from Classical Reform has not proceeded quite as smoothly as appears on the surface. When East European Jews joined the congregation in substantial numbers, a desire for Bar Mitzvah emerged. The board was unsure of how to proceed. It had agreed to add Hebrew classes one afternoon a week, but it had not thought through the question of Bar Mitzvah. On the one hand, it felt that a declaration in favor of Bar Mitzvah would push it solidly into the Neo-Reform camp and might ultimately detract from Confirmation. On the other hand, it did not want to alienate members who wanted a Bar or Bat Mitzvah for their children.

The matter was placed in Rabbi Levine's hands. In addition to a stipulation that the child must attend Hebrew school for three years, Rabbi Levine added requirements which included attendance at a stipulated number of religious services per year, writing book reports on volumes of Jewish interest, doing social-service projects, and attending services at a Conservative and an Orthodox synagogue. He even required attendance at services in a Protestant or Catholic church. His approach meant that if a family wanted to have a Bar or Bat Mitzvah, both the youngster and the parents would have to provide evidence of a special commitment. The board approved his plan. The congregation does not hold a public service on Saturday morning, but when there is a Bar or Bat Mitzvah a private service is held, to which the family and their guests are invited.

Rabbi Levine has retired. His successor appears to be moving the congregation further along the path he initiated. Adult education activities have been intensified, and increasing stress is being placed on Sabbath observance. A recent innovation has been a Saturday afternoon program culminating in *havdalah* (the ceremony marking the end of the Sabbath and the start of a new week). The ceremony highlights how the congregation has avoided sectarianism and moved with considerable rapidity into the mainstream of Reform Judaism.

The Samuel Hirsch Temple

The Samuel Hirsch Temple, the so-called "thinking man's congregation," is less distinctive today than when we originally studied it (see pp. 151–162). At that time, the attitude of the congregation was that it should not get involved in an "edifice complex," but should rent space in public or private buildings to accommodate its various activities (see

p. 160). As the years passed and activities increased, the arrangement proved increasingly unworkable.

After much soul-searching, the congregation came to the reluctant conclusion that it would have to erect a synagogue building. The structure was deliberately designed to be low-keyed and unimpressive. But in their eagerness to avoid the accusation of having an "edifice complex," the building committee failed to realize that the projected building's size was inadequate to the needs of a suburban congregation. As a result, space—particularly classroom space for the Sunday School—is at a premium in the new building. Classes must be scheduled on Saturday morning and Sunday afternoon, as well as Sunday morning, in order to accommodate all the students.

The Hirsch Temple experienced a crisis in the late 1960's, when Rabbi Samuel Aaron resigned. Rabbi Aaron was the congregation's first and only spiritual leader. He was chosen after the Hirsch Temple had failed to lure Rabbi Abraham Lubin to Lakeville from his congregation in Lake City (see pp. 151–153). Rabbi Aaron proved to be a happy choice. A devoted circle of admirers grew up around him, and he seemed to embody all the qualities which the Hirsch Temple stood for.

While affection for Rabbi Aaron increased as the years passed, his own contentment diminished. He wrote and lectured widely, and he no longer wished to be tied to a congregation. It was not that Hirsch was too small; he himself felt that congregations should be small in size and personal in approach. Even if he served a much larger congregation, his chances for the national exposure he desired would be limited.

Rabbi Aaron was active in Jewish communal affairs in Lake City as well as in liberal and radical politics. He sought to challenge the local Jewish establishment over the issue of the low wages paid to service personnel (most of whom were black) who worked at the leading Jewish hospital of Lake City. Thus he was widely known locally. However, for all intents and purposes Rabbi Aaron was just another suburban rabbi, albeit one of great talent, strong convictions, and radical opinions.

When the campus revolution started and when protests against the involvement of the United States in Vietnam mounted, Rabbi Aaron felt that if he remained at the Hirsch Temple his fate would be sealed; he would lose his last chance to move beyond the confines of being a congregational rabbi. Since the campus was where the action was, he sought a post as a Jewish chaplain. After some frustrating negotiations, he succeeded in locating a position at a first-class university whose Christian chaplains were noted for their radicalism and for their support of the campus revolution.

Rabbi Aaron's resignation angered some of the leaders of the Hirsch Temple. They felt that they had committed themselves to the congregation on the strength of his being the rabbi. Other members were more worried than angry. They feared that the congregation might not be able to discover a suitable replacement and would inevitably lose its unique character. And there were some who did not approve of Rabbi Aaron's radicalism and who were relieved by his resignation.

The congregation moved very cautiously and named an interim rabbi. Then, after considerable deliberation, Rabbi Ralph Berkowitz was chosen as the new spiritual leader. Rabbi Berkowitz's approach to Judaism is much the same as that of Rabbi Aaron. He is not as scintilating a personality, but the congregation has weathered the transition. There was every reason why it should; the Hirsch Temple was a going concern, with regular services, a large religious school, a very attractive program of adult Jewish study, and a building. The congregation has had no trouble maintaining its maximum membership, which was set at 500 families. There is a waiting list and no need for membership campaigns.

As before, Hirsch's worship program centers around the Friday evening service. However, emphasis has shifted somewhat from the preparation of original services to the role of the performing arts and more particularly to the introduction of new music into the service. Special services are held on various occasions; the congregation's Shoah service commemorating the Holocaust has become an annual event.

The Saturday morning service is a new feature of the worship program. This service has several significant features: it is more traditional than the Friday evening service, the use of Hebrew is emphasized, and it is entirely conducted by lay people. To see a man wearing a *kipah* is not unusual. The service, which is brief, is preceded by a study session which runs for one-and-a-half hours.

The congregation has sought to continue its stress on participation in Jewish study for every age-group. The emphasis on study is highlighted by the continued refusal to establish a Sisterhood or Brotherhood, despite periodic efforts of some congregants to win support for the formation of such groups. However, the congregation does sanction a youth group, with an active program of social activities.

Many members consider their Sunday School to be highly innovative. Indeed, many of them believe that Hirsch has the best such school on the Heights. Several years ago, in a surprise move, the congregation hired the principal of Lilienthal's Sunday School, leaving that institution to fend for itself.

When we first studied the Hirsch Temple, those who had taken mid-week Hebrew classes could have a Bar Mitzvah, though Rabbi Aaron made no secret of his distaste for the ceremony (see p. 156).

The congregation now has a two-day-a-week Hebrew school and places a good deal of emphasis on enrolling a small but dedicated group of students, but Bar Mitzvah has been abolished. The congregation was very proud of its decision. In the minds of those who pushed for its abolition, Bar Mitzvah stood for vulgarity, ostentation, and a mindless Judaism which emphasized lavish display rather than true religiosity. In addition, Rabbi Aaron always emphasized that Bar Mitzvah comes at the onset of adolescence, when young people are unprepared both psychologically and intellectually to cope with the demands he believed were inherent in the ceremony. Rabbi Berkowitz feels much the same way:

> What Bar Mitzvah does for the child is disastrous. A thirteen-year-old is not an adult. The Bar Mitzvah is ludicrous, and the implications for both the child and Judaism are often catastrophic.
>
> Judaism is reduced to the ability to read from the Torah. The sense of Mitzvah is neglected. The child is expected to display knowledge and linguistic skills. He is not expected to display commitment. Nor is a thirteen-year-old capable of doing so.

Families who still insist on a Bar Mitzvah are allowed to hold a private ceremony at the Temple. The ceremony is not announced in the Temple Bulletin, and it is understood that the congregation takes no responsibility in the matter.

In recent years, the Hirsch Temple has been seeking a substitute for the Bar Mitzvah. It is experimenting with what it calls the "Shomer Ha-Torah" ceremony. This ceremony would coincide with graduation from high school (or some later point in the life cycle) and would involve meeting a series of requirements, including regular attendance at religious services and "a personal prayer or brief statement of commitment to Judaism."

The program of adult Jewish studies includes courses co-sponsored with congregations in the area as well as Hirsch's own courses. The tradition of avoiding the use of outside speakers as much as possible is continued; the *Lehrhaus* idea obviously inspires much of Hirsch's continuing efforts in the area of adult Jewish learning. Because of the larger number of people able to handle simple Hebrew texts, courses based upon such texts have been introduced in recent years. There are also courses which tie in with trends in the general culture. For example, a course on "Transactional Analysis in Judaism" was introduced several years ago. Other new features of Hirsch's educational program include courses for college students during the summer and courses for a variety of age-groups on Saturday afternoon.

While the stress on social action was not very evident when we originally studied the Hirsch Temple (indeed, as noted on p. 152, one observer felt that the decay in liberal and radical politics which occurred during and after World War II motivated the affiliation of a substantial number of the congregation's members), Rabbi Aaron began to place great emphasis on social action, and the congregation was soon involved in a variety of causes: Vietnam, unionization of farm workers, and especially racial integration and civil rights. People in other congregations viewed these activities—particularly the support of racial integration— quite cynically. They pointed out that Hirsch was established by those who had left Lake City when blacks moved into their neighborhoods.

After Vietnam and after the peak of the civil rights struggle, the emphasis upon social action diminished considerably. Attention was focused on Jewish concerns such as support of Israel, the right of free emigration for Soviet Jews, and assistance to poor, elderly Jews in Lake City. Rabbi Berkowitz feels that the institution should seek a more even balance between its Jewish and its general concerns:

> Our social action thrust, while still present, seems to me to have diminished. And that seems to be true all over the country. There seems to be a pulling away from involvement in the affairs of others and a deeper concentration in the affairs of our own community. There is greater concern for Israel than ever before. We have sponsored two congregational trips within the past two years to Israel. We have a program to send our children to Israel when they've completed their Hebrew education. We have a great deal of emphasis on fund-raising for Israel.

The social action program which has survived is non-political in orientation. Rather, it focuses on acquainting Hirsch youngsters with black youngsters, having blacks and Jews encounter each other in non-stereotypic situations, and providing black children with remedial instruction. According to Rabbi Berkowitz:

The congregation has an ongoing relationship with St. Mary's Parish, a black Catholic church, where we've had a most meaningful exchange. Their youngsters will come out and use our playground, and we will provide teachers and staff for them at the playground program. We had a joint picnic with them. We've had meetings between the two groups, both at their church in the inner city and out here. Their children came out and presented a musical for us one Shabbat. Also, instead of a regular service one Shabbat, we had their people come out and entertain us with a show showing the development of black culture. So we've had that ongoing, and we've had some tutorial work going where some of the members of our congregation have gone into the city to teach and to work with reading skills.

Although the Hirsch Temple is still different from other congregations in the area, it has lost some of the sense of excitement which characterized its early years. The Hirsch Temple is not as unique as it once was. Indeed the recent publication of new prayer books and a new Haggadah by the Reform movement means that even staid congregations are becoming "experimental." Rabbi Berkowitz accurately reflected Hirsch's present mood when he said:

> Today I think that many of the things the congregation set out to do have been achieved, that many of the congregations in the area have adopted the vision that this congregation has had. That's partly the result of national and international events, but it's also partly the result of the presence in this community of a congregation like Hirsch. At the beginning, there was a feeling on the part of the small group that were active in this congregation that they were really achieving something and part of something. Today I think there is still the feeling that we are a unique congregation, but the pioneering aspects have been replaced by the sense of a need for an ongoing commitment. . . .
>
> Also, the congregation has become bifurcated in its interest. There are so many things going on that people don't feel part of the unity so much anymore. They feel part of the specific activity in which they are involved.

The Max Lilienthal Temple

At the time of our original study, the Max Lilienthal Temple was the weakest synagogue in Lakeville (see pp. 162–166). The prognosis for its survival was guarded. It had sought to merge with other congregations but none was interested.

In the intervening years, Lilienthal has emerged as one of the more prominent congregations in the area. It has had to limit its membership (it set the figure at 500 families). It has also discontinued membership drives, since it has a substantial waiting list.

What accounts for the congregation's success? As with all the other congregations, the fact that it provides a Jewish education for children is crucial. But, in addition, Lilienthal is the best exemplification of the Neo-Reform position in Lakeville. As the most traditional Reform temple in the area, it has benefited from the influx of couples reared in the heavily Jewish areas of Lake City, who have had some contact with traditional Judaism but prefer the latitudinarianism of Reform Judaism. When they settled in Lakeville, such couples were wary of joining a Conservative congregation lest they be expected, either by others or by their own conscience, to follow a traditional regimen.

Lilienthal's position as the most conservative of the Reform congregations is underscored by the fact that it has served as a haven for disaffected members of the Solomon Schechter Synagogue. In fact, Lilienthal's spiritual leader, Rabbi Joshua Cohen, began to wear a *kipah* during services when he noticed that families from Schechter were coming to his synagogue. He believed that his wearing the *kipah* (which congregants are free to wear as well) would ease the transition from Schechter to Lilienthal. While there are some instances where families from Lilienthal have joined Schechter, the predominant movement has been in the other direction.

Rabbi Cohen remains an asset, just as when he first came to the once-struggling congregation. His Orthodox background, his Talmudic education, and his racy Yiddish give congregants a feeling of nostalgia without burdening them with guilt feelings. When he first became the rabbi of the Lilienthal Temple, he was still a comparatively young man; over the years, his presence has given Lilienthal a continuity absent at the other congregations. Rabbi Cohen is in fact the senior rabbi in the area.

Other factors have played a role in Lilienthal's rise. The type of young family the congregation originally attracted has prospered financially in the intervening years. Those who did not left Lakeville, while those who remained rose in business or in the professions either by dint of their own efforts or because of family connections. New members have tended to be more prosperous than were the original families at the time when the congregation was formed; it became increasingly evident to Lake City Jews on the move that those in modest circumstances would find it difficult to make their way in Lakeville. The congregation has elicited financial support and in 1967, after a successful fund-raising drive, was able to erect its own building. One of the reasons for limiting membership is that its facilities were constructed to serve a smaller membership than it now has.

While Lilienthal is the most traditional Reform Temple in Lakeville, it has not made a serious attempt to alter the life-style of its members. Unlike the Schechter synagogue, it has not mounted campaigns for *sukkah*-building or for the observance of the Sabbath. Rather, it has sought to serve the felt religious needs of its membership.

The most obvious such need has been that of Jewish education for the young. The congregation conducts a nursery school, a Sunday school, and a Hebrew school that meets two afternoons a week. Unlike the staffs of other congregations, which have tried to avoid using Israelis as Hebrew teachers, most of Lilienthal's staff are Israelis.

But perhaps even more important to its members is that, instead of tolerating Bar and Bat Mitzvah, Lilienthal goes to great lengths to encourage the ceremony. The Saturday morning service is entirely centered on it. The child conducts the service from start to finish—only during the recitation of the mourner's Kaddish, which is conducted by Rabbi Cohen, is the spotlight off the child. Saturday morning services are brief and begin at 12 noon so that they can be followed with a luncheon. When there are two children having a Bar or Bat Mitzvah, it is not unusual for the congregation to schedule two services, one at 9:30 or 10:00 A.M. and the other at noon. On those few Saturdays during the active congregational year when no Bar or Bat Mitzvah is scheduled, the Sabbath morning service is canceled. One of the requirements of Bar or Bat Mitzvah is that the youngster remain for Confirmation; Rabbi Cohen has been successful in maintaining this requirement.

Lilienthal has also given a good deal of attention to *rites de passage* of a sad nature. It emphasizes the observance of *Yahrzeit* and, more particularly, the purchase of memorial tablets in the Temple. An article in the Temple bulletin puts the matter as follows:

> To keep alive the precious memory of our beloved departed is a sacred rite in Jewish tradition. A hallowed atmosphere permeates our House of God. One can choose no finer medium of perpetuating the memory of our dear ones than by inscribing their names in the sacred edifice on our beautiful Bronze Yahrzeit Memorial Tablet.

The Memorial Tablet in our Temple constitutes a permanent record of the names of men and women departed from this earth, yet cherished by surviving relatives and friends. Each individual bronze plaque is lighted on the Sabbath Eve and Sabbath Morning Services of the week of the Yahrzeit and at Memorial Services. In addition, the name of the departed is mentioned at the Kaddish Prayer during Yahrzeit week and published in the Temple Bulletin. A Yahrzeit reminder card is also sent to the family. Thus our beloved departed are never forgotten.

Lilienthal recently embarked on an even more ambitious project, offering to arrange funerals for deceased members of families affiliated with the congregation. The funeral and all associated expenses are paid for by the congregation—no charge is made to the family. According to Rabbi Cohen:

> . . . with all these changes taking place, what do you still have at a synagogue? A Bar Mitzvah and a wedding and that's it, fellow. So I started to take an interest and started to speak to my congregants, and my president who is a marvelous guy and a young millionaire said to me, "Rabbi, why don't we look into this funeral business?" We looked around and around, and we finally came up with a plan for the entire congregation. The funeral is held in my sanctuary, every box is a beautiful box, a mahogany-stained oak box. And every box is covered with a beautiful velvet thing with a menorah on it.
>
> Everyone who dies, we have a separate memorial fund set up in the name of the deceased. The money goes to the congregation to pay off the funeral costs of our old members—one hand washes the other. It pays for itself. We are making money, because I'll tell you what else happens. When a man dies, his friends and relatives will call up the office and say: "I want to make a contribution, who shall I make it out to?" Right now we're making a profit.
>
> I can't get the temples here to respond to this idea. I say the temple and the rabbi should reacquire all of the emotions that used to go to the funeral director. It's a real *mitzvah*.

Although the funeral is held in the congregation's sanctuary, all arrangements are made by a local funeral home which has agreed to handle them for a set fee much lower than that charged for regular funerals. This special fee made the project possible, helped by the donation of a Lilienthal member who was impressed with the plan and gave $5,000 to cover the costs of the initial funerals.

One of the advantages of Rabbi Cohen's plan is that it does not call for the active involvement of members of the congregation in preparing the body for burial. All necessary steps are taken care of by the funeral director and his staff, in cooperation with the Chevra Kadisha (Jewish burial society) of Lake City. It is too early to assess how many members will avail themselves of the plan and whether it will constitute a substantial force binding families closer to the congregation and to its rabbi, but the intent is clear.

Under Rabbi Cohen's direction, the synagogue has pioneered in other directions as well. For example, Rabbi Cohen believes that going to Israel once or twice in a lifetime is insufficient. In order to encourage congregants to go as a family at periodic intervals, he interested them in renting an apartment in Jerusalem. The apartment is available to congregants without charge, and they are encouraged to stay for a three-week period. He even succeeded in interesting the mayor's office in Jerusalem in the project. The trip is designed for those who have been in Israel before and are ready for the more intensive exposure to Israeli life that the very fact of living in an apartment rather than in the sheltered environment of a hotel provides.

In many aspects of its program, Lilienthal follows the usual pattern of Neo-Reform congregations. Its most active social group is the Sisterhood. Most of the courses in adult Jewish education are offered in cooperation with neighboring congregations. The main weekly service is held on Friday night. The regular group of worshipers is rather small, although attendance is larger at services held in honor of special occasions, when noted guests address the congregation, or when a Bat Mitzvah is held (some families prefer a Friday evening Bat Mitzvah to a Saturday morning one). Rabbi Cohen is convinced that little can be done to improve attendance at services, and his conviction in this matter has undoubtedly played a part in his seeking out other avenues to building congregational participation and loyalty.

Despite the traditionalism of Lilienthal, attendance at the High Holidays follows the pattern observable in other congregations. Two services are held on the evening of Rosh Hashanah, but only one is necessary during the day. The same is true for Yom Kippur; two services are held on Kol Nidre eve but only one on Yom Kippur day. The congregation also holds a *s'lichot* service on the Saturday night before Rosh Hashanah.

All the congregations on the Heights have a certain amount of turnover. Since a certain percentage of families are motivated to join a synagogue for a specific purpose, such as to have a Bar Mitzvah or a Confirmation, some will fail to renew their membership once the ceremony has been completed. Given its emphasis on serving the felt religious needs of families, the tendency to resign after such a ceremony is somewhat more pronounced at Lilienthal than at the other Reform congregations. Resignations are taken for granted; the congregation has been able to sustain itself by drawing on the large reservoir of unaffiliated families interested in what it offers. Because Lilienthal has improved its status position and does not have to contend with another congregation of the same ideological stance, its future now seems as secure as that of the other congregations in the area.

A Final Word

There is much that remains to be studied about the Jews of Lakeville. We have analyzed all the synagogues located there as well as several located in neighboring areas which draw heavily on Lakeville, but there are Lakeville Jews who belong to other synagogues. Perhaps the most striking is a small congregation devoted to "Humanistic Judaism," which is to be found in a suburb adjacent to Lakeville. The term "God" is not mentioned in any of the five principles espoused by this congregation, two of which are: "The major source of the solutions for man's problems lies within man," and "The most efficient method for the discovery of truth is the scientific (empirical) method."

Several new Jewish institutions have been established in the Lakeville area. They include a branch of the Jewish family service agency of Lake City (the establishment of the branch is not unconnected with the growth of problems within the Jewish family), as well as a small branch of the Lake City Jewish community center. Lakeville also now has a larger number of Jewish organizations than before, many of them women's organizations. They include chapters of B'nai B'rith, B'nai B'rith Women, the National Women's Committee of Brandeis University, Hadassah, the National Council of Jewish Women, Women's American ORT, and Pioneer Women. In addition, Lakeville Jews belong to organizations located in Lake City, as well as to national Jewish agencies which do not have local chapters.

It should also be pointed out that, at present, Jewish life in Lakeville is not confined to the private sphere. In the early 1970's, a group of rabbis, Jewish educators, and parents felt that Hebrew should be offered as a foreign language in the Lakeville High School. Since Italian was already in the curriculum, there was a precedent for adding Hebrew, and in 1972–73 the first Hebrew course was offered. The principal of the high school supported the program although he feared that so many Jewish students would take Hebrew instead of French and Spanish that he would be left with surplus faculty. His fears were not realized, however. A full-time Hebrew teacher was hired in 1973–74, and the school now offers four years of the language, but the demand has not escalated to the point where a second or third teacher is required.

Another manifestation of Jewishness in the public sphere is that schools are now closed on the High Holidays in several school districts. However, the initiative in this matter seems to have come from school officials, who concluded that it was of no educational benefit to hold classes when only a handful of children were in attendance and substitute teachers had to be recruited.

In our analysis of the Lakeville synagogues on the institutional level, the subject of attitudes toward Israel has occurred at numerous points. The response of Lakeville Jews to the Six-Day War of 1967 has been presented in a separate publication.* Our investigation, conducted in 1968, indicated a strong feeling of solidarity with Israel. The response to the Yom Kippur War of 1973 was even more intense. In 1973 the question we had asked when we collected our original data in 1957–58 —"If the Arab nations should succeed in carrying out their threat to destroy Israel, would you feel a very deep, some, or no personal sense of loss?" (see pp. 215–220)—was not theoretical in nature, but rather had direct relevance.

In respect to the friendship ties of the Lakeville Jew, we would expect them to be more strongly Jewish than before. Jews have many more Jewish neighbors than previously; moreover, newer residents, knowing the changing character of the community, would be likely to be part of a highly-Jewish clique, or eager to join one.

Intermarriage may be thought of as the soft underbelly of Jewish identity in Lakeville. In our original study, we focused on the threat of intermarriage (see pp. 306–320). If we were to interview a sample of Lakeville Jews today, we would focus not only on the threat of intermarriage but on its prevalency. The intermarriage rate in Lakeville is

---

* See Marshall Sklare, "Lakeville and Israel: The Six-Day War and its Aftermath," *Midstream*, Vol. 14, No. 8 (October, 1968), pp. 3–21.

substantial. In many cases, the desire of Jewish parents is to have a rabbi officiate, or at least co-officiate with a Christian minister. Reform rabbis in Lakeville who refuse to perform intermarriages have been criticized as being insensitive, disloyal to Jewish ideals, and even unconcerned with Jewish survival. This is particularly the case where the bride or groom is the offspring of a member of the rabbi's congregation.

This brief review of some of the changes which have occurred in Lakeville indicates that while acculturation has proceeded apace, a mood of Jewish affirmation and heightened Jewish ethnicity has emerged. The early Jewish suburbanites on the Heights made themselves as inconspicuous as possible and were prepared to speak softly in the face of Gentile prejudice and discrimination. The most they hoped for was that their Gentile hosts would tolerate their presence and understand that Jews were prepared to abide by community mores and had no intention of dominating the Gentile suburbs of the Heights.

But the prosperity of a segment of Lake City's Jewish population, together with the aspirations of some Jews to move to prime suburban locations in the Lake City metropolitan area, meant that increasing numbers were motivated to purchase homes in Lakeville. In the absence of organized Gentile resistance, Lakeville eventually came to be a community in which the majority of the population was Jewish.

Some Gentiles remained in Lakeville. Those who moved generally did not announce that they were doing so because of the Jews—the United States is a country where moving is an accepted phenomenon and where few urban (and now suburban) residents, particularly those who are prosperous, live out their lives in the same neighborhood in which they were born. But relatively few Gentiles moved into Lakeville, and it is apparent that Christians did not enjoy, and in some cases could not abide, being a minority.

We may ask the question whether, from a Jewish perspective, Lakeville is not already past its peak. It is evident that the Heights now has more Jewish residents than ever before. It is also evident that Lakeville has served as a kind of staging area, from which Jews have proceeded to invade a number of adjoining elite suburbs which historically have had few if any Jewish residents. For the moment, however, Jews who wish to sell and move to the Sun Belt, or to a luxury apartment in the suburbs, or into one of the plush apartment buildings located close to the business district of Lake City can find Jewish buyers eager to move into Lakeville, who do not reject the community because its supply of Gentiles of their social class is limited. They are content with the opportunity to locate in Lakeville and take advantage of the many opportunities which the community offers, and do not avoid settling in areas where most of their neighbors will be Jewish.

There are certain ironies and ambiguities one can discern in the behavior of the Lakeville Jew. On the one hand, he is highly acculturated. He appreciates Lakeville's traditional "Gentile" ambience and has no strong desire to recreate the character of the older Jewish neighborhoods in Lake City. But at the same time he is happy that a Jewish cathedral has been erected on the Heights that no one traveling on its most scenic drive can miss. The Lakeville Jew is proud to be Jewish, but at the same time he is pleased that there are still some non-Jews in the community and concerned that Gentiles are no longer moving in.

The final question is of course whether the Jews of Lakeville, and/or the American Jewish community as a whole, will long endure. We have noted many positive signs of Jewish survivalism: a new mood of Jewish affirmation, the establishment of a Jewish day school, the teaching of Hebrew at the high school, the organization of new congregations, the strengthening of existing congregations and the building of adequate facilities, the character of friendship ties, the support for Soviet Jewry, and the involvement with and support of Israel. On the other hand, there are negative signs, most obviously the rise in intermarriage.

A sociologist who has studied American-Jewish life has stated that the mood of the first edition of *Jewish Identity on the Suburban Frontier* was pessimistic—a pessimism which, as he put it, was "not even thinly veiled." He indicated that in subsequent writings my mood became considerably more optimistic.* Should one be optimistic or pessimistic about the prospects for survival of American Jewry? I confess that I am hesitant to declare myself. I will take my stand with that pious Jew who lived in Jerusalem during the desperate siege of 1947–48. He went through the streets warning the defenders not to rely on miracles to save Jerusalem from the Arab armies which surrounded the city. "Do not rely on miracles," he implored, "say *tehillim*" (psalms).

*See Chaim Waxman, "Psalms of a Sober Man: The Sociology of Marshall Sklare," *Contemporary Jewry,* Vol. 4, No. 1 (Fall/Winter, 1977–78), pp. 3–11.

What has been accomplished in Lakeville in the past twenty years is an encouraging sign of Jewish affirmation. Nevertheless, let us not neglect to say psalms. I am of course aware that there may be no unanimity on which psalms we should say, or even perhaps on whether our psalms are to be taken from *Sefer Tehillim*, the Book of Psalms, or some other source. Nevertheless, the saying of psalms is a wise precaution when the survival of a Jewish community is at stake.

APPENDIX

Selection of Sample

The selection of our sample—as any sample design—was at the outset determined by the purposes of the study. Since we were interested in studying Jewish identity in Lakeville, we wanted to select residents who considered themselves to be Jews. If we had been primarily interested in the total saga of Lakeville Jewry—in changes in its size and character as determined, for example, by its birth rate, its intermarriage rate, its patterns of mobility into and out of the community —we would have been obliged to select all persons of Jewish lineage who currently resided in the community as well as those who had moved away in recent times. Such a study was beyond the scope of our investigation. Our sample excludes former residents of the community as well as converts to another religion and individuals who—in contrast to their parents—no longer consider themselves to be Jewish.* We were aware, from our preliminary study of the community, that such exclusions would foreclose the possibility of studying certain significant problems that were ancillary to our main objective, as for example the problem of apostasy, conversion, and other types of leakage from the Jewish community. The fact that such leakage had occurred became known to us from a variety of sources, perhaps most strikingly from an interview with the minister of a Unitarian church in Lakeville. He estimated that in one-third of the families affiliated with his church one or both spouses were of Jewish origin. Our study design also required that we exclude intermarried couples; the interview schedule included many questions about family behavior and assumed a homogeneously Jewish household.

* The absence of such cases should be kept in mind when generational trends are analyzed.

In addition to studying Jewish identity our design also called for a supplementary investigation of Gentile attitudes to and relationships with Jews. These interviews with Gentiles are analyzed in Volume II as well as material in the interviews with Jews which concern Jewish–Gentile relationships.

The study's focus also influenced the decision regarding the relative sizes of the Jewish and Gentile samples. We desired to obtain representative samples of men and women among both Jews and Gentiles. But, because we wanted more detailed information about Jews and planned to analyze this more intensively, the sample of Jewish respondents had to be larger than that of Gentile respondents in spite of the fact that Lakeville's population was estimated to be about one-third Jewish. Given, on the one hand, the limitations of budget and, on the other hand, the statistical requirement of random sampling and of data analysis, we established a target of about 250 Gentile interviews. It was then possible to plan for a minimum of 400 Jewish interviews with provision for increasing this sample within the limits of feasibility.

For a variety of reasons—scientific and administrative—it was necessary that we first establish the religious identity of prospective members of our sample before we selected them for an interview. Desiring to maximize the reliability of the respondents' answers to our interview questionnaire, we decided that the Jewish sample would be approached by Jewish interviewers working under Jewish auspices and the Gentile respondents would be contacted by non-Jewish interviewers representing a non-sectarian research organization. In addition the design of the interview questionnaire varied for each sample.

The first step in selecting the sample was to construct an adequate sampling frame—a comprehensive list of all households in Lakeville from which the sample was to be drawn. Such a list, containing the street address and the name of the head of the household, was obtained. It proved to be an adequate frame, for a spot check of address listings on a random selection of streets revealed that our list contained 99 per cent of all Lakeville addresses.* We then drew a sample from this list using tables of random numbers. The size of this sample was sufficiently large—even if the minimum estimate of the Jewish population and the expected rate of attrition from the sample were applied—to allow us to attain the desired number of Jewish respondents. This procedure had the advantage of flexibility inasmuch as the pool of randomly selected households could

* The 1 per cent not listed were almost entirely new houses constructed between the time the list was compiled in January 1957 and our spot check in May 1957.

be enlarged or decreased in the event that original estimates proved to vary markedly from the actual situation.

The next step was to establish which households in the sample were Jewish or Gentile. We had access to membership lists of several Jewish organizations (primarily synagogues) and also a validated list of 250 most common American Jewish surnames. The name of each head of household was first checked against these lists. (These techniques are heavily relied upon in surveys of Jewish communities.) But, since our aim was to interview a true sample of the Jewish population of Lakeville, we sought a means of classifying those whose identity could not be determined by these methods. We decided upon the technique of a telephone interview survey. A brief questionnaire, concerned with interest in religious television programs, was devised. It led naturally to a question on the religious identity of both husband and wife.

These techniques of determining the identity of the head of the household and his spouse proved to be highly accurate. Thus, when later contacted for an interview, none of the cases identified as Jews proved to be non-Jewish while only five of those identified as non-Jews considered themselves to be Jewish. Furthermore the methods were effective in screening out the intermarried cases. Only a handful of such households turned up in the sample that was interviewed.

Households in the sample were contacted for interviews in the order in which they were drawn for the sample. The interviewing was organized as two independent administrative operations and conducted in two separate time periods. Jews were interviewed during the period from October 1957 to May 1958, the great majority of them in the late fall and winter. In preparation for this phase a committee of local community leaders and representative citizens had been formed. The actual interviewing of the Jewish sample was supervised by staff members of the Division of Scientific Research of the American Jewish Committee. Interviewers were recruited from the surrounding area. Prospective respondents were informed of the study's sponsorship when they were approached for interviews. The interviewing of non-Jews was done from February to June 1959; the field work was conducted by the National Opinion Research Center of the University of Chicago. No local sponsoring committee was formed for this phase of the study.

As the table below indicates, completed interviews were obtained from a total of 86 per cent of Jews in the sample. Only 10 per cent refused to cooperate, and 4 per cent were deceased or had moved. The 250 Gentile interviews which were obtained represented 65 per cent of all non-Jews with whom contact was attempted. Some 20 per cent refused or were unavailable. No limit was set on the number of call-backs required to contact respondents for interviews. An additional 2 per cent of the Gentile sample were deceased or ill. A large number, 13 per cent, had moved from Lakeville. The number of Gentiles moved considerably exceeds the proportion of Jews who had moved and is due in part to the greater time lag between the period in which the sample was established and the interviewing phase.

RESULTS OF ATTEMPTED CONTACTS FOR INTERVIEWS

Per Cent of Sample	Jews	Gentiles
Completed interview	86	65
Refused to cooperate; unavailable	10	20
Deceased or ill	2	2
Moved	2	13
TOTAL SAMPLE SELECTED	(500)	(387)

One adult in each household was interviewed. Adult children of married couples were excluded. In order to assure a random selection and approximately equal proportions of men and women, the male head of the household or his spouse was pre-designated in alternate succession. Such respondents—who were married and living with their spouse—comprised 96 per cent of all Jews interviewed and 83 per cent of all Gentiles interviewed. The other respondents were widowed, divorced, or unmarried heads of households. Since most of these were women, the overall sample that was interviewed contains a larger proportion of female respondents (52 per cent of the Jewish and 56 per cent of the Gentile respondents).

The more detailed questionnaire for the Jewish respondents resulted in longer interviews averaging 3½ hours in contrast to 1½ hours for the interviews with non-Jews. Aside from questions concerning Jewish life, the questionnaire contains somewhat more detail on intergroup issues than does the one for the Gentile respondents. However, a similar set of questions on intergroup relations was asked of both groups. It was sometimes necessary to split the longer Jewish interviews into two sessions. In any case both questionnaires were highly successful in engaging the attention and interest of the respondents: only one respondent terminated the interview before its completion.

NOTES

Chapter 1

1. Moshe Davis, *The Emergence of Conservative Judaism* (Philadelphia: The Jewish Publication Society of America, 1963), p. 318.
2. Isaac M. Wise, *Reminiscences*, trans. and ed. David Philipson (Cincinnati: Leo Wise and Co., 1901), pp. 23–24.
3. Abram Vossen Goodman, "A Jewish Peddler's Diary, 1842–1843," *American Jewish Archives*, III (June 1951), 85.
4. *Ibid.*, p. 99.
5. *Ibid.*, pp. 108–109.
6. Norman Bentwich, *Solomon Schechter: A Biography* (Philadelphia: The Jewish Publication Society of America, 1938), pp. 215–219. For an analysis of Jewish life on the Lower East Side during this period, see Moses Rischin, *The Promised City: New York's Jews, 1870–1914* (Cambridge: Harvard University Press, 1962).

Chapter 2

1. The ages of the adults who reside in our 432 households are slightly more heterogeneous than the figures in Table 2–1 suggest. Not all the adult children of our respondents have established their own homes, and very occasionally a respondent's parents will reside in his household.
2. Some 5 per cent of the Gentiles have five or more children. Differences in fertility between Jews and Gentiles may be reduced, should younger Jewish couples deviate from the pattern characteristic of the older Jews in the community. Data on the children refer to all living children, including adult children who do not reside in their parents' household.
3. See Erich Rosenthal, "Jewish Fertility in the United States," *American Jewish Year Book*, LXII (1961), 3–27.
4. Three of the five respondents in the craftsmen-foremen category reported an income of $10,000 per year or more. Upon reinvestigation, it became apparent that they should have been classified under the rubric "managers, officials, and proprietors." Their incorrect classification resulted from the fact that they had described themselves as craftsmen (thus one respondent had said he was an electrician), when in reality they were proprietors (this particular respondent was in actuality a partner in an electrical contracting concern).
5. By education we mean secular or general education. Jewish education is discussed in Chapter 9.

411

6. It could be argued that, given the occupations of our respondents, it is surprising that as many as 35 per cent have *not* graduated from college. The explanation is that very few of our managers, officials, and sales workers are employed by large corporations—companies which traditionally place emphasis on educational criteria and do considerable recruiting at schools of business administration and engineering and at the better liberal arts colleges.

7. In the parental generation (particularly among those reared in Eastern Europe), there is the possibility that some who are reported as having little or no formal training actually had such training in the course of their Jewish education. This possibility would be reduced if we were comparing our respondents with their mothers, instead of their fathers.

8. Like other researchers, we must consider the validity of the information which respondents volunteer in respect to the question on income. Our conclusions are as follows: (1) the figures do not perfectly reflect income; (2) the figures constitute an underestimate more often than they do an overestimate; and (3) while the figures have much more than a minimal margin of error, they are usable for our purposes.

   The problem of correct reporting is complicated by the fact that only a minority of our respondents derive all, or nearly all, of their income from wages. Since many of them are self-employed (and presumably also gain income from a variety of sources), there is greater indeterminacy about their income, as well as greater opportunity for concealing income, than there is for wage earners. Furthermore, our respondents may conceal income even from themselves: thus for some of them there is the problem of correctly estimating the worth of goods and services paid for by their firms, but utilized for non-business purposes. Additionally, there is the fact that income is on the rise for most of our respondents. We assume that a certain proportion of those just above a cutting point between two income categories may choose the lower category, thus reporting essentially what was their income during the previous year.

   Of perhaps greater importance than any of these considerations is the fact that over half of those who were asked to supply income figures were women. Since only in a minority of our families are wages the main source of income, the wife may not have an entirely accurate understanding of the facts of the family's economic life. Income is frequently derived, at least in part, from sources other than wages, and the husband's bonuses, commissions, and fees are ever changing, as is the amount of income derived from dividends and like sources. Accordingly, we find that there is a disparity of almost $2,000 between the median total family income reported by the males and the females, with the males presenting the higher figure. We assume that the figures supplied by the men are more accurate than those given by the women, for our presumption is that there is no actual income differential between those families in which men, rather than women, were interviewed. Because of the presumedly more accurate estimate of family income given by the men, cross tabulations in this chapter which use income are based on the 208 male respondents.

9. While it is possible that self-made Gentiles avoid settling in Lakeville, our general knowledge about social mobility reinforces rather than modifies our conclusion.

10. The respondent's generation in the United States was determined from information—ascertained in the course of the interview—on his birthplace and on the country of birth of his parents and of his grandparents. These data permitted a classification into four generations. They also yielded a number of

mixed-generation types, which were classified under the basic generational groupings. The first generation—the immigrant generation—consists of respondents who were born in a foreign country. American-born respondents whose parents are *both* known to be foreign-born are classified as second-generation. If one of the parents is American-born and the other foreign-born, the respondent is considered as partly third-generation. A fully third-generation respondent is one whose parents are both American-born and whose four grandparents are *all* known to be foreign-born. If at least one, but not all, of the grandparents was born in America, the respondent is considered as partly fourth-generation. Only if all four grandparents are known to be American-born is the respondent classified as fully fourth-generation. Only 3 per cent of the respondents could not be classified into these categories because of insufficient information on their parents' or grandparents' birthplaces.

The necessity for distinguishing those who have one American-born parent from those who are fully second-generation has been demonstrated by Lazerwitz. (See Bernard Lazerwitz and Louis Rowitz, "The Three-Generations Hypothesis," *American Journal of Sociology,* LXIX [March 1964], especially 535–537.) One would therefore also expect to find important distinctions between those who have one to three American-born grandparents and those who are fully third-generation. In general, we reasoned, in those cases where parents or grandparents were of mixed birth, that it was the American-born parent or grandparent that was more determinative of the generational status of his children, i.e., that the claim to more advanced generation status in the United States is generally allowed if at least one of the parents or the grandparents is American-born.

We found support for this assumption in our own data. The behavior of respondents whose parents were of mixed birth—particularly their pattern of religious observance and their attitudes about Israel—generally resembles that of fully third-generation respondents more than it does that of the fully second-generation respondents. Similarly, respondents classified as partly fourth-generation behave more like the fully fourth-generation respondents than like the fully third-generation respondents. In the classification of four generations used throughout this study, therefore, the third generation consists of the respondents who are partly third-generation as well as of those who are fully third-generation, and the fourth generation embraces the respondents who are partly fourth-generation as well as those who are fully fourth-generation.

11. From information on the birthplace of respondents, of their parents, and of their grandparents, the country of birth of the grandparents in both the maternal and paternal lines was determined and classified as follows:

German: Country of grandparents' birth was Germany or Austria.

East European: Country of grandparents' birth was located in Eastern or Central Europe.

Other: Country located in any other area.

Respondents were classified as of "German," "East European," or "mixed" descent, according to the country of birth of the grandparents. Where a grandparent was native-born, respondents were asked to identify his national origin. Information on both the maternal and paternal family line of the respondent was pooled to yield a classification of descent. In some 92 per cent of the cases in the paternal lines and 89 per cent in the maternal lines, the descent of both grandparents was ascertainable and identical.

Cross marriages and lack of information for one grandparent necessitated some presumption in ascribing descent. The extent of these presumptions was minor, however, for in 76 per cent of the cases classified as German and in 86 per cent of those classified as East European, the stock of all four grandparents is definitely known to be identical. In 92 per cent of those classified as East European or German, at least three grandparents are definitely known to be of the appropriate stock. In the other cases classified as East European or German, information is available for only one or two grandparents, and these are known to be of the appropriate stock. In all the cases classified as "mixed," the respondent has at least one German and one East European grandparent; in 76 per cent of such cases, two grandparents are of German stock and two of East European stock. Where the national stock of both grandparents in either the maternal or paternal line was unknown, descent has been considered indeterminate.

12. It is true that, since the German group is somewhat older, a slightly greater proportion of them were of college age during the bottom of the depression. As we shall see, however, most German parents were more prosperous than East European parents and thus should have been better able to keep their children in college even during difficult times.

13. In respect to educational attainment, the mixed group resembles the East Europeans, although, as we noticed earlier, they are closer to the Germans in terms of generational status.

14. It is interesting to speculate whether the choice of professions among the Germans portends a shift of Jews away from medicine and law. Interest in engineering, we may assume, is related to level of acculturation. Thus it is possible that, as they raise their level of acculturation, the East Europeans will become more interested in engineering, especially as anti-Jewish discrimination in this field wanes.

15. We use the term "class" or "social class" to refer to economic position based on income. Although amount of education is frequently included in calculations of class level, this would be unwarranted in the present study, where income and education are not positively correlated.

16. While the literature on values as they relate to mobility has included the study of Jewish culture, investigations have not sought to differentiate between German and East European Jews. See, for example, David C. McClelland, *The Achieving Society* (Princeton: D. Van Nostrand Co., 1961), pp. 364–367.

17. For some statistics on the rapid rise of the first generation of Germans and the contrasts between the occupational distribution of both groups, see the figures quoted in Nathan Glazer, "Social Characteristics of American Jews, 1654–1954," *American Jewish Year Book*, LVI (1955), especially 9–11.

18. The classification of economic mobility that we constructed from the responses was based on the respondent's comparison of his own present economic standing with the economic standing of his parents in two time periods: the 1950's (when unavailable, the 1940's was used) and the 1920's. Respondents were classified as follows:

> Higher: higher standing than that of the parents in both decades.
> Same: the same standing as that of the parents in both decades *or* the same for one but higher for the other decade.
> Lower: lower standing than that of the parents in either or both decades.

19. These differences would be further magnified if age were held constant.

20. If our study were centrally concerned with intragroup cleavages rather than with Jewish identity, we would study not only the sense of deprivation of the

Germans but also the reactions of East Europeans. Thus we would seek to ascertain whether the East European validates the status of "old money" and seeks to ingratiate himself with its holders, or rather chooses to esteem German businessmen while denigrating the self-made tycoons in his own descent group. If he is "intellectual" but of middling income, how does he react to those Germans who do not particularly value academic achievement? And what about the reaction of the most prosperous segment of the East European group—the self-made men of little education? Are they attracted to the Germans, but at the same time find they have little in common with men whose lives have been devoted to conserving a patrimony rather than to establishing a new family dynasty?

21. The respondent's own length of residence approximates that of the spouse. In a large majority of cases (89 per cent), they are identical.

22. For the SRC material, see Bernard Lazerwitz, "A Comparison of Major United States Religious Groups," *Journal of the American Statistical Association,* LVI (September 1961), 568–579. For the NORC data, see Donald J. Bogue, *The Population of the United States* (Glencoe, Ill.: The Free Press, 1959), pp. 697–709. Both sets of data combine material from more than one survey and thus increase the number of Jewish respondents.

Chapter 3

1. Jacob Katz, *Exclusiveness and Tolerance* (London: Oxford University Press, 1961), p. 28.

2. *Ibid.,* pp. 29–30.

3. Of course, the continued existence of various forms of traditional Judaism attests to the fact that some modern Jews have succeeded in the effort to observe halachah.

4. For a typology of religiosity, see Charles Y. Glock, "On the Study of Religious Commitment," *Religious Education,* LVII (July–August 1962, Research Supplement), 98–110.

5. The inclusion of observances that have fallen into disuse was avoided. With the possible exception of the item on smoking on the Sabbath, practices or prohibitions observed by only the most traditional elements in the Jewish community were similarly avoided.

6. Nonobservance and full observance of the eleven rituals on our list are excluded. These levels preclude any change in the pattern of observance of specific rituals.

7. The "Synagogue Attendance" index represents a combination of two subindices: one for attendance at holiday services, the other for attendance at Sabbath services. The "Holiday Attendance" measure is based on the number of holidays during which the respondent attended services during the past three years. Since we inquired about three holidays—Rosh Hashanah, Yom Kippur, and Sukkot—the total possible number of holidays is nine. The range of frequencies of holidays on which services were attended was arbitrarily collapsed to an index ordered from zero to 5, as follows:

Score Value	Number Holidays Attended
5	9
4	7–8
3	5–6
2	3–4
1	1–2
0	0

Since Festival attendance almost always presupposes High Holiday attendance, a score value of 3 typically represents regular annual attendance at High Holiday services only (6 times). This proved to be the modal pattern of holiday attendance, occurring among more than one in three respondents. The "Sabbath Attendance" index scores, arbitrarily ordered from zero to 4, stand for frequency of weekly attendance in the past year, as follows:

Score Value	Frequency
4	weekly or almost weekly
3	2 to 3 times per month
2	once a month
1	less than once a month
0	never

The two measures were combined into a single index by adding the respondent's scores on each index. Thus the range of possible score values extends from zero to 9.

While a certain degree of arbitrariness was necessary in assigning weights to attendance at holiday and Sabbath services, the resulting score values bear some relation to traditional norms. Although in the Holiday Attendance index each of the two High Holidays—the most sacred holidays in the Jewish calendar—has no greater value than do the Festivals, together they have twice as much value. (Attendance at *both* High Holiday services is by far more typical than at only one of them.) Regular attendance at services on Sabbath, which is traditionally considered no less sacred than Yom Kippur, receives only a slightly higher score than does regular attendance at High Holiday services (4 compared to 3).

8. National sample surveys conducted about the same time as our study show a similar level of nonattendance by Jews in the country at large. See Bernard Lazerwitz, "A Comparison of Major United States Religious Groups," *Journal of the American Statistical Association*, LVI (September 1961), especially Table 8. Nonattendance is also confined to less than one-fifth of the Jewish population in two metropolitan areas: Washington, D.C. (19 per cent), and Detroit (12 per cent). See Stanley K. Bigman, *The Jewish Population of Greater Washington in 1956* (Washington, D.C.: The Jewish Community Council of Greater Washington, May 1957), p. 100; and Harold L. Orbach, "Aging and Religion," *Geriatrics*, XVI (October 1961), 530–540.

9. Figures in national surveys conducted at about the same time as our study indicate that 39 per cent of Jewish men in the United States attended synagogue at least once a month. This statistic is greater than that for Lakeville men, but lower than that for their fathers. In view of the older age composition of Jews in the nation, Lakeville may foreshadow the national trend. See Bernard Lazerwitz, "Some Factors Associated with Variations in Church Attendance," *Social Forces*, XXXIX (May 1961), 301–309.

10. Some 61 per cent of Lakeville Jews seldom attend services (less than once a month, but not never). In both Washington and Detroit, the comparable figure is 56 per cent (see Bigman, *op. cit.*, and Orbach, *op. cit.*). The comparable nationwide figure is 51 per cent (see Lazerwitz, "A Comparison of Major U.S. Religious Groups"). In view of the lower nonattendance of Lakeville adults compared to their parents, it is likely that this pattern of very irregular attendance will grow in the nation as a whole. It remains to be seen whether regular monthly and weekly attendance can be sustained with the passing of the immigrant generation.

11. The pattern of parental influence occurs in regard to synagogue attendance as well as home observance.

12. There are, of course, gaps between actual childhood experience and adult memories. Adults remember only selective aspects of their childhood experiences; this selectivity is strongly influenced by experiences during adolescence and adulthood. What is notable about our respondents is that their post-childhood experiences have not made them negative about their earlier life as it relates to their Jewishness.

13. Such information was obtained from the respondent and was classified in the same manner as was comparable information about the respondent. See Chapter 2, footnotes 10 and 11.

14. For an interpretation in "child-oriented" terms, see Herbert J. Gans, "The Origin and Growth of a Jewish Community in the Suburbs: A Study of the Jews of Park Forest," in Marshall Sklare, ed., *The Jews: Social Patterns of an American Group* (Glencoe, Ill.: The Free Press, 1958), pp. 205–248.

15. Studies of adolescents and college students which provide information on religious behavior during the transitional period between the childhood home and the adult home uniformly agree on the relatively low levels of religious practice during these years. Many assign prognostic meaning to their findings, without further follow-up. For a comprehensive review of studies of American Jewish youth conducted primarily in the 1930's, when the average Lakeville respondent was in his adolescent and college years, see Nathan Goldberg, "Religious and Social Attitudes of Jewish Youth in the U.S.A.," *The Jewish Review*, I (December 1943), 135–168. See also Meyer Greenberg, "The Jewish Student at Yale: His Attitude Toward Judaism," *YIVO Annual of Jewish Social Science*, I (1946), 217–240. For more recent and more comprehensive college samples, see Andrew M. Greeley, *Religion and Career: A Study of College Graduates* (New York: Sheed and Ward, 1963), pp. 152–153; "A Survey of the Political and Religious Attitudes of American College Students," *National Review*, XV (October 8, 1963), especially pp. 291–301. Despite its serious methodological flaws, the findings in the *National Review* study appear to be consistent with other research.

Several studies of Jewish adolescents point to a cleavage from parental norms of religious practice especially during the later teen-age years, although it is no longer a complete break and does not assume the proportions of generation conflict. Thus in one eastern seaboard community a high proportion of adolescents approved of their parents' practices. Older adolescents approved less often, however, and more frequently voiced intentions to depart from their parents' norms than did their younger contemporaries. See Marshall Sklare and Marc Vosk, *The Riverton Study* (New York: American Jewish Committee, 1957), especially pp. 13–16. Bernard C. Rosen, "Minority Group in Transition: A Study of Adolescent Religious Conviction and Conduct," in Sklare, *op. cit.*, pp. 336–346, found that traditionalist attitudes and beliefs survived even when religious practice became minimal or nonexistent. See also B. C. Rosen, *Adolescence and Religion* (Cambridge, Mass.: Schenkman, 1965), pp. 192–195. This suggests one basis for a possible re-evaluation of and return to observance in later phases of the life cycle.

16. Since almost all of our respondents have at least one child, we cannot compare ritual behavior at all points in the life cycle of the adult. We cannot discover how the behavior of the unmarried and the childless compares with that of our respondents. However, comparisons can be made among respondents at different phases of the parental life cycle. One possible measure of life cycle is the

age of the parent. A more meaningful measure of the progress of the parental life cycle—and of the life cycle of the family—is the ages of the children. We distinguish the following stages in the parental life cycle, partly in relation to the ages at which children receive their general education and partly in relation to the ages at which children are expected to receive Jewish education:

1. Pre-school: all the children are under 6 years of age.

2. Early-school: at least one child is between ages 6 and 9, but none are between ages 10 and 14; the child may have begun religious education or postponed it to the next phase.

3. Peak-school: at least one child is between ages 10 and 14; the child is generally receiving religious education and/or preparing for the Bar Mitzvah or Confirmation ceremony.

4. Late-school: all the children are over 14 years of age, but the youngest is still between ages 15 and 17; there is some likelihood that the youngest may still be receiving some religious education.

5. Post-school: all the children are 18 years of age or older.

17. The progress of the life cycle is, of course, highly correlated with the aging of the parents, but the effects of the life cycle are not a function of aging. Differential religious performance of parents in various phases of the life cycle occurs even when the factor of age is controlled.

18. We have already noticed that child-centeredness is one criterion for ritual retention. However, if all observance were "child-oriented" in the simple sense of the term, observance should return to a lower level than it actually does. While the group which declines in observance may be thought of as "child-oriented," this phrase overlooks the fact that in the performance of their parental role they realize their own values.

19. See Will Herberg, *Protestant, Catholic, Jew* (rev. ed.; Garden City, N.Y.: Anchor Books, Doubleday and Co., 1960); also Marcus L. Hansen's classic essay "The Problem of the Third Generation Immigrant," conveniently available in *Commentary*, XIV (November 1952), 492–500.

20. Of course, it would be desirable to have data on the religious observance of grandparents as well, thus allowing for a three-generational presentation.

21. As is apparent in succeeding tables, the overlap between parents and respondents of the same generation is small: the parents of our second-generation East European respondents, for example, have quite a different level of observance than our first-generation respondents.

22. See, for example, Gerhard Lenski, *The Religious Factor* (Garden City, N.Y.: Anchor Books, Doubleday and Co., rev. ed., 1963), pp. 43–48, and Bernard Lazerwitz and Louis Rowitz, "The Three-Generations Hypothesis," *American Journal of Sociology*, LXIX (March 1964), 529–538. Both of these studies present generational data on attendance at worship. Their findings do not give support to the Hansen-Herberg generational approach, except for various subgroups of respondents. Their data on Jews are limited, but consistent: successive generations mean decreasing attendance. We believe, however, that if religious behavior were contrasted with the practices observed by the respondents' parents, a somewhat different picture of religious change might emerge. In any case, such parental data are a more valid measure of the historical dimension implied in the Hansen-Herberg approach.

23. Were this statistic, which includes mothers, calculated for fathers only, it would be noticeably higher. The religious pattern in which the parents of our first-generation respondents were reared did not encourage attendance of women at corporate worship.

24. There is one exception to this. The level of home observance of fourth-generation Germans not only equals but exceeds that of their parents. However, this rise must be understood in context: the majority of the parents of such respondents did not observe a single home ritual.

25. The only exception is the gap in synagogue attendance between third-generation Germans and their parents. This is slightly larger than the deviation from the parental pattern among the second generation.

    In most cases, it is mathematically possible for such deviations to be just as large as among the respondents of the preceding generation.

26. They have at least one child of age 6 to 14. Both life-cycle phases have been combined, inasmuch as a separate analysis for each results in too few cases.

27. While an insufficient number of cases are available for controlling parents' observance levels, we find that among those East Europeans in the earliest phase of the life cycle (children aged 1 to 5 only), the third generation, despite its lower level of childhood religious exposure, scores higher on home observance (30 per cent, compared to 6 per cent, practice five or more observances) and on synagogue attendance (58 per cent, compared to 44 per cent, score three or higher) than the second generation. Generational comparisons among families of East European origin in the last phase of the cycle (and among German-origin families in any phase), while often based on very few cases, yield similar results.

28. See Glock, *op. cit.*, for an analysis of these and other dimensions.

29. The responses to the probe "Why do you feel this way?" were coded, and then the codes were grouped under the categories of sacramentalism, moralism, religious feeling, and belief in God. Since it was often apparent whether or not the individual felt deficient or adequate in his observance of a particular criterion, this dimension was added to the coding.

30. Among those who are even more observant (seven or more rituals), the percentage who consider themselves "very religious" does not increase.

Chapter 4

1. The terms "Classical Reform" and "Neo-Reform" are used to distinguish between two different interpretations of Jewish tradition. While there is some variation within the Classical Reform school as it developed in the last half of the nineteenth and early part of the twentieth centuries in those American cities where sizable numbers of German Jews resided, such differences need not concern us. For our purposes, the "Pittsburgh Platform," adopted in 1885 by a group of American Reform rabbis, may be taken to represent the Classical Reform position. The "Columbus Platform," adopted in 1937 by the Central Conference of American Rabbis, may be taken to represent the Neo-Reform position (or, better, the shift to a Neo-Reform position).

    There is no up-to-date history of Reform Judaism in the United States. A popular presentation, *Reform Judaism in the Making,* by Sylvan D. Schwartzman (New York: Union of American Hebrew Congregations, 1955) is, however, helpful. See p. 143 for a table which highlights some of the differences between Classical Reform and Neo-Reform. Although they are not presented systematically, contrasts between the two positions, as reflected in documentary sources on the Reform movement, can be found throughout *The Growth of Reform Judaism,* by W. Gunther Plaut (New York: World Union for Progressive Judaism, 1965), especially pp. 31–36, 96–100, 145–159.

2. In retrospect, it could be claimed that the hesitancy to organize was not only un-

necessary but self-defeating: that if a congregation had *not* been established, Jewish integration into the community would have been diminished, rather than increased. This was, of course, not the view in the 1920's. Only several decades later did the view expounded by Will Herberg and others gain ascendancy: that the identification of the Jew as a member of a religious group constituted integration into the social fabric, rather than a tendency toward divisiveness.

3. The location selected by the founders became a considerable source of irritation and anxiety at a later period when the membership had increased substantially and the Temple generated considerable automobile traffic. Swarms of cars began to arrive from Lake City each Sabbath with relatives and friends coming to attend a Bar Mitzvah; the off-the-street facilities provided by the Temple could accommodate only a portion of the vehicles. On Sunday, the traffic clogged the narrow streets in order to deposit and pick up students at the religious school. Gentile (as well as Jewish) residents of the area became angry when they found their streets blocked by traffic and their lawns trampled by those who parked in front of their homes.

   Temple officials were forced to take strong measures. They printed stern warnings in the congregational bulletin and worked out a series of traffic regulations in consultation with local police officials. A volunteer traffic corps was recruited from the Temple membership to assist in enforcement procedures on Sunday mornings as well as at other busy times.

4. For the attitudes of longtime Jewish residents toward Jewish newcomers, see Volume II, Chapter 4.

5. The ostensible fears of some of the longtime residents turned out to be groundless. Because of the size of the estate, the Schechter Synagogue was able to arrange for off-the-street parking facilities. Also, the development of an arterial highway in another section of the community shifted through traffic away from the area in which the Synagogue was located. Ironically, whatever intergroup hostility could be traced to traffic problems was a result of the site selected by longtime residents for the Wise Temple, rather than of the location of the new Schechter Synagogue.

6. It can be claimed—with a good deal of justice, we think—that while the Einhorn group view themselves as the upholders of a tradition, their rigidity constitutes a departure from the Classical Reformism popular during the nineteenth and early twentieth centuries—the period when this particular version of the Jewish tradition was espoused by large segments of the American-Jewish upper-middle and upper classes. However, the analysis of the extent to which the Einhorn group have actually departed from what they conceive to be their tradition constitutes a matter considerably beyond our present concern.

7. On the formation of the Council and its relationship with Reform, see Samuel Halperin, *The Political World of American Zionism* (Detroit: Wayne State University Press, 1961), pp. 71–101, 282–284.

8. For the approach of the Jews of Park Forest to the same problem, see Herbert J. Gans, "The Origin and Growth of a Jewish Community in the Suburbs: A Study of the Jews of Park Forest," in Marshall Sklare, ed., *The Jews: Social Patterns of an American Group* (Glencoe, Ill.: The Free Press, 1958).

9. Preaching was traditionally the prerogative of the *maggid*, an office held to be inferior to that of rabbi.

10. The traditional role of the laity in Jewish worship bulks much larger than it does either in Catholicism or in many of the leading denominations of Protestantism. Since the Einhorn service maximizes the distinction between laity and clergy,

the service is from this point of view more acculturated than those held in the other temples in Lakeville.

11. While we were heartily welcomed at the Sunday morning service, when we inquired about the Friday afternoon service we were advised against attending. In order to preserve rapport, we did not press the matter.

12. This suggests that in Classical Reform it is the woman who is the most traditional and the most pietistic. A similar tendency has been repeatedly observed among the Catholic and Protestant laity. The sex composition of the vesper service thus demonstrates again the far-reaching acculturation of the Einhorn constituency to general religious norms. Significantly, the traditional Jewish service comparable to the vesper service at Einhorn—the *Kabbalat Shabbat* service—is attended only by men. (Since most Reform congregations have a Friday evening service, they do not ordinarily hold a service on Friday afternoon.)

13. Rabbi Isaacs would prefer only a single service on Rosh Hashanah and Yom Kippur, rather than an evening and morning service, but he has hesitated to press his views upon the congregation.

14. Other parts of the "Statement of Principles" bear out this theme of exalting the secular culture. Instead of stressing the paganism of secular culture and the necessary antagonism between religion and culture, the "Statement" emphasizes the increasing perfection of American culture as well as Reform Judaism's intimate connection with that culture: "American democracy with its hope for the brightest future man had ever known, inspired this reformation [Classical Reform Judaism]. . . . We believe these hopes have been justified in the steady evolution of American democracy, which is still in the process of removing inequities and injustices." The conservatism of the Einhorn approach, as well as its nationalism, is apparent in a further excerpt: "To this vision of America, the [Classical] Reformers . . . added the realization that the enduring, permanent values of our faith are its inner strengths, eloquently amplified by the Prophets in universal terms and restated in contemporary language through all the generations of Jewish religious experience. These early Reformers also eliminated secondary accretions—*bearing no permanent relevance either to America* or to those inner strengths of a Prophetic and universal Judaism— which had become appended to our faith in the course of centuries when Jews had lived in less enlightened lands and eras" [emphasis supplied].

15. The measure of "integration-mindedness" is a composite index summarizing several dimensions of Jewish attitudes and behavior vis-à-vis the Gentile community. The index has five component items: (1) attitudes with respect to whether it is essential for a Jew to promote civic improvement in the community and to gain the respect of Christian neighbors; (2) feelings and behavior with respect to having a Christmas tree in one's home; (3) the ratio of Gentiles to Jews desired in the neighborhood; (4) involvement in non-sectarian organizations; and (5) participation in leisure-time activities that are characteristic of non-Jews in Lakeville. For a more detailed description of the index and how it is constructed and scored, see Volume II, Chapter 7.

16. The status of the community's seven residential areas is based on respondents' evaluations of the area where the "most respected persons in the Jewish community live." The two areas which were most frequently mentioned are ranked "high," the two next most frequently mentioned are ranked "medium," and the three others are ranked "low." A more complex measure of residential status yields a similar ranking of these areas. This measure is based on two additional criteria: (1) the value of the houses in each area and (2) the "attractiveness" of

the area. The areas were ranked according to the median value of the homes of the respondents who reside in the respective area. The "attractiveness" of each area is based on a combination of the rankings with respect to two evaluations made by the respondents: the area they considered as "most attractive . . . in terms of the kinds of Jews living there" and the area they considered as "least attractive . . . in terms of the kinds of Jews living there." When the rankings of each area with respect to house value and attractiveness are added to the "reputational" ranking (in terms of where the "most respected persons in the Jewish community live"), the rank order of the combined scores for each area approximates the rank order on the latter criterion alone.

Chapter 5

1. Only one-fifth have no concern with a religious question.
2. This differential decline in synagogue membership among German Jews in the most advanced phase of the life cycle parallels their behavior in respect to religious observance. See above, p. 75.
3. Although analysis often yields few cases for comparison, the finding is strikingly consistent: in nine of seventeen possible comparisons between the peak-school and post-school phase, membership remains the same or increases. In six others it declines, but it does so by less than a 15 per cent margin.
4. Each of the three measures of synagogue-centered values is independently related to decreased membership. In seven out of nine possible comparisons, membership declines sharply (more than 20 per cent) between the peak-school and post-school phases.
5. Only 1 per cent of Lakeville Gentiles do not consider themselves either Protestant or Catholic.
6. Because of the difference in definition of what constitutes affiliation among Jews and in some Protestant denominations, were the Jewish definition applied to Protestants their proportion of church members would actually decrease.
7. While the Jewish proportion is slightly less than the Catholic figure, this may be largely an artifact of coding procedures. Most Catholic organizations were coded as church-connected, but only those Jewish organizations which had a direct connection with synagogue life were coded as synagogue-affiliated. As we shall see, there is a large network of extra-synagogual Jewish organizations.
8. The fact that Jews have a virtually similar or greater rate of membership in affiliated groups—as well as of activity—in the synagogue than do Protestants and Catholics in their respective churches is not due to the differences between them in age and income. For when we compare the segments from each of the three religious groups who most resemble each other in age (ages 40 to 59) and income (earn $10,000 or more), the results are similar.
9. Other major reasons are the synagogue's religious orientation, educational program, and rabbinical and lay leadership.
10. These are the regular worshipers, by Lakeville standards: they attend High Holiday services every year, come to Festival services occasionally or regularly, and attend Sabbath services at least twice a month. As we indicated in Chapter 3, only 13 per cent of all Lakeville Jews meet this standard of attendance.
11. While the figures for participation in Jewish study refer to total attendance at study groups, lectures, and Hebrew courses conducted under any Jewish auspices, there is sufficient evidence that the great bulk of this participation occurred under the sponsorship of the synagogues.
12. Home observance, in contrast to the other indicators of religiosity, can be used

here as an independent variable. Because of its family setting, it appears to be less subject to synagogue influences. While home observance may be stimulated by synagogue involvement, it generally has its roots in the personal background and life situation of the individual, as shown in Chapter 3.

13. These findings generally apply to members of Hirsch or Einhorn as well as to members of Wise, Schechter, or Lilienthal.

Chapter 6

1. The size of the "no-effect" group is large enough to make us wonder about the exact meaning of the response. It is difficult to evaluate whether this 33 per cent consists mainly of those who denied an implied bad effect because they believed the effect of Israel to be good, those who denied an implied good effect because they believed the effect of Israel to be bad, or those who, indeed, believed that Israel has not had any effect.

2. Only 1 per cent say the effect has been neither beneficial nor harmful.

3. Although the scale meets the criterion of reproducibility, it does not appear to fulfill other requirements of a Guttman scale. Nor was assignment of non-scale types done in the manner recommended by Ford (see Robert N. Ford, "A Rapid Scoring Procedure for Scaling Attitude Questions," in M. W. Riley, J. W. Riley, Jr., and J. Toby, eds., *Sociological Studies in Scale Analysis* [New Brunswick: Rutgers University Press, 1954], pp. 273–305). Non-scale types—those persons who did not respond according to this cumulative pattern, but preferred other combinations of aid—totaled 13 per cent. They have been classified together with the purer cumulative scale types possessing the same score value (see Table below). This was done because of the similarity of their behavior in respect to most, if not all, other attitude dimensions and orientations concerning Israel: comparisons were carried out for six other attitude items and with an index consisting of three of these items. (Among persons with scale value 1, congruence was noted in about half the items.) In addition, the cumulative scale types themselves were consistently associated with these items; that is, increasing support for Israel was related to other indicators of pro-Israel sentiment. Scale values 3 to 5 were combined into one category for analytic purposes. The resulting scale (see Table 6–4) yields four levels. The specified actions in this reduced scale actually apply to about nine in ten of the persons at the respective levels.

Scale Value	Levels of Support of Israel		
0	None at all	7%	
1	Money only	25	28
	Any other 1 action	3	
2	Money and influence U.S. policy	28	32
	Any other 2 actions	4	
3	Money, influence U.S. policy, join Zionist organizations	21	26
	Any other 3 actions	5	
4	Money, influence U.S. policy, join Zionist organizations, and give Israel financial priority	6	6
	Any other 4 actions	*	
5	All actions, including either type of immigration to Israel	1	1
	Any other 5 actions	*	

* Less than 0.5 per cent.

4. Our focus in this section is on level of support for Israel. We have already shown that such support reflects pro-Israel feeling and concern.

5. The index of involvement in synagogue life ranges from zero to 3. One point was assigned for each of the following characteristics: synagogue membership, membership in a synagogue-affiliated group, and any time spent weekly in non-devotional synagogue activities. The highest score is assigned to those with all three forms of participation, the lowest to those with none.

6. Our index of Jewish organizational involvement ranges from zero to 4 and consists of two elements: number of memberships in Jewish organizations (organizations which are independent of a synagogue) and hours spent each week in such groups. One or two memberships were scored as one point, while three or more were scored as two; one hour's activity was scored as one point, and two or more hours as two. Thus the highest position on the index is occupied by those holding three or more memberships and spending two or more hours each week in organizational activities; the lowest position is occupied by those with no memberships and no activity.

7. See footnote 15 of Chapter 4 for a brief description of the components of the "integration-mindedness" index and Chapter 7 in Volume II for the details of its construction.

8. The concept of alienation developed here most closely approximates the dimension of isolation specified by Seeman in his systematization of the diverse meanings of this concept found in the literature. The alienated person, according to this meaning, is estranged from society and its culture and devaluates socially valued goals and beliefs. This meaning of alienation can be found in the negative or indifferent orientation of minority group members to selective values and styles of life of the majority culture. See Melvin Seeman, "On the Meaning of Alienation," *American Sociological Review*, XXIV (December 1959), 783–791, and Gwynn Nettler, "A Measure of Alienation," *American Sociological Review*, XXII (December 1957), 670–677.

9. Members of Einhorn Temple, as expected, are highly integration-minded, more than three-fourths scoring six or higher. This compares to one-third of the others. However, differences in integration-mindedness do not appear to overcome ideological predispositions: the less integration-minded express only slightly more pro-Israel sentiment than the more integration-minded.

10. This finding differs somewhat from the situation we noticed with respect to religious observance (see above, p. 83). There we found a more definite stabilization of the decline in observance in the more advanced generations.

11. In this section, the first and second generation are combined. Attitudes of these two generations are basically similar.

12. The peculiar, albeit ambivalent, affinity between these two religious traditions among American Jews is explored in Marshall Sklare, *Conservative Judaism: An American Religious Movement* (Glencoe, Ill.: The Free Press, 1955).

13. Because of the small number of cases in some cells, this and subsequent tables do not include all the possible combinations of religious orientation. Thus Conservative respondents whose parents had a Reform or no religious orientation are rare, as are respondents with no religious orientation whose parents were Orthodox, Conservative, or Reform.

14. The designated levels of support in Figure 6–1 are, of course, cumulative. Approval of the action at a given level presupposes support of all actions at lower levels (see above, footnote 3). On each vertical line representing the respondent's generation, the respective median score value for each designated combination of parent-and-respondent orientation has been plotted. Adjacent

generations are connected by lines at all points where the religious orientation of the parents of respondents in a given generation matches that of respondents in the previous generation. Thus various patterns of intergenerational change in religious orientation across several generations are represented. This technique permits us to generalize trends in pro-Israel sentiment across four generations, although it is based on data on religious identification covering only the present respondent and his parent. A more ideal, although more complex, type of analysis would be possible if data for grandparents were available.

15. These generalizations are limited by the type of data available. Insufficient numbers of Orthodox respondents, of third- and fourth-generation Conservative respondents, and of those identifying with none of these movements limit us in studying the effects of intergenerational change. Thus, while the latter appear to have no less pro-Israel sentiment than Reform persons, their numbers are too few when intergenerational change is taken into account. An additional limitation is lack of data on the grandfather's religious orientation. Our generalizations regarding changes in religious orientation over three or more generations are projections from data based on two generations, the respondent's and the parent's. While we assume that the East European immigrant grandfathers of the third generation were predominantly Orthodox in orientation, we have no definite way of identifying such persons or distinguishing them from the possibly significant number whose grandfathers were Yiddish secularists or adherents of other non-traditional viewpoints.

Chapter 7

1. While we did not ask respondents to evaluate the agencies, we have several indications of their attitudes in our data. About nine in ten not only believe it important to give to a Jewish philanthropy but actually make an annual contribution. As many as two-thirds give at least $100 a year. Data on giving and on attitudes toward Jewish and non-sectarian philanthropies are not included in the present volume.

2. For a general discussion, see Robin M. Williams, Jr., *American Society: A Sociological Interpretation* (New York: Alfred A. Knopf, 2nd ed., rev., 1960), pp. 494–501.

3. These figures on the extent of affiliation help us to understand one of the important aspects of the multiplicity of Jewish associations. Given the heterogeneity of Lakeville Jewry, organizational multiplicity maximizes the possibility of involving residents in a Jewish voluntary association. Hence, multiplicity is far from being "inefficient" in the conventional sense.

4. If synagogue affiliates such as sisterhoods and men's clubs are included, this figure rises to 60 per cent.

5. Other types of Jewish organizations command smaller followings among our respondents. The Jewish community-relations groups count 8 per cent as members. A similar number belong to various educational and cultural groups. With the exception of Hadassah, only a small number are affiliated with a variety of Zionist and Israel-oriented groups. Affiliation with groups based on common economic or occupational interests, such as societies of Jewish lawyers, doctors, or dentists, is highly uncommon. Membership in Jewish veterans' groups is even more rare.

6. The significance of non-synagogue-centered Jewish organizational life has not been carefully explored by students of contemporary Jewish life. Commentators on contemporary Jewish religious life and on the Jewish "revival" have

concentrated on those aspects of the revival which seem to parallel developments in the Christian community. For example, see Will Herberg, *Protestant, Catholic, Jew* (rev. ed.; Garden City, N.Y.: Anchor Books, Doubleday and Co., 1960), Chapter 8, and Nathan Glazer, *American Judaism* (Chicago: University of Chicago Press, 1957), Chapter 7. Herberg, Glazer, and others who depict Jewish suburban life stress that it is dominated by religious institutions and influenced by the religious patterns of Christian neighbors; little is said of Jewish associational life outside the synagogue. When such associations are acknowledged, they tend to be interpreted as a manifestation of the activity of a religious community (for example, see Herberg, pp. 196–197, and Glazer, pp. 121–123).

One reason why little independent significance has been attached to contemporary non-synagogue organizational life is its lack of ideological content. Thus the decline of such movements as Zionism and Socialism, so important in the Jewish community several decades ago, appears to observers to herald the diminution and ultimate disappearance of any meaningful Jewish identity outside of the religious nexus (for example, see Herberg, pp. 185–186, 189–190, and Glazer, pp. 123–124).

7. While Table 7–4 compares the various levels of home observance, a comparison of the various levels of synagogue attendance yields similar results.

8. Comparisons between synagogue members and non-members do not include men and women in the pre-school and early-school phases of the life cycle. As pointed out in Chapter 5, the majority of such younger parents will become synagogue members when their oldest child approaches Bar Mitzvah or Confirmation age.

9. A somewhat similar pattern occurs among the women in social-recreational groups.

10. It may be that one of the functions of certain Jewish organizations is to offer a non-threatening environment for such proclamation.

11. Similar results regarding both affiliation and activity are obtained even when those at each extreme pole of the integration-mindedness index are compared with one another.

12. This pattern is also found among the women.

13. For a different approach to the significance of the Jewish club and lodge see Seymour Leventman and Judith R. Kramer, *Children of the Gilded Ghetto* (New Haven: Yale University Press, 1961).

14. See Volume II, Chapter 11, regarding interfaith social contacts in non-sectarian organizations.

Chapter 8

1. More than eight out of ten women and almost nine out of ten men had at least some college education (see above, p. 27).

2. While such terms as "friendship circle," "friendship group," or "clique" generally refer to a distinguishable set of persons who are bound together by friendship ties, our data refer only to the aggregate of persons considered as "close friends" by the respondent. These data do not tell us, of course, the extent to which such friendship choices are reciprocated or whether the respondent's collection of close friends constitutes a functioning group.

We employed the following item for the purpose of distinguishing between close friends and others: "When you think of all the persons you are friendly with at this moment, about how many of them are people you consider really close friends?" Respondents were then probed as to the religious identity of their close friends. They were also asked a series of questions regarding the type of relationship they had with the person whom they considered their closest Jewish friend as well as with the person whom they considered their closest Gentile friend.

3. Some 2 per cent did not know the religious identity of their close friends or did not report any close friends.

4. Four in ten of these respondents say that all such Gentile friends are married to Jews. Another one in ten say that *most* such Gentile friends are married to Jews. If these cases, which constitute about one-fourth of all respondents, are added to those whose friendship circle is exclusively Jewish, we find that as many as two-thirds of Lakeville Jews make all their close friendships either with Jews or with Gentiles who are all or mostly married to Jews.

5. The comparison with parents required that "most" friendships be defined as over 60 per cent, rather than over 50 per cent, and that "about half" be defined as 41 to 60 per cent (see Table 8–1). Therefore, the 89 per cent figure is slightly less than the comparable total of the relevant percentages in the previous paragraph.

6. When the most intimate Gentile friend who is not married to a Jew is entertained, in only a third of the cases are most or all of the other persons likely to be Jewish. Such information was gathered only in respect to the most intimate Gentile friend, the person who is referred to in the relevant questionnaire item as "the one with whom you are most friendly."

7. For an analysis of how the college sorority facilitates relationships that lead to endogamous courtship and marriage patterns, see John Finley Scott, "The American College Sorority: Its Role in Class and Ethnic Endogamy," *American Sociological Review*, XXX (August 1965), 514–527.

8. See Volume II, Chapter 8 for a discussion of the relationship between comfortableness, social anxiety, and integration-mindedness. It should be remembered, however, that this material refers to any social contact with Gentiles, rather than to close friendships.

9. The "most observant" group here are those who observe five or more home rituals. The finding remains the same even if we compare the unobservant with those who observe seven or more rituals. A strikingly similar finding emerges when those who never attend synagogue services are compared with those who attend quite regularly.

10. The "unaffiliated" are persons who do not hold membership in either a general Jewish organization or a synagogue-related organization. Some, however, may belong to a synagogue.

11. Only among a small segment who are consistently alienated from Jewish organizations is there a sizable proportion who participate in ethnically balanced or mostly Gentile cliques. Among those who are not affiliated with a Jewish organization or with a synagogue (despite the fact that their children have reached or passed the peak age for religious education), as many as 31 per cent claim such friendship circles, while only 54 per cent are part of homogeneously Jewish cliques.

12. See Volume II, Chapter 7.

13. Note, for example, our respondents' image of the "good Jew," particularly their feeling about gaining the respect of Christian neighbors. See Chapter 10, pp. 324–325.

14. Regarding the relevance of religious and ethnic identity in assimilating successful members of minority groups to elite social life, see E. Digby Baltzell, *The*

Protestant Establishment (New York: Random House, 1964). See also Richard L. Rubenstein, "The Protestant Establishment and the Jews," *Judaism*, XIV (Spring 1965), 131–145.

Chapter 9

1. See Eric Werner, *Mendelssohn: A New Image of the Composer and His Age* (New York: The Free Press of Glencoe, 1963), pp. 36–38.
2. All data on the parents' Jewish education refer only to the parents in our sample. No information was obtained about the Jewish education of the respondent's spouse.
3. The sex of the child exposed to Jewish schooling could be distinguished only in families where all the children were of the same sex.
4. The stratagem of advancing the age of Confirmation has tended to prolong the years of Jewish schooling somewhat. However, the problem of secondary, higher, and adult Jewish education remains.
5. Several temples in the community try to induce boys who have had a Bar Mitzvah to remain for Confirmation.
6. For the extent of religious observance in the home, see Chapter 3.
7. Parents whose children were all less than 4 years old were not asked this question. A handful of other parents who did not answer this question are also excluded from these tabulations.
8. Those observing two or less rituals generally constitute more than half of Lakeville Jews. If three to four rituals are also considered as minimal, about three-fourths of the population would be encompassed by this broader definition. See above, p. 51.
9. Although nostalgic parents who believe that their children will have less pleasant Jewish memories are less observant than those who feel that their children's memories will be just as pleasant or more pleasant than their own, their lower level of observance does not explain their self-critical attitudes toward the Jewishness of their homes; critical attitudes continue to be related to a less hopeful view of their children's memories, whatever the level of observance. Not only does this relationship persist among the less observant parents who are strongly attached to their Jewish childhood but we find that even among the more observant nostalgic parents self-critical attitudes are more frequent if they feel that the current religious experiences which will constitute their children's future memories do not match the richness and variety of their own Jewish childhood. Thus self-criticism occurs among some 46 per cent of such observant parents who feel that their children are missing out, but among only 20 per cent of those equally observant and nostalgic though more sanguine about their children's memories.
10. On contemporary Jewish attitudes toward intermarriage, see Marshall Sklare, "Intermarriage and the Jewish Future," *Commentary*, XXXVII (April 1964), 46–52.
11. A desirable characteristic of a marriage partner is understood here in relative terms as indicating a specific status and outlook more appropriate to the Lakeville Jew than are their opposites. Of course, in traditional Jewish culture it is inconceivable that a Gentile, irrespective of what desirable qualities he might have, should be preferred over a Jew. Conversely, it is inconceivable that a Jew, irrespective of what undesirable qualities *he* might have, should not be preferred over a Gentile.
12. This latter question was asked only of parents of girls.

13. Some 9 per cent could not decide between the Orthodox Jew and the non-religious Gentile, and 17 per cent as between the Jewish carpenter and the Gentile professional.

14. These are the same groups that opted for a love-based intermarriage in preference to a loveless intrafaith marriage.

15. Some 6 per cent do not indicate whether they would accept or reject the marriage.

16. The other 57 per cent who would accept the intermarriage do not express any reluctance or resistance.

INDEX

acculturation, of Jews: and generation, 241; and group identity, 21; rapidity of, 5; of respondents, 9; and social interaction, 251–252

adolescence, Gentile friends during, 274–275; Jewish friends during, 274–276; religious behavior, studies of, 276, 417

adult education, 20, 119, 130, 157–158, 326, 374

age distribution, and family income, 30; of Lakeville vs. nation, 43–44; of respondents, 22–24

alienation, from general community: meaning of, 424; and sacramentalism, 132–133; and support of Israel, 237–241

alienation, from Judaism; and associational ties, 263–265, 283–284; and friendship ties, 283–289

American Council for Judaism, 133, 135, 136, 142, 384, 420

American Jewish Committee, 409; and Riverton Study, 9 n.

American Legion, 268

American Technion Society, 229

Americanization, Educational Alliance and, 5; of immigrants, 5–6

anti-Jewish discrimination, in Lakeville, 11–12, 13

Armed Forces, friendship ties in, 271

assimilation, as an alternative for Jews, 100, 332

Baltzell, E. Digby, 427

Baptist churches, 18

Bar Mitzvah, in Conservative synagogue, 129; as motivation for synagogue affiliation, 185–186, 187; observance of, among respondents, 297; parental feelings toward, 298; preparation for, 295–296, 364, 378–379, 385, 390–391, 394, 398; in Reform synagogue, 109; see also post-Bar Mitzvah club

Bartholdy, Felix Mendelssohn, 291

Bat Mitzvah, 117, 296, 297; see also post-Bat Mitzvah club

Bentwich, Norman, 411

Bigman, Stanley G., 416

B'nai B'rith, 255, 259, 260, 263, 265

Bogue, Donald J., 415

casualness, as a way of life, 155–156

Catholic churches, membership of, in Lakeville, 18

Catholic parochial schools, 18

Catholics, organizational involvement of, 255; population of, 18

child-centeredness, 417; and retention of rituals, 58–59, 418; and synagogue affiliation, 181–192; see also Jewish education; synagogue affiliation

children, of respondents: ages of, 23–24; number of, 22–24

churches, in Lakeville, 18

civic groups, 16–17

class, see social class

Classical Reform Judaism, definition of, 419; Jewish education in, 135–137; vs. Neo-Reform, 106–114, 133–135; prayer book of, 141–142; and pro-

observances, *see* religious observances

occupations, and descent, 35; of Lakeville compared with nation, 42–43; of respondents, 24–27

Orbach, Harold L., 416

organizations, affiliation with, 262, 425–429; clique relationship and, 269; function of, 252, 352; Gentile enrollment in, 255; health and welfare, 19, 258, 259; involvement in, 254–255, 424; for Israel support, 235–237, 254; membership of, 252–255; non-synagogue, 261–263; social and recreational, 258–259; and social class, 259–261; social service, 263; synagogue-sponsored, 253, 254, 255; in traditional society, 251; types of, 254, 401; women in, involvement of, 255–259

ORT (Organization for Rehabilitation through Training), 230, 254, 258, 260, 261, 263, 267, 268

Orthodox Jews, attitudes to Israel support, 244–249; in Lakeville, 42, 44

Orthodox synagogue, efforts to establish, 167–171, 342

parent-child relationships, effect of educational gap on, 28; and Jewish home observance, 302–306

Parent-Teacher Association (PTA), 17

parental generation, education of, 412; *see also* generational differences

parental influence, on pro-Israel sentiment, 243–249

Passover, 50, 52, 53, 54, 55, 57, 58, 59, 118–119; in Reform Judaism, 115, 141

philanthropy, 18, 329–330; attitudes toward, 425; in image of "good Jew," 326, 327; to Israel, 225–228

Philipson, David, 411

Piaget, Jean, 348

Pirke Avot ("Sayings of the Fathers"), 291

"Pittsburgh Platform," of Reform Judaism, 419

Plaut, W. Gunther, 419

population, effect of World War II on, 14; of Jews, in Lakeville, 42

post-Bar Mitzvah Club, 130

post-Bat Mitzvah Club, 130

Presbyterian churches, 18

Protestant churches, 18; membership of, 422

Protestants, attitude toward Jews of, 12; organizational involvement of, 255; population of, in Lakeville, 18

public library, of Lakeville, 20

recreational facilities, 19–20

Red Cross, 19

Reform Judaism, Classical vs. Neo, 106–114, 360–361; "Columbus Platform," of, 419; "Pittsburgh Platform" of, 419; and pro-Israel sentiment, 244–249, 386–387, 387–388; program of, 114–119; *see also* Classical Reform Judaism; Neo-Reform Judaism

Reform synagogues, 98–105; Jewish education in, 101–102, 117, 135–137; *see also* Einhorn Temple; Hirsch Temple; Lilienthal Temple; Wise Temple

religion, in Lakeville, 45–96; role of women in, 62

religious groups, relationships of, 18

religious life, revival of, 425–426; voluntaristic character of, 180–181

religious observance, 46, 50–56, 329, 415; generational differences in, 50–56, 78–88, 418, 424; in home, 49–59, 61–64, 297–306; influences on, 65–78; and life cycle, 73–78, 422; and pro-Israel sentiments, 244–249; and synagogue affiliation, 184, 188

religious school, *see* Jewish education

respondents, acculturation of, 9; age distribution of, 22–24, 337; evaluation of area by, 421–422; family composition of, 22–24; interviews with, 409–410; number of, 21; occupations of, 24–27, 412; residence of, length of, 39–41

Riley, J. W., Jr., 423

Riley, M. W., 423

Rischin, Moses, 411

rituals, and child-centeredness, 58–59; frequency of occurrence of, 59; observance of, 368–370, 373–374, 428;

Date Due

JUL 29 97			